CARTER & HARRISON
ON
OFFENCES OF VIOLENCE

Second Edition

OTHER VOLUMES IN THE CRIMINAL LAW LIBRARY

Andrews and Hirst on Criminal Evidence (2nd ed.)
Arlidge and Parry on Fraud (2nd ed.)
Bucknell and Ghodse on Misuse of Drugs (3rd ed.)
Mitchell, Taylor & Talbot on Confiscation and the
Proceeds of Crime
Jones on Extradition Law and Practice
Offences Against Public Order (2nd ed.)
Rook and Ward on Sexual Offences (2nd ed.)
Stone and Johnson on Forensic Medicine (2nd ed.)
Wolchover & Heaton Armstrong on Confession Evidence

AUSTRALIA
LBC Information Services—Sydney

CANADA AND USA
Carswell—Toronto

NEW ZEALAND
Brooker's—Auckland

SINGAPORE AND MALAYSIA
Thomson Information (S.E. Asia)—Singapore

THE CRIMINAL LAW LIBRARY

CARTER & HARRISON
ON
OFFENCES OF VIOLENCE

Second Edition

Peter Carter Q.C., LLB(Lond),
of Gray's Inn, Barrister
Ruth Harrison, LLM(Lond)

LONDON
SWEET & MAXWELL
1997

First edition 1991
Second Edition 1997
Published in 1997 by Sweet & Maxwell Limited of
100 Avenue Road, Swiss Cottage, London NW3 3PF
Computerset by Wyvern 21 Ltd, Bristol.
Printed and bound in Great Britain by Hartnolls Ltd, Bodmin

No natural forests were destroyed to make this product; only farmed
timber was used and replanted.

A CIP catalogue record for this book is available from the British
Library

ISBN 0 421 53770 1

PREFACE

If rules are innate in any civilised society, so alas is violence. While violence seems to continue in depressingly familiar ways to those of use who practise in the criminal courts, the law is ever on the move. Despite the proven inadequacies of the Offences Against the Person Act 1861, it remains the governing statute for most of the offences of violence. It has in recent years been the subject of sustained judicial criticism, and attempts to interpret it in the light of contemporary needs. The efforts of the Law Commission to simplify and rationalise the law of violence have gone largely unheeded. We are left with the conundrum that defendants are presumed to know the law—that same law which perplexes academics and senior judges, and which has to be described in careful and basic terms to intelligent jurors to enable them to comprehend it in even simple cases.

In this Second Edition we have rationalised the format of the book. Problems of analysis or definition can arise in any case, however commonplace the facts, and so we have set out in chapter 1 such consistent threads as run through this subject and highlight various intellectual and practical problems involved. These problems of definition and analysis are important not only for the most serious cases, but also in more mundane cases where a trial of a violent incident charged as different alternative offences can cause real problems of definition.

We have concentrated on the most common offences of violence, and have excluded from this edition the more arcane offences still lurking in the Offences Against the Person Act 1861. Our intention is to make this book easy to use and helpful to the practitioner in search of an answer to a problem. We also seek to alert that practitioner to problems which may not be immediately apparent.

Thanks go to those (too many, unfortunately, to list) who have helped with advice and encouragement. Our thanks to our spouses for their patience and support. We are particularly grateful to Sweet and Maxwell for taking on this book and adding it to their formidable repertoire.

The law is stated as at June 1, 1997.

Peter Carter
18 Red Lion Court
EC4

Ruth Harrison
London

June 10, 1997

CONTENTS

Chapter 3 – ASSAULTS RESULTING IN INJURY   85

Chapter 4 – MURDER   155

TABLE OF CASES

TABLE OF STATUTES

1

TABLE OF STATUTORY INSTRUMENTS

CHAPTER 1

OFFENCES OF VIOLENCE—INTRODUCTION AND PRINCIPAL DEFINITIONS

I. INTRODUCTION

It should be easy to identify what the law regards as offences of violence. **1–001** It is not. For example, a threat to kill would normally be regarded as an offence of violence, but in *R. v. Ragg*[1] the Court of Appeal held that for the purposes of passing longer than normal sentences under section 2(2)(b) of the Criminal Justice Act 1991, such an offence is not necessarily a violent offence.

We have confined ourselves to an examination of the offences of violence **1–002** which do not clearly come into any other category. We include murder, manslaughter, the principal offences under the Offences Against the Person Act 1861, offences of violence against children (other than sexual offences), kidnapping and piracy. Other offences which involve violence, *e.g.* robbery and public order offences are included in separate works within this series. This edition of the book no longer seeks to deal with *all* the offences set out in the Offences Against the Person Act 1861. The minor ones can be regarded as covered by the same general principles as apply to the other offences in the Act as they tend to use similar terminology.

The governing statute, the Offences Against the Person Act 1861 has **1–003** recently come in for considerable judicial criticism. Lord Ackner in *R. v. Savage*; *D.P.P. v. Parmenter*[2] described it as "piece-meal legislation" containing "a rag-bag of offences brought together from a wide variety of sources with no attempt, as the draftsman frankly acknowledged, to introduce

---

[1] [1995] Crim. L.R. 664.
[2] [1992] A.C. 699 at 752C.

1

consistency as to substance or as to form". When *R. v. Parmenter*[3] was in the Court of Appeal Mustill L.J. said:

> "At a time when 'middle-rank' criminal violence is a dismal feature of modern urban life, and when convictions and pleas of guilty on charges under section 47 occupy so much of Crown Court lists it seems scarcely credible that 129 years after the enactment of the Offences Against the Person Act 1861 three appeals should come before [the Court of Appeal] within one week which reveal the law to be so impenetrable."

The cases of *R. v. Spratt*[4] and *R. v. Savage; D.P.P. v. Parmenter*[5] came before the Court of Appeal on the same day, but in front of differently constituted courts. The issue in each case was the mental element necessary to establish assault occasioning actual bodily harm under section 47 of the Act. The courts contradicted each other, and the issue had to go to the House of Lords. There it was decided that there is no requirement that the accused should have intended or even foreseen *any* injury; it is sufficient if he commits an assault (or battery) and *as a matter of causation* some injury follows.

1-004   Only in general terms can a hierarchy of offences with associated mental states be identified. Logic would demand that the mental states of each offence should be clearly defined, and the boundaries between them clearly marked; and that the distinctions in injury caused would similarly be clearly distinguished in the offences themselves. That was the intention in the Law Commission's report "Offences Against the Person and General Principles".[6] Paragraph 12.33 of that Report identified the muddle in which (despite recent judicial efforts) the law still rests:

> "The injustice and the inefficiency of the law under the 1861 Act combine to make the law an inept vehicle for conveying society's disapproval of violence, and the penalties with which violence will be met. At best, the 1861 Act contains a muddled message: that the same penalty is envisaged for causing both substantial (section 20) and minor (section 47) harm; and that although the law purports to punish and control the actual, subjective, fault of the accused, that fault is not linked to the damage caused, and is irrelevant to the punishment that the law provides. Such a law does not clearly single out those who contemplate violence as proper objects of deterrence and punishment because of the violence they contemplate rather than the harm that they accidentally cause; nor does it distribute punishment according to the subjective intentions, and thus the social fault, of the accused. Such a law, resting as much as it does on chance or the causing of unintended harm, does not properly convey society's message that a propensity to engage in violence is taken very seriously, and will be punished according to the seriousness of the harm that the accused consciously causes".

1-005   The Law Commission proposed a

> ". . . graded system of offences . . . which, unlike the 1861 Act, distributes liability rationally according to the seriousness of the injury that the defendant consciously causes—and therefore according to the seriousness of the risk that he consciously took."[7]

---

[3] [1992] A.C. 699 at 711H–712A.
[4] [1990] 1 W.L.R. 1073.
[5] (1992) Cr.App.R. 193.
[6] Law Com. No. 218, Cm. 2370.
[7] *ibid.* para. 12–031.

The Report went on to suggest that

"The interests both of justice and of social protection would be much better served by a law that was (i) clearly and briefly stated; (ii) based on the injury intended or contemplated by the accused, and not on what he happened to cause; and (iii) governed by clear distinctions, expressed in modern comprehensible language, between serious and less serious cases."[8]

Sadly, this call for clarity (coupled with suggested draft legislation to achieve that effect) has been ignored. Instead we have been inundated with a series of statutes and proposed statutes which do not address the central issues of definition and clarity, but concentrate on procedure and sentencing—making a confused picture even more bewildering for anyone trying to make sense of the criminal justice system insofar as it concerns violence against the person.

An example of the way in which the outdated legislation had to be stretched **1–006** to fit contemporary concerns was how to deal with the threatening phenomenon of "stalking". In those cases, physical injury is not usually inflicted upon the victim, and none is usually intended. Nor is it intended to put the victim in fear of *imminent* violence. The motive seems to be to terrify the victim; or sometimes only to unsettle. Whatever the intent, the result must be frightening for the victim. If the victim suffers a condition amounting to psychiatric illness then it will constitute actual (or, if sufficiently serious, grievous) bodily harm; whereas emotional disturbance, grief or fear will not.[9] In *Smith v. Chief Superintendent, Woking Police Station*[10] it was found to be an offence of common assault for a man persistently to stare through the windows of a woman's house even though he could not physically reach her at the time. That was because the court found as a fact that the accused intended to put the victim in fear of imminent violence. Such a conclusion of fact will often not be possible in cases of "stalking". In *R. v. Burstow*[11] the trial judge ruled that severe depression amounting to psychiatric injury caused by "stalking" was sufficient for the purposes of section 20 of the 1861 Act to amount to grievous bodily harm inflicted on the victim and the Court of Appeal agreed. There is an extraordinary decision in *R. v. Ireland*.[12] The Court of Appeal held that repeated silent telephone calls to female victims which caused them to suffer psychiatric harm amounted to assault occasioning actual bodily harm. The reasoning was that the defendant put himself in contact (by telephone) with his victims who were put in fear; putting someone in fear amounts to assault; and psychiatric illness is bodily harm. The difficulty with this decision is that it by-passes the established case law requiring there to be a fear of imminent physical harm caused by the defendant's proximity to the victim.[13] The court

---

[8] *ibid.* para. 12–034.
[9] *R. v. Chan-Fook* 99 Cr.App.R. 147. See also *R. v. Miller* (1953) 38 Cr.App.R. 1 (explained in *R. v. Chan-Fook*) and *R. v. Dawson* (1985) Cr.App.R. 150.
[10] (1983) 76 Cr.App.R. 234, D.C.
[11] [1997] 1 Cr.App.R. 144.
[12] [1996] 2 Cr.App.R. 426. See also *R. v. Constanza* (March 6, 1997, *Archbold News*, Issue 4, May 1, 1997).
[13] See *Smith v. Chief Superintendent, Woking Police Station*, above.

used the development in the law which sensibly acknowledges psychiatric injury as a species of bodily harm and extended it to create a new concept of "long-range" assault, as if the infliction of psychiatric injury suffices for the offence of assault even though there is no risk of any physical contact between defendant and victim. If A were to telephone B to announce that he or C was coming to the house to beat B, or that B would be assaulted next time he stepped through his door, that would itself be an assault. Any psychiatric injury suffered as a result would transform the offence into one of assault occasioning actual bodily harm.[14] Is the deliberate or reckless infliction of psychiatric injury an assault in the absence of any possibility of fear of any other injury? The case of *Ireland* indicates that the infliction of such harm is a direct assault (and therefore akin to a battery[15]) and any unlawful act causing such injury will amount to assault occasioning actual bodily harm. This raises the question whether it would be an assault to *threaten* to make repeated nuisance telephone calls intending or being reckless as to whether that will induce in the victim the *fear* of being subjected to psychiatric illness; it is not yet clear whether that can be the justification for the decision, or whether it has to be confined to its own facts—one of which was the defendant's plea of guilty. *Ireland* obviously poses problems of analysis and of application.

Stalking is now the subject of legislation making persistent harassment an offence, summary for minor harassment, indictable for more serious cases (the Protection from Harassment Act 1997, in force on June 16, 1997). This should avoid the need to use inappropriate fictions to counter the activity. There is a provision in the Criminal Justice and Public Order Act 1994 amending the Public Order Act 1986 by inserting an offence of behaving in a threatening abusive or insulting way "with intent to cause a person harassment, alarm or distress".[16] This new offence is purely summary.

1-007 Any generalisation about some single concept of offences of violence is therefore fraught with difficulty. Common features examined in this book are:—an unlawful act; interference (actual or threatened) with another's bodily integrity; an injury caused by the unlawful violence; a state of mind necessary to satisfy the definition of the offence. These generalisations are soon exposed as inadequate—for example omissions as well as acts can sometimes be the basis of an offence; and *no* particular state of mind is required for the offences of common assault and assault occasioning actual bodily harm.[17] However, of necessity the ingredients of the various offences of violence fall to be considered in this book under those features. One feature that might be expected to feature is some element of *hostility* towards the victim. This has been discounted as a necessary element in offences of violence. In *R. v. Brown*[18] the House of Lords had to consider whether consent to injury nullified the unlawfulness of what would otherwise be an assault. The House decided by a majority that it did not, except in the small category of exceptions already

---

[14] *R. v. Savage; D.P.P. v. Parmenter* (1992) 94 Cr.App.R. 193.
[15] See *D.P.P. v. Taylor* (1992) 95 Cr.App.R. 28.
[16] s.154 of the 1994 Act.
[17] *R. v. Savage, D.P.P. v. Parmenter* (1992) 94 Cr.App.R. 193.
[18] (1993) 97 Cr.App.R. 44.

established and condoned by the law. The argument raised the question whether an element of hostility was a necessary aspect of offences of assault. Hostility in the sense of ill-will or malevolence is not required, as Lord Lowry pointed out,[19] giving as an example the police officer stopping someone temporarily, but by doing so acting outside the execution of the officer's duty—that would be an unlawful assault. Lord Mustill (dissenting on the outcome, but agreeing with the majority on this principle) said[20]:

"The doctor who hastens the end of a patient to terminate his agony acts with the best intentions, and without hostility to him in any ordinary sense of the word, yet there is no doubt that notwithstanding the patient's consent he is guilty of murder. Nor has it been questioned on the argument of the present appeal that someone who inflicts serious harm, because, for example, he is inspired by a belief in the efficacy of pseudo-medical treatment, or acts in conformity with some extreme religious tenet, is guilty of an offence notwithstanding that he is inspired only by a desire to do the best he can for the recipient. Hostility cannot, as it seems to me, be a crucial factor which in itself determines guilt or innocence, although its presence or absence may be relevant when the court has to decide as a matter of policy how to react to a new situation."

II. RELATIONSHIP BETWEEN OFFENDER AND VICTIM

Offences of violence do not depend upon proof of particular relationships. **1–008** There is no specific offence in English law of patricide or fratricide. There is an offence of infanticide, but that exists to reduce what would otherwise be murder to an offence equivalent to manslaughter.[21] Acts of violence are treated for the purposes of the criminal law as the same whether they are perpetrated by strangers to the victims or relatives of them. Many (perhaps most) offences of serious violence are committed by persons living in close proximity to their victim. The law seeks to protect some of the most vulnerable, *i.e.* children, by imposing a duty on their parents or guardians, or others for the time being having charge of them, to care and protect them. A mother who does nothing while her partner mistreats her child will be guilty of wilful ill-treatment (subject to defences such as duress), even though not guilty of the act of violence itself.[22] There is no specific protection afforded to the elderly or the infirm. Patients in mental institutions are given protection similar to that afforded to children.[23] The particular vulnerability of some people within violent relationships causes problems not of legal analysis, but of proof. There are cases where even injuries to children have gone unnoticed until too late. Much more common are "domestic" injuries where the victim is too isolated, too frightened, or too fatalistic to seek redress. When a complaint is made, then

---

[19] At p. 58.
[20] At p. 72.
[21] See chap. 7, para. 7–028.
[22] See chap. 8, para. 8–015.
[23] s.127 of the Mental Health Act 1983. See chap. 3, para. 3–075.

there are often problems of proof, and the potential for intimidation by the perpetrator.

1–009   Cohabitation has recently featured as giving rise, not to a species of offence, but to a slightly more generous attitude towards the defence of provocation in murder cases. "Battered woman syndrome" has been accepted as a relevant characteristic and must be taken into account for the purposes of determining whether, if the woman charged had suffered a sudden and temporary loss of self-control which resulted in the man's death, her behaviour was reasonable for a woman possessing that characteristic.[24] This state of affairs reflects the way in which the criminal law of violence finds itself addressing the wrong problem. What the law should be concerned about is how to prevent the incidence of "battered wife syndrome". Recognising it only for the purposes of providing a restricted defence to murder is getting things the wrong way round. Young children do not normally suffer severe unexplained injuries at home; and when a child is found to have such injuries, the prosecution is likely either for assault if the perpetrator can be identified, or for wilful neglect if he or she cannot. The same is not true of adults. A black eye or broken bone in an adult does not necessarily cry out for an explanation. It also seems to be true that, perhaps as reflected in Mustill L.J.'s dictum set out at paragraph 1–003 above, there is a tolerance for some categories of violence which would not now be acceptable if committed against a child.

III. ACTIONS AND OMISSIONS

1–010   Offences of violence by their nature usually involve actions by the accused, ranging from a punch to setting an explosive device. In some cases, words will suffice, such as threats to kill. Words are sufficient in some assaults where the assault is the verbal threat of imminent violence—but there must also be physical proximity between accused and victim.

Liability for an offence of violence on the basis of joint enterprise might at first sight seem to be guilt by omission. But liability depends on proof that the accused was in the vicinity of where the offence occurred as part of an agreed plan.

1–011   Some offences against the young can be committed by omission. Wilful neglect requires no positive act. It requires a relationship of responsibility towards the child. Failure to act to protect the child's welfare (*e.g.* by failing to seek appropriate medical attention) will suffice.[25] It is in this category of case that standing by while the child is injured by someone else renders that parent or guardian guilty of neglect.

1–012   Omission in the sense of gross dereliction of duty can be the basis for an offence of manslaughter. The omission must rise out of a duty to exercise care

---

[24] *R. v. Thornton (No. 2)* [1996] 2 All E.R. 1023. The Court of Appeal ordered a retrial. She was convicted of manslaughter.
[25] See chap. 8, para. 8–020 below.

in circumstances where lack of care is dangerous. In *R. v. Adomako*[26] the House of Lords upheld the conviction for manslaughter of an anaesthetist who had failed to notice that an oxygen tube had come disconnected during an operation. The patient died of cardiac arrest. Lord Mackay, L.C., in a speech with which the rest of the House of Lords concurred, said:

> "The essence of the matter, which is supremely a jury question, is whether, having regard to the risk of death involved, the conduct of the defendant was so bad in all the circumstances as to amount in their judgement to a criminal act or omission."[27]

IV. INJURY

Injury—whether actual bodily harm, grievous bodily harm, or a wound— **1-013** means injury to the body, including the brain, the nervous system and any organ. Psychiatric illness such as anxiety neurosis or reactive depression is regarded as bodily injury; fear, distress, or panic are not.[28] Such injury requires proof by expert evidence.[29] This is a potentially developing area, as it should keep pace with developments in medical opinion. Lord Wilberforce said in *McLoughlin v. O'Brien*[30]:

> "Whatever is unknown about the mind-body relationship (and the area of ignorance seems to expand with that of knowledge), it is now accepted by medical science that recognisable and severe physical damage to the human body and system may be caused by the impact, through the senses, of external events on the mind. Thus may be produced what is as identifiable as illness as any that may be caused by direct physical impact."

It is possible that psychiatric illness caused by witnessing some horrific act of unlawful violence (*e.g.* a prison riot or an affray) would justify a prosecution for causing actual (or—if appropriate—grievous) bodily harm against the perpetrator.

As the words of Lord Wilberforce quoted above demonstrate, injury need not be directly inflicted by the accused; murder can be committed by poisoning as readily as by stabbing.

Some of the offences covered by this book do not require proof of any **1-014** injury. An offence of wilful cruelty to a person under 16[31] requires injury or "unnecessary suffering" which may mean that the child is distressed through cold or hunger. The offence of torture involves infliction of "severe pain or suffering" whether "physical or mental".[32] Threats to kill do not involve injury—the harm concerned is the deliberate causing of fear that the threat will be carried out.

---

[26] 99 Cr.App.R. 362.
[27] At p. 369.
[28] *R. v. Chan-Fook* (1994) 99 Cr.App.R. 147.
[29] *ibid.*
[30] [1983] 1 A.C. 410 at 418. This was adopted in *R. v. Chan-Fook.*
[31] See chap. 8, para. 8–010.
[32] s.134 of the Criminal Justice Act 1988.

V. JOINT ENTERPRISE

1–015   Acts committed as part of a joint enterprise are treated as the acts of all the participants, even for unusual consequences of that agreed joint enterprise.[33] However, if one of the parties goes beyond what has been tacitly agreed, then no-one else involved in the joint venture is liable for the consequences of that act.[34] This principle is simple to state but difficult to apply, especially since it has become over-complicated by recent decisions. What seems to have begun as a means of isolating responsibility for consequences unintended by at least some of the participants—so that in a robbery in which threats only were to be used, the infliction of fatal injuries by one of the group going beyond what had been expressly or tacitly agreed, would make him alone guilty of murder—has become a means of imposing greater responsibility on all present. The test ought to be what did each individual *intend*. Were that the case, then criminal liability for an act of violence would attract the label according not only to its consequences but to the appropriate mental capability of each participant in the acts which led to the assault. It is possible that during an attack, one person intends to inflict serious injury, while others intend only minor harm. If the victim dies, should the participants be found culpable for what they intended? It is possible that the person who kills does not intend serious injury, but another present as part of the joint enterprise does so intend. There is no mischief in holding each responsible for his respective intent, so that the killer would be guilty of manslaughter, while the other person would be guilty of murder. But a series of cases in the Privy Council and Court of Appeal have decided that what matters in joint enterprise cases is not what the persons who did not inflict the fatal injury themselves intended, but what they *foresaw* the killer might do. If they foresaw such an act or consequence, then they are guilty, even though it was not intended as part of the joint venture.[35] The consequence of this line of authorities is that the necessary intent to establish an offence of specific intent, *e.g.* causing grievous bodily harm, or murder, is less for the person who does not inflict the fatal injury than it is for the person who does. The latter must be proved to have intended death or serious injury. The former need only have foreseen it as an undesired possibility of associating in a criminal venture in which weapons were carried, or when it was known that one of their associates with whom they were committing the offence was capable of behaving in an unpredictable and violent manner.

     In the case of *R. v. Stewart & Schofield*, the Court of Appeal approved a direction that the jury could convict one of the participants of manslaughter

---

[33] *R. v. Anderson & Morris* [1966] 2 Q.B. 110. See especially at p. 118.
[34] *ibid.*
[35] See, *e.g. Chan Wing-Siu v. R.* (1984) 80 Cr.App.R. 117; *R. v. Hyde* (1991) 92 Cr.App.R. 131; *Hui Chi-Ming v. R.* (1992) 94 Cr.App.R. 236; *R. v. Stewart & Schofield* [1995] 1 Cr.App.R. 441; *R. v. Perman* [1996] 1 Cr.App.R. 24; and *R. v. Powell & Daniels* [1996] 1 Cr.App.R. 14 in which Lord Taylor, C.J. doubted the dictum of Lawton L.J. in *R. v. Reid* (1976) 62 Cr.App.R. 109 at 112 that "If such injury is not intended by the others, they must be acquitted of murder" insofar as it was inconsistent with the principles set out in the text and supported by the other authorities cited in this note.

if they concluded that "as part of the joint criminal enterprise he was agreeable to, or realised that, or *if he had thought about it must have realised* that [D1] might, in the heat of the moment or in the excitement or tension of the occasion, strike [the victim] with a piece of scaffolding bar and inflict some bodily injury on him."[36] This makes joint responsibility depend upon a test which sounds dangerously like an objective assessment of what an accused should have foreseen. Change the words "some bodily injury" to "really serious injury" and there is the possibility of participation in murder on that basis. That cannot be the proper test.

As a matter of law and of evidence, participation in any offence which involves the possibility of some violence means that, if the victim dies as a result of that violence—even if it is greater and of a different kind than others involved in the enterprise intended—then they are nevertheless guilty of murder or manslaughter depending upon whether they foresaw as possibilities really serious injury, or only a minor assault. This would extend to a person participating in an offence, say of robbery, who realises during the robbery that his accomplice is likely to inflict really serious injury and does nothing to prevent it or to extricate himself from the incident. He would be guilty of murder. However, where the one defendant believed that he was involved in a joint enterprise only to frighten with an unloaded gun in the course of a robbery, he was not guilty of murder or manslaughter when the other party had used a loaded gun to kill the victim during the robbery.[37]

In *Stewart & Schofield*,[38] Hobhouse L.J., giving the judgment of the court said:

1–016

> "The allegation that the defendant took part in the execution of a crime as a joint enterprise is not the same as an allegation that he aided, abetted, counselled or procured the commission of that crime. A person who is an aider or abettor, etc., is truly a secondary party to the commission of whatever crime it is that the principal has committed although he may be charged as a principle . . . In contrast, where the allegation is joint enterprise, the allegation is that one defendant participated in the criminal act of another. That is a different principle."

This is a surprising dictum. One of the appellants in that case had been standing watch outside the premises while the robbery occurred within. Such activity is normally given as an example of the meaning of aiding and abetting. The suggestion seems to be that an aider and abettor must have had knowledge

---

[36] *ibid.* at p. 445. Our emphasis.

[37] *R. v. Perman* [1996] 1 Cr.App.R. 24. In that case, the Court of Appeal thought that manslaughter could not result from these facts. This ignores the question whether robbery in such circumstances amounts to a sufficiently dangerous unlawful act for manslaughter to follow if death occurs in the course of it. The court also assumed that had the defendant known the gun to be loaded, but expected it not to be used to cause injury, he would have a defence. This conflicts with the established authorities if it is thought to indicate that the defendant would not be guilty of murder if he foresaw as a possibility that the gun would be used to inflict serious injury. In *R. v. Bamborough* [1996] Crim.L.R. 744 the Court of Appeal held that a defendant was guilty of murder when, during the course of a robbery, his co-defendant fired a gun which he thought was to be used to inflict serious injury by "pistol whipping" the victim. The court held that it was immaterial how the fatal injury was inflicted if serious injury was contemplated as apart of the joint enterprise.

[38] [1995] 1 Cr.App.R. 441 at p. 447.

of the actual offence committed to be liable for it, and can be liable for no other offence; whereas a person participating in a joint venture has a distinct criminal liability depending upon that person's intent or state of knowledge of what were the possible consequences. Whether this sophisticated distinction works in practice will have to be seen. A detailed criticism of the principle encapsulated in this dictum is to be found in the Commentary by Sir John Smith on the case of *R. v. Wan & Chan*.[39]

In *R. v. Powell*[40] the Court of Appeal confirmed the now established view that, where a secondary party realised, without agreeing to such conduct being used, that the principal might kill or intentionally inflict serious bodily injury and that secondary party nevertheless continued to participate in the venture, that amounted to the requisite intent for murder if the principal killed in the course of the venture with the requisite intent. In the course of the judgment of the court, Lord Taylor C.J. was fully aware of the concern that such a principle creates. He said[41]:

> "As a matter of principle, it has been strongly argued that there is an anomaly in requiring proof against a secondary party only of a lesser *mens rea* than needs to be provided against the principal who commits the *actus reus*. This was taken up by the Law Commission in their Consultation Paper No. 131 entitled 'Assisting and Encouraging Crime'. The Paper states at p. 63:
>
> > "First, it is one thing to think that a person should be guilty of murder if he engages in an unlawful enterprise and foresees that his co-adventurer may intentionally kill, but rather different to convict such a person of murder when he merely foresees that his co-adventurer may intentionally inflict serious injury. Secondly, it is anomalous that in such a case the law now requires a less blameworthy mental standard for the non-acting co-adventurer than for the person who actually commits the murderous act."
>
> Despite those observations, we feel bound to follow and apply the Hyde formulation having regard to the approval which it has received in a number of decisions in this court and to the fact that it is in accordance with the House of Lords' decision in *Maxwell*.[42] If the result is an unacceptable anomaly, it must now be for the House of Lords or the Legislature to say so."

It follows from these principles that the liability of a secondary party who foresees that the principal might inflict serious injury depends upon two facts beyond his control: (a) whether the victim dies from his injuries; (b) whether the principal himself intended to kill or inflict serious injury. If the principal had no such intent, then the secondary party's foresight will not be elevated to an "intent", even though the injury inflicted is precisely that which the secondary party foresaw (and maybe feared) as a possible consequence of the principal's actions.

---

[39] [1995] Crim.L.R. 296 at 298–301.
[40] [1996] 1 Cr.App.R. 14.
[41] At pp. 21 to 22.
[42] *Maxwell v. D.P.P. for Northern Ireland* (1978) 68 Cr.App.R. 128.

VI. WHICH OF TWO OR MORE CULPRITS?

It is sometimes the case that an injury is inflicted by one or other of several   1–017
people, and it is impossible to say who committed the assault which caussed
the injury. In cases such as fights where it can be shown that several people
were involved in a joint attack upon the victim, then it is proper to join all
those as defendants in a single count, *e.g.*, of assault occasioning actual bodily
harm on the basis that they were all participating in an assault which resulted
in injury.

. In other situations a real problem will arise where the offence must have
been committed by one or other of two people but it is impossible to say
which. If they were not party to a joint enterprise then in most situations
where that occurs, neither can be guilty of an offence of assault, nor of any
more serious offence based on an assault. In *R. v. Abbott*[43] Lord Goddard
said[44]:

> "If two people are jointly indicted for the commission of a crime and the evidence
> does not point to one rather than the other, and there is no evidence that they
> were acting in concert, the jury ought to return a verdict of Not Guilty in the
> case of both because the prosecution have not proved the case. If, in those circum-
> stances it is left to the defendants to get out of the difficulty if they can, that
> would put the onus on the defendants to prove themselves not guilty. My brother
> Finnemore J. remembers a case in which two sisters were indicted for murder,
> and there was evidence that they had both been in the room at the time of the
> murder; but the prosecution could not show that sister A or sister B had commit-
> ted the offence. Very likely one or other must have committed it, but there was
> no evidence which one. Although it is unfortunate that a guilty party cannot be
> brought to justice, it is far more important that there should not be a miscarriage
> of justice and that the law should be maintained rather than that there should be
> a failure in some particular case."

There is a limited exception to this rule which applies where a child has   1–018
suffered injuries at the hands of one or other of its parents or other persons
responsible for the child's welfare and while in their joint custody and control.
In *R. v. Gibson*[45] a five-week-old baby was admitted to hospital suffering very
severe injuries. The parents were charged with causing grievous bodily harm,
and an offence contrary to section 1 of the Children and Young Persons Act
1933. The prosecution case was that one or other had inflicted the injury, but
there was no evidence implicating one rather than the other. Following the
trial judge's ruling on joint enterprise neither accused gave or called evidence.
They were both convicted. Their appeals against conviction were allowed on
the basis that the trial judge had misdirected the jury on joint enterprise, and

---

[43] (1955) 39 Cr.App.R. 141. This was in fact a case of forgery, where the appeal was allowed
because the trial judge wrongly rejected a submission of no case to answer on the basis that to
do so would prejudice the co-defendant in a case there one or other of the defendants must
have been the perpetrator. See *R. v. Forman & Ford* [1988] Crim. L.R. 677 for an example of
a case where the jury were left to decide whether they were satisfied there had been a joint
enterprise; the alternative being to acquit both defendants.
[44] At pp. 148 to 149.
[45] (1984) 80 Cr.App.R. 24.

that the judge's direction was such as to deprive the accused of a free choice as to whether to give evidence. However, in the course of his judgment O'Connor L.J. said[46]:

> "Is the criminal law powerless in the situation presented by this case? We think not. In law and defendants had joint custody and control of their baby ... The evidence established that while in their joint custody and control the baby had sustained grievous bodily harm which had been inflicted by one, either or both parents. There being no explanation from either parent, and no evidence pointing to one rather than the other, the inference can properly be drawn that they were jointly responsible and so both guilty as charged. This is not reversing the burden of proof. The case is quite different from that envisaged in *Abbott*, in particular the two sisters charged with murder, because the deceased was not in their joint custody or control."

This dictum must be treated with caution. Despite O'Connor L.J.'s assurance that it does not shift the burden of proof, it seems to suggest that in cases such as this, either of those having joint care and custody of the child at the time it suffers injury can be convicted in the absence of explanation. The dictum would apply to cases where the victims are children, and also the elderly and infirm. The cases concentrate on children because they are the most vulnerable, and in the case of injury not resulting in death are likely to be too young to give evidence.

1–019   In *R. v. Lane & Lane*[47] the Court of Appeal described the passage from *Gibson* cited above as *obiter*, and held that where the injury was caused by a single blow, then participation had to be proved in the normal way, *i.e.* the prosecution must prove which person struck the blow and that the other party was aiding and abetting; or if it could not be proved which of them struck the blow, that they were acting in concert. In the absence of such proof, both were to be acquitted. In particular, the court was concerned at the suggestion that joint custody and care coupled with lack of explanation could prove even that the accused was present at the time the injury was inflicted. Croom-Johnson L.J. said[48]:

> "Evidence of general custody and care does not establish presence; it is only a step towards proof. Failure to give an acceptable explanation of what happened does not fill the gap in the evidence."

In *Lane & Lane* husband and wife were both convicted of manslaughter of the wife's 22-month-old child by a previous marriage. Death had been caused by a single blow. During the period within which the fatal blow had been struck, the child was alone from time to time with each of the defendants. There was no evidence as to which of them had inflicted the injury. Their appeal against conviction for manslaughter was allowed on the grounds that the principle in *Abbott* applied, and a submission of no case to answer should have succeeded. The court said that *Gibson* should be confined to offences under section 1 of the Children and Young Persons Act 1933, and even then

---

[46] At p. 30.
[47] (1985) 82 Cr.App.R. 5.
[48] At p. 17.

not for allegations of ill-treatment or neglect which relied on proof of a single incident. In *Lane & Lane* there had been three previous injuries which had not contributed to the child's death and there was no appeal against the conviction for wilful ill-treatment contrary to the 1933 Act which were based upon those injuries.

The Court of Appeal expressed further reservation about *Gibson* in *R. v. Russell*[49] where the defendants were both heroin addicts who on occasions dipped the dummy of their 15-month-old daughter in methadone to placate her. She died as a consequence of a massive overdose, probably administered as a single dose. She had otherwise been well cared for. Both parents denied administering the fatal dose to her. Their convictions for manslaughter were upheld by the Court of Appeal on the basis that a jury could infer joint responsibility for that fatal dose from the fact that they had both been responsible for administering the same drug to the child on previous occasions, and from the absence of any other explanation as to the cause of death. The court said that as a general rule, parents were in no different position from any other persons, and so the principle in *Abbott* applies. However, parents are under a positive duty towards their children which includes intervening to prevent ill-treatment of that child by another.

The case of *Lane & Lane* points the distinction which can properly be **1–020** drawn by a jury when a child in the defendant's joint care and custody on the one hand suffers injury or death from a single unlawful act, and, on the other, when it results from a course of conduct. In the former case, the principle in *Abbott* applies; in the latter the inference can be drawn that both are criminally responsible for the injury or death resulting either at their own hands or from their wilful failure to interfere and protect the child from the conduct causing the injury. An example of the "course of conduct" liability is *R. v. Gibbins & Proctor*.[50] In that case the two defendants were living together, and in the household were several children of one of them. All but one of the children were properly cared for; one was deliberately starved to death. (This is a case which still finds modern echoes. Evidence in child abuse cases frequently discloses that one of the children is picked out for ill-treatment while the rest are cared for properly). Both were convicted of murder, and G's appeal against conviction was dismissed since the jury could infer from his conduct that he intended the child to suffer really serious injury as a result of being starved, and although he did no positive act to the child, he did nothing to interfere on that child's behalf. If in *Lane & Lane* there had been no evidence that the parents had previously given the child methadone, then as death resulted from a single act which could not be attributed to one rather than the other, there would have been insufficient evidence against either of them.

This principle in *Abbott* was confirmed and applied in *Aston*[51] where the **1–021** prosecution had asserted that the first defendant had inflicted the injuries while the second defendant had encouraged him, or vice versa. The Court of

---

[49] (1987) 85 Cr.App.R. 388.
[50] (1918) 13 Cr.App.R. 134.
[51] (1992) 94 Cr.App.R. 180.

Appeal held that at the close of the prosecution case, the trial judge should have withdrawn the case from the jury. The two defendants were indicted with murder of and with cruelty to a child. There was nothing in the evidence to suggest that one rather than the other had inflicted the injuries, and nothing to indicate that they had acted in concert.

1-022   It may be that as the offences of wilful ill-treatment and wilful neglect of a child contrary to section 1 of the Children and Young Persons Act 1933 are now punishable with up to 10 years' imprisonment, rather than two years which applied before September 29, 1988,[52] cases involving injuries inflicted upon children under the age of 16 by those having care of them will be charged under that section, rather than with offences contrary to sections 18, 20 or 47 of the Offences Against the Person Act 1861.

1-023   In cases of multiple acts of violence in the course of a fight, it is sometimes impossible to establish who struck whom, or which blow caused what injury. Such cases are often better dealt with as offences under the Public Order Act 1986.[53]

VII. UNLAWFUL ACT

1-024   To amount to an offence of assault, or any of the offences set out in this work, the act must be unlawful. The activity itself need not be unlawful, it is sufficient if the act alleged transforms what would otherwise be a lawful act into one that is unlawful, *e.g.* a policeman going beyond the limits of his powers, or a parent or teacher using excessive force in the course of correcting or restraining a child.

1-025   Touching someone to attract their attention, or in the course of conversation or other social activity is not unlawful, nor are the sort of physical contacts which are the consequences of everyday living, such as being in a crowded shop or train.[54] The definition of assault requires a deliberate act intended to cause the victim to apprehend immediate and unlawful violence, or being reckless as to whether such apprehension is caused.[55] It follows that accident is a defence. This would include the acts of third parties, *e.g.* someone rushing for a bus causes A to stop suddenly and collide with B. It would afford a defence, for example, to two people engaged in horseplay in a public street where one caused the other to bump into a pedestrian knocking him into the road; it would amount to an assault by both participants in the horseplay if they realised that there was the possibility of such a thing happening, as then

---

[52] ss.45 and 171(6) Criminal Justice Act 1988; and see para. 8–010.
[53] See *R. v. Smith* [1988] Crim. L.R. 616 for an example of the problems in proving participation in a single act of violence in the course of a fight. For the liability of all participants for injury caused by one of them in the course of a joint enterprise see *Chan Wing-Siu v. R.* (1985) 80 Cr.App.R. 117 and *R. v. Hyde* (1991) 92 Cr.App.R. 131.
[54] *Tuberville v. Savage* (1669) 1 Mod. Rep. 3; *R. v. Kimber* (1983) 77 Cr.App.R. 225; *Collins v. Wilcock* (1984) 79 Cr.App.R. 229.
[55] *R. v. Venna* [1976] Q.B. 421; *R. v. Savage, D.P.P. v. Parmenter* (1992) 94 Cr.App.R. 193.

they would be reckless and their recklessness would supervene the defence otherwise open to them.[56]

1–026
Acts which would otherwise be assaults are lawful if they amount to the use of reasonable force while exercising a right. Reasonable force may be used by any person "in the prevention of crime, or in effecting or assisting in the lawful arrest of offenders or suspected offenders or of persons unlawfully at large."[57] Police officers have extended powers of arrest set out under the Police and Criminal Evidence Act 1984, and further exceptional powers under the Prevention of Terrorism (Temporary) Provisions Act 1989 and the Prevention of Terrorism (Additional Powers) Act 1996. The exercise of those powers is lawful if exercised in accordance with the following principles:—(i) the factual basis for the exercise of the police office's power exists (*e.g.* an offence has been committed, or there are circumstances giving rise to reasonable suspicion); (ii) the officer gives the correct reason for his action when he is required to do so (*e.g.* when arresting someone); and (iii) his actions were reasonable.[58] The ordinary citizen is in a different position. In his case the "lawful arrest" referred to in section 3(1) of the Criminal Law Act 1967 is confined to three circumstances. Firstly, anyone who is or whom he has reasonable grounds for thinking is committing an arrestable offence (in general, an offence carrying a maximum penalty of five years' imprisonment[59]). Secondly, where an arrestable offence has been committed, anyone who is guilty of the offence, or whom he has reasonable grounds for believing to be guilty of it.[60] Thirdly, where there is a breach of the peace and reasonable action is taken to prevent it, including arrest if necessary.[61] In addition, any person may use reasonable force to protect themselves or another from unlawful assault[62] and to protect his own property from criminal violation.[63] Reasonable force may be used in carrying out a court order (*e.g.* a sentence of imprisonment, or remand in custody—an order of a court is sufficient answer even to applications for habeas corpus[64]).

1–027
A number of general defences prevent what would otherwise be an unlawful assault from being an offence. Some of these defences apply generally, some

---

[56] This proposition is based upon general principles of liability for offences of assault. The case of *R. v. Bruce* (1847) 2 Cox C.C. 262 (see para. 1–038) seems to be contrary to this proposition; but is not likely now to be applied so as to exonerate those engaged recklessly in dangerous, boisterous behaviour—see *R. v. Adomako* 99 Cr.App.R. 362 (para. 1–012 above).

[57] Criminal Law Act 1967, s. 3(1).

[58] These principles are gleaned from *Christie v. Leachinski* [1947] A.C. 573; *Steel v. Goacher* [1973] RTR 98; *Rice v. Connelly* [1966] 2 Q.B. 414; *Donnelly v. Jackman* [1970] 1 W.L.R. 562; and *Edwards v. D.P.P.* [1993] C.O.D. 378 together with the Codes of Practice issued under s.66 of the Police and Criminal Evidence Act 1984.

[59] See Police and Criminal Evidence Act 1984, s.24(4). For the precise definition and the extended offences to which it applies see s.24(1)–(3) of that Act. The action is only lawful if an arrestable offence has actually been committed or is being committed however reasonable may be the person's belief that it is being or has been committed—see *R. v. Self* 95 Cr.App.R. 42.

[60] *ibid.*, s.24(5). No such arrest is lawful unless an arrestable offence has actually been committed—*R. v. Self* (see previous footnote).

[61] *Albert v. Lavin* (1981) 74 Cr.App.R. 150.

[62] *Palmer v. R.* [1971] A.C. 814.

[63] Criminal Law Act, 1967, s.3.

[64] *e.g. R. v. Liverpool City Justices, ex p. D.P.P.* [1992] 3 W.L.R. 20.

only to certain categories of offence especially consent. Attempts to rationalise these exceptions within a consistent principle have failed. Lord Mustill in his exemplary (though dissenting) speech in *R. v. Brown*[65] analysed the historical basis for these exceptions founded on the theory of consent to determine whether there is some consistent principle behind them. He considered that the issue of whether a set of facts, not previously decided upon, fell within the prohibition of the criminal law of assault depended upon the starting point:

> "As I have ventured to formulate the crucial question, it asks whether there is good reason to impress upon section 47 [of the Offences Against the Person act 1861] an interpretation which penalises the relevant level of harm irrespective of consent, *i.e.* to recognise sado-masochistic activities as falling into a special category of acts, such as duelling and prize-fighting, which the law says shall not be done." This is very important, for if the question were differently stated it might well yield a different answer. In particular, if it were to be held that as a matter of law all infliction of bodily harm above the level of common assault is incapable of being legitimated by consent, except in special circumstances, then we would have to consider whether the public interest required the recognition of private sexual activities as being in a specially exempt category . . . I ask myself, not whether as a result of the decision in this appeal, activities such as those of the appellants should *cease* to be criminal, but rather whether the Act of 1861 (a statute which I repeat once again was clearly intended to penalise conduct of a quite different nature) should in this new situation be interpreted so as to *make* it criminal."[66]

He decided that such consensual activities were not offences, and he was not prepared to say that the law should make them offences. The majority took the view that as the activities (sado-masochistic activities of a particularly unpleasant kind) were not covered by any existing category of exemption, they were unlawful irrespective of consent. Much discussion concerned whether it was possible to define the extent of physical injury to which consent was a valid defence, and injury of such gravity that it could not. Such an exercise was fraught with difficulty—the differences between "wound" and "actual bodily harm" being technical rather than indicating gravity; and section 20 of the 1861 Act prohibiting wounding (which might be a minor injury) as well as infliction of grievous bodily harm. Consequently there was no means of distinguishing certain injuries or certain sections which give rise to a defence of consent as a matter of principle, as opposed to those which do not. The House of Lords decided the issue by ruling that consent is only a defence to common assault. Injury precludes a defence of assault except in those cases falling within one of the established categories. Despite Lord Mustill's efforts to keep those categories open[67] we must accept that all violence inflicting injury is an assault unless it falls within an established exception. Those exceptions below which are sometimes said to be based on consent (*e.g.* lawful sports) must be regarded as *sui generis* rather than an expression of a larger principle.

---

[65] (1993) 97 Cr.App.R. 44 at 68–84.
[66] At p. 82.
[67] "I prefer to address each individual category of consensual violence in the light of the situation as a whole. Sometimes the element of consent will make no difference and sometimes it will make all the difference. Circumstances must alter cases." (at p. 79).

VIII. DEFENCES

(1) CONSENT

As a result of the House of Lords' decision in *Brown*,[68] consent is in general 1–028 only a defence to common assault. Except in the limited categories of established exceptions set out below, it does not apply where any injury more than "transient or trifling" is inflicted.

In *Brown* the existing categories of cases where consent *will* afford a defence were expressly preserved. It will be seen that they cannot properly be explained on the basis of consent, and must be regarded as exceptions to the principle that inflicting any substantial injury amounts to an offence. These exceptions referred to in *Brown*[69] are set out below in paragraphs 1–029 to 1–045. No person can lawfully consent to their own death, and anyone who causes a person to die or assists in their death is guilty of an offence.[70]

(a) Properly conducted sports and tests of skill.

Sports injuries are common and accepted as an inevitable consequence. Any 1–029 theory of criminal law which prohibited properly conducted sports would not command respect. In fact, what is and what is not permitted is an odd mixture. Football and other such sports are of course lawful (although prohibited during the 17th century). Boxing is permitted if properly conducted, even though the intention of each participant is to inflict such injury on his opponent so as to render him unconscious, or so badly injured as to be unable to continue. Prize fighting is not lawful even with consent.[71] Even within sporting contests, if one participant acts with intolerable violence and intends to inflict injury and does an act which is contrary to the rules of the sport then consent will not provide a defence.[72]

(b) Reasonable surgical interference.

In such cases consent is normally sought from the patient in advance. In 1–030 cases where consent is not given, *e.g.* because the patient is too young, too ill or is suffering from mental incapacity, the surgery is nevertheless lawful provided it is in the patient's best interests, and surgery is necessary to save the patient's life, or prevent deterioration.[73] In *Airedale NHS Trust v. Bland*[74] Lord Mustill expressed the exception for medical treatment in these terms:

---

[68] (1993) 97 Cr.App.R. 44.
[69] At pp. 72 to 79.
[70] Euthanasia is either murder, or aiding and abetting suicide—see chaps 4 and 6 below. Only when death occurs in the course of proper medical treatment (*e.g.* the administration of pain-killing drugs) will acceleration of death be lawful:—see, *e.g. Airedale NHS Trust v. Bland* para. 1–030 below.
[71] *R. v. Coney* (1882) 8 Q.B.D. 534; *R. v. Orton* (1878) 39 L.T. 293.
[72] *R. v. Bradshaw* (1878) 14 Cox C.C. 83.
[73] In *Re T* [1988] 2 W.L.R. 189 and *F. v. West Berkshire Health Authority* [1989] 2 All E.R. 545.
[74] [1993] A.C. 789.

"How is it that, . . . a doctor can with immunity perform on a consenting patient an act which would be a very serious crime if done by someone else? The answer must be that bodily invasions in the course of proper medical treatment stand completely outside the criminal law. The reason why the consent of the patient is so important is not that it furnishes a defence in itself, but because it is usually essential to the propriety of medical treatment. Thus, if the consent is absent, and is not dispensed with in special circumstances by operation of law, the acts of the doctor lose their immunity."[75]

That there is a limit to this immunity is shown by *R. v. Adomako*[76] where it was held that negligence of sufficient gravity in the performance of a medical operation can take it outside the immunity and render the acts criminal.[77]

(c) Lawful correction.

1–031   Whether this is an example of consent when the correction is carried out by a teacher or someone else in *loco parentis*, or whether the child is deemed in some perverse Victorian way to consent to its own punishment is immaterial. It is an exception recognised by law. A parent or other person exercising authority in *loco parentis* is entitled to use reasonable force to discipline or chastise a child or young person under his care.[78] In *R. v. Hopley*[79] Cockburn C.J. directed the jury as follows:

"A parent or schoolmaster (who for this purpose represents the parent and has parental authority delegated to him) may for the purpose of correcting what is evil in the child inflict moderate corporal punishment, always, however, with this condition, that it is moderate and reasonable. If it be administered for the gratification of passion or of rage, or if it be immoderate or excessive in its nature or degree, or if it be protracted beyond the child's powers of endurance, or with an instrument unfitted for the purpose or calculated to produce danger to life or limb; in all such cases the punishment is excessive, the violence is unlawful, and if evil consequences to life or limb ensue, then the person inflicting it is answerable to the law . . ."

In that case, a schoolmaster beat a pupil in his early teens with a stick and rope for two and a half hours. At the end of it, the boy died of exhaustion. The schoolmaster was convicted of manslaughter.

1–032   As subsequent cases show, what is regarded as "moderate and reasonable" does not remain static. What is reasonable depends not only upon moral views prevalent at the time, but also upon the facts of the case—a teacher confronted by a burly and violent sixteen-year-old will be entitled to use more force than with a wilful and disobedient six-year-old. Whatever the circumstances, any serious injury (and possibly anything beyond a temporary mark) will in practice require exceptional circumstances to justify it.

1–033   What constitutes reasonable chastisement depends upon the ordinary standards of this country. Consequently it is no defence to say that the local

---

[75] At p. 891.
[76] 99 Cr.App.R. 362.
[77] See para. 1.12.
[78] *R. v. Donovan* (1934) 25 Cr.App.R. 1 at 12.
[79] (1860) 2 F. & F. 202 at 206.

customs of the place from which the child or defendant originate, tolerate or require chastisement more severe than is lawful according to the law of England and Wales.[80] However, cultural and philosophical practices should be taken into account by a school when acting in *loco parentis*—but possibly only to the extent of alleviating rather than exacerbating the type and gravity of punishment inflicted.[81]

A parent is deemed to give authority to a teacher to make reasonable regulation for the running of the school, and to administer punishment where appropriate. This authority extends to regulation of the pupil's behaviour outside school premises.[82] The school's authority is not completely substituted for that of the parents—The European Court of Human Rights decided in *Campbell & Cosans v. U.K.*[83] that the school should respect the parents' philosophical convictions about the use of corporal punishment. In that case the parents objected to the school's policy of administering corporal punishment, and took the case to court when their child was beaten.

1–034

Section 47 of the Education (No. 2) Act 1986[84] restricts a teacher's right to use corporal punishment. Section 47(1) provides that:

1–035

> "Where in any proceedings, it is shown that corporal punishment has been given to a pupil to whom this subsection applies by or on the authority of a member of the staff, giving the punishment cannot be justified on the ground that it was done in pursuance of a right exercisable by the member of staff by virtue of his position as such."

The subsection applies to pupils at any publicly funded schools, and also to pupils at independent schools whose fees are paid wholly or partly out of public funds. This includes schools maintained by local authorities, special schools, grant maintained schools, independent schools maintained or assisted out of public funds, direct grant independent schools, Ministry of Defence schools, city technology colleges, and to pupils at independent schools whose fees are paid by a local authority.[85] However, this section does not automatically mean that any teacher using corporal punishment in any circumstances is guilty of an offence of assault. Section 47(4) of the Act provides that no offence is committed:

> "by reason of any conduct . . . which would, apart from this section, be justified on the ground that it is done in pursuance of a right exercisable by a member of staff by virtue of his position as such."

The combined effect of these provisions seems to be that corporal punishment cannot be justified simply by asserting that the teacher was entitled by rules and practices of the school to administer such punishment; however, it

---

[80] *R. v. Derriviere* (1969) 53 Cr.App.R. 637.
[81] See *Campbell & Cosans v. U.K.* below.
[82] *R. v. Newport (Salop) Justices, ex p. Wright* [1929] 2 K.B. 416.
[83] (1982) 4 E.H.R.R. 293.
[84] As amended by regs S.I. 1987 No. 1183, S.I. 1989 No. 1233 and S.I. 1989 No. 1825 and by the Education Act 1993, Sched. 19, para. 101.
[85] Education (No. 2) Act 1986, s.4(5) and (6) and amendments—see previous footnote. Corporal punishment is subject to similar restriction in children's homes—see S.I. 1991 No. 1506, reg. 8(2)(a).

will be a defence in criminal proceedings to show that the punishment was no more than reasonable chastisement in the particular case. This probably means that in practice an evidential burden is placed on the defence to justify the act.

1-036   Throwing an object at a pupil in class so that injury is caused is unlawful.[86] If a person exercising care or authority of a child puts that child in fear of unlawful punishment so that he runs away to escape that is assault; and if he sustains injury in so doing, it will be assault occasioning actual bodily harm.[87]

The use of corporal punishment by way of three whacks with a rubber soled gym shoe on the bottom of a seven-year-old boy at an independent private school which had a policy of administering corporal punishment was held by the European Court of Human Rights not to amount to degrading punishment within Article 3 of the European Convention on Human Rights.[88] However, a single stroke of a cane by the headmaster in presence of his deputy adminis- tered to a sixteen-year-old girl as punishment for smoking was found by the European Commission of Human Rights to be degrading. She had been caned on the hand, and the caning had caused bruising. The Commission's concerns were the age of the girl and the fact that the teachers were male. The Council of Ministers did not endorse that finding.[89]

1-037   A requirement that a pupil do homework is not a matter of school discipline, and so keeping a pupil behind at school for that purpose is unlawful—it amounts to false imprisonment.[90] A person is entitled to restrict a child's free- dom of movement in the exercise of parental discipline. But there is no rule of law to prevent a parent committing an offence of false imprisonment in respect of his own child if that restriction of the child's freedom exceeds the demands of reasonable control. In *R. v. Rahman*[91] the defendant, a Banglade- shi national, placed his teenage daughter with foster parents after his wife had returned to Bangladesh. In due course he too decided to return there and abducted his daughter against her will with the intention of returning with her to Bangladesh. It was argued on his behalf that a parent could not commit an offence of false imprisonment of his own child unless he were acting in breach of a court order or contrary to the rights of the other parent. The Court of Appeal rejected that argument and decided that where detention is for such a period or in such circumstances as to take it outside the realms of reasonable parental discipline it is unlawful and therefore amounts to false imprisonment. Inevitably, whether the bounds of reasonable parental disci- pline have been exceeded depends upon the circumstances of each case.

(d) Rough and undisciplined horseplay

1-038   It is a defence that the victim consented to such behaviour—or that the defendant genuinely believed that he did. It is not confined to adolescents,

---

[86] *R. v. Taylor, The Times*, December 28, 1983.
[87] *R. v. Mackie* (1973) 57 Cr.App.R. 453.
[88] *Castello-Roberts v. U.K.* (1993) 19 E.H.R.R. 112.
[89] *Warwick v. U.K..* Resolution DH (89) 5 of March 2, 1989.
[90] *Hunter v. Johnson* (1884) 13 Q.B.D. 225.
[91] (1985) 81 Cr.App.R. 349.

although "adolescent" is the type of behaviour with which this defence is concerned. In *R. v. Bruce*[92] the defendant, who was drunk, went into a shop and playfully spun round a boy who was inside. The boy realised it was a game and consented to it. As a result of spinning the boy round, the defendant staggered into the road and collided with a woman who was passing. She fell and later died of her injuries. Erle J. held that the defendant must be acquitted of manslaughter because there was nothing unlawful in what the defendant did, since the boy had consented. This type of robust view of lawful activity must be contrasted with other situations giving rise to an offence of manslaughter by recklessness.[93] It is notable that the defendant's drunkenness did not affect the availability of the defence.

In *R. v. Jones*[94] the defendants (who were schoolboys) were indicted with maliciously inflicting grievous bodily harm on a fellow schoolboy. They threw him in the air and let him fall to the ground—an extreme form of the "bumps". He suffered serious injury as a result. The defences were that the victim consented, or that the defendants genuinely believed he was consenting to rough horseplay. The trial judge refused to allow those defences to go to the jury. The Court of Appeal quashed the convictions, saying that those defences should have been left to the jury. There is of course a great deal of difference between consensual horseplay, which is not unlawful, and bullying which is.

(e) Consensual sexual activity involving only trifling injury

Most consensual sexual conduct is lawful even if it results in some minor **1–039** injury, *e.g.* a transient mark or bruise. The House of Lords in the case of *Brown*[95] was concerned with activity which caused more than trivial injury and can be categorised as atypical sexual conduct. However, even where the injury is permanent, consent may afford a defence. The Court of Appeal in *R. v. Wilson*[96] avoided the effect of a literal interpretation of *Brown*. The defendant had branded his wife's buttocks with his initials. The act was at her instigation and with her consent. The trial judge ruled that her consent afforded no defence and directed a conviction. The Court of Appeal quashed the conviction. They did so on the basis that there was no aggression nor sado-masochistic element. The court pointed out that the act was akin to tattooing which attracts no criminal penalty when carried out consensually. The court said public policy considerations require each case to be decided on its own facts in determining what activity amounts to criminal conduct. Insofar as this is an application of the majority decision in *Brown* it applies common sense to an area which would otherwise bring the law into disrepute. It seems that the only difference in approach between the Court of Appeal and Lord

---

[92] (1847) 2 Cox C.C. 262. See also *R. v. Lamb* (1967) 51 Cr.App.R. 63, and *R. v. Brown* (1993) 97 Cr.App.R. 44 (para. 1–027 above).
[93] See chap. 5.
[94] (1986) 83 Cr.App.R. 375.
[95] See para. 1–027 above.
[96] [1996] Crim.L.R. 573.

Mustill dissenting in *Brown* is that the former will start from the proposition that such activity requires public policy justification, whereas Lord Mustill's approach was that in the absence of established prohibition of certain conduct (*e.g.* killing), all consensual activity was in principle lawful. There remains the case of *R. v. Donovan*[97] in which Swift J. said that inflicting physical harm for sexual gratification (in that case with a prostitute) could be an offence because "As a general rule, although it is a rule to which there are well established exceptions, it is an unlawful act to beat another person with such a degree of violence that the infliction of bodily harm is a probable consequence, and when such an act is proved, consent is immaterial".[98] The current law is that it is immaterial whether the physical injury which results is probable or adventitious.[99] These cases show the confusion in which the law now stands when dealing with consensual sexual activity. It seem that the law has generally taken a prudish attitude towards any sexual deviancy and will regard any substantial injury resulting from it to be outside the scope of a defence of consent.

1-040   Where consent is raised as a defence that consent must be real. If it is obtained by duress or fraud it is no defence.[1] Whether consent is a valid defence when one person infects another with a sexually transmitted disease in the course of consensual acts when that person is aware of the infection and the other party is not, is open to doubt. In *R. v. Clarence*[2] the Court of Crown Cases Reserved decided that when a husband knowingly infected his wife with gonorrhoea he committed no offence. Now that a wife may withdraw her consent[3] this case is of limited authority.

1-041   A defendant's genuine mistake that the other party is consenting will afford a defence in those cases where actual consent would be a defence.[4]

1-042   A child or young person who does not appreciate what he is doing cannot validly consent to an act resulting in injury to himself.[5]

1-043   Consent is no defence where the assailant strikes in anger or intends to do physical harm beyond that regarded as inherent in the lawful activity.[6] In situations where any injury is not regarded as an acceptable part of the lawful activity (*e.g.* street fights) then consent is no defence where anything beyond transient and trifling injury is inflicted.[7] Prizefighting with bare fists is unlaw-

---

[97] (1934) 25 Cr.App.R. 1.
[98] *ibid.* at p. 10.
[99] *A.-G.'s Reference (No. 6 of 1980)* (1981) 73 Cr.App.R. 63.
[1] *R. v. Elbekkay* [1995] Crim. L.R. 163. Whether the fraud must relate to the identity of the person or the nature of the act as in rape cases is open to question.
[2] (1888) 22 Q.B.D. 23.
[3] *R. v. R.* [1992] 1 A.C. 599.
[4] *R. v. Gladstone Williams* (1983) 78 Cr.App.R. 276 and *D.P.P. v. Morgan* [1976] A.C. 182.
[5] *Burrell v. Harmer* [1967] Crim. L.R. 169.
[6] *R. v. Coney* (1882) 8 Q.B.D. 534; *R. v. Jones* (1986) 83 Cr.App.R. 375 and *A.-G.'s Reference (No. 6 of 1980)* (1981) 73 Cr.App.R. 63. In *R. v. Coney* it was said that consent could not be a defence to a scuffle which amounted to a breach of the peace. The Court of Appeal in *A.-G.'s Reference (No. 6 of 1980)* disagreed where the scuffle was minor and no injury resulted. This conclusion was approved in *R. v. Brown* (1993) 97 Cr.App.R. 44.
[7] *R. v. Brown* (1993) 97 Cr.App.R. 44 and *A.-G.'s Reference (No. 6 of 1980)* (1981) 73 Cr.App.R. 63.

ful irrespective of consent.[8] In *R. v. Orton*[9] the two defendants fought in a roped off ring; each wore boxing gloves and each had a second. During the fight, they beat each other severely and one bit through the ear of the other. That was held to be an unlawful fight, *i.e.* the nature of the fight made it unlawful for both participants. A distinction was drawn between genuine tests of skill and fights (however supervised) in which it is the intention of the parties to beat the other until he collapses from exhaustion or injury. This is different from those cases where one party exceeds the level of violence acceptable in the lawful sport, in which case only that person is guilty of assault, *e.g.* a footballer who deliberately aims a hard kick at an opponent.

(2) ACTS DONE BY PERSONS TREATING PATIENTS IN MENTAL HOSPITALS

The Mental Health Act 1983 contains provisions as to treatment and man- **1-044** agement of the affairs of those suffering from mental disorder. Confining these patients in a hospital or other institution and their day-to-day management involve acts which would be assaults in the absence of the lawful authority provided by the Act. In order to protect those treating such patients or engaged in their care, section 139 of that Act provides two limits on prosecution for any offence:

> "(1) No person shall be liable, whether on the ground of want of jurisdiction or on any other ground, to any ... criminal proceedings to which he would have been liable apart from this section in respect of any act purporting to be done in pursuance of this Act or any regulations or rules made under this Act, or in, or in pursuance of anything done in, the discharge of functions conferred by any other enactment ... unless the act was done in bad faith or without reasonable care.
> (2) ... no criminal proceedings shall be brought against any person in any court in respect of such an act except by or with the authority of the Director of Public Prosecution."

In *R. v. Bracknell Justices, ex p. Griffiths*[10] Lord Edmund-Davies adopted **1-045** the following definition of the acts which fall within the protection of section 139:

> "In my judgement where a male nurse is on duty and exercising his functions of controlling the patients in the hospital, acts done in pursuance of such control, or purportedly in pursuance of such control, are acts within the scope of section [139], and one is thus protected by the section."[11]

R. v. Bracknell Justices is an example of the type of protection afforded by section 139. The defendant was a male nurse at Broadmore. He was alleged to have punched a patient on the shoulder. The patient prosecuted him under section 42 of the Offences Against the Person Act 1861 and he was convicted. Leave to prosecute had not been given under what is now section 139(2). The House of Lords quashed his conviction because he was acting in the course of

---

[8] *R. v. Coney* (1882) 8 Q.B.D. 534.
[9] (1878) 39 L.T. 293.
[10] [1976] A.C. 314.
[11] *ibid.* at p. 336. The principle of course applies irrespective of the gender of the nurse.

his duties at the time, and so failure to obtain the necessary consent was fatal to the prosecution. That consent must be obtained before he first appears in court, but it need not be obtained before he is charged.[12] Section 139 does not apply to offences of ill-treating patients, contrary to section 127 of the Mental Health Act[13] as the consent of the Department of Public Prosecution is required for such prosecutions in any event.

(3) SELF DEFENCE

1-046   A person is entitled to use reasonable force to defend himself against an unlawful attack. He is equally entitled to use reasonable force to protect his family or his property from unlawful attack. In addition, section 3(1) of the Criminal Law Act 1967 provides that "A person may use such force as is reasonable in the circumstances in the prevention of crime, or in effecting or assisting in the lawful arrest of offenders or suspected offenders or of persons unlawfully at large." Therefore reasonable force can be used to prevent an unlawful attack upon anyone, or a breach of the peace.[14]

1-047   Self-defence is a complete defence to any charge, including murder. In a case of alleged murder, a successful defence of self-defence entitles the defendant to a verdict of not guilty. Unlike provocation it does not have the effect of reducing the charge from murder to manslaughter. If the force used is excessive, the defence fails. Use of excessive force resulting in deliberate killing (either by intending death or really serious bodily injury) is murder, not manslaughter.

1-048   The defence consists of two ingredients: (i) the defendant must have genuinely believed at the time that he was being attacked (or someone else was being attacked, etc., as the case may be) or was in imminent danger of being attacked; and (ii) his response must have been proportionate to the perceived threat. The principles of the law of self-defence and guidance on how a judge should direct a jury on the issue are set out in the speech of Lord Morris of Borth-y-Gest giving the judgment of the Privy Council in *Palmer v. R.*[15]:

> "In their Lordships' view, the defence of self-defence is one which can be and will be readily understood by a jury. It is a straightforward conception. It involves no abstruse legal thought. It requires no set words by way of explanation. No formula need be employed in reference to it. Only common sense is needed for its understanding. It is both good law and good sense that a man who is attacked may defend himself. It is both good law and good sense that he may do, but only may do, what is reasonably necessary. But everything will depend upon the particular facts and circumstances. Of these a jury can decide. It may in some cases be only sensible and clearly possible to take some simple avoiding action. Some attacks may be serious and dangerous. Others may not. If there is some relatively minor attack, it would not be common sense to permit some action of retaliation which was wholly out of proportion to the necessities of the situation. If an attack is serious so that it puts someone in immediate peril, then immediate defensive

---

[12] *R. v. Elliott* (1984) 81 Cr.App.R. 115.
[13] s.139(3).
[14] *Albert v. Lavin* (1981) 74 Cr.App.R. 150.
[15] [1971] A.C. 814 at 831–832.

action may be necessary. If the moment is one of crisis for someone in imminent danger, he may have to avert the danger by some instant reaction. If the attack is all over and no sort of peril remains, then the employment of force may be by way of revenge or punishment or by way of paying off an old score or may be pure aggression. There may no longer be any link with a necessity of defence. Of all these matters the good sense of the jury will be the arbiter. There are no prescribed words which must be employed or adopted in a summing up. All that is needed is a clear exposition, in relation to the particular facts of the case, of the conception of necessary self-defence. If there has been no attack, then clearly there will have been no need for defence. If there has been attack so that defence is reasonably necessary, it will be recognised that a person defending himself cannot weigh to a nicety the exact measure of his necessary defensive action. If the jury thought that in a moment of unexpected anguish a person attacked had only done what he honestly and instinctively thought was necessary, that would be most potent evidence that only reasonable defensive action had been taken. A jury will be told that the defence of self-defence, where the evidence makes its raising possible, will fail only if the prosecution show beyond reasonable doubt that what the accused did was not by way of self-defence. But their Lordships consider, that if the prosecution have shown that what was done was not done in self-defence, then that issue is eliminated from the case. If the jury consider that an accused acted in self-defence or if the jury are in doubt as to this, then they will acquit. The defence of self-defence either succeeds so as to result in an acquittal or it is disproved, in which case as a defence it is rejected."

A genuine mistake about the existence of a threat entitles a defendant to be treated as if his belief were true, and his response judged according to that perceived threat. Whether his belief was reasonable is only material insofar as it enables the jury to assess whether his belief was genuinely held.[16] A mistake cannot be relied upon if it results from self-induced intoxication by alcohol or drugs.[17] But if the mistake is a genuine, sober mistake the defendant is entitled to rely upon it, not only as to the existence of the imminent threat but also as to its severity in determining how reasonable was his response.[18]   **1-049**

A person need not wait until he is struck before using force in his own defence. In *R. v. Deana*[19] the trial judge had directed the jury that self-defence was limited to warding off blows. The Court of Appeal said that direction was incorrect, and that a defendant is entitled to use self-defence by striking his assailant before he himself is struck. In exceptional circumstances he may even arm himself against imminent attack. The Court of Appeal expressed the view in *Attorney-General's Reference (No. 2 of 1983)*[20] that it could be lawful for a person to arm himself with a petrol bomb with the object of protecting himself and his family from an imminent attack of great ferocity. A defendant is expected to exercise reasonable restraint. He is not required to retreat or demonstrate an unwillingness to stand his ground or fight.[21] Such matters are   **1-050**

---

[16] *R. v. Gladstone Williams* (1983) 78 Cr.App.R. 276, approved by the Privy Council in *Beckford v. R.* [1988] A.C. 130.
[17] *R. v. O'Grady* (1987) 85 Cr.App.R. 315; *R. v. Lipman* (1969) 53 Cr.App.R. 600; *R. v. O'Connor* [1991] Crim. L.R. 135.
[18] *R. v. O'Grady* (1987) 85 Cr.App.R. 315.
[19] (1909) 2 Cr.App.R. 75.
[20] (1984) 78 Cr.App.R. 183.
[21] *R. v. McInnes* (1971) 55 Cr.App.R. 551 at 560–561 *per* Edmund-Davies L.J. and *R. v. Bird* (1985) 81 Cr.App.R. 110.

evidence which the jury must assess in deciding whether the defendant's fear was genuine and whether he reacted commensurately with that genuine fear. Voluntary involvement in an unlawful fight is not self-defence; and self-defence ceases at the point where reasonable protection ends and retaliation begins.

1-051   The defendant's actions must be proportionate to the threat. His own genuine belief in the heat of the moment as to what is a reasonable reaction carries great weight, and will often be the critical issue.[22] If a defendant is under attack and reaches for the first object to hand, the use of that object is likely to be more reasonable than if he deliberately chooses a lethal weapon when others are available and the attack upon him is not such as to require the use of extreme violence to repel it. But if the attack upon the defendant is of murderous ferocity, then he may be entitled to use extreme violence in defence if that, in the heat of the moment, is the reasonable course to adopt. Many of the authorities on self-defence arise from murder cases, and there is no doubt that self-defence is a complete defence to such a charge, *e.g.* killing someone about to detonate a bomb. If the defence fails for whatever reason, then, subject to the existence of some other defence, the defendant is guilty of the full offence. It was argued in *Palmer v. R.* and *R. v. McInnes*[23] that if the defence of self-defence to a charge of murder fails because excessive force was used, then the jury should convict of manslaughter. This argument was rejected. That argument was rejected by the House of Lords in *R. v. Clegg*[24] in which a soldier in Northern Ireland had fired at and fatally struck a person in a moving car. It was argued on the defendant's behalf that where the death resulted from the defendant using excess force in attempting to arrest an offender or prevent crime, then that excess force reduced the offence from murder to manslaughter. The House of Lords rejected that argument, and held that there is no special rule for soldiers or anyone seeking to enforce law and order, and that if the defence of self-defence fails because the jury find that the defendant used excessive force then the verdict has to be guilty of murder.

1-052   In *R. v. Fennell*[25] the defendant assaulted a police officer who was arresting his son. The son had been involved in a fight outside a public house. The defendant thought the officer was using excessive force to arrest his son. The trial judge directed the jury that if the officer had not in fact used excessive force, then he was acting lawfully and the defendant was not entitled to use force in his son's aid. The Court of Appeal said that where a person honestly and reasonably believed that he or his child was in imminent danger of injury, then he was entitled to use reasonable force to avert that danger. The requirement that the belief of reasonable is no longer necessary as a matter of law following the decisions in *Gladstone Williams* and *Beckford*.[26] In *Fennell* the Court of Appeal decided (as a matter of fact not law) that as the defendant's

[22] *R. v. Gladstone Williams* (1983) 78 Cr.App.R. 276; [1971] A.C. 814 at 831–832.
[23] [1971] A.C. 814 and (1971) 55 Cr.App.R. 551 respectively.
[24] [1995] 1 A.C. 482.
[25] (1970) 54 Cr.App.R. 451.
[26] (1983) 78 Cr.App.R. 276 and [1988] A.C. 130 respectively, and see para. 1–049 above.

son was in police custody he was not in any imminent danger of injury. This sanguine view of police conduct must be a matter for review on the facts in each case, and in appropriate circumstances excessive use of force by a police officer would certainly entitle a defendant to use reasonable force on his own or another's behalf. In *R. v. Ball*[27] the Court of Appeal held that a mistaken belief that a police officer was using excessive force to restrain a prisoner did not amount to a defence. The point in that case was that there was no mistake about the amount of force being used, merely a misconception about whether that force was reasonable. A mistake of law will not avail a defendant. However, *Ball* must be confined to its own facts. Neither *Gladstone Williams* nor *Beckford* were cited to the court. In *R. v. Ryan*[28] the defendant slightly injured one of two men who entered his house with a sledgehammer. He believed they had come to assault him or his family or to damage his property. In fact they were police officers acting lawfully. The defendant was convicted of assault occasioning actual bodily harm. His appeal was allowed, as he was entitled in the circumstances to rely on the defence of self-defence based on his genuine but mistaken belief. The case of *Ball* must be viewed with care, and in *Ryan* it was distinguished. It can effectively now be disregarded and confined to its own facts.

In *R. v. Scarlett*[29] the defendant was a licensee who ejected L, a trespasser, **1–053** from his bar after closing time. L was bigger than the defendant and had made what the defendant took to be an aggressive gesture. The defendant used force to eject L and L fell into the street where he was fatally injured. The defendant was convicted of manslaughter. His conviction was quashed. The Court of Appeal held that the trial judge should have allowed a submission of no case to answer at the close of the prosecution case. This case confirms that the defendant's belief of the circumstances in which he found himself—even if mistaken—is to be used as the basis for judging his actions provided his belief was genuine and not the result of self-induced intoxication; and that the defendant's belief as to all the circumstances, including his belief about the degree of force necessary, is material in deciding whether the defendant's use of force was reasonable.

In giving the judgment of the court, Beldam L.J. said[30]:

> "If the mental element necessary to prove an assault is an intention to apply unlawful force to the victim, and the accused is to be judged according to his mistaken view of the facts, whether that mistake was on an objective view reasonable or not, we can see no logical basis for distinguishing between a person who objectively is not justified in using force at all but mistakenly believes he is and another who is in fact justified in using force but mistakenly believes that the circumstances call for a degree of force objectively regarded as unnecessary.
>
> Where . . . an accused is justified in using some force and can only be guilty of an assault if the force used is excessive, . . . the jury should be directed that the accused is not to be found guilty merely because he intentionally or recklessly used force which they consider to have been excessive. They ought not to convict

---

[27] (1990) 90 Cr.App.R. 378.
[28] Unreported, February 19, 1993, see *Archbold News*, Issue 4, April 30, 1993.
[29] (1993) 98 Cr.App.R. 290.
[30] At p. 295.

him unless they are satisfied that the degree of force used was plainly more than was called for by the circumstances as he believed them to be and, provided he believed the circumstances called for the degree of force he used, he is not to be convicted even if his belief was unreasonable."

Insofar as this dictum might give the impression that any objective element is no longer necessary, the Court of Appeal made clear in *R. v. Owino*[31] that what was meant was that the jury applied the test of whether the defendant had acted reasonably on the basis of the circumstances as he believed them to be—and it was this question of belief which was addressed in the above passage. Once that has been determined by the jury, they then go on to consider whether the defendant's acts were reasonable on that basis of perceived fact.

1–054   In *R. v. O'Connor*[32] the defendant was convicted of murder after headbutting a man in a public house in the course of an argument. The victim died as a result of the blows. The defence was that the defendant believed he was acting in self-defence. His appeal was allowed because the trial judge failed to direct the jury that alcohol could affect the specific intent required in murder. The Court of Appeal said that self-defence would fail where it was based upon a mistaken belief formed as a result of self-induced intoxication. This dictum is criticised in the commentary at [1991] Crim.L.R. 136. It is, however, in line with the authorities which establish (i) that intoxication—even self-induced—can be a defence to any offence of specific intent; (ii) where the offence only requires basic intent, then self-induced intoxication affords no defence, whereas involuntary intoxication does.[33]

(a) Burden of proof

1–055   Once the issue of self-defence (or any other defence except insanity) is raised on the evidence, the defendant is entitled to be acquitted unless the prosecution prove beyond reasonable doubt that he was *not* acting in self-defence. A model direction was given by Edmund-Davies L.J. in *R. v. Abraham*,[34] in which he said the trial judge should:

> "give a clear, positive, and unmistakable general direction as to the onus and standard of proof; then immediately follow it with a direction that in the circumstances of the particular case there is a special reason for having in mind how the onus and standard of proof applies and go on to deal in, for example, the present case, with the issue of self-defence by telling the jury something on these lines: 'Members of the jury, the general direction which I have just given to you in relation to onus and standard of proof has a particularly important operation in the circumstances of the present case. Here the accused has raised the issue that he acted in self-defence. A person who acts reasonably in self-defence commits no unlawful act. By his plea of self-defence the accused is raising in a special form the plea of Not Guilty. Since it is for the Crown to show that the plea of Not Guilty is unacceptable, so the Crown must convince you beyond reasonable doubt that self-defence has no basis in the present case.' Having done that, the trial

---

[31] [1996] 2 Cr.App.R. 128.
[32] [1991] Crim. L.R. 135.
[33] See *D.P.P. v. Majewski* (1976) 62 Cr.App.R. 262; *R. v. Kingston* (1994) 99 Cr.App.R. 286; and *R. v. O'Grady* (1987) 85 Cr.App.R. 315.
[34] (1973) 57 Cr.App.R. 799 at 803. See also *R. v. Wheeler* (1968) 52 Cr.App.R. 28 at 30.

judge can then proceed to deal with the facts of the particular case. The last thing I seek to do is to lend support to the misconception that any prescribed words have to be used in giving the direction."

(4) DURESS

If the defendant committed a criminal act when under the threat of death or serious injury to himself, or so that his will was overborne, then he is entitled to acquittal on all charges of violence except murder, and attempted murder.[35] The threat must be an immediate one so that it compels the defendant to act against his will. The more remote the threat (*e.g.* in the distant future or by some person who is overseas) the more likely is the defence to fail. Unlike self-defence, which renders lawful an otherwise unlawful act, duress is an excuse. The act itself remains unlawful, so those aiding and abetting or involved in some other ancillary capacity will be guilty of the offence in the absence of some defence particular to them. Whether the person who causes the defendant to act as he did is guilty of the offence by reason of inciting it or as principal acting through an innocent agent is perhaps not material— what matters is that the acquittal of a defendant successfully relying upon a defence of duress does not avail any other party to the offence.[36]

1-056

In *R. v. Hudson and Taylor*[37] two girls had given false evidence at a trial. They were charged with perjury. Their defence was that they had given false evidence because they were frightened of a man who had assaulted one of them and was in the public gallery of the court while they gave false evidence. The Court of Appeal held that the defence of duress should have been left to the jury. Lord Parker C.J. set out the principles which apply.[38]

1-057

"The threat must be a 'present' threat in the sense that it is sufficient to neutralise the will of the accused at that time. Hence an accused who joins a rebellion under compulsion of threats cannot plead duress if he remains with the rebels after the threats have lost their effect and his own will has had a chance to re-assert itself ... a threat of future violence may be so remote as to be insufficient to overpower the will at the moment when the offence was committed, or the accused may have elected to commit the offence in order to rid himself of a threat hanging over him and not because he was driven by immediate and unavoidable pressure. In none of these cases is the defence of duress available because a person cannot justify the commission of a crime merely to secure his own peace of mind.

When, however, there is no opportunity for delaying tactics, and the person threatened must make up his own mind whether he is to commit the criminal act or not, the existence at that moment of threats sufficient to destroy his will ought to provide him with a defence even though the threatened injury may not follow instantly, but after an interval ... it is always open to the Crown to prove that the accused availed himself of some opportunity which was reasonably open to him to render the threat ineffective, and that upon this being established the threat

---

[35] *R. v. Howe* [1987] A.C. 417; *R. v. Gotts* [1992] A.C. 412.
[36] *R. v. Howe* [1987] A.C. 417; *R. v. Bourne* (1952) 36 Cr.App.R. 125. In the latter case the defendant forced his wife to submit to buggery with the family dog. He was held to be guilty as principal.
[37] (1971) 56 Cr.App.R. 1.
[38] At pp. 4–6, giving the judgment prepared by Widgery L.J.

in question can no longer be relied upon by the defence. In deciding whether such an opportunity was reasonably open to the accused, the jury should have regard to his age and circumstances and to any risks to him which may be involved in the course of action relied upon."

1-058   The threatened injury must be severe, so as to overwhelm the will of the defendant.[38a] A defendant is expected to show the resilience of a sober person of reasonable firmness. The test, as set out by Lord Lane C.J. and approved by the House of Lords in *R. v. Howe*[39] is: "Would a sober person of reasonable firmness sharing the defendant's characteristics have responded to the threats by taking part in the [offence]?" There is a subjective element to this test— as with self-defence the facts must be viewed as the defendant genuinely believed them to be.[40] Low I.Q. (which falls short of a mental defect or to mental impairment) creating a character profile which means that the defendant is unusually weak and suggestible is *not* a special characteristic of the defendant which the jury must take into account.[41] Such persons must be judged by the standards of ordinary people of reasonable firmness; were it otherwise the whole basis of duress, namely the objective test of how someone in the defendant's position *but* possessing reasonable firmness of character would react, would be undermined.[42]

1-059   However severe the threat, duress is not a defence to murder or attempted murder, whether the defendant is charged as principal or as secondary party, and notwithstanding that the threats may be to members of the defendant's family.[43] There is an illogicality in this. If the defendant acts under duress, perhaps because his wife or child have been threatened with imminent death if he refuses, and he deliberately inflicts serious injury on the victim, he is entitled to an acquittal if the victim lives, but not if he dies, even though the defendant's actions and intentions are identical whatever the outcome to the victim. In such cases, the choice of charge between attempted murder and inflicting grievous bodily harm with intent would be very important—the former would not be amenable to a defence of duress while the latter would. If a terrorist group forced a defendant to drive a vehicle loaded with explosives to a place where the defendant knew there would be people present, the defence of duress would be unavailable if one person died of their injuries; but if many were seriously—but not fatally—injured, he would be able to rely on duress.[44] Whether the defence succeeds in a particular case depends upon the jury's conclusion about whether the defendant has shown sufficient resilience in resisting the threat.

1-060   Evidence of words used in issuing the threat are admissible without calling

---

[38a] In *R. v. Baker & Wilkins* the Court of Appeal held that fear of serious psychological injury did not qualify for the purposes of duress. *cf.* para. 1–006 above.

[39] [1987] A.C. 417 at 458 E-F.

[40] See para. 1–049 above.

[41] *R. v. Bowen*, [1996] 2 Cr.App.R. 157.

[42] *ibid.*

[43] *R. v. Howe* [1987] A.C. 417, overruling *Lynch v. D.P.P.* [1975] A.C. 653.

[44] See the Law Commission report on Offences Against the Person and General Principles (Law Com No. 218) paras 29.1 to 31.8 in which the problems of principle are addressed. The recommended solution is to extend duress to every offence, including murder, but to transfer the burden of proof to the defendant.

the person who spoke or made them.[45] This proposition should be obvious, but is occasionally overlooked by advocates and judges.[46]

A defendant who voluntarily joins a gang or criminal organisation knowing **1-061** its nature, and knowing that he is likely to come under pressure to commit offences, cannot rely upon duress if that risk becomes realised.[47] If he joins such an organisation without appreciating that violence might be used to compel him to commit offences, then he is entitled to rely upon the defence of duress.[48] However, if he joins such an organisation and fails to leave it as soon as he realises its nature, he will not be able to rely upon duress as a defence as he will have failed to take the opportunity of removing the threat or the potential threat. Participation in an offence of violence with people known to the defendant to be violent does not deprive him in all cases of the right to rely on duress as a defence. In *R. v. Lewis*[49] the defendant was serving a sentence of 12 years' imprisonment for robbery. He was attacked and seriously injured by the man with whom he had committed the robbery. He refused to give evidence on the trial of that assault because he was too frightened. He was convicted of contempt. The Court of Appeal quashed his conviction and said that he should have been given an opportunity of giving evidence about the reason for his refusal to give evidence of the assault. Only where the coercion was closely connected to the enterprise which the defendant had joined could he be deprived of a possible defence of duress. The court said that if there were evidence to satisfy the jury that the defendant was aware that he was exposing himself to the risk of serious threats by joining the enterprise or group, then he could not rely upon duress as a defence. On the other hand, where duress is relied upon, the threat must relate directly to the offence committed. In *R. v. Cole*[50] the defendant admitted a robbery of two building societies. His defence was that he and his family had been threatened with violence if he did not immediately repay a debt which he had no means to repay. The trial judge ruled there was no evidence of duress to go to the jury. His conviction was upheld. Duress by threats can only apply when the defendant is required by the threats to commit the offence with which he is charged. Duress of circumstances was not available because the urgency fell short of the directness and immediacy required. The court considered that, pending legislation, the defence of duress should be rigidly confined to its present limits.

One situation yet to be determined by the courts is whether duress applies **1-062** to a person who joins an initially peaceful demonstration which develops into violence. If the reason the defendant remained with the group or even joined in acts of violence was the psychological effect of group pressure short of implied or express threats of violence, then it will afford no defence.[51]

---

[45] *Subramaniam v. Public Prosecutor* [1956] 1 W.L.R. 965.
[46] See, *e.g. R. v. Willis* (1959) 44 Cr.App.R. 32 and *Woodhouse v. Hall* (1980) 72 Cr.App.R. 39.
[47] *R. v. Sharp* (1987) 85 Cr.App.R. 207.
[48] *R. v. Shepherd* (1988) 86 Cr.App.R. 47.
[49] (1993) 96 Cr.App.R. 412.
[50] *Archbold News*, July 1, 1994.
[51] For an example of a study of group dynamics see the essay by Harrington in "*Violence*", ed. Norman Tutt, (HMSO) at pp. 168–171.

(a) Burden of proof

1–063   Once the issue has been raised, the burden lies on the prosecution to prove that the defence of duress has not been made out.[52]

(5) DURESS OF CIRCUMSTANCES, OR NECESSITY

1–064   "Necessity" in a broad sense has never been a defence to any offence of violence. However, something akin to a defence of necessity has evolved in the shape of "duress of circumstances". In *R. v. Martin*,[53] Simon Brown J., giving the judgment of the Court of Appeal, said[54]:

> "The principles may be summarised thus: first, English law does, in extreme circumstances, recognise a defence of necessity. Most commonly the defence arises as duress, that is pressure on the accused's will from the wrongful threats or violence of another. Equally however it can arise from other objective dangers threatening the accused or others. Arising thus it is conveniently called 'duress of circumstances'.
>
>   Second, the defence is available only if, from an objective standpoint, the accused can be said to be acting reasonably and proportionately in order to avoid a threat of death or serious injury.
>
>   Third, assuming the defence to be open to the accused on his account of the facts, the issue should be left to the jury, who should be directed to determine these two questions: first, was the accused, or may he have been, impelled to act as he did because as a result of what he reasonably believed to be the situation he had good cause to fear that otherwise death or serious injury would result; second, if so, would a sober person of reasonable firmness sharing the characteristics of the accused have responded to that situation by acting as the accused acted? If the answer to both these questions is Yes, then the jury should acquit; the defence of necessity would have been established."

1–065   That case concerned an offence of driving whilst disqualified; but the principles are clearly expressed to be of general application. The reference in the passage quoted above to what the accused "*reasonably* believed" must be read as if it were a reference to what the accused actually and genuinely believed in the light of the cases of *Gladstone Williams* and *Beckford*.[55]

1–066   The Court of Appeal in *R. v. Pommell*[56] again endorsed the existence of a defence of duress of circumstances, and equated it to the type of situation where duress would apply. In other words, if the defendant is confronted by some emergency which requires action of a kind which would otherwise be an offence, then he is entitled to rely upon the defence of duress of circumstances provided that his actions are such as would be taken by a sober person of reasonable firmness. It might, for example, justify pushing someone out of the way with considerable force in order to prevent a child running into a busy

---

[52] *R. v. Hudson and Taylor* (1971) 56 Cr.App.R. 1.
[53] (1989) 88 Cr.App.R. 343. See also *R. v. Conway* (1989) 88 Cr.App.R. 159. The history of the development of this defence is studied in the commentary in [1992] Crim. L.R. at 177, and the article by Padfield [1992] Crim. L.R. 778.
[54] At pp. 345–346.
[55] (1983) 78 Cr.App.R. 276 and [1988] A.C. 130 respectively. See para. 1–049 above.
[56] [1995] 2 Cr.App.R. 607.

road. It would not justify pushing someone out of the way and causing injury because, *e.g.* the defendant was late for work. The test of "proportionality" referred to in *R. v. Martin* above is simply another way (taken from E.C. law) of saying "reasonableness". See *R. v. Cole* at paragraph 1–061 above.

Like duress by threats, duress of circumstances affords no defence to   1–067
murder whether as principal or as secondary party. In *R. v. Dudley and Stephens*[57] shipwrecked sailors were adrift and they thought they would die unless they received nourishment. They killed and ate one of their number so that the rest should survive. It was held that even in such extremes, they had no defence to a charge of murder. The result would be the same if the person killed had volunteered to be sacrificed to save the others, like Count Ugolino's sons in Dante's *Divine Comedy*.[58]

(a) Burden of proof

As the passage from the judgment of Simon Brown J. in *Martin* quoted   1–068
above makes clear, once the defence is raised, the burden is on the prosecution to disprove it.

(6) Marital Coercion

This offence remains in a diluted form as an anachronism. There was a   1–069
presumption that a wife acted under the coercion of her husband if she committed an offence in his presence. That presumption was abolished by section 47 of the Criminal Justice Act 1925 which provides:

> "Any presumption of law that an offence committed by a wife in the presence of her husband is hereby abolished, but on a charge against a wife for any offence other than treason or murder, it shall be a good defence to prove that the offence was committed in the presence of, and under the coercion of, the husband."

The defence is only available to a wife; only in respect of coercion by her   1–070
husband;[59] and only when the offence was committed by her in his presence.

Coercion means less than duress in that it need not involve physical force   1–071
or threats; what must be proved is that the wife's will was overborne by her husband by pressure of some kind.[60]

(a) Burden of proof

The burden of proof lies on the defendant. The standard is the balance of   1–072
probabilities as in all cases where the burden lies on the defence.[61]

---

[57] (1884) 14 Q.B.D. 273. Approved by the majority in *R. v. Howe* [1987] A.C. 417. See para. 4–022 below.
[58] *Hell*, Canto XXXIII.
[59] *R. v. Ditta, Hussain and Kara* [1988] Crim. L.R. 42.
[60] *R. v. Shortland* [1996] 1 Cr.App.R. 116.
[61] *R. v. Dunbar* [1958] 1 Q.B. 1.

(7) AUTOMATISM AND INSANITY

1–073   Where the act alleged to constitute the offence is committed by the defendant involuntarily so that he has no conscious control over his physical acts, he
may be able to rely upon the defence of *automatism*. When successful it is a
complete defence to any charge, including murder. As it involves an absence
of any conscious act, it should not be surprising that it extends to murder.
Although it applies to any offence, the scope of the defence is extremely
narrow. It only applies to some external factor causing the body to act without
control by the defendant's conscious will. The clearest examples are when
someone is struck on the head by a stone or is stung by a wasp, or suffers a
stroke.[62] In each case their reaction will be uncontrollable and should they
strike someone in the course of their reaction then they are entitled to rely on
automatism. Similarly, a person undergoing medical treatment will have no
control of his body while under anaesthetic.[63] In *R. v. T.*[64] a trial judge left
the issue of automatism to a jury when there was evidence that the defendant
was suffering post-traumatic stress disorder as a result of being recently raped.

1–074   In *Hill v. Baxter*[65] Devlin J. considered that medical evidence is necessary
before a defence of automatism can properly be raised. While this is a sensible
point, it cannot be a condition of raising the defence and sometimes it is raised
in the absence of medical evidence.[66] Inevitably when there is no medical
evidence called by the defence, the issue of automatism is more easily rebutted
by the prosecution, *e.g.* by relying upon acts consistent with the defendant's
proper self-control, or by proof that the defendant's lack of conscious co-
ordination was the result of self-induced intoxication.

1–075   Where loss of self-control results from self-induced intoxication by drink
or drugs, then the defendant cannot rely upon the defence of automatism as
a matter of public policy.[67] A person whose actions are conditioned by self-
induced intoxication is not entitled to claim that his actions were unconscious
or that he is exempt from all responsibility.[68] However, if a person takes thera-

---

[62] These are examples given by Lord Goddard C.J. in *Hill v. Baxter* (1958) 42 Cr.App.R. 51 at
56. His other example of a qualifying incident, namely an epileptic fit, is now more problematic
as a result of the case of *R. v. Sullivan* below.

[63] *R. v. Sullivan* [1984] A.C. 156.

[64] [1990] Crim. L.R. 256.

[65] (1958) 42 Cr.App.R. 51.

[66] See, *e.g. R. v. Bingham* [1991] Crim. L.R. 433 in which the Court of Appeal held that the trial
judge should have left the defence of automatism to the jury on the basis that the defendant
was suffering from hypoglycaemia (*i.e.* insufficient sugar in the blood) as a result of taking
insulin. The evidence fit to raise that issue was the defendant's bizarre behaviour at the time
of and immediately after the incident—he was accused of theft from a shop.

[67] *R. v. Lipman* (1969) 53 Cr.App.R. 600.

[68] *D.P.P. v. Majewski* (1976) 62 Cr.App.R. 262 (H.L.); *R. v. Kingston* (1994) 99 Cr.App.R. 286
(H.L.). In *Kingston*, Lord Mustill, giving the judgment of the House of Lords, pointed out
that case was not concerned with automatism; however he developed the principle that the
criminal law is not concerned with "blame" or moral judgment. He said (at pp. 291–292):
"Each offence consists of a prohibited act or omission coupled with whatever state of mind is
called for by the statute or rule of common law which creates the offence . . . In respect of
some offences the mind of the defendant, and still less his moral judgment, may not be engaged
at all . . . Certainly, the "mens" of the defendant must usually be involved in the offence; but

peutic drugs on prescription which cause uncontrollable actions; or if he eats something apparently innocuous which causes him to suffer a spasm, he is entitled to rely upon automatism.[69] Even in the case of therapeutic drugs, if the prosecution prove that the effects were known to the defendant (*e.g.* if he drove while under the effect of medication contrary to advice and had an accident because of a black-out caused by the drug); or if the defendant's lack of control of his actions was the result of a wilful failure to take prescribed medication, then the defence of automatism will fail.[70]

Automatism must be contrasted with disinhibition caused by external fac-   **1-076** tors, *e.g.* drink or drugs administered by another. Provided the defendant possessed the requisite state of mind to commit the offence, then automatism does not apply, and he is guilty of the offence; lack of moral blame as a result of disinhibition even *not* self-induced is a matter of mitigation only.[71]

The relationship between automatism and insanity can give rise to difficult-   **1-077** ies. Section 2(1) of the Trial of Lunatics Act 1883 (as amended by section 1 of the Criminal Procedure (Insanity) Act 1964) provides for a verdict of not guilty by reason of insanity:

> "Where in any indictment or information any act or omission is charged against any person as an offence, and it is given in evidence on the trial of such person for that offence that he was insane, so as not to be responsible, according to law, for his action at the time when the act was done or omission made, then, if it appears to the jury before whom such person is tried that he did the act or made the omission charged, but was insane as aforesaid at the time when he did or made the same, the jury shall return a special verdict that the defendant is not guilty by reason of insanity."

Medical evidence is essential before a jury can return a verdict of not guilty by reason of insanity. Section 1(1) of the Criminal Procedure (Insanity and Unfitness to Plead) Act 1991 provides:

> "A jury shall not return a special verdict under section 2 of the Trial of Lunatics Act 1883 (acquittal on grounds of insanity) except on the written or oral evidence of two or more registered medical practitioners at least one of whom is duly approved [*i.e.* under the Mental Health Act 1983]."

The effect of a verdict of not guilty by reason of insanity is that the defendant is ordered to be admitted and detained in a hospital; or (except in respect of offences for which the sentence is fixed by law, *i.e.* murder) a guardianship or supervision order or absolute discharge.[72]

---

the epithet "rea" refers to the criminality of the act in which the mind is engaged, not to its moral character."

[69] *R. v. Bailey* [1983] 1 W.L.R. 760.

[70] *R. v. Bailey* [1983] 1 W.L.R. 760.

[71] *D.P.P. v. Majewski* (1976) 62 Cr.App.R. 262 (H.L.); *R. v. Kingston* (1994) 99 Cr.App.R. 286 (H.L.). The reference to mitigation is of limited value in cases of murder: see *Practice Direction (Crime: Life Sentences)* (1993) 96 Cr.App.R. 397. This fact was acknowledged by Lord Mustill who gave the leading speech in *R. v. Kingston* who said he was not prepared to let that "anomalous relic of the history of the criminal law" stand in the way of sensible principle—see (1994) 99 Cr.App.R. 286 at 302.

[72] s.5 of the Criminal Procedure (Insanity) Act 1964. See s. 5 of and Sched. 1 to that Act for the procedures which follow such orders.

1-078   "Insanity" has a specific meaning in law which is different from that recognised by psychiatrists.[73] The House of Lords decided in *R. v. Sullivan*[74] that insanity means "a disease of the mind". Although medical evidence is usually necessary to raise the issue of automatism, that medical opinion cannot determine the legal category of the condition from which the defendant was suffering. In *Sullivan*, the defendant was suffering from epilepsy. The House of Lords decided that his actions while in the throes of an epileptic fit did not amount to automatism. Instead they decided that it fell within the definition of insanity because it brought about a temporary defect of reason. This is so even though it was acknowledged by the House of Lords that it flies in the face of medical opinion. Their Lordships held that a condition amounts to a disease of the mind and so to insanity in law if its effect is to impair the defendant's mental faculties so severely that he did not know what he was doing; or if he did, he did not know that it was wrong. It is immaterial whether the condition was organic, as in epilepsy, or functional; nor whether the condition was transient and intermittent or of longer duration. The reason for this was a policy decision, namely that section 2 of the Trial of Lunatics Act 1883 was to protect society against the recurrence of a dangerous state. In order to preserve the existing categories in which automatism is a defence (*e.g.* being struck by something), the definition of insanity that there must be some condition affecting the defendant distinguishes the sudden temporary trauma by an external force from an internal physiological condition which might appear intermittently. In *R. v. Horseferry Road Magistrates' Court, ex p. K*[75] the Divisional Court held that the common law defence of insanity remains a defence to all offences, whether tried summarily or on indictment. The court held that the Criminal Procedure (Insanity and Unfitness to Plead) Act 1991 does not affect either the definition of insanity nor the range of offences to which it can apply.

1-079   For further details on insanity, see paragraphs 5–048 to 5–065 below.

1-080   The problems created by the principles set out in *Sullivan* can be illustrated by the problem of diabetes. In *Broome v. Perkins*[76] the medical evidence suggested that the defendant had acted while suffering from hyperglycaemia, despite taking all reasonable steps by way of medication to avoid it. The doctor said that the defendant could only react to gross stimuli, and then only imperfectly. The Divisional Court directed the magistrates to convict on the basis that, as he was shown to have some control over his actions, automatism could not apply. In *R. v. Hennessy*[77] the Court of Appeal decided that hyperglycaemia caused by the defendant's failure to take medication was a disease of the mind; therefore automatism did not arise and insanity was the appropriate defence. However, if the act was caused by the defendant taking something to relieve his condition—and so his unconscious acts are the result of an external

---

[73] A point made by Lord Lane C.J. in *R. v. Burgess* (1991) 93 Cr.App.R. 41.
[74] [1984] A.C. 156. See also *R. v. Hennessy* (1989) 89 Cr.App.R. 10.
[75] [1996] 3 W.L.R. 68.
[76] (1987) 85 Cr.App.R. 321. This case was distinguished in *R. v. T.* [1990] Crim. L.R. 256 (see above at para. 1–073).
[77] (1989) 89 Cr.App.R. 10.

stimulus—he will be able to rely upon automatism as a defence in the absence
of proof by the prosecution that he realised that taking this medication would
make him more aggressive or liable to violent outbursts.[78] It follows from what
was said in *Hennessy* that if the defendant fails to take prescribed prophylactic
medicine due to some factor outside his control, then he may well be able to
rely upon the defence of automatism even though the act is committed in a
state which the law would otherwise regard as giving rise to insanity rather
than automatism. In *Hennessy* it was held that anxiety and depression are not
external factors creating a state of automatism. In that case the defendant had
claimed he had failed to take appropriate medication due to his depression
and anxiety. The trial judge had ruled that, on those facts, he would not have
a defence of automatism, but if proved he would be found not guilty by reason
of insanity. Faced with the consequences of such a verdict he pleaded guilty
(he was indicted with taking a vehicle and driving whilst disqualified). The
Court of Appeal said that the judge's ruling was correct.

An effect of the test in *Sullivan* is shown in *R. v. Burgess*.[79] The Court of   **1–081**
Appeal held that where an offence was committed while sleep-walking, that
amounted in law to insanity. The Lord Chief Justice pointed out that the test
of insanity the law requires courts to impose is not that recognised by psychiatrists. This area of the law is causing difficulty and some apparent contra-
dictions. In *R. v. Toner*[80] the Court of Appeal allowed the defendant's appeal
against convictions for attempted murder and wounding with intent on the
ground that the trial judge had not allowed his counsel to adduce evidence of
the effect of mild hypoglycaemia (caused by a protracted fast) upon the
defendant's ability to form judgments or any specific intent. In *R. v. Bingham*[81]
the Court of Appeal held that odd behaviour by the defendant, who was diabetic, at the scene of the alleged offence and subsequently at the police station
was sufficient for the defence of automatism on the grounds of hypoglycaemia
to be left to the jury. That was a case of theft, and Lord Lane C.J. said that
in cases involving specific intent, evidence of automatism can be sufficient to
show that the necessary intent is lacking without raising the spectre of a possible verdict of insanity. The Court distinguished between hypoglycaemia (*i.e.*
insufficient sugar in the blood) as a result of taking insulin and hyperglycaemia
(too much sugar in the blood) which is an incidence of the disease of diabetes
and therefore, on the authority of *Hennessy*, a disease of the mind.

There is a distinction between automatism or insanity on one hand, and   **1–082**
unfitness to plead on the other. Unfitness to plead is not a defence but a bar
to trial—see *R. v. O'Donnell*[82] for the practice in such cases.

---

[78] *R. v. Bailey* [1983] 1 W.L.R. 760. This case was referred to in *R. v. Hennessy* but the court in
the latter case found it unnecessary to consider it in detail.
[79] (1991) 93 Cr.App.R. 41.
[80] (1991) 93 Cr.App.R. 382.
[81] [1991] Crim. L.R. 433.
[82] [1996] 1 Cr.App.R. 286.

(a) Burden of proof

1–083   The burden of proving insanity lies on the party asserting it.[83] For practical reasons this will usually be the prosecution when confronted by a defence of automatism, or (in murder cases) of diminished responsibility. The evidential burden of raising the defence of automatism lies on the defence. Once the issue is raised, the burden is upon the prosecution to disprove it, either by proving that the defendant's acts were voluntary (as in *Hill v. Baxter*[84]), or that the circumstances do not amount to automatism (*e.g.* because of self-induced intoxication), or that the condition amounts to insanity.[85]

IX. EVIDENCE OF A SPOUSE

1–084   Section 80 of the Police and Criminal Evidence Act 1984 makes a wife or husband of the defendant a competent witness for the prosecution, for the accused, or for a co-accused; and compellable on behalf of the accused. A spouse is compellable on behalf of the prosecution or a co-accused of the person on trial

"if and only if—

(a) the offence charged involves an assault on, or injury or threat of injury to, the wife or husband of the accused or a person who was at the material time under the age of sixteen; or
(b) the offence charged is a sexual offence alleged to have been committed in respect of a person who was at the material time under that age; or
(3) the offence charged consists of attempting or conspiring to commit, or aiding, abetting, counselling, procuring or inciting the commission of, an offence falling within paragraph (a) or (b) above."[86]

If the wife or husband is himself or herself on trial jointly charged together with the spouse, then the spouse is a competent witness for the wife or husband; but not competent for the prosecution nor any other co-accused; and not compellable on behalf of anyone. These restrictions only apply where the parties are married at the time when the evidence is to be adduced—so, for example, a former wife (married at the time of the alleged offence but since divorced) would be compellable on behalf of any party, unless she herself were a defendant in the proceedings.[87]

Section 80(8) prohibits adverse comment by the prosecution on the failure of a spouse to give evidence. On the wording of the subsection this prohibition

---

[83] *R. v. M'Naghten* (1843) 10 Cl. & F. 200.
[84] (1958) 42 Cr.App.R. 51.
[85] *Bratty v. A.-G. for Northern Ireland* [1963] A.C. 386.
[86] Police and Criminal Evidence Act 1984, s.80(3).
[87] Police and Criminal Evidence Act 1984, s.80(4) and (5). The restriction on the competence of a spouse "jointly charged with an offence" in subs. (4) is odd, because at common law and by s.1(a) of the Criminal Evidence Act 1898 a defendant in a joint trial is a competent witness for a co-accused but not a competent witness for the prosecution against himself or a co-accused irrespective of their relationship. See also *R. v. MacDonell* 2 Cr.App.R. 322.

applies to comment adverse to the spouse defendant whether or not the husband or wife would have been relevant to his own case or that of a co-defendant:

> "The failure of the wife or husband of the accused shall not be made the subject of any comment by the prosecution."

Curiously, this prohibition survives the provisions of the Criminal Justice and Public Order Act 1994 which remove a defendant's right to say nothing at trial immune from adverse comment from the prosecution and adverse inference from the jury.[88]

X. EVIDENCE OF CHILDREN

Children are defined for as being either under 14 years for some purposes, **1-085** and under 17 years for others. A child under the age of fourteen years must give evidence unsworn; and the child's evidence "shall be received unless it appears to the court that the child is incapable of giving intelligible testimony".[89] Note that the test is "intelligible" testimony, not reliable testimony. However, if the child demonstrates incompetence in the sense that the judge decides, *e.g.* that the witness does not understand the significance of telling the truth or is suffering from some medical condition which renders the witness' evidence inherently unreliable, the judge may refuse to allow the evidence to be given.[90] Subject to these general requirements (which apply to any witness) any child is a competent and compellable witness—although where the child is a ward of court then it is desirable that the child should be interviewed in order to provide a statement (presumably this would include a video statement) in the presence of a representative of the Official Solicitor. Subject to that, it is for the trial judge alone to determine whether a child who is a ward of court is a competent witness.[91]

Children will usually give evidence via live television link, or (where they **1-086** may have reason to fear the defendant but a television link is not used) from behind a screen so that they are visible to the jury, the judge and the advocates, but not to the defendant. See Chapter 8 for further details.

---

[88] See ss.35 and 38 of and Scheds 9, 10 and 11 to that Act. In particular, para. 2 of Sched. 10 repeals the immunity from adverse comment by the prosecution on the defendant's failure to give evidence provided by s.1(b) of the Criminal Evidence Act 1898. The provision relating to comment on a spouse's failure to give evidence had originally been part of that section, but was amended by the Police and Criminal Evidence Act 1984 Sched. 7, pt VI. Whether the retention of this prohibition on prosecution comment is the result of carefully considered policy or merely a sloppy oversight no doubt time will reveal.

[89] s.33A of the Criminal Justice Act 1988 as amended by the Criminal Justice and Public Order Act 1994.

[90] *R. v. Hampshire* [1995] 2 Cr.App.R. 319; and for the judge's general discretion see s. 82(3) of the Police and Criminal Evidence Act 1984.

[91] *Re R (a minor) (Wardship: Witness in Criminal Proceedings)* [1991] 2 W.L.R. 912.

XI. EXTRATERRITORIAL OFFENCES AGAINST
INTERNATIONALLY PROTECTED PERSONS

1–087   Section 1 of the Internationally Protected Persons Act 1978 gives courts in
England and Wales extended jurisdiction to try offences committed abroad
against any of the class of persons listed in section 1(5). The people protected
include heads of state, ambassadors, ministers of foreign affairs and their
attendant families. The offences to which the Act applies are set out in section
1(1). These offences are:—assault occasioning actual bodily harm; maliciously
wounding or inflicting grievous bodily harm; wounding with intent; attempt
to choke, etc. [section 21 of the Offences Against the Person Act 1861]; administering drugs with intent to commit an indictable offence [section 22 of the
Offences Against the Person Act 1861]; maliciously administering poison, etc.
[sections 23 and 24 of the Offences Against the Person Act 1861]; and explosives offences [sections 28–30 of the Offences Against the Person Act 1861,
and section 2 of the Explosive Substances Act 1883].

By section 1(2), jurisdiction applies to inchoate forms of the offences, except
conspiracy. For any of these offences, a person charged is dealt with as if
the act alleged to constitute the offence had been committed in England and
Wales.

(1) MAKING A THREAT TO AN INTERNATIONALLY PROTECTED PERSON

1–088   In addition to extending the jurisdiction of the Courts, section 1(3) of the
Internationally Protected Persons Act 1978 creates an offence of threatening
to commit one of the substantive offences against such a person. Jurisdiction
is conferred irrespective of where the threat was made or communicated or
intended to be carried into effect and it imposes liability on those who participate in the threat or attempted threat. The maximum penalty provided by
section 1(3) for an offence of making a threat is 10 years' imprisonment unless
the substantive offence carries a lower penalty in which case the lower maximum prevails. It is an offence triable only on indictment.

1–089   The question whether a person is or was a protected person is determined
conclusively, by section 1(5), by a certificate issued by or under the authority
of the Secretary of State. Section 1(4) provides that it is immaterial for the
purposes of the extended jurisdiction and the offence of making threats
whether or not the accused knew the status of the victim or intended victim.

Section 2 of the 1978 Act provides that the Attorney-General's consent is
required for proceedings for any offence based on section 1 of the Act.

XII. GENERAL DEFINITIONS—MENTAL INGREDIENTS OF OFFENCES

(1) INTENT

The law distinguishes between crimes of "basic" intent and crimes of **1–090** "specific" intent. Crimes of specific intent require some particular intention (*e.g.* to inflict serious injury) to accompany the act. Crimes of basic intent do not. Crimes of basic intent (such as assault) are not offences of strict liability and do require some element of *mens rea*.

An intent remains an intent even if it is formed under the influence of drink **1–091** or drugs.[92] The significance of drink or drugs is that (a) it may prevent a person from forming the requisite intent[93]; (b) it may, in extreme cases, result in such damage to the brain as to amount to insanity, or to an abnormality sufficient to amount to diminished responsibility in murder cases[94]; and (c) it may, if intoxication is induced by drugs or alcohol administered by another without the defendant's knowledge, so remove his capacity to control his actions as to amount to a defence even to offences of basic intent (akin to a defence of automatism).[95] The fact that the defendant forms an intent as a result of intoxication induced by a third party without that defendant's knowledge does not provide any defence—an intent remains an intent however formed. In *R. v. Kingston*[96] the defendant had paedophiliac tendencies. Two associates decided to blackmail him. One of them invited a 15-year-old boy to a flat where he was given a soporific drug in a drink and fell asleep. The defendant went to the room where the boy lay unconscious and performed acts of gross indecency with him. The activities were recorded and photographed by one P with the intention of using the material for the planned blackmail. Both the defendant and P were indicted with indecently assaulting the boy. P pleaded guilty. The defendant claimed that P had also laced his drink with some drug so that he had no recollection of the events. The trial judge directed the jury that it was open to them to find him not guilty if they concluded drugs had been secretly administered to him; but only if the effect of the drugs was to obliterate any intent which the evidence otherwise indicated must have driven the defendant's actions and that a drugged intent was still an intent. The Court of Appeal quashed his conviction and held that involuntary intoxication negatived *mens rea*.[97] The House of Lords restored the conviction and held that an intent induced by involuntary intoxication was nevertheless a sufficient intent in law. The case concerned the disinhibiting effect of the drug—it was not suggested that the drug caused the defendant to act in a way which was totally out of character[98]; not that that factor would

[92] *D.P.P. v. Majewski* (1976) 62 Cr.App.R. 262.
[93] *R. v. Bingham* [1991] Crim. L.R. 433.
[94] *R. v. Tandy* (1988) 87 Cr.App.R. 45; *D.P.P. v. Beard* [1920] A.C. 479; *R. v. Kingston* (1994) 99 Cr.App.R. 286 at 295.
[95] *D.P.P. v. Majewski* (1976) 62 Cr.App.R. 262.
[96] (1994) 99 Cr.App.R. 286. See para. 1–075 above.
[97] (1993) 97 Cr.App.R. 401.
[98] (1994) 99 Cr.App.R. 286 at 291.

have availed him unless he could show either he had no intent, or, in a case of basic intent, that his actions were not even conscious.

Lack of memory induced by intoxication is not the same as absence of intent.

1-092   Intent must be distinguished from a desire to achieve a particular outcome. Murder cases provide frequent examples of cases where the defendant inflicts serious injury, hoping that death will not result; or else joins in a robbery knowing that serious injury might result but hoping that it will not.[99]

1-093   Section 8 of the Criminal Justice Act 1967 provides the following test (which does not differentiate between degrees of participation):

> "A court or jury, in determining whether a person has committed an offence—
> (a) shall not be bound in law to infer that he intended or foresaw a result of his actions by reason only of its being a natural and probable consequence of those actions; but (b) shall decide whether he did intend or foresee that result by reference to all the evidence, drawing such inferences from the evidence as appear proper in the circumstances."

1-094   Intention is different from motive, although sometimes evidence of motive may be relevant to intent. In *R. v. Bryson*[1] the defendant was involved in an altercation with some pedestrians, and drove off, hitting and seriously injuring three of them. The Court of Appeal followed *R. v. Moloney*[2] and held that what the jury had to decide was whether the defendant's intention *included* serious injury to anyone who happened to be in his way and if it did, it was immaterial what his motive may have been. The court considered it desirable that the trial judge should explain the difference between motive and intent. That may not always be simple. In *R. v. Purcell*[3] the Court of Appeal followed *Moloney* and *Hancock* and suggested that in a case of a section 18 offence the proper direction was:

> "You must feel sure that the defendant intended to cause serious bodily harm to the victim. You can only decide what his intention was by considering all the relevant circumstances, and in particular what he did and said about it."

1-095   Is evidence of motive included among "all the relevant circumstances" which the jury must take into account? In *R. v. Berry*[4] the Court of Appeal said not. But that was an unusual case in that it involved a murder which the prosecution said was motiveless. Nevertheless, the prosecution adduced evidence of comments made by the defendant some considerable time before the murder indicating he was jealous of the victim and would kill her rather than lose her to a rival. The Court of Appeal held that the evidence was inadmissible because it was too remote from the offence to be relevant and had only prejudicial effect. The Court of Appeal held that such evidence should not generally be admissible to prove the defendant's state of mind at

---

[99] *R. v. Moloney* [1985] 1 A.C. 905; *R. v. Hancock* [1986] A.C. 455.
[1] [1985] Crim. L.R. 669.
[2] [1985] A.C. 905; and see *R. v. Hancock* [1986] A.C. 455 for the House of Lords' refinement of the *Moloney* principle.
[3] (1986) 83 Cr.App.R. 45 at 48.
[4] (1986) 83 Cr.App.R. 7. The court found in favour of the defendant's argument on the admissibility of the evidence but applied the proviso.

the time of the killing. That general proposition was disapproved in *R. v. Williams*[5] where the case of *Berry* was distinguished. *Williams* was a case concerning threats to kill. The Court of Appeal held that evidence of the defendant's previous violence towards the victim was admissible, even as evidence of motive, because it was relevant to the issue of whether the defendant intended the victim to take his threat seriously. The court in *Williams* agreed with the outcome in *Berry* on the basis that the threats made by the defendant in that case were too remote to be admissible; and in any event there was no relevance in evidence of motive in what was said to be a motiveless crime. *Williams* confirms that evidence of motive can be admissible if relevant to the issue of intent.

The result is that the jury must be directed that in deciding the defendant's   **1–096**
intent, they must look at all the relevant circumstances, including what the defendant said and did, and in appropriate cases whether his motive as displayed by his words and actions indicates his intention at the time of the alleged offence. But the jury must be warned that evidence of motive is only relevant if it shows the defendant's intention at the material time, and motive is not to be confused with intention.

The words "intend or foresee" in section 8 have become sufficient tests for   **1–097**
intent in cases of joint enterprise where the foresight by defendant A that defendant B *might* use violence is sufficient to constitute an "intent" by A to commit the violence. In *R. v. Roberts*[6] the two defendants agreed to commit a robbery at the house of an elderly man. They both realised he would be at home and they both contemplated the use of some violence in the course of the robbery. The victim was struck over the head either with an axe or a spade and was killed. Each defendant denied responsibility for the killing and blamed the other. There was no independent evidence as to which of them had struck the fatal blow. Both were convicted of murder. Only Roberts appealed. In evidence he had said that he foresaw the risk of really serious injury. The Court of Appeal followed the Privy Council decision of *Chan Wing-Siu v. R.*[7] and held that it is enough for a defendant to foresee or realise that the other might inflict injury of a particular degree of gravity for him to be taken to have consented to that injury as part of the joint enterprise. If lethal weapons such as knives or guns are carried, then it will inevitably be easier for the prosecution to prove that really serious injury is contemplated. The realisation of the possible risk must be a real one; Lord Taylor C.J. said[8]

> ". . . we are doubtful whether the defendant B, who fleetingly thinks of the risk of A using violence with murderous intent in the course of a joint enterprise only to dismiss it from his mind and go on to lend himself to the venture, can truly be said, at the time when he so lends himself, to 'foresee' or 'realise' that A might commit murder. In such a case B can hardly have such foresight or realisation at the time he lends himself to the venture because he has banished the risk from his mind . . . to realise something may happen is surely to contemplate it as a real

---

[5] (1986) 84 Cr.App.R. 299.
[6] (1993) 96 Cr.App.R. 291.
[7] [1985] A.C. 168.
[8] (1993) 96 Cr.App.R. 291 at 298.

not fanciful possibility. Accordingly, we are inclined to the view that seeking to distinguish between a fleeting but rejected consideration of a risk and a continuing realisation of a real risk will, in most cases, be unnecessary. It would over-complicate directions to juries and possibly lead to confusion."

An extreme example of the application of the principle of the participant's liability for the principal's acts was *Hiu Chi-Ming v. R.*[9] where the acquittal of the principal in a murder case was held by the Privy Council to be immaterial to the conviction of the aider and abettor; and the principles set out in *Chan Wing-Siu* was approved. In *R. v. Woollin*[9a] the defendant was convicted of the murder of his infant son who had died of severe head injuries. The prosecution case was that the defendant's intent arose from his realisation that serious injury was almost certain to result from his admitted act of throwing the child against a hard object in a fit of temper. The Court of Appeal held that, provided the jury was directed they had to find the defendant intended serious injury, how they reached that conclusion was immaterial—and precise formulae such as "virtual certainty" were unnecessary. The defendant's intent had to be judged on the evidence of what he did and any explanation he gave.

See paragraphs 1–015 to 1–016 above and paragraphs 4–022 to 4–024, and 4–064 to 4–083 below.

(2) Maliciously

1-098   This word appears repeatedly in the Offences Against the Person Act 1861. Its meaning is not consistent. In murder, "malice aforethought" means intent to kill or cause serious bodily injury.[10] In Offences of inflicting grievous bodily harm with intent or wounding with intent "the word maliciously adds nothing".[11] In *R. v. Savage*; *D.P.P. v. Parmenter*[12] Lord Ackner adopted the argument that the word "maliciously" "was a term of legal art which imported into the concept of recklessness a "reckless" or "recklessly" in modern "revising" statutes then before the House of Lords, where those words bore their popular or dictionary meaning."[13] He went on to say that the harm envisaged in the term "maliciously" is harm to the person as opposed to harm to property.[14] For the purposes of an offence contrary to section 20 of the Offences Against the Person Act 1861 (maliciously wounding or inflicting grievous bodily harm) he said "[I]t is quite unnecessary that the accused should either have intended or foreseen that his unlawful act might cause physical injury of the gravity described in section 20, *i.e.* a wound or serious physical injury. It is enough that he should have foreseen that some physical harm to some person, albeit of a minor character might result."[15]

"Maliciously" is sometimes equated with "recklessly" in cases of offences

[9] [1992] A.C. 34.
[9a] [1997] 1 Cr.App.R. 97.
[10] See para. 4–061 below.
[11] *Per* Diplock L.J. in *R. v. Mowatt* (1967) 51 Cr.App.R. 402 at 406.
[12] (1992) 94 Cr.App.R. 193.
[13] At p. 214.
[14] At p. 215.
[15] At p. 215.

of basic intent such as offences contrary to section 20 or assault occasioning actual bodily harm. But as the case of *R. v. Savage; D.P.P. v. Parmenter* makes clear, in the former it means actual foresight of some injury or else absence of such foresight as a result of self-induced intoxication[16]; and in offences of assault (whether or not actual bodily harm follows) it means either intending to strike the victim or induce fear of being struck, or deliberately taking the risk of such consequences, or else acting under the influence of self-induced intoxication.[17]

Judges have been told that they should not give juries a direction on the **1–099** meaning of "maliciously" unless the defendant's state of mind is in issue.[18] This is a sorry reflection upon the confusion which still exists as to the meaning of this word. As Diplock L.J. said in *R. v. Mowatt*[19]:

> "In s.18 the word maliciously adds nothing. The intent expressly required by that section is more specific than such element of foresight of consequences as is implicit in the word 'maliciously' and in directing a jury about an offence under this section the word 'maliciously' is best ignored.
> In the offence under s.20 . . . the word 'maliciously' does import upon the part of the person who unlawfully inflicts the wound or other grievous bodily harm an awareness that his act may have the consequences of causing some physical harm to some other person. That is what is meant by 'the particular kind of harm' in the citation from Professor Kenny. It is quite unnecessary that the accused should have foreseen that his unlawful act might cause physical harm of the gravity described in the section *i.e.* a wound or serious physical injury. It is enough that he should have foreseen that some physical harm to some person, albeit of a minor character, might result."

The reference to the citation from Professor Kenny is to the following passage from Kenny's Outlines of Criminal Law which was approved in *R. v. Cunningham*[20]

> "In any statutory definition of a crime, malice must be taken not in the old vague sense of wickedness in general but as requiring either (1) An actual intention to do the particular kind of harm that in fact was done; or (2) Recklessness as to whether such harm, should occur or not (*i.e.* the accused has foreseen that the particular kind of harm might be done and yet has gone on to take the risk of it). It is neither limited to nor does it indeed require any ill will towards the person injured."

The case of *Cunningham* concerned a defendant who broke open a gas meter, **1–100** took it away and stole the contents. In doing so, he unknowingly fractured the gas main causing gas to seep through the wall to an adjoining house. The occupant of that house inhaled a considerable amount of gas and her life was endangered. The defendant was convicted of unlawfully and maliciously causing her to take a noxious thing so that her life was endangered contrary to section 23 of the Offences Against the Person Act 1861. His conviction was

---

[16] See, *e.g. R. v. Cunningham* (1957) 41 Cr.App.R. 155; *D.P.P. v. Majewski* (1976) 62 Cr.App.R. 142.
[17] *ibid.*
[18] *R. v. Mowatt* [1968] 1 Q.B. 421 *per* Diplock L.J.
[19] *ibid.* at 426.
[20] (1957) 41 Cr.App.R. 155 at 159.

quashed, as the jury should have been directed to consider whether, even if he did not intend injury, he foresaw that removing the meter might cause injury to someone, and nevertheless went ahead and did it. Although dissenting from the precise formulation of Professor Kenny, the Court of Appeal in *Mowatt* agreed with the general principle expressed in *Cunningham*. Diplock L.J. said of that decision[21]:

> "No doubt upon these facts the jury should be instructed that they must be satisfied before convicting the accused that he was aware that physical harm to some human being was a possible consequence of his unlawful act in wrenching off the gas meter. In the words of the court, 'maliciously' and upon this proposition we do not wish to cast any doubt."

1–101   Recklessness in the sense explained in *Cunningham* and *Mowatt* can satisfy the requirement that the defendant acted "maliciously", namely that he foresaw that physical injury of some kind might result. This was confirmed by Lord Diplock in *Commissioners of Metropolitan Police v. Caldwell*[22]:—if the defendant never turned his mind to an obvious risk he would not be acting maliciously.[23]

It is not necessary that the defendant should foresee the particular injury inflicted; he is acting "maliciously" if he was aware that the probable consequence of his act was to cause *some* injury.[24]

1–102   The cases of *D.P.P. v. Majewski*[25] and *R. v. Roberts*[26] can be reconciled with this principle. In the former case, the House of Lords held that offences of assault (including assault occasioning actual bodily harm, and section 20 offences) required no specific intent. Lord Elwyn Jones adopted[27] this passage from the speech of Lord Simon of Glaisdale in *D.P.P. v. Morgan*[28]:

> "I take assault as an example of a crime of basic intent where the consequence is very closely connected with the act. The actus reus of assault is an act which causes another person to have apprehension of immediate and unlawful violence, or would possibly have that consequence, such being the purpose of the act, or that he was reckless as to whether or not his act caused such apprehension. This foresight (the term of art is 'intention') or recklessness is the mens rea of assault. For an example of a crime of basic intent where the consequences of the act

---

[21] *R. v. Mowatt* at p. 425.

[22] [1982] A.C. 341 at 351 where Lord Diplock said that *R. v. Cunningham* was concerned with the meaning of "maliciously" in the Malicious Damage Act 1861 and the Offences Against the Person Act 1861. This included recklessness in the sense that the consequences had been foreseen as a possibility by the defendant; whereas when the word "reckless" appears in a modern statute such as the Criminal Damage Act 1971 it extended to an act by a defendant who never turned his mind to a risk which sober and reasonable people would regard as obvious.

[23] See also *R. v. Martin* [1881] 8 Q.B.D. 54 at 58 where Stephen J. said: "... a man acts 'maliciously' when he wilfully and without lawful excuse does that which he knows will injure another." See also *W. v. Dolbey* [1983] Crim. L.R. 681 where the Divisioinal Court allowed an appeal against conviction of an offence of unlawful wounding when the magistrates had found (i) that the defendant should have realised there was a risk of injury, (ii) but that he did not in fact do so.

[24] *R. v. Sullivan* [1981] Crim. L.R. 46.

[25] (1976) 62 Cr.App.R. 262.

[26] (1972) 56 Cr.App.R. 95.

[27] (1976) 62 Cr.App.R. 262 at 267.

[28] (1975) 61 Cr.App.R. 136 at 153.

involved in the actus reus as defined in the crime is less immediate, I take the crime of unlawful wounding. The act is, say, the squeezing of a trigger. A number of consequences (mechanical, chemical, ballistic and psychological) intervene before the final consequence involved in the defined actus reus—namely, the wounding of another person in circumstances unjustified by law. But again here the mens rea corresponds closely to the actus reus. The prosecution must prove that the accused foresaw that some physical harm would ensue to another person in circumstances unjustified by law as a probable (or possible or desired) consequence of his act, or that he was reckless as to whether or not such consequence ensued."

The House of Lords decided in *Majewski* that self-induced intoxication (by alcohol or drugs) provided the requisite degree of recklessness for offences of basic intent. On this interpretation, *Majewski* is authority for the proposition that whatever degree of recklessness is required to satisfy section 20, self-induced intoxication will suffice. Any broader interpretation of *Majewski* would mean that the dictum cited above conflicted with the other authorities on the point, principally *Cunningham*, *Mowatt* and *Caldwell*. It was not necessary in *Majewski* to determine the precise elements of recklessness so as to constitute an act done "maliciously" for the purposes of section 20—it sufficed to say that if the defendant failed to foresee the risk because of his self-induced intoxication, that self-induced intoxication was substituted for actual foresight to provide the required ingredient of *mens rea* both in offences of assault, and offences contrary to section 20. **1-103**

Roberts[29] is concerned with foresight of the acts resulting in injury when the victim tries to escape from unlawful assault—it is therefore directed to the nexus between the defendant's act and the injury, and establish that it is not necessary that the defendant foresaw *how* the injury would happen. It should not affect the principle that (subject to self-induced intoxication) he foresaw that some injury was a possible consequence. An example would be where the defendant strikes P so hard that he knocks him to the ground. It would be no defence for the defendant to say that P suffered an injury to his head as a result of striking an object on the ground which the defendant did not know was there, when the force of the blow was such that he realised some injury, perhaps a bruise or a bloody nose, might result. **1-104**

An intention merely to frighten is not malicious, unless the accused actually foresaw that some injury might result.[30] Inducing panic in a crowd so that some will be injured in the crush would be malicous for the purposes of section 20 if the accused realised there was a risk of some injury. In *R. v. Martin*[31] the defendant extinguished the lights in a theatre at the end of a performance, and put a bar across the doorway to obstruct the exit. Some of **1-105**

---

[29] (1972) 56 Cr.App.R. 95.
[30] *R. v. Sullivan* [1981] Crim. L.R. 46. Contrast *R. v. Ward* (1872) 11 Cox 123. The defendant in that case was in a punt wildfowling. He fired at the victim with the intention of frightening him and to deter him from returning to that spot. As he fired, his punt slewed round so that the victim was struck by the shot. Had the punt not moved, the victim would not have been hit. It was held that the defendant was acting maliciously. That decision must be considered in the light of the foresight test expounded in the more recent cases. See also para. 1–016 above for apparent exceptions to this proposition.
[31] (1881) 8 Q.B.D. 54.

the audience panicked when the lights went out, and rushed to the exit, forcing those in front of them against the iron bar, with the result that some people were seriously injured. The defendant's actions were held to be malicious. In that case, foresight or intent was assumed from the principle that a person was presumed to intend the natural and probable consequence of his act. Section 8 of the Criminal Justice Act 1967 abolished that presumption, and the intent or foresight would now have to be proved. In a case like *Martin* a jury would be entitled to infer intent or foresight, but it cannot be presumed as a matter of law.

1-106   Any lingering question whether "maliciously" is equivalent to a subjective test of recklessness has been removed by the House of Lords' decision in *R. v. Savage*; *D.P.P. v. Parmenter*.[32] In *Martin* and *R. v. Farrell*[33] the Court of Appeal in each case had held that where the word "maliciously" appears in a statute, it requires proof that the defendant foresaw the risk of the type of harm envisaged by the section, and yet went on to take the risk. The House of Lords in *Savage & Parmenter* did not accept that "maliciously" required any foresight quite so precise, but that the prosecution must prove that the defendant intended to inflict some injury, or else that he realised some injury was a possible consequence of his acts. The defendant need not have foreseen the actual injury suffered so long as he intended or foresaw some injury. The House of Lords decided that in order for there to be a conviction under section 20, the defendant must be proved to have either intended some harm or to have foreseen that his act would cause some harm. It is not enough for the prosecution to prove that the defendant *ought* to have foreseen injury as a possible consequence.[34] Lord Ackner adopted the argument that the word "maliciously" "was a term of legal art which imported into the concept of recklessness a special restricted meaning, thus distinguishing it from 'reckless' or 'recklessly' in modern 'revising' statutes then before the House of Lords, where those words bore their popular or dictionary meaning."

(a) Transferred malice

1-107   If a defendant aims a blow at A, but misses and unlawfully strikes B, then he is guilty of an offence against B, even though he never intended to injure or strike him.[35] Where the offence is one contrary to section 20 there is no problem in framing the charge—it is sufficient to allege that the defendant unlawfully and maliciously wounded (or inflicted grievous bodily harm upon) B. But where the offence is one contrary to section 18, it is necessary to allege the appropriate intent, *i.e.* wounded or inflicted grievous bodily harm on B with intent to wound or inflict grievous bodily harm upon A (as the case may be).[36] Where there is doubt as to the defendant's intended victim in a section 18 case, he will have to be charged with alternative charges, each identifying

---

[32] (1992) 94 Cr.App.R. 193.
[33] [1989] Crim. L.R. 376.
[34] (1992) 94 Cr.App.R. 193 *per* Lord Ackner at 214.
[35] *R. v. Latimer* (1886) 17 Q.B.D. 359.
[36] *R. v. Monger* [1973] Crim. L.R. 301.

his possible intended victim. Where a defendant does an act intending to cause serious injury to someone, but having no particular victim in mind, *e.g.* shooting at a crowd, he can properly be charged with intending to wound (or to inflict grievous bodily harm upon) his actual victim.[37] If the defendant wounds B mistakenly thinking that B is A, he should be charged with an intent towards B.[38]

Malice cannot be transferred from one type of offence to a totally different offence: *e.g.* throwing a stone at a window which misses and strikes A by mistake.[39] That would not constitute malice for the purposes of sections 18 and 20 (although in some circumstances it may be reckless so as to amount to an assault). **1–108**

(3) RECKLESSLY

This is considered above as part of the interrelationship with maliciously at paragraphs 1–098 to 1–107. **1–109**

---

[37] *R. v. Fretwell* (1864) L. & C. 443.
[38] *R. v. Smith* (1855) 1 Dears 559; *R. v. Stopford* (1870) 11 Cox 643.
[39] *R. v. Pembliton* (1874) 11 Cox 607; and *R. v. Savage*; *D.P.P. v. Parmenter* (1992) 94 Cr.App.R. 193 (H.L.).

CHAPTER 2

ASSAULT OFFENCES

In this chapter we deal with offences of assault which do not necessarily **2–001** result in injury, and which do not require proof of injury for conviction. The simplest form of assault is common assault. An assault is the basis of many offences in this book, but by no means all. For example, grievous bodily harm can be caused (contrary to section 18 of the Offences Against the Person Act 1861) by any number of ways which do not involve an assault, such as tampering with the victim's car, or causing the victim to take poison. The law dictating which lesser offences are inherent in the more serious ones has become complex. This issue is not only of academic interest in trying to achieve an acceptable synthesis of the law, but has considerable practical importance. In deciding what offence to charge or indict, the offences which might be proved as alternatives must be considered. A mistake can result in a defendant's acquittal in circumstances where—had there been the appropriate charge—there would have been a conviction for some lesser offence. Alternatively, where a single offence contains within it the possibility of conviction of an alternative less serious offence, it avoids a multiplicity of charges. Many offences of violence occur in a very short space of time, and it does not inspire confidence in the law if an essentially simple incidence of violence requires multiple charges or counts in an indictment to cater for legal nuances of causation, injury or intent.

I. COMMON ASSAULT

(1) DEFINITION

An assault is committed when a person does a deliberate act intending that **2–002** it should cause another to fear immediate and unlawful violence to his person;

or he is reckless whether it will have that effect.[1] Assault is the act which induces fear, although it is often used to mean the actual use of force applied against another's person. Unlawfully striking another person is a battery. Assault and battery are distinct offences and should be charged as such. Both offences are now contrary to section 39 of the Criminal Justice Act 1988 which provides:

> "Common assault and battery shall be summary offences and a person guilty of them shall be liable to a fine not exceeding level 5 on the standard scale, to imprisonment for a term not exceeding six months, or to both."

This section does not affect the definition of either assault or battery, but it makes them into statutory offences. The use of the plural "offences" makes it clear that they are distinct offences.[2] The use of the word "beat" rather than "battery" in framing the charge is acceptable—"beat" is an offence known to law and means the same as battery.[3] The Divisional Court in *D.P.P. v. Taylor*[4] suggested that where violence was used against the person the offence should be charged as "assault by beating" to distinguish it from a charge of "assault" where no violence to the person was inflicted.

2-003   The situation is not, however, free from confusion. Section 40 of the same Act provides for specified summary offences to be triable on indictment in certain circumstances. Section 40 provides:

> "(1) A count charging a person with a summary offence to which this section applies may be included in an indictment if the charge—
>
>   (a) is founded on the same facts or evidence as a count charging an indictable offence; or
>
>   (b) is part of a series of offences of the same or similar character as an indictable offence which is also charged,[5]
>
> but only if (in either case) the facts or evidence relating to the offence were disclosed in an examination or deposition taken before a justice in the presence of the person charged.[6]
>
> (2) Where a count charging an offence to which this section applies is included in an indictment, the offence shall be tried in the same manner as if it were an indictable offence; but the Crown Court may only deal with the offender

---

[1] *Fagan v. Metropolitan Police Commissioner* (1968) 52 Cr.App.R. 700; *R. v. Kimber* (1983) 77 Cr.App.R. 225 at 228. As assault is an offence of basic intent, self-induced intoxication is no defence and will itself provide the necessary element of recklessness—*D.P.P. v. Majewski* (1976) 62 Cr.App.R. 262.

[2] *D.P.P. v. Taylor* (1992) 95 Cr.App.R. 28 (D.C.).

[3] *Cross v. D.P.P.* [1995] C.O.D. 382 (D.C.). The Divisional Court reiterated that, by s. 39, assault and battery are separate offences.

[4] (1992) 95 Cr.App.R. 28 (D.C.).

[5] The words in (a) and (b) are taken from the Indictments Rules 1971, r. 9. The basic principles from cases decided on those words are:—(i) two incidents may constitute a series—*R. v. Kray* (1969) 53 Cr.App.R. 569; (ii) both fact and law must be considered in deciding whether the conditions are satisfied—*Ludlow v. Metropolitan Police Commissioner* [1971] A.C. 29. There is a distinction between offences founded on the same facts and those which form offences of the same or similar character. In the former case there need be no similarity in law in the nature of the charge, so that a common assault might for example arise from the facts of a road traffic offence. If not based on the same facts, then the offences must be similar in law and in fact— it is not enough that they share certain common features—see *R. v. Williams* [1993] Crim. L.R. 533.

[6] In cases where proceedings are transferred, then these conditions apply with appropriate adjustment to accommodate those proceedings.

in respect of it in a manner in which a magistrates' court could have dealt with him."

The section applies to a limited number of offences of which the only offences with which this book is concerned are "common assault"[7] and offences of assault upon prisoner custody officers and secure training centre custody officers.[8] Therefore, although section 39 dictates that assault and battery are treated as separate offences, identical in terms of sentence, section 40 specifies assault, but not battery, as an offence which can be tried on indictment.[9]

In *R. v. Lynsey*[10] the Court of Appeal decided that there is a distinction between the use of the words "common assault" in sections 39 and 40. Section 39, it was said, creates separate offences so that the word "assault" does not embrace "battery", whereas in section 40(3)(a) the words "common assault" include "battery". The result is that an offence of battery can also be tried on indictment provided the other conditions of section 40 are satisfied. This is an example of the court adopting a rule of construction which in effect amounts to redrafting the statute so as to avoid an absurdity which a literal reading would cause.[11]

In *R. v. Savage, D.P.P. v. Parmenter*[12] the House of Lords had to decide a   **2–004**
number of fundamental questions relating to assault:

(1) "Is a verdict of guilty of assault occasioning actual bodily harm a permissible alternative verdict on a count alleging unlawful wounding contrary to section 20 of the act?"[13]

(2) "Can a verdict of assault occasioning actual bodily harm be returned upon proof of an assault together with proof of the fact that actual bodily harm was occasioned by the assault, or must the prosecution also prove that the defendant intended to cause actual bodily harm or was reckless as to whether such harm would be caused?"[14]

(3) "In order to establish an offence under section 20 of the Act, must the prosecution prove that the defendant actually foresaw that his act would cause harm, or is it sufficient to prove that he ought so to have foreseen?"[15]

---

[7] s.40(3)(a).

[8] s.40(3) as amended by Sched. 9 para. 35 to the Criminal Justice and Public Order Act 1994.

[9] s.41 of the 1988 Act provides for any summary offence which carries a sentence of imprisonment to be committed to the Crown Court together with any other offence triable either way (but not, apparently, if the other offence is indictable only) if it "arises out of circumstances which appear to the court to be the same as or connected with those giving rise to the offence, or one of the offences, triable either way" (section 41(1)(b)). This would apply to battery, even were it not included in the word "assault" in s.40. However, the procedure for dealing with summary offences committed to the Crown Court under s.41 precludes their trial on indictment—if not the subject of a guilty plea or disposed of by the prosecution indicating they do not intend to proceed, the charge must be remitted to the magistrates' court to try (section 41(4)–(9)).

[10] [1995] 2 Cr.App.R. 667.

[11] In giving judgment in *Lynsey*, Henry L.J. expressed dissatisfaction with this state of affairs resulting from the wording of the two sections.

[12] (1992) 94 Cr.App.R. 193.

[13] At p. 202.

[14] At p. 205.

[15] At p. 207.

(4) "In order to establish an offence under section 20 is it sufficient to prove that the defendant intended or foresaw the risk of some physical harm or must he intend or foresee either wounding or grievous bodily harm?"[16]

This case was a consolidated appeal. The facts of the *Savage* case were that the defendant went into a public house where her husband's former girlfriend, the victim, was sitting. She threw the contents of a glass of beer over the victim, and as she did so she let go of the glass which struck the victim and cut her wrist. By their verdict of guilty of unlawful wounding, the jury concluded either (a) that she had deliberately thrown the glass; or alternatively (b) that the glass had accidentally slipped from her hand and cut the victim, the defendant having no intention to hit the victim with the glass.

Lord Ackner delivered the judgment of the House of Lords in a speech which all their Lordships adopted. He said[17] "It was of course common ground that Mrs Savage was guilty of common assault". It was argued that, even though common assault was established on the evidence, the prosecution had to prove that the defendant was reckless as to the injury in order to secure a conviction of assault occasioning actual bodily harm.

The facts of the Parmenter case were that the defendant had injured his baby son. The issue for the jury was whether he had intended to injure the child, or whether he had caused injury through ignorance of the fact that rough handling of a baby could cause injury.

The House of Lords decided the grounds of appeal as follows:

(1) Assault occasioning actual bodily harm is a permissible alternative verdict on a count of unlawful wounding, though not on a count of "inflicting grievous bodily harm" (see *R. v. Wilson*[18]).

(2) An offence of assault occasioning actual bodily harm is proved by proof of an assault from which, as a matter of causation, actual bodily harm results. "The prosecution are not obliged to prove that the defendant intended to cause some actual bodily harm or was reckless as to whether such harm would be caused."[19]

(3) This question raised the "subjective/objective" argument. The House of Lords decided that in order for there to be a conviction under section 20, the defendant must be proved to have either intended some harm or to have foreseen that his act would cause some harm. It is not enough for the prosecution to prove that the defendant *ought* to have foreseen injury as a possible consequence.[20] Lord Ackner adopted the argument that the word "malicious" "was a term of legal art which imported into the concept of recklessness a special restricted meaning, thus distinguishing it from "reckless" or "recklessly" in modern "revising" statutes then before the House

---

[16] At p. 214.
[17] At p. 197.
[18] (1983) 77 Cr.App.R. 319.
[19] At p. 207.
[20] At p. 214.

of Lords, where those words bore their popular or dictionary meaning".[21]

(4) The harm envisaged in the term "maliciously" is harm to the person as opposed to harm to property.[22]

"... it is quite unnecessary that the accused should either have intended or foreseen that his unlawful act might cause physical injury of the gravity described in section 20, *i.e.* a wound or serious physical injury. It is enough that he should have foreseen that some physical harm to some person, albeit of a minor character, might result."[23]

The result was that the defendant's appeal in *Savage* was dismissed and in the case of Parmenter verdicts of guilty of actual bodily harm were substituted for the verdicts of guilty of the section 20 offences. The distinctions drawn between offences of wounding and the offence of common assault demonstrate the principle that no foresight of potential injury is necessary to prove assault—it is sufficient that there is an unlawful act which is deliberate or reckless (in the sense that the defendant foresaw the possibility of some physical contact or only failed to do so as a result of self-induced intoxication).

(2) MODE OF TRIAL AND PUNISHMENT

As set out in the preceding paragraphs, sections 39 and 40 of the Criminal Justice Act 1988 make the offences of assault and battery triable summarily, with a maximum sentence of a fine not exceeding level 5 and/or imprisonment for up to six months. They are both triable on indictment if the conditions in section 40 of that Act as set out above are satisfied. This means that the accused has no right to elect trial by jury on a charge of assault or battery, but may make representations to the magistrates if he is charged with an either way offence of the same or similar nature, or such an offence arising out of the same facts as the assault/battery charge.[24]   **2–005**

On an indictment for a more serious offence, including assault occasioning actual bodily harm a defendant cannot be convicted of common assault as an alternative to that count in the indictment. In order for a defendant to be convicted on indictment of common assault there must be a specific count of common assault included in the indictment.[25]   **2–006**

(3) INGREDIENTS OF OFFENCE

There must be a deliberate act. The defendant must intend to strike or alarm the victim into thinking he will be subjected to immediate violence, or be reckless as to whether it will have this effect. Words or threats can constitute assault if accompanied by some act or gestures, *e.g.* shaking a clenched   **2–007**

---

[21] At p. 214.
[22] At p. 215.
[23] At p. 215.
[24] This seems to be the interpretation required of s. 9 of the Magistrates' Courts Act 1980 and s.40 of the Criminal Justice Act 1988.
[25] *R. v. Mearns* (1990) 91 Cr.App.R. 312.

fist.[26] If the words make it clear that the threat is not to be carried out, or at least not in the immediate future, there is no assault. In *Tuberville v. Savage*[27] the defendant was found to have committed no assault even though he had placed his hand on his sword hilt while saying in the course of an argument "If it were not assize time, I would not take such language from you." As the defendant made it clear that there was no immediate risk of battery there was no assault. The extent to which physical proximity between defendant and victim is now essential, is open to question as a result of the decision in *R. v. Ireland*[28] in which a series of telephone calls was found to amount to an assault.

2-008   The assault must result from a positive act. There is no assault by omission.[29] In *Fagan v. Metropolitan Police Commissioner*[30] the Divisional Court affirmed this principle, but decided that the defendant, who had inadvertently parked his car on the foot of a police officer was nevertheless guilty of an assault by allowing the car to remain there. The court decided that to do so amounted to a positive act, not merely an omission. It seems from this decision that if a person sets in train a course of events which would amount to an assault if done deliberately, he is held responsible for the consequences of that deliberate act if he fails to take remedial action.

2-009   An assault can be committed by the use of some instrument under the defendant's control as in the example of the car in *Fagan*, in which James L.J. said "Where an assault involves a battery, it matters not, in our judgment, whether the battery is inflicted directly by the body of the offender or through the medium of some weapon or instrument controlled by the action of the offender".[31] Throwing a stone at someone who fears they may be struck is an assault, even though it happens to miss or fall short. If the intended victim is unaware that the defendant was throwing the stone intending to strike, then it would be an attempted battery.

2-010   Battery is the unlawful application of force to the person of another; assault is an unlawful act causing the victim to fear imminent and unlawful violence.[32] In cases of battery, it does not matter whether the victim is conscious of the violence. A battery can be made on a sleeping or unconscious victim. It is battery to strike someone from behind when they are not looking. Assault need involve no actual violence—it is the threat of imminent violence by words and/or actions which amounts to an assault. In *Tuberville v. Savage*[33] the court said "If one strikes another upon the hand or arm or breast in discourse, it is no assault, there being no intention to assault; but if one, intending to assault, strikes at another and misses him this is an assault; so if he held up his hand

---

[26] *Logden v. D.P.P.* [1976] Crim. L.R. 121; *Ansell v. Thomas* [1974] Crim. L.R. 31.
[27] (1669) 1 Mod. Rep. 3.
[28] *The Times*, May 22, 1996, and see para. 1–006 above. *Ireland* has been followed in *R. v. Constanza* (unrep., March 6, 1997, C.A.—see *Archbold News*, Issue 4, May 1, 1997).
[29] Injury or suffering resulting from omission to provide care is in certain circumstances a specific offence, *e.g.* wilful neglect of a child.
[30] (1968) 52 Cr.App.R. 700.
[31] *ibid.* at p. 703.
[32] *D.P.P. v. Taylor* (1992) 95 Cr.App.R. 28.
[33] (1669) 1 Mod. Rep. 3. See also *Collins v. Wilcock* [1984] 1 W.L.R. 1172.

in a threatening manner and says nothing, it is an assault". In *R. v. Lamb*[34]
two men were fooling with a loaded gun. Both mistakenly thought the gun
would not fire. That was no assault.

There are cases where the courts have found an assault even though there   **2-011**
was no threat nor likelihood of violence being inflicted there and then. In
Logden v. D.P.P.[35] the defendant was visited by a female officer of Customs
and Excise to discuss his VAT affairs. The defendant told her that he was
owed money by the Customs and he intended to hold her hostage until something was done. He showed her a pistol in his desk drawer and said it was
loaded. He telephoned her office and repeated his demand and the threat. She
was obviously frightened. He then told her that the gun was a replica and
gave it to her. He was charged with assaulting her. His defence was that he
had no intention of frightening her and it was all a joke. He was convicted by
the magistrates and his conviction was affirmed by the Divisional Court. That
court held that it amounted to an assault where a person deliberately or recklessly caused another to fear that force was about to be used. The fact that the
defendant did not intend to use any violence against her was immaterial—
what mattered was the fear he had induced by his deliberate and unlawful act.
The commentary on the case in the Criminal Law Review points out that the
threat of violence was as to the future. But that is a question of degree. She
was then and there subjected to the threat of force in that she believed she
could not leave the defendant's premises without risk of violence to herself.

In *Smith v. Chief Superintendent, Woking Police Station*[36] the defendant went
late at night to a house where a lady lived alone. He stood outside her window
and stared in. He then moved to another window and did the same. The
occupant of the house was frightened. The Divisional court held that he had
been rightly convicted of assault because his actions had been intended to
frighten the lady into believing that he would use some violence in the
immediate future, even though he was at that stage outside the house.

It is an assault to strike the clothing worn by another.[37] Whether, for   **2-012**
example, throwing a stone at a car amounts to an assault will depend on the
circumstances. If it causes an occupant of the car to fear that it might break
the window and strike him, then that is an assault. If the occupant's fear is
that the car will be damaged, then that is not an assault. If the driver takes
evasive action and causes serious injury to himself or another, then that might
amount to an offence contrary to sections 20 or 18 of the Offences Against
the Person Act 1861 by the stone thrower.

(4) CONSENT

Consent is a defence to common assault and battery.[38] Physical contact is   **2-013**
part of everday life, and no offence is involved in the natural hustle and bustle

---

[34] (1967) 51 Cr.App.R. 417.
[35] [1976] Crim. L.R. 121.
[36] (1983) 76 Cr.App.R. 234.
[37] *R. v. Day* (1845) 1 Cox C.C. 207.
[38] *R. v. Brown* (1993) 97 Cr.App.R. 44.

of community, shopping, etc.[39] See chapter 1 paragraphs 1–028 to 1–043 above.

II. ASSAULT ON A CONSTABLE

(1) DEFINITION

2–014   By section 51(1) of the Police Act 1964:

"Any person who assaults a constable in the execution of his duty or a person assisting a constable in the execution of his duty shall be guilty of an offence."

(2) MODE OF TRIAL AND PUNISHMENT

2–015   This offence is triable only summarily. It carries a maximum penalty of imprisonment for six months or a fine not exceeding level 5 on the standard scale, or both.[40]

(3) INGREDIENTS OF OFFENCE

2–016   For "assault" see paragraphs 2–002 to 2–013 above. Taking hold of a police officer's uniform can be an assault,[41] but would not be if it was done for some lawful purpose, *e.g.* to attract his attention.[42]

2–017   The prosecution must prove that, at the material time, the constable was acting in the execution of his duty at the time he, or the person assisting him (*i.e.* a member of the public) was assaulted.

2–018   Every police officer in England and Wales holds the office of constable, whatever his rank.[43] Sections 136 to 141 of the Criminal Justice and Public Order Act 1994 provide that police officers from England and Wales may exercise their powers in certain circumstances in Scotland or Northern Ireland, and vice versa. Section 51(1) of the Police Act is applied to any officer from Scotland or Northern Ireland while exercising such powers in England by Schedule 10 paragraph 14 to the Criminal Justice and Public Order Act 1994.

(a) In the execution of his duty

2–019   No court has ever defined a police constable's powers and duties, and various statutes created a bewildering range of local variations. Wien J. in *Johnson v. Phillips*[44] said "The powers and obligations of a constable under the

---

[39] *Tuberville v. Savage* (1669) 1 Mod. Rep. 3 and *Collins v. Wilcock* [1984] 1 W.L.R. 1172.
[40] Police Act 1964, s.51(1) as amended by the Criminal Law Act 1977 Sched. 1 and the Criminal Justice Act 1982, ss.37 and 46.
[41] *R. v. Day* (1845) Cox C.C. 207.
[42] *Collins v. Wilcock* (1984) 79 Cr.App.R. 229.
[43] *Lewis v. Cattle* [1938] 2 K.B. 454.
[44] [1976] RTR 170 at 174L.

common law have never been exhaustively defined and no attempt to do so has ever been made." It is the duty of the police to give adequate protection to all persons and their property.[45] In the course of the debates in House of Commons on the Police and Criminal Evidence Bill, the then Home Secretary said: "The present state of the law is unclear and contains many indefensible anomalies".[46] The Police and Criminal Evidence Act 1984 provided more uniform provision of the extent of the duties and powers of a police officer—but the common law will continue to govern the manner in which those powers and duties are exercised. Legislation subsequent to the Police and Criminal Evidence Act, in particular the Criminal Justice and Public Order Act 1994, has added to the complexity of determining the extent of a constable's duties. In the context of an offence contrary to section 51 of the Police Act a constable is treated as acting within the scope of his duty if he is lawfully exercising a power (*e.g.* a power of arrest) given to him by law. Most of the lawful acts of constables are in fact the exercise of a power rather than a duty. It might be said that it is a constable's duty to exercise his powers; and provided those powers are exercised reasonably he is within the scope of his duty.[47]

The powers and duties of police officers, and limits on the way in which   **2–020** those powers and duties may lawfully be exercised is now subject to much learning, both judicial and academic. This chapter does no more than give the basic principles underlying the lawful exercise of a police constable's duties. For more detailed analysis resort must be had to the specialist books on the topic.

(b) Breach of the peace

A constable is under a duty to take reasonable steps to end a breach of the   **2–021** peace which is taking place, or to prevent a breach of the peace which he reasonably believes is about to take place.[48] Both a constable and a private citizen have the power to take reasonable steps to end or prevent a breach of the peace, but only a constable is under a duty to do so. As Lord Diplock said in *Albert v. Lavin*[49]:

> ". . . every citizen in whose presence a breach of the peace is being, or reasonably appears about to be, committed, has the right to take reasonable steps to make the person who is breaking or threatening to break the peace refrain from doing so; and those reasonable steps in appropriate cases will include detaining him against his will. At common law this is not only the right of every citizen, it is also his duty, although, except in the case of a citizen who is a constable, it is a duty of imperfect obligation."

---

[45] *Glasbrook Brothers Ltd v. Glamorgan County Council* [1925] A.C. 270 at 285; *Steel v. Goacher* [1983] RTR 98 at 102.

[46] Hansard H.C., vol. 48, col. 25.

[47] *e.g. Shaaban Bin Hussein v. Chong Fook Kam* [1970] A.C. 942; *Holgate-Mohammed v. Duke* [1984] A.C. 437; and *G v. Chief Superintendent of Police, Stroud* (1988) 86 Cr.App.R. 92 applying to the exercise of police officers' powers the principles found in *Associated Provincial Picture Houses v. Wednesbury Corporation* [1948] 1 K.B. 223.

[48] *Albert v. Lavin* (1981) 74 Cr.App.R. 150; *Joyce v. Hertfordshire Constabulary* (1984) 80 Cr.App.R. 298.

[49] (1981) 74 Cr.App.R. 150 at 152.

In that case the defendant attempted to jump the queue at a bus stop. A police officer in plain clothes tried to stop him, fearing a breach of the peace. He told the defendant his identity, but the defendant disbelieved him, and punched him in the stomach. The case was initially argued on the question whether it was necessary for a mistaken belief to be a reasonable one for the purposes of self-defence. The House of Lords found it unnecessary to decide the matter as on the proper view of the powers of any citizen to prevent a breach of the peace, the question was hypothetical.

2–022   The power and duty to prevent a breach of the peace, and if need be arrest the offender or potential offender exists, (i) when the breach of the peace has been committed in the presence of a constable; (ii) when the constable reasonably believes a breach of the peace would be committed in the immediate future by the person arrested, even though no such breach had been committed[50]; and (iii) where a breach of peace has occurred and has ceased, and the constable reasonably believes that a renewal of the breach was threatened.[51] Scenes of violence among football crowds provide examples of circumstances in which such justifications may arise. In *Joyce v. Hertfordshire Constabulary*[52] a police officer had used force to restrain the defendant, a spectator at a football match who was struggling with another officer. There was a fight taking place in the crowd. In the Divisional Court it was argued that the detention was unlawful because the officer had not given evidence that he feared a breach or further breach of the peace. Giving judgment Kerr L.J. said:

> "One can visualise the scene at a football match with a good deal of fighting going on. It is unnecessary for the police officer, or indeed anybody else who is placed in that position, to say expressly that it was because of the breach of the peace that was going on, and that which was apprehended, that he intervened. That is self-evident."

The case also illustrates that it is lawful for a constable to remove, if need be by force, the person from the scene of the breach of the peace (in this case to the far end of the football ground). It should be noted that under (iii), the constable will be empowered to detain a person who was not involved in the initial breach of the peace, but whose behaviour indicates that he may become involved or precipitate a further breach. This constitutes a common law power of preventive detection, and under this power, although the constable must have reasonable belief that a breach of the peace is threatened, he may detain or arrest at common law even though the person has not behaved in a way which is threatening, abusive or insulting so as to make it likely that a breach of the peace would occur.

2–023   It does not follow from the above definition that the threatened breach of the peace must be imminent in time and place. In *Moss v. Charles McLochlan*[53] police officers stopped a coach at the junction of the M1 motorway in Not-

---

[50] *Lewis v. Chief Constable for Greater Manchester*, *The Independent*, October 23, 1991; [1991] C.L.Y. 704.
[51] *R. v. Howell* (1981) 73 Cr.App.R. 31.
[52] (1984) 80 Cr.App.R. 298.
[53] [1985] IRLR 76.

tingham. It was during the 1984 miners strike and the coach carried striking miners on their way to a picket at a pit or pits where miners were working. There were four pits within a five mile radius of the point at which the pickets were stopped. There had been reports in the press and on television of incidents of violence involving striking miners. While waiting at the junction, some of the striking miners had shouted angrily at passing National Coal Board vehicles, and so the police had reasonable grounds for fearing that there was a substantial risk of a breach of the peace. The Divisional Court held that the constables had acted lawfully within their powers in stopping the coach and preventing the pickets proceeding. The court found that in the context of the strike, the presence of such a large body of men justified the action of the police. Provided the police honestly and reasonably formed the opinion that there was a real risk of a breach of the peace in close proximity both of place and time, then preventative action by the police was justified. Here, it was found that the presence of a pit approximately one and a half miles away was in sufficiently close proximity to justify the action by the police. It was also held that the constables did not have to rely on what they saw or heard at the scene to enable them to come to the reasonable conclusion that there was a real risk of a breach of the peace—they were entitled also to take into account what they had heard and read about the situation. Whether this decision will have any general application, or will be confined to its own facts arising as it did from unusual circumstances remains to be seen.

A "breach of the peace" is an act done (or threatened to be done) which **2-024** actually harms a person, or his property in his presence, or puts someone in fear of such harm being done.[54] A breach of the peace is not to be regarded as synonymous with a "disturbance".[55]

A breach of the peace can take place on private premises, and a constable **2-025** is entitled to arrest without warrant anyone whom he reasonably believes is or is about to become involved in a breach of the peace on private premises, even where the only people likely to be affected are those in the premises.[56]

(c) Power to detain and arrest

At common law, whenever a constable stops a person going on his way, that **2-026** is an arrest; there is no halfway stage between arrest and liberty.[57] In a sense, the distinction between arrest and detention is artificial, and it is now subject to many statutory exceptions. Police officers have in certain circumstances a power to detain a person without arresting him for an offence. But unless they have such power at common law or conferred by statute then they are not

---

[54] *R. v. Howell* (1981) 73 Cr.App.R. 31.
[55] *ibid*; *Parkin v. Norman* [1982] 3 W.L.R. 523.
[56] *McConnell v. Chief Constable of Greater Manchester Police* (1990) 91 Cr.App.R. 88. The argument in that case might have been substantially shorter had *Albert v. Lavin* (no. 48 above) been referred to.
[57] *Grant v. Gorman* [1980] RTR 119. It is now subject to the common law rule that a police officer can detain a person to prevent or restrain a breach of the peace without arresting that person—see *Albert v. Lavin* (1981) 74 Cr.App.R. 150 and para. 2–029 below.

acting in the execution of their duty by so detaining a citizen, and the citizen is lawfully entitled to resist.[58]

2-027   The importance of identifying an officer's powers of arrest and detention can be assessed from two passages in the speech of Lord Simonds in *Christie v. Leachinsky*:

> (1) "... it is the right of every citizen to be free from arrest unless there is in some other citizen, whether a constable or not a power to arrest him. And I would say next that it is the corollary of the right of every citizen to be thus free from arrest that he should be entitled to resist arrest unless that arrest is lawful. ... Blind, unquestioning obedience is the law of tyrants and slaves; it does not yet flourish on English soil"[59];

> (2) "... the liberty of the subject and the convenience of the police or of any other executive authority are not to be weighed in the scales against each other. This case will have solved a useful purpose if it enables your Lordships once more to proclaim that a man is not to be deprived of his liberty except in due course and process of law."[60]

2-028   There is no general power in a constable to detain a person for questioning.[61] If the constable has reasonable grounds for suspecting a person had committed an arrestable offence, he may arrest him for that offence with the intention of questioning him; and the arrest is nevertheless valid, if the constable's motive for arresting him is the belief that he will more readily confess after arrest.[62] But arrest will be unlawful unless there exist reasonable grounds for suspecting that the person has committed the offence.[63] If there is a warrant in existence for the arrest of that person, then the constable may arrest on that warrant.[64]

(d) Detention without formal arrest

2-029   In a number of circumstances, police officers are acting in the execution of their duty when they detain a person without formally arresting him. At common law, where there is a breach of the peace, or a threatened breach of the peace, a constable can detain a person causing the breach, or whose conduct leads the constable reasonably to fear that a breach of the peace is threatened.[65] In *Coffin v. Smith*[66] for example, police officers were called to a boys'

---

[58] *Christie v. Leachinsky* [1947] A.C. 573.
[59] [1947] A.C. at 591.
[60] *ibid*. at p. 595.
[61] *Lodwick v. Sanders* (1984) 80 Cr.App.R. 304; *Steel v. Goacher* [1983] RTR 98; *Pedro v. Diss* (1980) 72 Cr.App.R. 193.
[62] *Holgate-Mohammed v. Duke* [1984] A.C. 437.
[63] *Haywood v. Commissioner of Police for Metropolis, The Times*, March 24, 1984.
[64] He need not have the warrant in his possession unless the warrant is for a matter not included in s.125 of the Magistrates' Courts Act 1980 as amended by s.33 of the Police and Criminal Evidence Act 1984: see *De Costa Small v. Fitzpatrick* (1978) 68 Cr.App.R. 186.
[65] *Albert v. Lavin* (1981) 74 Cr.App.R. 150.
[66] (1980) 71 Cr.App.R. 221. In *R. v. Roxburgh* (1871) 12 Con. C.C. 8 it was held that although acting lawfully, an officer was not acting in the execution of his duty when he assisted a publican by ejecting a customer. This must either be distinguished on the grounds that in the case there were no grounds for suspecting a breach of the peace; or it must be regarded as wrongly decided in the light of subsequent authorities including *Albert v. Lavin*; *Coffin v. Smith*; and *Thomas v. Sawkins* [1935] 2 K.B. 249.

club to assist a youth leader to ensure that certain people, including the defendants, left the premises. One of the defendants returned to the youth club immediately and struck one of the officers. He was arrested. The other defendants tried to secure the release of this defendant and they in turn were arrested. It was held that the officers' presence at the club was part of their duty to keep the peace as they thought that their presence would assist in keeping the peace. This was so even when there had been no breach of the peace prior to the officer being struck.

A police officer's power to detain a person in order to protect the peace and prevent crime applies equally to his power to detain a vehicle. He is entitled to require a vehicle to stop, to enable him to make enquiries of the driver and/or passenger, provided of course he has reasonable grounds for doing so.[67] However, unless he has reasonable grounds for believing a breach of the peace is being committed or threatened, the constable's powers extend only to making enquiries, not to detention of the vehicle or occupants. It was said in *Steel v. Goacher*[68] that a constable's duty included taking steps which appeared to be necessary to keep the peeace, prevent crime, and protect property, and that: 2-030

> "The police could not carry out those duties unless they had the power to make reasonable enquiries of members of the public and the decision in *Rice v. Connelly*[69] makes it clear that in making such enquiries a police officer is acting within the scope of his duties, and, thus, lawfully and within the execution of his duty. Of course, this power does not carry with it a power to detain or arrest and if the member of the public refuses to answer the police officer's questions he cannot be detained unless the officer has grounds for arresting him."

It was held in *Lodwick v. Sanders*[70] that an officer, in addition to his powers under what was then section 159 of the Road Traffic Act 1972, had a common law power to stop a motor vehicle where he reasonably suspected the commission of a crime, and to cause it to stop for a reasonable period of time, *i.e.* sufficient to allow him to effect an arrest if he reasonably believed an offence had been committed, and explain the reason to the driver. 2-031

(e) Powers to stop and search under statute

Various statutes confer on police powers to stop and search and/or question a person.[71] The principal public general acts conferring such powers are the Firearms Act 1968, and the Misuse of Drugs Act 1971. By section 47(3) of the Firearms Act, a constable may stop and search any person, (or vehicle) when he has reasonable cause to suspect the person of having a firearm in a 2-032

[67] *Steel v. Goacher* [1983] RTR 98.
[68] *ibid.* at p. 102 *per* Griffiths L.J.
[69] [1966] 2 Q.B. 414. See also *Donnelly v. Jackman* [1970] 1 W.L.R. 562 where it was held that a trivial interference with the citizen's liberty by tapping him on the shoulder to attract his attention did not take the constable outside the execution of his duty.
[70] (1984) 80 Cr.App.R. 304.
[71] See for further details The Royal Commission on Criminal Procedure, Law and Procedure vol., Appendix 1 (1981 Cmnd 8092–1); subject to the repeals set out in s.7 of the Police and Criminal Evidence Act 1984.

public place and of committing or about to commit certain offences under the Act.

2–033   The second, and more generally used power, is conferred by section 23(2) Misuse of Drugs Act 1971:

> "If a constable has reasonable grounds to suspect that any person is in possession of a controlled drug in contravention of this Act or any of the regulations made thereunder, the constable may—
> (a) search that person, and detain him for the purposes of searching him;
> (b) search any vehicle or vessel in which the constable suspects that the drug may be found, and for that purpose require the person in control of the vehicle to stop it;
> (c) seize and detain, for the purposes of proceedings under this Act, anything found in the course of the search which appears to the constable to be evidence in an offence under this Act.
>
> ... and nothing in this subsection shall prejudice any power of search or any power to seize or detain property which is exercisable by a constable apart from this subsection."

2–034   In addition, there are specific powers for terrorism and allied offences. The Prevention of Terrorism (Temporary Provisions) Act 1989 by section 13 makes provision for statutory instrument to confer on "examining officers" the power to detain, examine and arrest any person entering or leaving Great Britain to determine whether or not he has been involved in acts of terrorism or is subject to an exclusion order under section 4.

By Schedule 3 paragraph 1(2): "The following shall be examining officers— (a) constables; ..." The Prevention of Terrorism (Additional Powers) Act 1996, as its name suggests, provides additional powers of stop and search, and the power to impose police cordons and to place restrictions on the use of vehicles; and this has been further extended by section 81 of the Criminal Justice and Public Order Act 1994.

Section 7 of the Aviation Security Act 1982 confers on a constable power to stop and arrest and detain any person embarking or on board an aircraft in the United Kingdom whom he has reasonable cause to suspect intends to commit any offence contrary to sections 1 to 3 of that Act. For offences under sections 2 and 3 of that Act see paragraphs 3–162 to 3–172 below. For section 1 see paragraph 9–035 below.

2–035   Part I of the Police and Criminal Evidence Act 1984 contains powers to stop and search for stolen items or "prohibited articles", *i.e.* bladed weapons, offensive weapons and items for use in theft, *etc.* The Criminal Justice and Public Order Act 1994 extends the powers to stop and search for offensive weapons or dangerous articles in situations where an officer of the rank of superintendent or above has authorised it in the belief that incidents involving serious violence may take place in his area.[72] In addition, the same Act gives police officers powers to stop, detain, and remove persons involved in certain acts of trespassing (including meetings on land over which rights of way exist), squatting, and raves.[73]

---

[72] Criminal Justice and Public Order Act 1994, s.60.
[73] Criminal Justice and Public Order Act 1994, ss.61–80.

A special power is conferred[74] on a constable to take and detain a child into   **2–036**
police protection to protect that child from harm. The officer may take the
child to suitable accommodation, or prevent his removal from a place where
he is then accommodated. The grounds for taking this emergency action are
that the officer has reasonable cause for believing that the child would otherwise be likely to suffer significant harm. Once a child is taken into police
protection, the police do not acquire parental responsibility for the purposes
of section 17 of the Children and Young Persons Act 1933 (see paragraph
8–017 below).

A child can be kept in police protection for 72 hours and, if it is desired to   **2–037**
keep the child under protection for any longer, an application for an emergency protection order must be made. The constable who takes the child into
protective custody must, as soon as reasonably practicable, inform a number
of persons of the actions he has taken and the reasons for them. These are:
the local authorities in whose area the child normally resides and was found;
the child himself if capable of understanding, and must ascertain the child's
own wishes; the parents or anyone with parental responsibility; and the persons with whom the child was living immediately before being taken into
protective custody.[75]

In addition, road traffic legislation empowers police officers to stop vehicles   **2–038**
in a variety of circumstances. Where a constable exercises his power to stop a
vehicle on the ground that an offence may have been committed by the driver
or occupants, he is entitled to detain it for such a period as will enable him to
effect an arrest, or to formulate such road traffic offences as become apparent.
In *Lodwick v. Sanders*[76] a lorry was showing no excise licence, index plate or
brake lights. A police officer stopped the lorry to investigate. The driver
refused to say whether he owned the vehicle, and when asked about the excise
licence he gave his name and address and then started the engine and tried to
drive off. The officer was not satisfied with the driver's answers, and, suspecting the lorry may have been stolen he took the key from the ignition. The
driver grabbed the officer's hand and made him drop the key. He was arrested
for assaulting the constable in the execution of his duty. The magistrates
dismissed the charge on the basis that section 163 of the Road Traffic Act
1988 entitled a police officer to stop a vehicle, but did not authorise him to
do any act which was an interference with the individual's liberty or property
for the purpose of causing the vehicle to remain stationary. The prosecutor's
appeal was allowed by the Divisional Court, which held that when an officer
had stopped a motor vehicle, he was acting in the exercise of his duty if he
detained it for such a reasonable time as was necessary to enable him to effect
an arrest (if he suspected the vehicle had been stolen), and explain the reason
for the arrest. In addition, according to Watkins L.J.,[77] as by sections 161 and
162 of the Road Traffice Act 1972, a constable was entitled to ask questions
about driving documents, date of birth and name and address of driver, the

---

[74] By s.46 of the Children Act 1989.
[75] *ibid.*
[76] (1984) 80 Cr.App.R. 304.
[77] *ibid.* at pp. 310–311.

officer was acting in the execution of his duty in detaining the lorry to do so. Both Watkins L.J. and Webster J. took the view that the driver's conduct was such as to cause the officer reasonably to suspect that the vehicle was stolen, and that the officer would have arrested the driver and informed him of the reason had not the assault intervened.

2-039   Section 4 of the Police and Criminal Evidence Act 1984 provides an officer of the rank of superintendent (58) or above with power to conduct a road check over a period not exceeding a total of 14 days. Section 4(2) states:

> "For the purposes of this section a road check consists of the exercise in a locality of the power conferred by [s.163 of the Road Traffic Act 1988] in such a way as to stop during the period for which its exercise in that way in that locality continues all vehicles selected by any criterion."

2-040   By section 4 a road check can be authorised to enable a constable to check whether a vehicle contains a suspect or a witness if the authorising officer reasonably believes the offence is a "serious arrestable offence",[78] and (in the case of a suspect of an offence committed or intended) that the suspect is or will be in the specified locality. Alternatively, a road check can be set up if he reasonably suspects that a person unlawfully at large (whatever the offence he is otherwise alleged to have committed) is or will be in the locality. In cases of urgency, a road check can be authorised by an officer below the rank of superintendent; but if so, it must be reported to the appropriate officer who may authorise its continuance.

2-041   The difficulty facing any motorist stopped by virtue of this power is that there seems to be no requirement that he be told *at the time* the power by which he is required to stop, nor the purpose. Instead, he may obtain a written statement of the purpose of the road check (but not the reason for stopping him) if he applies within 12 months.[79] Whether such an obligation will be imposed on the exercise of this power as was the case with the power to stop and search under section 66 of the Metropolitan Police Act 1839[80] remains to be seen.

(f) Effecting an arrest

2-042   An arrest is touching or seizing a person with a view to their restraint. An arrest is effected even though the person does not submit to the arrest and is not brought under physical control. So when a man was told he was being arrested, and the constable took hold of him, that was an arrest even though the man immediately freed himself from the constable's grasp and fled indoors.[81] However, it would not be sufficient to constitute an arrest if the constable saw the suspect some way away (*e.g.* at an upstairs window while the constable was in the street) and said words to the effect, "I am arresting

---

[78] For the wide definition of "serious arrestable offence" see s.116 of and Sched. 5 to the Police and Criminal Evidence Act 1984 and additions made by subsequent statutes.
[79] s.4(15).
[80] *Pedro v. Diss* (1980) 72 Cr.App.R. 193 and see *Lodwick v. Sanders* (1984) 80 Cr.App.R. 304 for s.163 of the Road Traffic Act 1988.
[81] *Hart v. Chief Constable of Kent* [1983] RTR 484.

you for ...." because in those circumstances there is no possibility of the officer immediately taking the person into his custody.[82] Words can constitute arrest but only if they are calculated to bring to the accused's notice, and do bring to his notice the fact that he is under compulsion, and he submits to that compulsion.[83] No particular form of words need be used, provided their effect is sufficient to indicate that the person's status has changed from free man to prisoner.[84]

To constitute a *lawful* arrest, not only must there be a lawful cause to arrest;   **2–043** the person must be told he is being arrested at the time of his arrest; or if he is arrested without being informed he is under arrest he must be told as soon as is practicable.[85] This is so in the case of an arrest by a constable even if the fact of arrest is obvious.[86] The person arrested must be informed of the ground for the arrest at the time of or as soon as practicable after the arrest.[87] One of the circumstances making it impracticable for the person to be informed of the fact or or reason for his arrest is that he escapes before he can be told.[88] The reasons for the arrest must be given with sufficient detail to identify the circumstances of the alleged offence in order that the person arrested can make a proper answer. However, it is not necessary that such details be given at the moment of arrest, provided they are given as soon as is practicable.[89] When arresting, the proper reason for arrest must be given.[90] Provided the reason given is a genuine one, it is perfectly proper for the arrested person to be interviewed about other matters.[91] This is sometimes necessary to avoid

---

[82] *ibid.*

[83] *Alderson v. Booth* [1969] 2 Q.B. 216.

[84] *R. v. Inwood* (1973) 57 Cr.App.R. 529. Where a constable standing outside a person's door said to the person just inside the open door "I arrest you" and the person then tried to shut the door, that did not constitute a valid arrest; and so the officer was not entitled to enter the premises forcibly: see *Nichols v. Bulman* [1985] RTR 236.

[85] Police and Criminal Evidence Act 1984, s.28(1); *Christie v. Leachinsky* [1947] A.C. 573; *R. v. Kulyncyz* [1971] 1 Q.B. 367.

[86] s.28(2) of the Police and Criminal Evidence Act 1984 and s.28(4), reversing the position at common law: see *Christie v. Leachinsky* n.85. In *Nichols v. D.P.P.* [1987] RTR 199 the Divisional Court said that it was not sufficient in the case of arrest under s.25 of the Police and Criminal Evidence Act 1984 to say that the person had failed to give his name and address; the nature of the offence suspected which caused the officers to ask for the name and address must be indicated.

[87] *ibid.*, s.28(3). Failure to do so makes the arrest unlawful; however it becomes lawful with effect from the moment the person detained is informed of the proper reason for his arrest—see *Lewis v. Chief Constable for South Wales* [1991] 1 All E.R. 206.

[88] *ibid.*, s.28(5).

[89] *Murphy v. Oxford* (unreported) February 15, 1985, C.A. no. 56 (referred to in [1985] 8 C.L. 5). The plaintiff was arrested in Liverpool by an officer and told that he was being arrested on suspicion of committing burglary in Newquay. The plaintiff was detained in the police station for four hours without being given further particulars of the reasons for his arrest. It was held by the Court of Appeal (Civil Division) that detention beyond an hour was unlawful as the plaintiff was entitled to fuller details so that he could make an answer to them.

[90] *Christie v. Leachingsky*, n. 85 above.

[91] *ibid.* It was held by the Division Court in *Edwards v. D.P.P.* [1993] C.O.D. 378 that a police officer must give the correct reason for arrest. A valid arrest involves two elements—(1) an objectively valid reason for arrest; and (2) the officer must have had that reason in mind at the time he decided to arrest and communicated that decision to the detained person. Where, as in that case, it was practicable for the officer to give a reason for the arrest and he chose to give an invalid reason, then the arrest was unlawful. In that case, officers had tried to search three men whom they suspected of being in possession of drugs. One of the men—F—put

inflammatory situations or a possible breach of the peace—if an arrest takes place in a public place reciting the full details of alleged sex offences in the course of an arrest may prove prejudicial alike to the accused and to public peace.

2-044   Proper steps must be taken to bring the fact of and reasons for the arrest to the attention of the person arrested. Section 28 of the Police and Criminal Evidence Act 1984 states that it is necessary that the person "is informed". This may require greater diligence on the part of the arresting officer than under the pre-existing common law where it was sufficient to take reasonable steps to bring matters to the person's notice; and the arrest was still lawful even though the person did not understand because, for instance, he was deaf.[92] In *Abbassy v. Newman*[93] the Court of Appeal, Civil Division held that informal words were sufficient to constitute sufficient reason for arrest. In that case the officer told the suspect he had been arrested for "unlawful possession" and that was held to be enough. However, that case involved an incident in 1983 and so section 28 did not apply. Where a person is not told of the reason for his arrest, that arrest becomes unlawful. But where a person could not reasonably be told the reason because he was too violent and assaulted the officers, subsequent failure to inform him of the reason after he calmed down did not make the arrest unlawful *ab initio*, and so the officers were acting lawfully at the time of the arrest when they were assaulted.[94]

2-045   The Police and Criminal Evidence Act 1984 puts beyond doubt the position of a person at a police station "helping the police with their inquiries". If a person attends at a police station or any other place voluntarily without being arrested, he is free to leave at any time; and if at any stage the decision is taken to prevent him leaving at will, he must be informed at once that he is under arrest.[95]

(g) Arrest with warrant

2-046   By section 1 of the Magistrates' Courts Act 1980 where information is laid before a justice of the peace that a person has committed or is suspected of

---

something in his mouth and an officer told him he was arresting him for obstruction under the Misuse of Drugs Act 1971—a power of arrest which does not exist. A bystander—P—intervened in the "arrest" and was herself arrested. The appellant was in turn arrested for obstructing the arrest of P. The magistrate had decided that although the officer had no power to arrest F for obstruction under the Misuse of Drugs Act, he could have arrested him under section 25(3) on the grounds that F would not have given his correct name and address and would have assaulted the officer if he had tried to retrieve from F's mouth whatever he had put in it. The Divisional Court held that the magistrate was not entitled on the evidence to make any such assumptions. This should be contrasted with the decision in *Lunt v. D.P.P.* [1993] C.O.D. 430 in which it was held that police officers exercising their power to enter premises by force to arrest a driver who had failed to stop after an accident need not give to an occupier of those premises the reasons why they were exercising that power.
[92] *Wheatley v. Lodge* [1971] 1 W.L.R. 29. It should be noted that the European Convention on Human Rights by Article 5 imposes an exacting standard: "Everyone who is arrested shall be informed promptly, in a language which he understands, of the reasons for his arrest and of any charge against him."
[93] [1990] 1 All E.R. 193.
[94] *D.P.P. v. Hawkins* [1988] 1 W.L.R. 1166. This was a case decided by reference to s.28 of the Police and Criminal Evidence Act.
[95] s.29; and see *R. v. Inwood* (1973) 57 Cr.App.R. 529.

committing an offence in respect of which the magistrates' court for that area has or will have jurisdiction (whether as a court of trial or examining justices) then the justice may issue a warrant for the arrest of that person. Where the person named in the warrant has reached the age of 18 years, a warrant may only be issued if the offence alleged is indictable or punishable with imprisonment; or the person's address "is not sufficiently established for a summons to be served on him".[96]

Warrants may be issued in other circumstances, *e.g.* by a court before which a defendant fails to appear in answer to his bail[97]; or under the Extradition Act 1989; or for non-criminal matters such as the magistrates' domestic legislation (*e.g.* the Child Support Acts).

Once issued, the warrant authorises any police officer (or any other person **2–047** to whom the warrant is directed) to execute the warrant anywhere in England and Wales or Scotland or Northern Ireland.[97a] The warrant once issued remains in force until executed or withdrawn.[98] To effect a lawful arrest,[99] an officer need not have the warrant in his possession at the time provided it falls within one of a number of specific categories including a warrant to arrest for a criminal offence.[1]

(h) Arrest without warrant

At common law, an officer may arrest any person causing or threatening a **2–048** breach of the peace in his presence.[2] By statute, arrest without warrant falls into three categories:

(a) "arrestable offences";

(b) non-arrestable offences;

(c) offences for which a power of arrest exists by virtue of a particular statute.

By section 24(1) of the Police and Criminal Evidence Act 1984, an **2–049** "*arrestable offence*" is defined as any offence for which a person who is 21 or over could be sentenced to five years' imprisonment (ignoring the provisions of section 33 of the Magistrates' Courts Act 1980, *i.e.* penalties for offences which are triable summarily if their value is small); or one of a list of offences set out in section 24(2).[3] A conspiracy or attempt to commit such offence, or inciting, aiding, abetting, counselling or procuring them is also arrestable.[4]

Any person may arrest for an "*arrestable offence*": **2–050**

---

[96] Magistrates' Courts Act 1980, s.1(4)(b) as amended by Sched. 8 para. 6 of the Criminal Justice Act 1991.

[97] Bail Act 1976, s.7(1).

[97a] *ibid.*

[98] Magistrates' Courts Act 1980, s.125(2) and Criminal Justice and Public Order Act 1994, s.136.

[99] *ibid.*, s.125(1).

[1] *ibid.*, s.125(3) as amended by s.33 of the Police and Criminal Evidence Act 1984.

[2] *Albert v. Lavin* [1982] A.C. 546; *R. v. Howell* (1981) 73 Cr.App.R. 31.

[3] These are offences for which a person may be arrested under the Customs and Excise Acts; offences under the Official Secrets Acts 1911 and 1920 not otherwise arrestable by virtue of s.24(1); offences under s.14, s.22 and s.23 of the Sexual Offences Act 1956; offences under s.12(1) and s.25(1) of the Theft Act 1968; and offences under s.1 of the Public Bodies Corrupt Practices Act 1889 or s.1 of the Prevention of Corruption Act 1906.

[4] Police and Criminal Evidence Act 1984, s.24(3) and Criminal Attempts Act 1981, s.2.

    (i)   anyone who is, or whom he has reasonable grounds for suspecting to be committing an arrestable offence[5];

    (ii)   where an arrestable offence has been committed, any person guilty of the offence, or whom he has reasonable grounds for suspecting to be guilty of it.[6]

A constable may in addition arrest:

    (iii) when he has reasonable grounds for suspecting that an arrestable offence has been committed, anyone whom he has reasonable grounds for suspecting to be guilty of the offence[7];

    (iv) anyone who is, or whom he has reasonable grounds for suspecting to be about to commit an arrestable offence.[8]

2–051   By section 25(1) of the Police and Criminal Evidence Act 1984:

> "where a constable has reasonable grounds for suspecting that any offence which is not an arrestable offence has been attempted or committed, or is being committed or attempted, he may arrest the relevant person[9] if it appears to him that the service of a summons is impracticable or inappropriate because any of the general arrest conditions is satisfied."

2–052   The "general arrest conditions" are defined in section 25(3) and cover three categories:—the person's name and address are unknown or such as make service of a summons impracticable; arrest is necessary to prevent injury, loss or damage to property, an offence against public decency, or unlawful obstruction of the highway; or the officer has reasonable grounds for believing arrest is necessary to protect a child or other vulnerable person from the "relevant person".

2–053   Section 26 of the Police and Criminal Evidence Act 1984 repeals existing statutory powers of arrest, except insofar as they are preserved by Schedule 2.

2–054   Frequently, one of the tests of the lawfulness of an arrest without warrant is whether the officer had reasonable grounds to believe or suspect certain facts. Reasonable suspicion is not the same as prima facie proof. As Lord Devlin said in *Saaban Bin Hussein v. Choong Fook Kam*[10]:

> "Prima facie proof consists of admissible evidence. Suspicion can take into account matters that could not be put in evidence at all . . . suspicion can take into account also matters which, though admissible, could not form part of a prima facie case."

So, it is perfectly proper for a constable to arrest on the word of an informer, provided that the informer is thought reliable; or on information supplied by a member of the general public.[11]

---

[5] Police and Criminal Evidence Act 1984, s.24(4).

[6] *ibid.*, s.24(5).

[7] *ibid.*, s.24(6).

[8] *ibid.*, s.24(7). Section 2 of the Criminal Law Act 1967 which contained similar provisions has been repealed—see s.119 and Sched. 7 of the Police and Criminal Evidence Act 1984.

[9] *i.e.* "Any person whom the constable has reasonable grounds to suspect of having committed or attempted to commit the offence or of being in the course of committing or attempting to commit it."—s.25(2).

[10] [1970] A.C. 942 at 949B; and see *Holgate-Mohammed v. Duke* [1984] A.C. 437, and *O'Hara v. Chief Constable of R.U.C.* [1997] 2 W.L.R. 1.

[11] As happens, for example, when a person has been the victim of a robbery and accompanies a police officer on a search of the area and identifies a person whom he alleges is the offender.

The suspicion must be *reasonable* to justify arrest. If, on being accosted, the suspect gives a full and satisfactory account of himself, such as to allay suspicion, then if the constable persists in carrying out the arrest, he will be doing so unlawfully.[12]

Where the grounds exist to effect a lawful arrest, the constable has a discretion whether or not to do so, and he must exercise that discretion on the same principles as all executive discretion,[13] *i.e.*, not perversely, and taking into account relevant considerations and only relevant considerations.[14] It is for this reason that the officer must pay regard to what account the suspect gives. It is perfectly proper to exercise this executive discretion to arrest in the belief that the suspect is more likely to confess if interviewed under arrest, at a police station than if questioned in his own home.[15] If necessary, an officer is entitled to use reasonable force to effect an arrest.[16]   **2–055**

The fact that the person arrested is subsequently released without further proceedings against him does not itself invalidate the arrest.[17]   **2–056**

(i) Entry and search without warrant

The common law powers of entry to effect arrest have been abolished by section 17(5) of the Police and Criminal Evidence Act 1984, except for "any power of entry to deal with or prevent a breach of the peace". How far this entitles a constable to enter to arrest for breach of the peace is unclear. In *R. v. Richards and Leeming*[18] the Court of Appeal quashed the conviction of a man charged with assault occasioning actual bodily harm (the victim being a police officer) when officers had forced entry to the defendant's house after receiving information that the defendant was assaulting his wife. On arrival, the officer saw through the window the defendant washing blood from his hands. The officer demanded entry on the grounds that they wished to make sure no-one was injured; they did not say they intended to enter to effect an arrest. The defendant refused them entry and when they used force to gain entry he resisted violently and was arrested for assault. The Court of Appeal held that a constable has no power to enter to satisfy himself that no-one is injured. Although constables are entitled to enter to prevent a breach of the peace, and if need be arrest for that purpose, the facts of this case did not   **2–057**

---

[12] *Haywood v. Commissioner of Police for Metropolis, The Times*, March 3, 1984, but the constable is under no duty to prove every explanation given before effecting arrest, if the explanation appears, on reasonable grounds, untrue: see *Ward v. Chief Constable of Avon and Somerset Constabulary, The Times*, June 26, 1988, and *Castorina v. Chief Constable of Surrey, The Independent*, June 16, 1988. In *G. v. Chief Superintendent of Police, Stroud* (1988) 86 Cr.App.R. 92, it was held that circumstances must be taken into account in determining the reasonableness of the belief; and that where the arrest was for an actual breach of the peace, allowance must be made for the situation in which the arresting officer finds himself and the fact that the decision to arrest has been made on the spur of the moment.

[13] *Holgate-Mohammed v. Duke* (above) and *Saaban Bin Hussein v. Choong Fook Kam* [1970] A.C. 942 at 948 *per* Lord Devlin.

[14] *Associated Provincial Picture Houses Ltd v. Wednesbury Corp.* [1948] 1 K.B. 223.

[15] *Holgate-Mohammed v. Duke* (above).

[16] Criminal Law Act 1967, s.3; and Police and Criminal Evidence Act 1984, s.117.

[17] *Wiltshire v. Barrett* [1966] 1 Q.B. 312.

[18] (1985) 81 Cr.App.R. 125.

support any suggestion that there was occurring or imminent a breach of the peace. The court therefore declined to decide (though they raised the question) whether a constable can lawfully use force to enter premises to effect an arrest for breach of the peace in circumstances where the breach of the peace does not also constitute an arrestable offence. Although section 117 of the Police and Criminal Evidence Act 1984 allows an officer to use reasonable force if necessary, that section only applies to a power conferred on a constable "by any provision of this Act". Section 17(6) does not confer a power, it preserved the common law, and therefore section 117 does not apply to the common law power to enter to deal with or prevent a breach of the peace.[19]

2-058 Section 17 of the Police and Criminal Evidence Act 1984 is headed "Entry and search without warrant" and provides powers for police officers to do that in the circumstances prescribed in that section. The powers provided by this section are only powers to search "to the extent that is reasonably required for the purpose for which the power of entry is exercised".[20] Where a police officer has reasonable grounds to suspect that a person, who is suspected of having committed an arrestable offence, is on certain premises, he is entitled to enter, search for and arrest that person.[21]

(j) Search after arrest

2-059 These powers are now regulated by sections 18 and 32 of the Police and Criminal Evidence Act 1984, with a broadly similar effect. By section 18:

> "(1) Subject to the following provisions of this section, a constable may enter and search premises occupied or controlled by a person who is under arrest for an arrestable offence, if he has reasonable grounds for suspecting that there is on the premises evidence, other than items subject to legal privilege that relates—
>> (a) to that offence; or
>> (b) to some other arrestable offence which is connected with or similar to that offence.
>> (2) A constable may seize and retain anything for which he may search under subsection (1) above."

These powers may only be exercised with the written authorisation of an inspector or above, unless it is necessary for the effective investigation of the offence to search the premises before taking the person to a police station.

2-060 These powers permit search of premises names in section 18(1) even though the person has been arrested far from them. By contrast, section 32(2)(b) empowers a constable: "to enter and search any premises" in which he (*i.e.* the arrested person) was when arrested or immediately before he was arrested for evidence relating to the offence for which he has been arrested. This power of entry may only be exercised where the constable has reasonable grounds

---

[19] For a similar reason, the Court of Appeal in *R. v. Richards and Leeming* thought that the provisions of s.2(6) of the Criminal Law Act 1967 (now repealed by Sched. 7 of the Police and Criminal Evidence Act 1984) allowing entry by force to effect an arrest "under any power conferred by this section" would not apply to a common law power. While s.3 of the Criminal Law Act 1967 allows the use of "such force as is reasonable in the circumstances . . . in effecting . . . the lawful arrest of offenders" it makes no reference to any power of entry.

[20] s.17(4).

[21] *Kynaston v. D.P.P.* (1988) 87 Cr.App.R. 200.

for believing such evidence will be found on the premises.[22] In either case, the powers of search are limited to a search "to the extent that is reasonably required for the purpose" of discovering such evidence.[23] Therefore, there is no general power of search; and certainly no power

> "to ransack a man's house, or to search for papers and articles therein, or to search his person, simply to see if he may have committed some crime or other. If police officers should do so, they would be guilty of trespass".[24]

By section 32(1), a constable may search an arrested person elsewhere than **2-061** at a police station if he has reasonable grounds for believing the arrested man may present a danger to himself or others. He may also search that person for anything which he might use to escape from lawful custody, or which might be evidence relating to an offence[25] (not necessarily the one for which he has been arrested) provided that decency is observed in that only the outer garments can be removed in public. Any item found on the person may be seized if the constable has reasonable grounds for believing that the person searched might use it to cause physical injury to himself or any other person; or any item (other than an item subject to legal privilege), which the constable reasonably believes he might use to escape from lawful custody, or is evidence of or the proceeds of any offence.[26]

Nothing is provided in section 32 as to any power of seizure of items found **2-062** following the search of the premises in pursuance of section 32(2)(b). But by section 19, a constable who is lawfully on premises may seize anything he there finds which he has reasonable grounds for believing to be evidence or the proceeds of any offence,[27] and seizure is necessary to prevent it being concealed, lost, damaged or destroyed. Items which the constable has reasonable grounds for believing to be subject to legal privilege may not be seized,[28] and it would be unlawful for the constable to extend his stay on the premises to search for such items. Subject to that, the power of entry provided by section 32(2)(b) may allow the constable to avoid the procedures of applying for a search warrant for certain types of material. If the person is arrested when he emerges from his doctor's surgery, his accountant's office, his solicitor's office, or even his barrister's chambers, those premises can be searched—subject of course to the exclusion of items subject to legal privilege; and sub-

---

[22] s.32(6).
[23] s.18(3) and s.32(3).
[24] *Per* Lord Denning M.R. in *Ghani v. Jones* [1970] 1 Q.B. 693 at 706. See also *Entick v. Carrington* 19 State Tr. 1029.
[25] s.32(2)(a)—the constable must have reasonable grounds for believing that the arrested person may have such an item concealed upon him—s.32(5).
[26] s.32(8) and (9).
[27] It seems that it does not matter by whom the offence has been committed. So if a constable searches such premises and comes upon items implicating in some offence the occupant of the premises who had until then been suspected of nothing, the constable may seize those items provided those items were discovered while the officer was lawfully on the premises—and he would be if exercising his powers under s.32(2)(b). Section 19 deals with power of seizure. It does not authorise a more extensive search. See also *Foster v. Attard*, *The Times*, January 4, 1986.
[28] s.19(6).

ject to the requirement that the search be limited in extent to that necessary to carry out the proper objects of the search.[29]

(k) Powers of entry with warrant

2-063   A constable may obtain a warrant to search premises under a number of statutes.[30] In addition, section 8 of the Police and Criminal Evidence Act 1984 provides that a justice of the peace may issue a search warrant authorising a constable to enter and search premises if he is satisfied that there are reasonable grounds for believing a serious arrestable offence has been committed, and he is further satisfied that the other conditions set out in that section are satisfied. However, if a constable is lawfully on premises, he may seize any item (except items subject to legal privilege) if he has reasonable grounds for believing:

> "(a) that it has been obtained in consequence of the commission of an offence; and
>
> (b) that it is necessary to seize it in order to prevent it being concealed, lost, damaged, altered or destroyed".[31]

This power is not limited to items which are the proceeds of the offence in respect of which the warrant has been issued. A similar power exists to seize items the constable reasonably believes to be "evidence in relation to an offence which he is investigating or any other offence" and the same condition as (b) above is satisfied.[32]

2-064   An application for a warrant which mis-states the items sought or the grounds for application; or seizure of items when the conditions in section 19 had not been satisfied renders the constable's presence on the premises unlawful.[33] In the nature of things, this issue will only be determined *ex post facto*.[34]

(l) Searches of arrested persons

2-065   Section 54 of the Police and Criminal Evidence Act 1984 makes the custody officer at a police station responsible for ascertaining and recording everything which a person who is at a police station under arrest, or has been committed to custody by order or sentence of a court has with him. The section allows the person to be searched for this purpose by a constable of the same sex as the prisoner; but this does not include an intimate search.

Any property which such a search reveals may be retained by the custody officer, except clothing or personal effects which may only be seized if the custody officer:

---

[29] s.18(3) and s.32(3).
[30] *e.g.* Theft Act 1968, s.26; Misuse of Drugs Act 1971; and see Royal Commission on Criminal Procedure, Law and Procedure vol., Appendix 5 (1981 Cmnd. 8092-1).
[31] s.19(2).
[32] s.19(3).
[33] s.15.
[34] The notice of application must give a sufficiently clear description of the documents or other material sought: see *R. v. Central Criminal Court, ex p. Adegbesan* (1987) 84 Cr.App.R. 219 and *R. v. Central Criminal Court, ex p. Carr, The Independent*, March 5, 1987. The latter case suggests that an appeal from an order should be by way of case stated.

"(a) believes that the person from whom they are seized may use them—
    (i) to cause physical injury to himself or any other person;
    (ii) to damage property;
    (iii) to interefere with evidence; or
    (iv) to assist him to escape; or
(b) has reasonable grounds for believing that they may be evidence relating to an offence."

(m) Intimate searches, samples etc.

Section 55 of the Police and Criminal Evidence Act 1984 as amended by sections 54, 58 and 59 of the Criminal Justice and Public Order Act 1994 allows intimate searches of and the taking of intimate samples from persons in custody in the circumstances set out in that section. In addition, non-intimate searches and the taking of non-intimate samples (including fingerprints) are allowed by sections 63 and 65 of the Police and Criminal Evidence Act 1984 as amended by sections 55 to 59 of the Criminal Justice and Public Order Act 1994.   **2–066**

Section 107 of the Police and Criminal Evidence Act 1984 provides that where any provision of the Act requires the exercise of the power to be author-ised by an officer of a particular rank, that power can be exercised by an officer of an immediately inferior rank if authorised by a chief superintendent or above.   **2–067**

(n) Use of force

Section 117 of the Police and Criminal Evidence Act 1984 provides: **2–068**

"Where any provision of this Act—
    (a) confers a power on a constable; and
    (b) does not provide that the power may only be exercised with the consent of some person, other than a police officer,

the officer may use reasonable force, if necessary, in the exercise of the power."

In *Swales v. Cox*,[35] the Divisional Court considered the meaning of section 2(6) of the Criminal Law Act 1967[36] which provided that a constable could enter a premises to effect an arrest "if need be by force". The court held that "force" meant the application of energy, and accordingly opening a closed but unlocked door was use of force; and that where force was used, it was for the constable to justify its necessity.   **2–069**

By section 3(1) of the Criminal Law Act 1967 a police officer and any other person   **2–070**

"may use such force as is reasonable in the circumstances in the prevention of crime, or in effecting or assisting in the lawful arrest of offenders or suspected offenders or persons unlawfully at large."

[35] [1981] Q.B. 489.
[36] Now repealed by Police and Criminal Evidence Act 1984, Sched. 7 and replaced by s.17.

(o) Mental element

2–071   The mental element is the same as for assault. Knowledge that the person is a constable or is assisting a constable is not a necessary ingredient of this offence; nor is knowledge that the constable was acting in the exercise of his duty.[37] However, genuine belief that the officer was acting unlawfully would justify the use of reasonable force to prevent what would have been an unlawful assault or arrest had the person's mistaken view of the facts been accurate.[38]

III. OBSTRUCTING A CONSTABLE IN THE EXECUTION OF HIS DUTIES

(1) DEFINITION

2–072   Section 51(3) of the Police Act 1964 provides:

> "Any person who resists or wilfully obstructs a constable in the execution of his duty or a person assisting a constable in the execution of his duty, shall be guilty of an offence."

(2) MODE OF TRIAL AND PUNISHMENT

2–073   This offence is triable only summarily. It carries a maximum penalty of imprisonment for one month or a fine not exceeding level 3 on the standard scale, or both.[39]

(3) INGREDIENTS OF OFFENCE

(a) Obstructs

2–074   To obstruct is to make it more difficult for the police to carry out their duties.[40] A positive act which impedes the constable's duty is an obstruction, *e.g.* a motorist who takes a drink knowing that the police are intending to take a sample of his breath,[41] or someone who persists in opening the door of a police car containing his friend whom the police have arrested and intend to

---

[37] *Kenlin v. Gardner* [1967] 2 Q.B. 510.
[38] *R. v. Gladstone Williams* (1983) 78 Cr.App.R. 276 and see para. 1–052 above.
[39] Police Act 1964, s.51(3) as amended by the Criminal Law Act 1977, Sched. 6, and the Criminal Justice Act 1982, ss.37 and 46.
[40] *Rice v. Connolly* [1966] 2 Q.B. 414 at 419 B–E; *Lewis v. Cox* (1984) 80 Cr.App.R. 1. The officer must in fact be acting in the execution of his duty before the defendant's actions can amount to an obstruction. This is subject to an objective test. If the constable is acting outside his authority, then there can be no offence contrary to this provision however difficult it makes the constable's task. In *Kerr v. D.P.P.* [1995] Crim.L.R. 394 the defendant was convicted of obstructing a constable who had hold of her in the mistaken belief that she had been arrested by another constable—she had not and her detention was unlawful. The test is an objective one.
[41] *Dibble v. Ingleton* [1972] 1 Q.B. 480.

remove from the scene.[42] There is in general no obligation to answer a constable's questions, and silence in answer to a constable's enquiries is not obstruction. Fine distinctions have been drawn in the authorities between the bare exercise of a right of saying nothing, and saying something which amounts to an obstruction. In *Rice v. Connolly*[43] it was said that silence is not an obstruction, but telling a lie could be. A person who is abusive and antagonistic towards a constable can be guilty of obstruction even if he is in effect refusing to answer the constable's questions in an offence manner.[44] In *Lewis v. Cox*[45] Webster J said:

> "the simple facts which the court has to find are whether the defendant's conduct in fact prevented the police from carrying out their duty, or made it more difficult for them to do so . . ."

In that case a positive act was involved—opening the door of the police car.

It is not obstruction to tell someone whom the police are seeking to interview in the street not to say anything, because that only amounts to a reminder of the right to silence.[46]

In *Dibble v. Ingleton*[47] the Divisional Court distinguished between positive   2–075
acts which can amount to obstruction in law, whether or not they are independently unlawful, *e.g.* as assault, and failure to act which only amounts to an obstruction if there is a positive obligation to act. This principle lies behind the decision in *Johnson v. Phillips*.[48] In that case a constable was called to an incident in a narrow one-way street. He asked the defendant, a motorist, to reverse the wrong way down the street to allow access for emergency vehicles. The defendant refused. His conviction for obstruction was upheld. He had argued that he was under no obligation to defy the one-way sign. The court decided that it is part of a constable's duty to preserve life and property, and he is entitled to take reasonable steps to do so, including instructing a motorist to disobey a traffic sign. This implies that there must be a corresponding duty in the citizen to obey such reasonable requests. Sections 14 and 14A of the Public Order Act 1986[49] substantially restricts the rights of groups of individuals to engage in peaceful protest on land, and there is therefore in cases covered by those sections a positive duty on the citizen to move when requested by the police even though there is no risk of serious injury or substantial damage to property.

Refusing to open the door to a constable who had a right of entry would   2–076
be an obstruction. It is no obstruction if he has no such right but is simply making enquiries. Warning an offender or suspected offender that the police are in the vicinity may amount to an obstruction. On the other hand, a general

[42] *Lewis v. Cox* (1984) 80 Cr.App.R. 1 and *Liepens v. Spearman* [1986] RTR 24.
[43] [1966] 2 Q.B. 414.
[44] *Ricketts v. Cox* (1981) 74 Cr.App.R. 298. ·
[45] (1984) 80 Cr.App.R. 1 at 6.
[46] *Green v. D.P.P.* [1991] Crim. L.R. 784. It is possible, as a result of ss.34, 36, and 37 of the Criminal Justice and Public Order Act 1994 that such conduct could amount to obstruction if it impeded the constable administering the appropriate caution.
[47] [1972] 1 Q.B. 480.
[48] (1976) RTR 170. *Dibble v. Ingleton* was cited to the court but not referred to in the judgment.
[49] s.14A is inserted by s.70 of the Criminal Justice and Public Order Act 1994.

warning to obey the law because there are police in the area who might detect any crime is not obstruction. The distinction is between warning people not to commit offences at all, and advising them to desist while the police are in the vicinity to avoid detection.[50]

2–077   The defendant's actions must in fact obstruct the constable. In *Bennett v. Bale*[51] the defendant was a customer in a restaurant being investigated for licensing offences. Uniformed officers arrived. He told an undercover constable, ignorant of her identity, that if she had not had a drink after midnight and had eaten a meal she would be alright. He intended to obstruct, but did not do so. The Divisional Court quashed his conviction.

(b) Resists

2–078   There is little authority on the meaning of this word. It must mean physical resistance short of assault.[52]

(c) A constable in the execution of his duty

2–079   See paragraphs 2–014 to 2–070.

(d) Mental element

2–080   Obstruction must be "*wilful*". Resistance need not. To be wilful, the obstruction must be a deliberate act and intended to impede the constable in the execution of his duty. It is therefore different from assaulting a constable in that the defendant's belief that the constable is not acting in the execution of his duty is relevant to the issue of whether what in fact amounts to obstruction was committed wilfully.[53] There is no need to prove hostility towards the police—in fact well-meaning interference which deliberately impedes the police, such as trying to persuade them that they have arrested the wrong person, still amounts to wilful obstruction.[54] If, however, the act which obstructs is intended to assist, then there is no wilful obstruction. An example of this principle is *Willmot v. Atack*.[55] In that case a constable arrested a motorist who then began to struggle. The defendant, who knew the motorist, tried to assist the constable by telling the motorist not to struggle. In fact his interference impeded the constable, but because his intention was to assist, he was not guilty of wilful obstruction.

2–081   Obstruction cannot be wilful unless the defendant appreciates the person

---

[50] *Hinchliffe v. Sheldon* [1955] 1 W.L.R. 1207; *Bastable v. Little* [1907] 1 K.B. 59. See also *Betts v. Stevens* [1910] 1 K.B. 1. These cases concerned warnings given to motorists of a speed trap. In the former case the defendant was acquitted, and in the latter his conviction was upheld. *Bastable v. Little* has been confined to its own facts—see *Green v. Moore* (1982) 74 Cr.App.R. 250.
[51] [1986] Crim. L.R. 404.
[52] *Kerr v. D.P.P.* [1995] Crim.L.R. 394.
[53] *Lewis v. Cox* (1984) 80 Cr.App.R. 1.
[54] *Hills v. Ellis* (1983) 76 Cr.App.R. 217.
[55] [1977] Q.B. 498.

he is obstructing is a constable.[56] It is no defence that the defendant did not appreciate that the constable was acting in the exercise of his duties, unless the defendant's genuine belief—had it been correct—would have entitled him to act in the way he did.[57]

(e) Powers of arrest

An offence contrary to section 51(3) of the Police Act is not an arrestable **2–082** offence. Arrest is therefore only possible if one of the arrest conditions in section 25 of the Police and Criminal Evidence Act 1984 is present, or the situation demands the defendant's arrest to prevent a breach of the peace, or the constable has reasonable grounds to believe that the person will prevent the lawful arrest of another.[58]

IV. ASSAULTS ON AND OBSTRUCTION OF OTHER DESIGNATED PERSONS

A number of other particular persons are protected by statute from assault, **2–083** *e.g.* Customs Officers, Inland Revenue Officers, officers of the court, and prisoner escort officers.[59] The Court of Appeal (Civil Division) confirmed that a genuine mistake of fact, either as to whether the person assaulted is an officer of the court, or was acting in the execution of his duty, will afford a defence to this charge.[60] This should apply equally to other instances of assault on particular persons.

V. ASSAULT WITH INTENT TO RESIST ARREST

(1) Definition

By section 38 of the Offences Against the Person Act 1861: **2–084**

> "Whoever shall assault any person with intent to resist or prevent the lawful apprehension or detainer of himself or any other person for any offence, shall be guilty . . ."

---

[56] *Ostler v. Elliott* [1980] Crim. L.R. 584.
[57] See *R. v. Gladstone Williams* (1983) 78 Cr.App.R. 276 for the general principle that a genuine mistake of fact means that, where relevant, the facts are treated as if the defendant's perception were correct.
[58] *Wershof v. Commissioner of Police for Metropolis* (1978) 68 Cr.App.R. 82.
[59] See Customs and Excise Management Act 1979, s.156(1); Inland Revenue Regulation Act 1890, s.11; County Courts Act 1984, s.14; and Criminal Justice and Public Order Act 1994, Sched. 9, para. 35.
[60] *Blackburn v. Bowering* [1994] 3 All E.R. 380.

(2) MODE OF TRIAL AND PUNISHMENT

2–085 The maximum penalty provided by section 38 is two years' imprisonment. It is triable either way.[61] On indictment, an alternative verdict of guilty of common assault or battery is not available.[62] For the jury to return such a verdict, the alternative count must, if appropriate, be added to the indictment.

2–086 If a person guilty of this offence (or of attempting to commit it, or aiding and abetting or counselling and procuring its commission) has in his possession, at the time of committing the offence, any firearm or imitation firearm he is guilty of a further offence under section 17(2) of the Firearms Act 1968 which is triable only on indictment and carries a maximum penalty of imprisonment for life.[63] Guilt of the assault offence is a pre-condition of guilt of the firearms offence.[64]

(3) INGREDIENTS OF OFFENCE

2–087 For "assault" see above. The offence is not confined to an assault upon the person executing the arrest or assisting in it. An offence under this section could, for example, be committed by someone assaulting another constable or any other person with intent to cause a diversion so that the person being arrested can escape.

2–088 This offence applies as much to an arrest by a private citizen as to an arrest by a constable. However, section 24 of the Police and Criminal Evidence Act 1984 requires there to have been an offence committed or in the course of commission for a citizen to have the power of arrest. Therefore there is no offence under this section against a citizen who mistakenly believes that an arrestable offence has been committed, however reasonable that belief may be.[65]

2–089 This offence requires a specific intent to resist or prevent apprehension or detention. It is no defence to show that the defendant thought the detention was unlawful,[66] unless that belief is genuine, and, had the facts been as the defendant believed them, he would have been entitled to act as he did.[67]

2–090 Where the assault is a minor one, and the victim is a constable, the purely summary offence of assaulting a constable in the execution of his duty is frequently charged rather than this offence.

---

[61] Magistrates' Courts Act 1980, Sched. 1, para. 5.
[62] Criminal Justice Act 1988, s.40.
[63] Firearms Act 1968, Sched. 6 as amended by ss.44 and 171(6) of the Criminal Justice Act 1988.
[64] *R. v. Baker* (1961) 46 Cr.App.R. 47.
[65] *R. v. Self* (1992) 95 Cr.App.R. 42.
[66] *R. v. Fennell* (1970) 54 Cr.App.R. 451 at 453.
[67] *R. v. Gladstone Williams* (1983) 78 Cr.App.R. 276.

VI. THREATS TO KILL

(1) DEFINITION

By section 16 of the Offences against the Person Act 1861:   **2–091**

> "A person who without lawful excuse makes to another a threat, intending that that other would fear it would be carried out, to kill that other or a third person shall be guilty of an offence and liable on conviction on indictment to imprisonment for a term not exceeding ten years."

Section 16 in this form was substituted by section 65(4) and Schedule 12 of the Criminal Law Act 1977. In its original form, section 16 read as follows:

> "Whosoever shall maliciously send, deliver or utter or directly or indirectly cause to be received, knowing the contents thereof, any letter or writing threatening to kill or murder any person, shall be guilty of felony."

This material difference in wording should be borne in mind when considering any of the pre-amendment authorities.

(2) MODE OF TRIAL AND PUNISHMENT

This offence is triable either way.[68] The maximum penalty on conviction   **2–092** on indictment is 10 years' imprisonment.

(3) INGREDIENTS OF OFFENCE

A threat to kill must be proved. It is not necessary that the threat should   **2–093** be explicitly to kill; any threat which carries by implication a threat to kill will suffice. A letter containing the message "I shall be with you shortly and then you shall nap it" signed "cut throat" was sufficient,[69] as was a letter sent by the defendant to a probation officer containing a threat about the defendant's wife—"I do not wish to take her life, but . . . the law will take its course after the act, but I hope my children will be looked after".[70] It is not an offence under this section to threaten to kill an unborn child,[71] although if the threat were made to an expectant mother so as to put her in fear of immediate attack upon herself, that would be an assault on her. The threat must be a threat to kill; a threat to injure will not suffice.

Whether the threat amounts to a threat to kill is a question for the jury.   **2–094** The threat may be made orally or in writing. In *R. v. Cousins*,[72] the defendant went with a shotgun to the house of R whom he believed intended to cause him serious injury, and told R's parents that he intended to blow off R's head.

The case of *Cousins* illustrates the point, made clear by the wording of   **2–095**

---

[68] Magistrates' Courts Act 1980, s.17 and Sched. 1.
[69] *R. v. Boucher* (1831) C. & P. 562. See also *R. v. Tyler* (1835) 1 Mood. 428.
[70] *R. v. Solanke* (1969) 54 Cr.App.R. 30.
[71] *R. v. Tait* (1990) 90 Cr.App.R. 44.
[72] (1982) 74 Cr.App.R. 363.

section 16, that it is an offence for a defendant to make a threat to A that he intends to kill B. Equally, it is an offence where the defendant makes a threat that the killing will be carried out by someone else. Section 16 prohibits "a threat . . . to kill", not "a threat that *he* will kill". Where defendant A passes on a threat issued by defendant B, and does so intending the recipient to fear it will be carried out, then in the absence of lawful excuse defendant A is guilty as a principal. Defendant B is guilty as a principal in respect of the threat he conveyed to A, if he intended A to fear it would be carried out; he is guilty as a counsellor and procurer if he uses A as his messenger in respect of the threat conveyed by A. In cases of kidnapping[73] where a ransom is demanded, a threat to kill will often be involved either explicitly or by implication.

(4) Without Lawful Excuse

2–096   The threat must be made "without lawful excuse". It is a lawful excuse to make such a threat in self-defence. In *Cousins* the defendant issued the threat because he believed he was likely to be a victim of violence at the hands of the person whose life he threatened. The trial judge withdrew the issue of lawful excuse from the jury, on the ground that the defendant's life was not in immediate jeopardy and the Court of Appeal held that he was wrong to do so. The court held that since section 3 of the Criminal Law Act 1967 allows reasonable force to be used to prevent crime, and such force may also be used in self-defence, it should be left to the jury to determine whether the threat could amount to a lawful excuse on similar principles. The Court of Appeal also pointed out that the words "without lawful excuse" are part of the definition of the offence, and one of the elements which the prosecution must prove.[74] Unless there was no evidence capable of amounting to lawful excuse, that issue must be left to the jury. A defendant has a lawful excuse where

(i)   he is labouring under a genuine mistake of fact; and

(ii) if matters were as he believed them to be, he would be acting lawfully.[75]

So, a threat directed at the life of a man whom the defendant genuinely but mistakenly thought was threatening him could amount to a lawful excuse; but only if that threat would have been reasonable had the defendant's belief been true. Reporting a threat to the police, or handing the police a written threat in order to assist them in their duties of investigating crime would be a lawful excuse.[76] Although factually unlikely, a threat to be taken seriously momentarily, but made as a joke, might amount to a lawful excuse. The matter is not

---

[73] See para. 9–011 below.

[74] This should be contrasted, *e.g.* with s.5.1(1) of the Prevention of Crimes Act 1953 where the burden of proving reasonable excuse lies upon the defendant.

[75] *Cambridgeshire and Isle of Ely County Council v. Rust* [1972] 2 Q.B. 426. See also *R.. v .Harvey* (1871) L.R. I C.C.R. 284; and *Dickins v. Gill* [1896] 2 Q.B. 310. In the first of these cases, the Divisional Court held that the belief had to be reasonable as well as genuine. This must now be read in the light of *R. v. Gladstone Williams* (1983) 78 Cr.App.R. 276, where the Court of Appeal held that a mistake of fact did not need to be reasonable so long as it was genuine.

[76] *R. v. Solanke* (1969) 54 Cr.App.R. 30.

clear because an innocent motive is not tantamount to lawful excuse. In *Houghlon v. Chief Constable of Greater Manchester*[77] the plaintiff had attended a fancy dress party in the uniform of a police constable complete with truncheon. He was arrested for having an offensive weapon (the truncheon) and in an action for false arrest the Court of Appeal, Civil Division held that the plaintiff had a reasonable excuse as provided in section 1(1) of the Prevention of Crimes Act 1953 for having the truncheon, since it formed part of his fancy dress. However, reasonable excuse is not the same as lawful excuse.[78]

(5) MENTAL ELEMENT

The defendant must intend[79] that the person to whom the threat is made will fear that the threat will be carried out. It does not matter for the purposes of this offence whether or not the defendant intends to carry out the threat, nor whether or not the recipient of the threat takes it seriously. Evidence of a defendant's previous acts of violence towards the same victim is admissible to show that he intended that the victim would take his threats seriously.[80]

2–097

---

[77] (1987) 84 Cr.App.R. 319.
[78] *Dixon v. Atfield* [1975] 1 W.L.R. 1171.
[79] See paras. 1–090 to 1–097 above.
[80] *R. v. Clarence Ivor Williams* (1986) 84 Cr.App.R. 299.

CHAPTER 3

ASSAULTS RESULTING IN INJURY

(1) INTRODUCTION

The title to this chapter is a little misleading. As will be made clear in the **3–001** course of the chapter, certain offences resulting in injury, *e.g.* maliciously administering a noxious thing contrary to section 23 of the Offences Against the Person Act 1861, or causing grievous bodily harm contrary to section 18 of that Act, do not require an assault. They do however form a convenient group of offences and have as their base some unlawful act of violence affecting the person of another.

I. ASSAULT OCCASIONING ACTUAL BODILY HARM

3-002   Section 47 of the Offences Against the Person Act 1861 provides:

> "Whoever shall be convicted upon an indictment of any assault occasioning actual bodily harm shall be . . ."

guilty of an offence.

(1) Mode of Trial and Punishment

3-003   This offence is triable either way,[1] and on conviction on indictment the maximum penalty is five years imprisonment.[2]

3-004   By section 17(2) of the Firearms Act 1968:

> "If a person, at the time of his committing or being arrested for an offence specified in Schedule 1 to this Act, has in his possession a firearm or imitation firearm, he shall be guilty of an offence under this subsection unless he shows that he had it in his possession for a lawful object."

Where a person is charged with an offence under section 17(2) of the Firearms Act in conjunction with an offence of assault occasioning actual bodily harm, then by Schedule 6 of the Firearms Act the assault charge is triable only on indictment. The maximum penalty for an offence under section 17(2) of the Firearms Act is 14 years' imprisonment.[3] The penalty for the Firearms Act offence is in addition to any penalty imposed for the principal offence.[4]

(2) Indictment

3-005   An indictment alleging this offence should include in the words of the statement of offence "contrary to section 47 of the Offences Against the Person Act 1861". A defendant indicted for this offence cannot be convicted of an alternative offence of common assault; if there is an issue as to whether the assault resulted in injury a separate count of common assault must be added to the indictment.[5]

---

[1] Magistrates' Courts Act 1980, s.17 and Sched. 1.
[2] Penal Servitude Act 1891, s.1 and Criminal Justice Act 1948, s.1.
[3] Firearms Act 1968, s.51 and Sched. 6 as amended by Criminal Justice Act 1988, ss.44 and 171.
[4] Firearms Act 1968, Sched. 6.
[5] *R. v. Mearns* (1990) 91 Cr.App.R. 312.

(3) ASSAULT

See paragraphs 2–002 to 2–004.

3–006

(4) OCCASIONING ACTUAL BODILY HARM

"Occasioning" is a synonym for "resulting in" or "causing". The injury need not be the direct effect of a blow. It is sufficient if the victim suffers injury as a result of the assault, *e.g.* as a result of stumbling while avoiding a blow. In *R. v. Roberts*[6] the defendant molested a young woman who was a passenger in his car. To escape, she opened the door and jumped out while the car was in motion. She suffered grazing and concussion. The Court of Appeal held that the defendants had been properly convicted of assault occasioning actual bodily harm. In the words of Stephenson L.J.[7]:

3–007

> "The test is: was it the natural result of what the alleged assailant said and did, in the sense that it was something that could reasonably have been foreseen as the consequence of what he was saying or doing."

This test is not in conflict with section 8 of the Criminal Justice Act 1967, as it deals with causation not intent, a distinction which was explained fully in *D.P.P. v. Majewski*.[8]

"Actual bodily harm" means any type of injury however minor or temporary which is "calculated to interfere with the health or comfort of the prosecutor".[9] It is usual for there to be medical evidence of the injury, but this is not necessary to prove the injury. Although the words "bodily injury" might seem to exclude such things as nervous shock, it was held in *R. v. Miller*[10] to include a nervous or hysterical condition which resulted from the shock. That case also shows that if a husband assaults his wife for the purpose of having intercourse against her will, he is guilty of an assault upon her.

3–008

(5) MENTAL ELEMENT

The House of Lords in *R. v. Savage, R. v. Parmenter*[11] decided that the mental element is the same as for common assault, *i.e.* a deliberate act intended by the defendant to cause the victim to apprehend immediate violence; or an act done being reckless as to whether it will have that effect. The defendant need not have foreseen the risk of any injury actually occurring. The offence is made out if there is an assault and/or battery and injury follows as a consequence whether as a direct result of the blow or for example as a result of the

3–009

---

[6] (1971) 56 Cr.App.R. 95.

[7] *ibid.* at p. 102. In *R. v. Notman* [1994] Crim. L.R. 518 it was held that a direction to the jury that the defendant's actions must be the substantial cause of the injury was a convenient expression to indicate that the link between the defendant's actions and the injury must be more than *de minimis* and it avoided the need to go into a lengthy exposition about causation.

[8] (1976) 62 Cr.App.R. 262, H.L. see also para. 1–102 and 4–022.

[9] *R. v. Miller* [1954] 2 Q.B. 282 *per* Lynskey J. at 292.

[10] (1953) 38 Cr.App.R. 1. See also paragraph 1–006 above. Where it is alleged that the injury is psychiatric harm then expert medical evidence is essential—*R. v. Chan-Fook* (1994) 99 Cr.App.R. 147.

[11] (1992) 94 Cr.App.R. 193.

victim suffering injury while trying to escape (providing the steps taken to escape were proportionate to the apparent threat—see *R. v. Williams*; *R. v. Davis*).[12]

II. WOUNDING OR INFLICTING GRIEVOUS BODILY HARM

3-010   Section 20 of the Offences Against the Person Act 1861 provides:

"Whoever shall unlawfully and maliciously wound or inflict any grievous bodily harm upon any other person either with or without any weapon or instrument, shall be guilty . . ."

of an offence.

(1) MODE OF TRIAL AND PUNISHMENT

3-011   This offence is triable either way[13] and on conviction on indictment the maximum penalty is five years imprisonment.[14] This is an offence to which section 17(2) of the Firearms act 1968 applies.[15]

(2) INDICTMENT

3-012   There are two offences created by section 20, namely unlawfully and maliciously wounding; and unlawfully and maliciously inflicting grievous bodily harm. Wounding involves an assault, and on an indictment for malicious wounding, it is open to a jury to find the accused not guilty of that offence, but guilty of assault occasioning actual bodily harm.[16] Before the jury can consider that alternative verdict, they have to find the accused not guilty of the offence indicted, so they could not return a verdict of guilty of assault occasioning actual bodily harm where they could not agree on a verdict on the section 20 count.[17] It is also open to a jury to convict of assault occasioning actual bodily harm on a count for maliciously inflicting grievous bodily harm; and this is so even though Lord Roskill giving the judgment of the House of Lords in *R. v. Wilson*[18] considered that it is possible to envisage cases where grievous bodily harm was inflicted without an assault; however as an offence contrary to section 20 may involve an assault, then assault is included within the allegations of such an offence for the purpose of section 6(3) of the Criminal Law Act 1967.[19] This judgment seems to resolve a problem raised in *R.*

---

[12] (1992) 95 Cr.App.R. 1. In order for the defendant to be held responsible for the injury caused to the victim while escaping from the assault, the victim's conduct must be reasonably foreseeable.
[13] Magistrates' Courts Act 1980, s.17 & Sched. 1.
[14] Penal Servitude Act 1861, s.1 and Criminal Justice Act 1948, s.1.
[15] See para. 3–004 above.
[16] *R. v. Wilson* (1984) 77 Cr.App.R. 319 (H.L.); *R. v. Austin* (1973) 58 Cr.App.R. 163.
[17] This is the effect of the wording of s.6(3) of the Criminal Law Act 1967.
[18] [1984] A.C. 242.
[19] See *R. v. Collison* (1980) 71 Cr.App.R. 249.

v. Beasley[20] where the Court of Appeal held that the trial judge had misdirected the jury when he told them that on an indictment for an offence contrary to section 20 it was open to them to find the accused guilty of simple assault in the sense of causing the victim to apprehend violence. The Court of Appeal held that wounding or inflicting grievous bodily harm did not necessarily involve an allegation of assault in that sense. However, Lord Roskill's speech in *Wilson* suggests that, although such a direction adds unnecessary confusion, it is not wrong to leave to the jury an offence based upon assault on an indictment for a section 20 offence. In *R. v. Savage, R. v. Parmenter*[21] the House of Lords confirmed that assault is included in an allegation of an offence contrary to section 20. In most cases, this problem does not arise. Where it does arise, there are two practical alternatives. Either the particulars of offence can include the words "by assaulting him/her", a practice which received the approval of Lawton L.J. in *R. v. Ready*[22]; or a count of assault occasioning actual bodily harm can be added to the indictment. Of the two, the latter is preferable as it would enable the jury to return a verdict on that offence even if unable to reach a verdict on the section 20 offence. Where there is a real issue as to whether the injury amounts to a wound or grievous bodily harm (as the case may be) it simplifies the jury's task if they are able to consider an allegation of assault occasioning actual bodily harm as a separate count. Common assault can no longer be an alternative verdict, an express count needs to be added if appropriate—see paragraph 2–006 above.

Magistrates have no power to convict of a lesser offence; and on appeal to the Crown Court against conviction by magistrate, the Crown Court does not have power to substitute a conviction for a lesser offence.[23]   **3–013**

For the principles which apply where one of two or more people may have been responsible for the injury see paragraphs 1–017 to 1–023 above. Where a defendant joins in an attack which is so severe as to involve the infliction of grievous bodily harm, then that defendant is liable to be indicted for the full extent of the injuries, even though it cannot be proved that they were all inflicted at a time when he was participating in the attack; see *R. v. Grundy*[24] In that case, a group of men were involved in a concerted attack upon a police officer. The appellant joined in half-way through. He was indicted for inflicting grievous bodily harm—the injury being a broken nose. There was no evidence to show at what point during the fight that injury was inflicted nor whether the appellant was even involved in the attack at the time or whether it has been inflicted before he joined in. It was argued on his behalf that on the basis of *R. v. Abbot*[25] there was no sufficient evidence to say that he was responsible for the grievous bodily harm. The Court of Appeal held that the trial judge had correctly directed the jury that they must look at the totality of the injury suffered in deciding whether it amounted to grievous   **3–014**

---

[20] (1980) 73 Cr.App.R. 44.
[21] (1992) 94 Cr.App.R. 193.
[22] (1978) 67 Cr.App.R. 345.
[23] *Lawrence v. Same* [1968] 2 Q.B. 93.
[24] (1989) 89 Cr.App.R. 333.
[25] (1955) 39 Cr.App.R. 141.

bodily harm, and that included but was not confined to the broken nose in that case; and that the appellant was aiding and abetting the commission of an offence as soon as he joined in, and that there was ample evidence that the police officer had suffered grievous bodily harm as a result of the whole assault. That case is subject to proof that the defendant was participating in such an attack. It will also cause problems where there are several injuries not amounting to grievous bodily harm in totality, and only one of them is capable of being a wound. In those circumstances, the test in *Grundy* might be difficult to apply. In such a case, the alternative verdict of assault occasioning actual bodily harm would only be available in respect of that one injury (*e.g.* there may be a dispute whether it amounts to a wound), and so any other injuries would require an additional count of assault occasioning actual bodily harm if the prosecution are to avoid falling foul of a possible lacuna. There was no need for the Court of Appeal in *Grundy* to decide that the appellant was responsible for injuries inflicted prior to his involvement—his involvement must have aggravated whatever injury had been sustained before he participated.

(3) WOUND

3–015   A "wound" is an injury which breaks the whole skin—the fact that the injury bleeds is not enough; an abrasion does not amount to a wound.[26] It is a wound if the whole skin is broken whether the skin be external, or internal such as on the inside of the mouth[27] or the membrane of the urethra.[28] Subject to that, an injury, *e.g.* a kick, causing internal bleeding is not a wound because there would be no breaking of the skin.[29] It is therefore important to establish the nature of the injury by medical evidence where there is an allegation of wounding.

3–016   The wound can be caused "either with or without any weapon or instrument" according to the wording of section 20. The wound can be inflicted indirectly, *e.g.* by pushing the victim onto an object which causes the wound. It need not be the result of direct contact between assailant and victim; it would be wounding for the purposes of section 20 if the assailant threw a glass or bottle at the victim, or such objects as a dart or a sharpened coin which are sometimes used as weapons by rival football supporters. In *R. v. Sheard*,[30] the victim was struck on the head. He was wearing a hat with a hard rim, and the effect of the impact was that the hard rim caused a wound. That was a wounding.

---

[26] *R. v. McLoughlin* (1838) 8 C. & P. 635; *R. v. Wood* (1830) 1 Moo. 278; *Moriarty v. Brooks* (1834) 6 C. & P. 684; *R. v. Jones* (1849) 3 Cox C.C. 441.

[27] *R. v. Smith* (1837) 8 C. & P. 173.

[28] *Moriarty v. Brooks* (1834) 6 C. & P. 684.

[29] In *C. v. Eisenhower* [1984] 1 Q.B. 331 the victim was struck near his eye by an air gun pellet. It caused a black eye and redness in the eye due to the rupture of an internal blood vessel. The Divisional Court held that there was no wound, and quashed the defendant's conviction for a section 20 offence. The court affirmed the principles set out in the 19th Century cases at n. 26 above.

[30] (1837) 2 Moo. 13.

(4) GRIEVOUS BODILY HARM

"Grievous" means serious. "It is not necessary that such harm should . . .   3–017
be either permanent or dangerous, if it be such as seriously to interfere with
comfort or health, it is sufficient."[31] Juries are usually directed that it means
really serious bodily injury, though not necessarily posing a danger to life,[32]
although the absence of the qualifying "really" from the definition does not
constitute a misdirection, according to the Court of Appeal in *R. v. Saunders*[33]
in which it was said that on any view a broken nose was grievous bodily harm.
It is a misdirection to say that grievous bodily harm is established where there
has been an injury sufficient to interfere with the victim's health and comfort[34]—something more serious than that is required. The expression is apt
to include such injuries as fractures, injury to any organ, and disfiguring or
incapacitating injuries.

In *R. v. Ashman*[35] a clergyman was struck on the temple by some powder   3–018
which had been discharged from a gun by the defendant. There was no
wound, but he was peppered with grains of powder, and his eye was weak
with the effect of the blow for some two months. That was a sufficient injury
to constitute grievous bodily harm.

Psychiatric illness, if sufficiently severe, can amount to grievous bodily   3–019
harm,[36] since the brain is part of the body. It can be inflicted without assault
for the purposes of an offence contrary to section 20[37]; and it is possible that
an assault can cause a head injury which is in itself not serious, but which
results in serious psychiatric illness either as a result of trauma to the brain,
or as a result of the psychological reaction to the assault.

In contrast to a "wound", grievous bodily harm does not require medical   3–020
evidence to establish whether the injury is of the type alleged; but as a matter
of practice it is most desirable that there be such evidence, and it is unusual
for it to be absent.

(5) INFLICTS

The word "inflicts" encompasses an injury caused indirectly as well as   3–021
directly; it is not necessary to prove a battery.[38] The test is: was the injury a
natural consequence of the defendant's act? Examples are where the victim
suffers injury as a result of escaping from the defendant who is threatening or
using violence. In both *R. v. Halliday*[39] and *R. v. Beech*[40] the victim was
injured when escaping. In *Halliday* Lord Coleridge C.J. said:

---

[31] *Per* Wills J. in *R. v. Ashman* (1858) 1 F. & F. 88.
[32] Following Viscount Kilmuir L.C. in *D.P.P. v. Smith* [1861] A.C. 290 at 334, and see also *R. v. Cunningham* [1982] A.C. 566.
[33] [1985] Crim. L.R. 230.
[34] *R. v. Brown* [1994] 1 A.C. 212.
[35] See n. 31 above.
[36] *R. v. Burstow* [1997] 1 Cr.App.R. 144.
[37] *ibid.*
[38] *R. v. Wilson*; *R. v. Jenkins* [1984] A.C. 242.
[39] (1889) 61 L.T. 701.
[40] (1912) 7 Cr.App.R. 197.

"If a man creates in another man's mind an immediate sense of danger which causes such person to try and escape and in so doing he injures himself, the person who creates such a state of mind is responsible for the injuries which result."[41]

An extension of this principle is seen in *Cartledge v. Allen*[42] which is criticised in the commentary in the *Criminal Law Review* as imposing responsibility on the defendant for consequences which were too remote. In that case the victim was threatened by a group of people including the defendant. The victim panicked and ran off. He was pursued by some of the group, but not by the defendant. In an endeavour to escape he entered a public house, and in his panic put his hand through a glass panel in the door. The defendant was convicted by the magistrates' court, and the Divisional Court upheld that conviction, deciding that the magistrates were entitled to find that the victim suffered his injuries while under a well-grounded apprehension of violence induced by the acts of the defendant and others, and that there was a nexus between the defendant's acts and the injury such as to justify the magistrates in finding that the injury was the natural consequence of the defendant's acts.

(6) Unlawfully

3–022   See paragraphs 1–024 to 1–083 above.

(7) Maliciously

3–023   See paragraphs 1–098 to 1–107 above.

(8) Extended Jurisdiction

3–024   By section 1 of the Nuclear Material (Offences) Act 1983, an act (or omission) committed abroad by a person of whatever nationality which would have amounted to an offence contrary to section 20 of the Offences Against the Person Act 1861 if committed in England and Wales, can be tried here if the offence was committed "in relation to or by means of nuclear material". "Nuclear material" is defined in section 6(1). A scientific definition of nuclear material is set out in the Schedule to the Act, at paragraph 3–218 below.

3–025   Where jurisdiction is based on section 1 of the Nuclear Material (Offences) Act 1983, proceedings can only be begun with the consent of the Attorney-General.[43]

3–026   This is an offence to which the Internationally Protected Persons Act 1978 applies.[44]

---

[41] See also *R. v. Roberts* (1972) 56 Cr.App.R. 95 and paragraph 3–005 above. See also paras. 3–012 to 3–014 for possible problems with alternatives verdicts such situations create.
[42] [1973] Crim. L.R. 530.
[43] s.3(1).
[44] See paras. 1–087 to 1–089 above.

(9) Offences Committed on Aircraft

By section 6(1) of the Aviation Security Act 1982, any act done on an   3–027
aircraft outside the United Kingdom which if committed in England and
Wales would constitute any of a number of offences, including an offence
contrary to section 20 of the Offences Against the Person Act, shall be triable
here as such an offence if the act was done "in connection with the offence of
hijacking committed or attempted by him on board that aircraft". Section 6(1)
confers jurisdiction on the courts of the United Kingdom irrespective of (i)
the nationality of the offender, and (ii) the country in which the aircraft is
registered.

III. WOUNDING, ETC., WITH INTENT

(1) Definition

Section 18 of the Offences Against the Person act 1861 provides: 3–028

> "Whosoever shall unlawfully and maliciously by any means whatsoever wound or
> cause any grievous bodily harm to any person . . . with intent . . . to do some
> grievous bodily harm to any person, or with intent to resist or prevent the lawful
> apprehension of any person, shall be guilty . . ."

of an offence.

(2) Mode of Trial and Punishment

This offence is triable only on indictment, and carries a maximum penalty   3–029
of life imprisonment.

(3) Indictment

Where the person injured is not the person intended (*i.e.* transferred   3–030
malice—see paragraph 1–106 above) the indictment should state that the
defendant wounded (or inflicted grievous bodily harm on) A with intent to do
grievous bodily harm to B. Section 18 creates a single offence which may be
committed in a variety of ways.[45]

(4) Alternative Verdicts

Where the indictment alleges wounding with intent, that allegation includes   3–031
an allegation of assault, and so a jury would be entitled to return a verdict of
not guilty on the section 18 offence, but guilty of either assault occasioning
actual bodily harm, or malicious wounding. If the indictment alleges causing
grievous bodily harm with intent, then it used to be the law that the jury

---

[45] *R. v. Naismith* [1961] 2 All E.R. 735; *R. v. Hayles* (1969) 53 Cr.App.R. 36; *R. v. Beard* (1987)
85 Cr.App.R. 395.

could not return any alternative verdict as grievous bodily harm can be caused without an assault.[46] However, the House of Lords in *R. v. Mandair*[47] held that the word "cause" in section 18 was wide enough to encompass any method of inflicting grievous bodily harm under section 20, and accordingly such an alternative verdict was open to a jury. The defendant in that case was indicted with causing grievous bodily harm with intent contrary to section 18. He was alleged to have thrown acid at his wife, some of which had burnt her face. Counsel and the recorder agreed that the lesser offence under section 20 should also be left to the jury, but the indictment was not amended to add such a count, nor were the particulars of the section 18 count amended to allege that the grievous bodily harm was caused by inflicting it. When the jury returned their verdict of guilty to the section 20 alternative, the clerk asked them if they agreed on their verdict "of *causing* grievous bodily harm contrary to section 20". The Court of Appeal quashed the conviction and refused either to apply the proviso or substitute a conviction for inflicting grievous bodily harm contrary to section 20. Their reason was that the defendant had been convicted of an offence unknown to the law. The House of Lords restored the conviction, saying that the difference between "cause" and "inflict" was a mere technicality, but that, when the alternative is put to a jury, it is desirable for the actual words of section 20 to be used. Even in cases where such an alternative is open to the jury, the House of Lords thought it desirable that the alternative count should be added to the indictment. See paragraph 3–012 above.

(5) WOUND

3-032   See paragraphs 3–015 to 3–016 above.

(6) GRIEVOUS BODILY HARM

3-033   See paragraph 3–017 to 3–020.

(7) CAUSATION

3-034   The injury can be caused "by any means whatsoever" which includes injuries not caused by assault such as causing the victim to fall, or to take poison, or interfering with a vehicle so as to make it unsafe.

(8) UNLAWFULLY

3-035   See paragraphs 1–024 to 1–083.

---

[46] *R. v. McReady* (1978) 67 Cr.App.R. 345; *R. v. Collison* (1980) 71 Cr.App.R. 249.
[47] (1994) 99 Cr.App.R. 250, Lord Mustill dissenting.

(9) MALICIOUSLY

See paragraphs 1–098 to 1–107.   3–036

(10) WITH INTENT

Either of two intentions are required: 3–037
  (i) to do some grievous bodily harm; or
  (ii) to resist or prevent the lawful apprehension of any person.
  (i) This intent is the same as suffices for murder.[48] See paragraphs 4–061   3–038
to 4–083 below. In *R. v. Purcell*,[49] Lord Lane C.J. said that the proper direction on intent in a case under section 18 was:

> "You must feel sure that the defendant intended to cause serious bodily harm to
> the victim. You can only decide what his intention was by considering all the
> relevant circumstances and in particular what he did and what he said about it."

As in cases of murder, there is a problem in distinguishing intent to cause
grievous bodily harm from foresight of the possibility that such harm will
result.[50] There is the further dilemma of knowing what intent must be proved
against participants in the injury. The person who causes the injury must
intend to do some grievous bodily harm. But what of those who aid and abet?
They are equally guilty of a section 18 offence if they did not "intend" that
really serious bodily injury would be caused to someone, but foresaw it as a
possible consequence of their joint venture.[51] In *R. v. Slack*[52] the defendant
and another man went to the home of a frail old widow intending to rob her.
She was later found with her throat cut. In an interview with the police, the
defendant said that the other had told him to get the money, or to stand
outside until told that the coast was clear. The defendant further said that he
had taken a knife from the kitchen and given it to the other man (who was
holding the victim) to threaten her if need be, but he had no idea that he was
going to use the knife on her. At his trial, the defendant did not give evidence.
The trial judge directed the jury that the defendant was guilty of murder if
they found (i) that he contemplated and foresaw that the other man might kill
or inflict grievous bodily harm as part of the robbery; and (ii) that she died as
a result of such conduct by that person. He was convicted of murder and his
appeal was dismissed. Giving the judgment of the Court of Appeal, Lord Lane
considered what intent had to be proved in the case of "A" (the principal
party) compared with the necessary intent to be proved against "B" (the
secondary party)[53]:

---

[48] *R. v. Cunningham* [1982] A.C. 566.
[49] (1986) 83 Cr.App.R. 45.
[50] See, *e.g. R. v. Hancock* [1986] A.C. 455 explaining *R. v. Maloney* [1985] 1 A.C. 905 and *R. v.
Fry, The Independent*, October 17, 1988.
[51] *Chan Wing-Siu v. R.* [1985] A.C. 168 (P.C.); *R. v. Ward* (1986) 85 Cr.App.R. 71.
[52] (1989) 89 Cr.App.R. 252.
[53] At p. 257. For a discussion of some of the problems arising on the issue of intent see Norrie
"Oblique Intention and Legal Politics" [1989] Crim. L.R. 793.

"A must be proved to have intended to kill or do serious harm at the time he killed. B may not be present at the time of the killing; he may be a distance away, for example, waiting in the getaway car; he may be in another part of the house; he may not know that A has killed; he may have hoped (and probably did) that A would not kill or do serious injury. If, however, as part of their joint plan it was understood between them expressly or tacitly that if necessary one of them would kill or do serious harm as part of their common enterprise, then B is guilty of murder . . . Provided it is made clear to the jury that for B to be guilty he must be proved to have lent himself to a criminal enterprise involving the infliction, if necessary, of serious harm or death or to have had an express or tacit understanding with A that such harm or death should, if necessary, be inflicted, the precise form of words in which the jury is directed is not important."

See paragraphs 1–015 to 1–016, 1–097 and 4–089 to 1–095.

3-039 (ii) The intent to resist the lawful apprehension of himself or another must be proved in the same way as an intent to cause grievous bodily harm. It is no defence that the attacker believed, due to his ignorance of the law, that the apprehension was unlawful; but it is a defence where he is labouring under a genuine mistake of fact, such that if facts were as he believed them to be, the apprehension would be unlawful, *e.g.* where he sees one man knock another to the ground and believes it to be an assault, whereas it is a lawful arrest for an offence.[54]

3-040 For "lawful apprehension" see paragraphs 2–019 to 2–057.

(11) EXTENDED JURISDICTION

3-041 The Internationally Protected Persons Act 1978[55] applies to this offence, as does the Aviation Security Act 1982,[56] and section 1 of the Nuclear Material (Offences) Act 1983.[57]

IV. ATTEMPTING TO CHOKE, ETC., IN ORDER TO COMMIT OR ASSIST IN THE COMMITTING OF ANY INDICTABLE OFFENCE

(1) DEFINITION

3-042 Section 21 of the Offences Against the Person Act 1861 provides:

"Whosoever shall, by any means whatsoever, attempt to choke, suffocate, or strangle any other person, or shall by any means calculated to choke, suffocate, or strangle, attempt to render any other person insensible, unconscious, or incapable of resistance, with intent in any of such cases thereby to enable himself or any other person to commit, or with intent in any such case thereby to assist any other person in committing any indictable offence, shall be guilty . . ."

of an offence.

---

[54] *R. v. Gladstone Williams* (1983) 78 Cr.App.R. 276, approved in *Beckford v. R.* [1988] A.C. 130 (P.C.).
[55] See para. 1–087 to 1–089 above.
[56] See para. 3–027 above.
[57] See para. 3–024 above.

(2) MODE OF TRIAL AND PUNISHMENT

This offence is triable only on indictment, and carries a maximum penalty **3–043** of life imprisonment. It is an offence to which section 17 of the Firearms Act 1968 applies.[58]

(3) ATTEMPT

This offence is unusual in that the offence lies in the attempt. By section 3 **3–044** of the Criminal Attempts Act 1981 this offence is called a "special statutory provision", and what constitutes an attempt for such an offence is defined in section 3(2)–(4) as follows:

> "(2) For the purposes of this Act an attempt under a special statutory provision is an offence which
> (a) is created by an enactment other than section 1 above . . .; and
> (b) is expressed as an offence of attempting to commit another offence (in this section referred to as "the relevant full offence").
> (3) A person is guilty of an attempt under a special statutory provision if, with intent to commit the relevant full offence, he does an act which is more than merely preparatory to the commission of that offence.
> (4) A person may be guilty of an attempt under a special statutory provision even though the facts are such that the commission of the relevant full offence is impossible."

Even though choking or rendering a person insensible are not themselves offences, they would amount to murder, manslaughter or at least assault if carried out, and so section 3 of the Criminal Attempts Act will apply to this offence.

(4) ANY INDICTABLE OFFENCE

That is defined by the Interpretation Act 1978, Sched. 1 as meaning "an **3–045** offence, which, if committed by an adult, is triable on indictment, whether it is exclusively so triable or triable either way". This includes offences falling within section 22 of the Magistrates' Courts Act 1980 (by which the value of the item determines whether offences are purely summary or triable either way). However, the effect of the Criminal Justice Act 1988, Sched. 15 para. 59 is that offences of common assault, and taking a motor vehicle without consent (which become summary offences by sections 37 and 39 of that Act), together with driving whilst disqualified (which are all capable of being tried on indictment if founded on the same facts as, or forming part of a series of offences with, an indictable offence by section 40 of that Act) are excluded from the definition of indictable offences.

---

[58] See para. 3–004 above.

(5) Extended Jurisdiction

3–046   The Internationally Protected Persons Act 1978 and the Aviation Security Act 1982 apply to this offence.[59]

V. USING CHLOROFORM, ETC., TO COMMIT OR ASSIST IN COMMITTING ANY INDICTABLE OFFENCE

(1) Definition

3–047   Section 22 of the Offences Against the Person Act 1861 provides:

> "Whosoever shall unlawfully apply or administer or cause to be taken by, or attempt to apply or administer to or attempt to cause to be administered to or taken by, any person, any chloroform, laudanum, or other stupefying or over-powering drug, matter, or thing, with intent in any of such cases thereby to enable himself or any other person to commit, or with intent in any such case thereby to assist any other person in committing, any indictable offence, shall be guilty"

of an offence.

(2) Mode of Trial and Punishment

3–048   This offence is triable only on indictment, and section 22 provides a maximum penalty of life imprisonment. Section 17(2) of the Firearms Act 1968 applies.[60]

(3) Unlawfully

3–049   See paragraphs 1–024 to 1–083 above.

(4) With Intent

3–050   See paragraphs 1–090 and 1–097 above.

(5) Any Indictable Offence

3–051   See paragraph 3–045 above.

(6) Extended Jurisdiction

3–052   The Internationally Protected Persons Act 1978 and the Aviation Security Act 1982 apply to this offence.[61]

---

[59] See paras. 1–087 to 1–089 and 3–027 respectively.
[60] See para. 3–004 above.
[61] See paras. 1–087 to 1–089 and 3–027 respectively.

VI. MALICIOUSLY ADMINISTERING POISON, ETC., SO AS TO ENDANGER LIFE OR INFLICT GRIEVOUS BODILY HARM

(1) DEFINITION

Section 23 of the Offences Against the Person Act 1861 provides: 3–053

> "Whosoever shall unlawfully and maliciously administer to or cause to be administered to or taken by any other person any poison or other destructive or noxious thing, so as thereby to endanger the life of such person, or so as thereby to inflict upon such person any grievous bodily harm shall be guilty"

of an offence.

(2) MODE OF TRIAL AND PUNISHMENT

This offence is triable only on indictment, and is punishable with a maximum penalty of imprisonment for 10 years.   3–054

(3) ALTERNATIVE VERDICTS

A defendant may be convicted of an offence contrary to section 24 of the   3–055
Offences Against the Person Act[62] when tried for an offence under this section. Section 25 of the Act provides that if the jury trying an accused for a section 23 offence "are not satisfied that he is guilty thereof" but are satisfied that he is guilty of the section 24 offence, the jury may acquit him of the offence charged and convict him of the section 24 offence. The wording of section 25 is different from that of section 6(3) of the Criminal Law Act 1967 which deals with alternative verdicts in general. That subsection applies only where "the jury find him not guilty of the offence specifically charged"[63]; whereas section 25 of the 1861 Act seems to envisage the possibility of the jury failing to agree on a verdict on the offence charged, but agreeing that the accused is guilty of the section 24 offence.

(4) UNLAWFULLY

See paragraphs 1–024 to 1–083 above. In *R. v. McShane*[64] the Court of   3–056
Appeal held that it was unlawful to administer a noxious substance to a person intending to commit suicide, as aiding and abetting suicide is an offence. It might have been different had the defendant and the victim been willing parties to a suicide pact, when the act might not have been unlawful.[65]

---

[62] See para. 3–066 below.
[63] See *R. v. Saunders* (1987) 85 Cr.App.R. 334.
[64] [1977] Crim. L.R. 737.
[65] For the Suicide Act see paras. 6–001 to 6–002 below.

(5) MALICIOUSLY

3-057   See paragraphs 1–098 to 1–107 above, and especially *R. v. Cunningham*[66] which was a case concerning section 23. Note that this offence does require the defendant to act "maliciously", unlike sections 21 and 22 of the Offences Against the Person Act.

(6) ADMINISTER

3-058   It is not necessary for the prosecution to prove that the defendant introduced the noxious thing directly into the victim's body by, *e.g.* injection. In *R. v. Harley*[67] the defendant put arsenic in a cup of coffee and presented it to the victim who drank some and felt ill. The defendant was convicted, and appealed arguing that "administer" did not include leaving poison for the victim to take. The appeal was dismissed. It was held that it was not necessary for the poison to be delivered by hand to the victim. Spraying a noxious substance such as CS gas into the face of a victim is administering it; "administer" does not require that there be any form of entry into the victim's body either by absorption or through an orifice, and it encompasses an act which brings the noxious thing into contact with the victim's body, even if not by direct force.[68]

(7) INTENT

3-059   Once causation is proved, the prosecution need not prove that the defendant intended the consequences provided he acted "maliciously".[69]

(8) DESTRUCTIVE THING

3-060   Boiling water is capable of being a destructive thing[70]; as are acid and other such substances—although these are properly covered by section 29.[71]

(9) NOXIOUS THING

3-061   These fall into two categories—(i) those which are capable of doing harm irrespective of the quantities taken and are therefore analogous to poison; and

---

[66] (1957) 41 Cr.App.R. 155.
[67] (1880) 4 C. & P. 369. Contrast *R. v. Dalby* [1982] 1 W.L.R. 621 where a conviction for manslaughter was quashed on the ground that there was no "direct act" committed by the defendant towards the victim. They were both drug addicts, and the defendant had supplied part of the drugs he obtained on prescription to his friend. They both injected themselves. The quantity taken by the friend contributed to his death. However, there is no reference in the judgment to ss.23 or 24 of the Offences Against the Person Act; and it cannot affect the general principle in *Harley*.
[68] *R. v. Gillard* [1988] Crim. L.R. 531 disapproving *R. v. Dones* [1987] Crim. L.R. 682 (squirting with dilute ammonia contained in a plastic lemon was held at first instance not to be an "administering").
[69] *R. v. Cato* (1976) 62 Cr.App.R. 41.
[70] *R. v. Crawford* (1845) 1 Den. & P. 100.
[71] See para. 3–101 below.

(ii) those which are innocuous in small quantities or in particular form, but are likely to cause injury because of the nature or quantity administered, or the physical characteristics of the person to whom they are administered. In *R. v. Hennah*[72] Cockburn C.J. said:

> "... unless the thing is a noxious thing in the quantity administered, it seems exceedingly difficult to say logically there has been a noxious thing administered. The thing is not noxious in the form in which it has been taken; it is not noxious in the degree or quantity in which it has been given and taken ... It would be very different if the thing administered, as regards either its characteristics or degree were capable of doing mischief. But because it happens to fail in a particular instance, from any collateral or unforeseen cause, owing, maybe, to the vigour of the constitution of the person to whom it was administered, or some cause of that description, if it was capable of doing mischief at all it would be within the statute."

In *R. v. Cramp*[73] the defendant caused a pregnant woman to take half an ounce of juniper oil with intent to procure a miscarriage. The evidence was that quantities of the oil could be taken medicinally without ill-effect if in quantities substantially less than half an ounce, but that the amount administered in this case produces ill-effects, and is particularly dangerous for pregnant women. It was held that the quantity made the substance noxious. A more recent authority is *R. v. Marcus*.[74] In that case the defendant put some sedative and sleeping pills into a neighbour's bottle of milk. Expert evidence was called to the effect that the drugs would have evidence was called to the effect that the drugs would have caused little harm, but would have caused sedation and possibly sleep, and therefore were potentially dangerous if the person drove a car while affected by the drugs. The trial judge left to the jury the issue whether the drugs were of such a quantity and quality as to amount to a noxious thing. The Court of Appeal approved that approach, holding that the quantity as well as the quality of the substance had to be taken into account in deciding whether it was noxious, and something harmless in small quantities could be noxious if administered in greater amounts. The court reiterated the point that the characteristics of the victim are relevant, so that lacing the drink of an adult with alcohol might not amount to administering a noxious thing, whereas it might if administered to a child.[75] Lacing the drink of an adult, if done to excess, could on this principle amount to administering a noxious thing. The court in that case also held that a "noxious thing" was not limited to something causing direct injury to bodily health, so that, as in *Marcus* itself, a substance which makes a person more vulnerable to accident and injury by impairing their faculties is capable of being a "noxious thing". Tudor Evans J. made clear that the category of "noxious thing" is not limited to substances similar to poison.[76] He also suggested, *obiter*, that nervous shock suffered as a

---

[72] (1887) 13 Cox 547 at 549. According to Culpeper's *The Complete Herbal* many plants with medicinal properties are noxious if taken in quantity; conversely many poisonous plants have remedial qualities if taken in minute quantities.
[73] (1880) 5 Q.B.D. 307. See also *R. v. Wilkins* (1861) L. & C. 89.
[74] (1981) 73 Cr.App.R. 49.
[75] *ibid.* at p. 54 *per* Tudor Evans J.
[76] *ibid.* at p. 54.

result of some substance could render it noxious, quoting the example of *Donoghue v. Stevenson*[77] and suggesting that the snail in the ginger beer bottle was capable of being a noxious thing. Heroin is a noxious substance, even when administered to someone with a high degree of tolerance towards it.[78]

(10) ENDANGER

3–062   No actual danger need materialise, provided that there was a potential danger in that the victim's life was put at risk[79]; otherwise, offences against those whose constitution is so robust as to suffer no ill-effects would not be covered by this section, which would be contrary to Cockburn C.J.'s dictum in *Hennah*.[80] Therefore it would amount to endangering a person's life to give them a drink containing poison, which the intended victim accidentally spilled instead of drinking. To that extent, the element of endangering life encompasses acts which would otherwise be attempts; but as the accused need not intend that life be endangered, this offence is more extensive than an attempt.

(11) INFLICT

3–063   See paragraph 3–021 above.

(12) GRIEVOUS BODILY HARM

3–064   See paragraphs 3–017 to 3–020 above.

(13) EXTENDED JURISDICTION

3–065   The Internationally Protected Persons Act 1978 and the Aviation Security Act 1982 apply to this offence.[81]

VII. MALICIOUSLY ADMINISTERING POISON, ETC., WITH INTENT TO INJURE, AGGRIEVE OR ANNOY ANY OTHER PERSON

(1) DEFINITION

3–066   Section 24 of the Offences Against the Person Act 1861 provides:

"Whosoever shall unlawfully and maliciously administer to or cause to be admin-

---

[77] [1932] A.C. 562.
[78] *R. v. Cato* (1976) 62 Cr.App.R. 41.
[79] *R. v. Pearce* (1967) 50 Cr.App.R. 305.
[80] See para. 3–061 above.
[81] See paras. 1–087 to 1–089 and 3–027 respectively.

istered to or taken by any other person any poison or other destructive or noxious thing, with intent to injure, aggrieve, or annoy such person, shall be guilty"

of an offence.

(2) MODE OF TRIAL AND PUNISHMENT

This offence is triable either way[82] and carries a maximum penalty of five   **3–067**
years' imprisonment.

(3) ALTERNATIVE VERDICTS

By section 25 of the Offences Against the Person Act, a jury can convict of   **3–068**
this offence on a trial for an offence contrary to section 23.[83]

(4) UNLAWFULLY

See paragraphs 1–024 to 1–083 above.   **3–069**

(5) MALICIOUSLY

See paragraphs 1–098 to 1–107 above.   **3–070**

(6) ADMINISTER

See paragraph 3–058 above.   **3–071**

(7) DESTRUCTIVE OR NOXIOUS THING

See paragraphs 3–060 and 3–061 above.   **3–072**

(8) WITH INTENT

See paragraphs 1–090 to 1–097 above. The courts have given a wide   **3–073**
interpretation to what it is that must be intended. Any adverse inference with
a person's metabolism will be enough if done unlawfully and maliciously. In
R. v. Hill[84] the defendant had administered tablets (which were for a medicinal
purpose) to some boys with the purpose of making them more susceptible to
his homosexual advances. The House of Lords affirmed his conviction on the
basis that the defendant intended to injure the boys by causing harm to their
metabolism by overstimulating them. What had to be proved was an intention
to cause harm to the health of the boys. In that case, the boys did suffer harm.
However, had the intention been benevolent, *e.g.* to enable the boys to stay
awake to watch a firework display, that would not necessarily have been an

---

[82] Magistrates' Courts Act 1980, s.17 and Sched. 1.
[83] See para. 3–053 above.
[84] (1986) 83 Cr.App.R. 386.

intention caught by section 24. In *R. v. Wilkins*[85] the defendant put a quantity of "Spanish fly" in P's tea with the intention of stimulating her sexual passions. It was held that was a sufficient intention. In fact, due to the quantity administered, the woman suffered pain and was very ill. Old cases on intention must be approached with caution. Although it was said in *R. v. Marcus*[86] that the *eiusdem generis* rule of interpretation did not apply so as to limit "noxious thing" to poisons, it may well be that the intention to "aggrieve or annoy" should be construed *eiusdem generis* with "injure", including causing shock as described in *Marcus* which was a case concerning section 24.

(9) Extended Jurisdiction

3–074   The Internationally Protected Persons Act 1978 applies to this offence.[87]

VIII. ILL-TREATMENT OF MENTALLY DISORDERED PERSONS

(1) Definition

3–075   Section 127 of the Mental Health Act 1983 provides:

"(1) It shall be an offence for any person who is an officer on the staff of or otherwise employed in, or who is one of the managers of, a hospital or mental nursing home—
  (a) to ill-treat or wilfully to neglect a patient for the time being receiving treatment for mental disorder as an in-patient in that hospital or home; or
  (b) to ill-treat or wilfully to neglect, on the premises of which the hospital or home forms part, a patient for the time being receiving such treatment there as an out-patient.
(2) It shall be an offence for any individual to ill-treat or wilfully to neglect a mentally disordered patient who is for the time being subject to his guardianship under this Act or otherwise in his custody or care (whether by virtue of any legal or moral obligation or otherwise)."

(2) Mode of Trial and Punishment

3–076   The offences created by section 127 are triable either way, and carry on summary conviction a maximum penalty of six months' imprisonment and/or a fine not exceeding the statutory maximum; and on indictment two years' imprisonment and/or a fine.[88]

(3) Restrictions on Prosecution

3–077   No proceedings for an offence under this section may be instituted without the consent of the Director of Public Prosecutions.[89] Provided that the consent

---

[85] (1861) L. & C. 89.
[86] See para. 3–061 above.
[87] See paras. 1–087 to 1–089 above.
[88] Mental Health Act 1983, s.127(3).
[89] *ibid.*, s.127(4).

is obtained before the accused first appeared in court, it does not matter that it was not obtained before he was charged.[90]

(4) INDICTMENT

The offences of ill-treatment and wilful neglect are not synonymous and should be separately indicted.[91] Section 127 therefore creates six separate offences: **3–078**

   (i)   ill-treating an in-patient receiving treatment for a mental disorder;

  (ii)   wilfully neglecting an in-patient receiving treatment for a mental disorder;

 (iii)   ill-treating while on hospital or nursing home premises an out-patient receiving such treatment on those premises;

 (iv)   wilfully neglecting while on hospital or nursing home premises an out-patient receiving such treatment on those premises;

  (v)   ill-treating a mentally disordered patient who is subject to the defendant's guardianship or on his custody or care;

 (vi)   wilfully neglecting a mentally disordered patient who is subject to the defendant's guardianship or in his custody or care.

The last two offences are not confined to conduct on the premises of a hospital or mental nursing home. If the indictment alleges only ill-treatment or wilful neglect, or alleges those two offences in two separate counts it is likely that the jury must be directed that, before they can convict, they must be unanimous (or have reached the appropriate majority) as to which of the different ways in which the offences has been committed.[92]

(5) JOINT LIABILITY

Where a person to whom section 127 applies is ill-treated or neglected, then in the absence of explanation, all those responsible for his care at the material time are liable to be convicted even if it cannot be established which of several people having care of the patients actually committed the act or default; unless the ill-treatment or neglect consisted of a single isolated act.[93]   **3–079**

(6) ILL-TREAT

This must involve a deliberate act or omission. It is noticeable that "ill-treat" is not qualified by "wilfully", but it cannot be that the offence is intended to apply to anything less than cruel or at least callous conduct. Although there is no specific requirement that the ill-treatment must arise   **3–080**

---

[90] *R. v. Elliott* (1985) 81 Cr.App.R. 115.
[91] *R. v. Newington* (1990) 91 Cr.App.R. 247.
[92] See *R. v. Brown* (1984) 79 Cr.App.R. 115. This principle is applied inconsistently by the Court of Appeal. See, *e.g. R. v. Asquith* [1995] 1 Cr.App.R. 492, *R. v. Hancock & Warner* [1996] 2 Cr.App.R. 554.
[93] See paras. 1–017 to 1–022 above.

from an act done in bad faith or without reasonable care,[94] it is implicit that ill-treatment requires some deliberate act contrary to the patient's welfare. Any other interpretation would mean that any act or omission which in fact caused suffering to a patient, *e.g.* bruising while restraining him or administering medication would be an offence, and a matter for the D.P.P.'s discretion as to whether it should be prosecuted. This proposition is supported by the case of *R. v. Newington*[95] in which the Court of Appeal decided that the offence of ill-treatment consists of (i) deliberate conduct amounting to ill-treatment whether or not injury results, and (ii) an appreciation by the defendant that his conduct amounted to inexcusable ill-treatment, or that he was reckless as to whether his conduct was of that character. The court went on to say that ill-treatment and wilful neglect are not synonymous as the latter requires a particular state of mind which need not be proved in a case of ill-treatment.

(7) WILFULLY

3–081   In *Lomas v. Peek*[96] Lord Goddard said:

> "If a man permits a thing to be done, he means that he gives permission for it to be done, and if a man gives permission for a thing to be done, he knows what is to be done or is being done, and if he knows what is to be done or is being done, and if he knows that, it follows that it is wilful."

This is not very helpful as it begs a number of questions such as—was he wilful as to the way the thing was to be done?

3–082   In *R. v. Sheppard*[97] the 16-month-old child of a young couple of low intelligence living in deprived conditions died of hypothermia and malnutrition. The allegation was that they had failed to provide the child with medical assistance on several occasions. The defendants said that they had not realised that the child was so ill as to require medical attention. The trial judge directed the jury that the offence was one of strict liability, judged on the standard of the reasonable parent. The House of Lords held the direction was wrong, and that "wilful" indicated deliberate or reckless failure to provide proper care, and being reckless in this context means either knowing that the child (or patient) might be at risk as a result of the accused's acts or defaults, or not caring whether harm might result.

3–083   In *R. v. Senior*[98] Lord Russell of Killowen C.J. defined "wilfully" as follows:

> " 'Wilfully' means that the act is done deliberately and intentionally, not by accident or inadvertence, but so that the mind of the person who does the act goes with it."

In *Senior* the defendant was charged with an offence contrary to the Preven-

---

[94] This is a requirement imposed by s.139 of the Mental Health Act before any other offences of assault may be prosecuted—see para. 1–044 above.

[95] (1990) 91 Cr.App.R. 247.

[96] [1947] 2 All E.R. 574 at 575.

[97] [1981] A.C. 394. This case concerned s.1 of the Children and Young Persons Act 1933.

[98] [1899] 1 Q.B. 283 at 290–291.

tion of Cruelty Act 1894, which is materially similar to section 1 of the Children and Young Persons Act 1933. He belonged to a religious sect which did not believe in obtaining medical assistance. He refused to call a doctor to attend his child who was dangerously ill and died. In all other respects he cared properly for the child. Had a doctor been called, the child would probably have lived. The Court of Crown Cases Reserved decided that his neglect was "wilful" and he was guilty of manslaughter.

(8) NEGLECT

According to Lord Russell of Killowen C.J. in *R. v. Senior*.[99]   **3–084**

> "Neglect is the want of reasonable care—that is, the omission of such steps as a reasonable parent would take, such as are regularly taken in the ordinary experience of mankind—that is, in such a case as the present, provided the parent had such means as would enable him to take the necessary steps."

It includes failure to obtain medical help or treatment when normal reasonable care would require it.[1] There is no definition of "neglect" in the Mental Health Act, and to adopt that provided by section 1(2) of the Children and Young Persons Act 1933[2] is not strictly necessary, although it gives more indication of the type of conduct commonly regarded as neglect.

(9) PATIENT

This is defined in section 145 of the Mental Health Act 1983 as "a person   **3–085**
suffering or appearing to be suffering mental disorder".
"Mental disorder" is then defined by section 1(2) as meaning "mental illness, arrested or incomplete development of mind, psychopathic disorder and any other disorder or disability of mind and 'mentally disordered' shall be construed accordingly".

(10) HOSPITAL AND MENTAL NURSING HOME

These are defined by section 145 of the Mental Health Act, and mean   **3–086**
premises provided or used as a hospital by the National Health Service, or a registered mental nursing home.

(11) CORROBORATION

Where the prosecution evidence consists of or includes the testimony of   **3–087**
mentally disordered patients, corroboration is not required as a matter of law; nor is it necessary for the trial judge to give the normal direction on corroboration. He may tailor the warning he gives to the facts of the particular case, provided he makes it clear that it is dangerous to convict on such evidence.[3]

---

[99] [1899] 1 Q.B. 283 at 290–291 a case involving wilful neglect of a child by its parent.
[1] *Oakey v. Jackson* [1914] 1 K.B. 216.
[2] See chap. 8 below.
[3] *R. v. Spencer* [1987] A.C. 128; *R. v. Makanjuola* [1995] 2 Cr.App.R. 469.

3-088   For restrictions on prosecuting other allegations of assault committed by those engaged in the care of mentally disordered patients, see paragraphs 1-044 and 1-045 above.

IX. TERRORISM AND EXPLOSIVES

3-089   There is no offence of terrorism in English law. A definition of terrorism is succinctly provided by section 14(1) of the Prevention of Terrorism (Temporary Provisions) Act 1984:

> " 'terrorism' means the use of violence for political ends, and includes any use of violence for the purpose of putting the public or any section of the public in fear."

This definition only applies to that Act, but it provides a convenient generic description of offences commonly charged in cases of terrorism.

The provisions of the Suppression of Terrorism Act 1978 and the Prevention of Terrorism (Temporary Provisions) Act 1989, (as amended by the Criminal Justice act 1993, the Criminal Justice and Public Order Act 1994, and the Prevention of Terrorism (Additional Powers) Act 1996) contain provision as to procedure, powers of detention, extradition and jurisdiction. Where jurisdiction to try a particular offence is extended beyond the normal jurisdiction of criminal courts in England and Wales, that is set out in the section of this work dealing with the particular offence.

3-090   Murder, kidnapping, taking hostages, assault and offences contrary to sections 18, 20, 28 to 30 and 47 of the Offences Against the Person Act 1861, and the Explosive Substances Act 1883 can all be appropriate, depending on the circumstances, in cases involving acts of terrorism. Set out below are offences usually associated with terrorism, although they are not confined to terrorism.

3-091   As our celebrations every fifth of November remind us, terrorism is not a modern phenomenon. The term "terrorist" probably derives from the Reign of Terror during the French Revolution.

X. CAUSING BODILY INJURY BY GUNPOWDER

(1) Definition

3-092   Section 28 of the Offences Against the Person act 1861 provides:

> "Whosoever shall unlawfully and maliciously, by the explosion of gunpowder or other explosive substance, burn, maim, disfigure, disable, or do any grievous bodily harm to any person, shall be guilty"

of an offence.

(2) MODE OF TRIAL AND PUNISHMENT

This offence is triable only on indictment, and carries a maximum penalty   3–093
of life imprisonment.

(3) INDICTMENT

Section 28 creates a single offence which may be committed in a variety of   3–094
different ways, and therefore it is proper to allege any or all of the alleged
types of injury in a single count,[4] although it is desirable that in appropriate
cases the prosecution specify that which they allege occurred.[5] From their very
nature, explosives are likely to cause injury to more than one person. In such
cases, there must be a separate count for each person injured, subject to the
sensible course of relying on sample counts where any explosion has caused
many casualties.

(4) EXPLOSIVE SUBSTANCE

There is no definition in the 1861 Act of "explosive substance". However,   3–095
it was held in *R. v. Wheatley*[6] and *R. v. Bouch*[7] that the definition set out in
section 3 of the Explosives Act 1875 applied equally to the meaning of
"explosive substance" in the Explosive Substances Act 1883. It is more difficult to say that definition must be incorporated into the earlier statute, but it
does at the very least give a guide to the material which can be covered by the
term "explosive". Section 3 of the Explosives Act 1875 provides:

> "The term "explosives" in this Act
> (1) Means gunpowder, nitro-glycerine, dynamite, guncotton, blasting pow-
>   ders, fulminate of mercury or of other metals, coloured fines, and every
>   other substance, whether similar to those above mentioned or not, used or
>   manufactured with a view to produce a practical effect; and
> (2) Includes fog-signals, fireworks, fuses, sockets, percussion caps, detonators,
>   cartridges, ammunition of all descriptions and every adaptation of prep-
>   aration of an explosive as above defined."

A petrol bomb is an explosive substance within this definition as, whether
or not it explodes, it has a pyrotechnic effect.[8] The definition is wide enough
to cover any explosive device or substance, including modern innovations.

(5) UNLAWFULLY

See paragraphs 1–024 to 1–083 above. The possession or use of explosives   3–096
can be lawful if genuinely done for the protection of person or property,

---

[4] *R. v. Naismith* [1961] 2 All E.R. 735; *R. v. Hayles* (1969) 53 Cr.App.R. 36.
[5] *R. v. Beard* (1987) 85 Cr.App.R. 395. See n. 92 above for the problems when an offence may
    be committed in one of several ways.
[6] (1979) 68 Cr.App.R. 287.
[7] (1983) 76 Cr.App.R. 11.
[8] *R. v. Bouch* (1983) 76 Cr.App.R. 11.

provided that the possession or use of the explosive is in reasonable proportion to the perceived threat. In *Attorney-General's Reference (No. 2 of 1983)*[9] the Court of Appeal held that self defence was available in a case involving explosives provided the means used for protection (in that case a petrol bomb) were no more than the accused believed at the time were reasonably necessary to meet the force used or threatened against him. However, the court stressed that only in exceptional circumstances could possession of an object like a petrol bomb be justified. The Explosives Act 1875 contains detailed provisions about the lawful manufacture and use of explosives.

(6) BURN, MAIM, DISFIGURE, DISABLE

3-097 These injuries are not restricted to permanent injury, nor to injuries which result in grievous bodily harm—section 28 says "do any grievous bodily harm" as an alternative to the specific injuries set out in the section, not "do any *other* grievous bodily harm".[10] Consequently, throwing a corrosive liquid into someone's face to disable them for sufficient time to commit a crime or effect an escape, *e.g.* by causing temporary blindness, is sufficient to fall within the definition of "disable" for the purposes of section 29 of the Offences Against the Person Act[11]; and on that basis an explosion which renders a victim unconscious, or causes him temporary blindness or deafness would suffice.

(7) ANY GRIEVOUS BODILY HARM

3-098 See paragraphs 3–017 to 3–020 above.

(8) CAUSATION

3-099 The injury must result from the explosion, or its immediate consequences, *e.g.* the collapse of a building.[12] What is not clear is whether the explosion must have been activated or caused by the defendant or persons with whom he was acting in concert. In contrast to section 29[13] the words "cause . . . to explode" are not used, and it would probably be an offence contrary to section 28 unlawfully and maliciously to lure a victim into the vicinity of an explosion caused by someone else who was acting lawfully, *e.g.* an Army firing range. On the other hand, the clause "or do any grievous bodily harm to any person" suggests some causative link between the defendant and the explosion whether the injury is inflicted directly or indirectly by the defendant.

---

[9] (1984) 78 Cr.App.R. 183.
[10] *R. v. James* (1980) 70 Cr.App.R. 215, distinguishing *R. v. Boyce* (1824) 1 Moo. C.C. 29.
[11] See para. 3–101 below.
[12] See *R. v. Steer* (1987) Cr.App.R. 352 (H.L.) which concerned a case of danger to life caused by criminal damage. The House of Lords drew the analogy with damage by fire which could be indirect as well as direct, *e.g.* due to the smoke or fumes. They also referred to s.3 of the Explosive Substances Act 1883 (below at para. 3–095) in passing as though no comparable issue of causation would arise in the case of injury or danger to life resulting from an explosion.
[13] See para. 3–101 below.

(9) Extended Jurisdiction

The Internationally Protected Persons Act 1978[14] and section 6(1) of the   **3–100**
Aviation Security Act 1982[15] apply to this offence. The Suppression of Terrorism Act 1978[16] confers extended jurisdiction for any act committed in a "convention country" by a person of whatever nationality which if committed in
England or Wales would have constituted one of a number of offences, includ-
ing this one. "Convention country" is defined by section 8(1) as "a country
for the time being designated in an order made by the Secretary of State as a
party to the European Convention on the Suppression of Terrorism signed at
Strasbourg on the 27th January 1977". The convention countries are: Austria,
Belgium, Cyprus, Czech Republic, Denmark, Finland, France, Germany,
Greece, Iceland, Italy, Liechtenstein, Luxembourg, Netherlands, Norway,
Portugal, Republic of Ireland, Slovakia, Spain, Sweden, Switzerland, and
Turkey, and it has also been extended to the United States of America and to
India.[17]

XI. CAUSING EXPLOSION, OR SENDING EXPLOSIVE SUBSTANCE, OR THROWING CORROSIVE FLUID

(1) Definition

Section 29 of the Offences Against the Person Act 1861 provides: **3–101**

> "Whosoever shall unlawfully and maliciously cause any gunpowder or other cor-
> rosive substance to explode, or send or deliver to or cause to be taken or received
> by any person any explosive substance or any other dangerous or noxious thing,
> or put or lay at any place or cast or throw at or upon or otherwise apply to any
> person, any corrosive fluid or any destructive or explosive substance, with intent
> in any of the cases aforesaid to burn, maim, disfigure or disable any person, or to
> do some grievous bodily harm to any person, shall, whether any bodily injury be
> effected or not, be guilty of"

an offence.

(2) Mode of Trial and Punishment

This offence is triable only on indictment, and carries a maximum penalty   **3–102**
of life imprisonment.

---

[14] See paras. 1–087 to 1–089 above.
[15] See s.4(1) of that Act, and para. 3–027 above.
[16] See s.4(1) of and Sched. 1 to that Act and para. 3–089 above.
[17] For the Convention Countries see the statutory instruments under that Act, currently S.I. 1978
No. 1245; 1979 No. 497; 1980 Nos. 357 and 1392; 1981 Nos. 1389 and 1507; 1986 Nos. 271
and 1137; 1987 No. 2137; 1989 No. 2210; 1990 No. 1272; 1994 No. 2978.

(3) Indictment

3–103   Section 29 seems to create four separate offences, namely:

    (i)   causing any gunpowder or other explosive substance to explode;

   (ii) sending, delivering, etc., any explosive substance or other dangerous or noxious thing;

  (iii) putting or laying at any place any corrosive fluid or destructive or explosive substance; and

  (iv) casting or throwing at or applying to any person any corrosive fluid or destructive or explosive substance.

In each case, those offences can be committed with a number of different intents, but those different intents can be charged as a single offence.[18]

(4) Unlawfully

3–104   See paragraphs 1–024 to 1–083 above.

(5) Maliciously

3–105   See paragraphs 1–098 to 1–107 above.

(6) Cause

3–106   The defendant must cause the gunpowder or other explosive substance to explode. In *R. v. Saunders*[19] the defendant threw a detonator from a train in which he was travelling. P., who was working near the railway went up to the detonator and kicked it. It exploded and injured him. The trial judge held that there was a case to go to jury on whether the injury was too remote from the defendant's act, as well as on the issue of intent.

3–107   The wording of this section, and particularly "whether any bodily injury be effected or not" make it clear that, in contrast with an offence contrary to section 28[20] the explosion need not cause any injury. Section 29 is of course not confined to explosives, and is concerned with intent rather than consequences.

(7) Explosive Substance

3–108   See paragraph 3–095 above.

(8) Dangerous or Noxious Thing

3–109   See paragraphs 3–061 to 3–062 above.

---

[18] There is no specific authority for this demarcation. For the principle as to when a single offence is created which may be committed in several ways see *R. v. Naismith* [1961] 1 W.L.R. 952; *R. v. Hayles* (1969) 53 Cr.App.R. 36; *R. v. Beard* (1987) 85 Cr.App.R. 395. For the potential problems which arise about directing a jury on issues about which they must agree when an offence may be committed in different ways see para 3–078 and n. 92 above.

[19] (1879) 14 Cox 180.

[20] See para. 3–092 above.

(9) INTENT

See paragraphs 1–090 to 1–097 above, and 4–069 to 4–082 below.   **3–110**

(10) EXTENDED JURISDICTION

The Internationally Protected Persons Act 1978[21] and section 4(1) of the   **3–111**
Suppression of Terrorism Act 1978[22] apply to this offence.

XII. PLACING GUNPOWDER NEAR A BUILDING WITH INTENT TO DO BODILY INJURY

(1) DEFINITION

Section 30 of the Offences Against the Person Act 1861 provides: **3–112**

> "Whosoever shall unlawfully and maliciously place or throw in, into, upon,
> against, or near any building, ship or vessel any gunpowder or other explosive
> substance, with intent to do bodily injury to any person shall, whether or not any
> explosion takes place, and whether or not any bodily injury be effected, be guilty
> of"

an offence.

(2) MODE OF TRIAL AND PUNISHMENT

This offence is triable only on indictment and carries a maximum penalty   **3–113**
of 14 years' imprisonment. Section 17(2) of the Firearms Act 1968 applies to
this offence.[23]

This offence covers conduct not specifically dealt with by sections 28 and   **3–114**
29.[24] Section 30 does not require that any explosion take place; nor, if it does,
that any injury should result. In addition, the intent is to do any bodily injury
so it is apt to deal with the activities of a malevolent prankster intent on
causing some slight injury, *e.g.* throwing a firework at someone, as well as
those whose motives may be political or industrial.

(3) UNLAWFULLY

See paragraphs 1–024 to 1–083 above.   **3–115**

(4) MALICIOUSLY

See paragraphs 1–098 to 1–107 above.   **3–116**

---

[21] See paras. 1–087 to 1–089 above.
[22] See para. 3–100 above.
[23] See para. 3–004 above.
[24] See paras. 3–092 to 3–111 above.

(5) Building, Ship or Vessel

3–117   It is not clear whether "vessel" is to be construed *eiusdem generis* with "ship" or is to be given a wider interpretation. It is noticeable that the section does not refer to conveyance or vehicle, so that placing an explosive on or near a car would not be covered by this section.[25] Bearing in mind the likely effects of an explosion in or near a car, the appropriate offence would be contrary to section 2 or section 3 of the Explosive Substances Act 1883,[26] or section 29 of the Offences Against the Person Act.[27] Whether or not an aircraft is a "vessel", placing an explosive on board an aircraft is more appropriately dealt with by one of the latter charges, or a charge contrary to section 2(2) of the Aviation Security Act 1982.[28]

(6) Explosive Substance

3–118   See paragraph 3–095 above.

(7) With Intent

3–119   See paragraphs 1–090 to 1–097 above and 4–069 to 4–082 below.

(8) Any Bodily Injury

3–120   See paragraphs 3–007 to 3–008 above.

(9) Extended Jurisdiction

3–121   The Internationally Protected Persons Act 1978,[29] section 4(1) of the Suppression of Terrorism Act 1978[30] and section 6(1) of the Aviation Security Act 1982[31] apply to this offence.

XIII. CAUSING EXPLOSION LIKELY TO ENDANGER LIFE OR PROPERTY

(1) Definition

3–122   Section 2 of the Explosive Substances Act 1883 as substituted by section 7(1) and (3) of the Criminal Jurisdiction Act 1975 provides:

---

[25] Compare the definition of "conveyance" in s.12(7) of the Theft Act 1968: " 'conveyance' means any conveyance constructed or adapted for the carriage of a person whether by land, water or air, except that it does not include a conveyance constructed or adapted for use only under the control of a person not carried in or on it" (*e.g.* a pram or supermarket trolley with a child seat).
[26] See para. 3–134 below.
[27] See para. 3–101 above.
[28] See para. 3–162 below; and, by way of contrast, para. 3–157 below.
[29] See paras. 1–087 to 1–089 above.
[30] See para. 3–100 above.
[31] See para. 3–027 above.

"A person who in the United Kingdom or (being a citizen of the United Kingdom and Colonies) in the Republic of Ireland unlawfully and maliciously causes by any explosive substance an explosion of a nature likely to endanger life or to cause serious injury to property shall, whether any injury to person or property has been actually caused or not, be guilty of an offence".

(2) MODE OF TRIAL AND PUNISHMENT

This offence is triable only on indictment and carries a maximum penalty of life imprisonment. It is made a serious arrestable offence by Part II of Schedule 5 to the Police and Evidence Act 1984.   **3–123**

(3) RESTRICTIONS ON PROSECUTION

No proceedings for this offence may be initiated without the Attorney-General's consent.[32]   **3–124**

(4) UNLAWFULLY

See paragraphs 1–024 to 1–083 above.   **3–125**

(5) MALICIOUSLY

See paragraphs 1–098 to 1–107 above. It is interesting to note that when amending this section, the Criminal Jurisdiction Act 1975 retained "maliciously" as the *mens rea* rather than substituting "recklessly" as had been done in the Criminal Damage Act 1971.   **3–126**

(6) EXPLOSIVE SUBSTANCE

Section 9(1) of the Explosive Substance Act 1883 contains the following definition: **3–127**

"(1) In this Act, unless the context otherwise requires—The expression "explosive substance" shall be deemed to include any materials for making any explosive substance; also any apparatus, machine, implement, or materials used or intended to be used, or adapted for causing, or aiding in causing, any explosion in or with any explosive substance; also any part of any such apparatus, machine or implement."

This is an inclusive rather than exhaustive definition, and it was held in *R. v. Bouch*[33] that the definition contained in the Explosives Act 1875 was incorporated into the meaning of "explosive substance" for the purpose of the Explosive Substance Act. See paragraph 3–095 above.

Because the definition in section 9 includes apparatus, etc., for use in caus-   **3–128**

---

[32] s.7(1) of the Explosive Substances Act 1883 as substituted by s.63 of the Administration of Justice Act 1982. The consent must be obtained before the accused appears in court; it need not precede charge—*R. v. Elliott* (1984) 81 Cr.App.R. 115.
[33] (1983) 76 Cr.App.R. 11, following *R. v. Wheatley* (1979) 68 Cr.App.R. 287.

ing an explosion, it covers timing devices.[34] In the case of items in the hands of several persons, each of which is innocuous in itself, but together constitute a substance or device within section 9 then each of those persons is liable to be convicted of an offence under the Explosive Substances Act if he has the appropriate *mens rea*.[35]

(7) LIKELY TO ENDANGER LIFE

3–129   See paragraph 3–062 above.

(8) EXTENDED JURISDICTION

3–130   The Internationally Protected Persons Act 1978[36] and section 6(1) of the Aviation Security Act 1982[37] apply to this offence. In addition the Suppression of Terrorism Act 1978 confers extended jurisdiction for offences committed contrary to this section. The effect of section 4(1) of the Suppression of Terrorism Act (acts committed in "convention countries") is set out at paragraph 3–100 above.

3–131   Section 4(3) of the Suppression of Terrorism Act confers jurisdiction on courts in the United Kingdom to try as any offence contrary to sections 2 or 3 of the Explosive Substances Act 1883 acts which would have constituted such an offence if committed here, but were committed overseas by a citizen of a convention country. The requirements are:

  (i)   that the acts were committed outside the country of which he was a citizen;

  (ii) that country has itself extra-territorial jurisdiction to try him for those acts;

  (iii) had he been a citizen of the United Kingdom and Colonies, the United Kingdom Courts would have had jurisdiction.

Section 4(2) provides:

"If a person who is a national of a convention country but not a citizen of the United Kingdom and Colonies does outside the United Kingdom and that Convention Country commit any act which makes him guilty in that Convention Country of an offence and which if he had been a citizen of the United Kingdom and Colonies, would have made him guilty of an offence mentioned in paragraph 1, 2 or 13 of Schedule 1 to this Act [which includes offences contrary to sections 2 and 3 of the Explosive Substances Act], he shall, in any part of the United Kingdom, be guilty of the offence or offences aforesaid of which the act would have made him guilty if he had been such a citizen."

3–132   Section 2 of the Explosive Substances Act does not itself confer jurisdiction for acts committed abroad, whereas sections 3 and 5 do. The Attorney-General's consent is required for any prosecution of an offence triable only as

---

[34] *R. v. Berry* [1985] A.C. 246.
[35] *R. v. Charles* (1892) 17 Cox 499.
[36] See paras. 1–087 to 1–089 above.
[37] See para. 3–027 above.

a result of section 4 of the Suppression of Terrorism Act[38] (disregarding the effects of the Internationally Protected Persons Act 1978).

(9) ACCESSORIES

Section 5 of the Explosive Substances Act makes special provision for the   3–133
liability of accessories:

> "Any person who within (or being a subject of Her Majesty) without Her Majesty's dominions by the supply of or solicitation for money, the providing of premises, the supply of materials, or any manner whatsoever, procures, counsels, aids, abets, or is accessory to, the commission of any crime under this Act, shall be guilty of felony, and shall be liable to be tried and punished for that crime, as if he had been guilty as a principal."

XIV. ATTEMPT TO CAUSE EXPLOSION

(1) DEFINITION

Section 3 of the Explosive Substances Act 1883 as substituted by section   3–134
7(1) and (3) of the Criminal Jurisdiction Act 1975 provides:

> "(1) A person who in the United Kingdom or a dependency or (being a citizen of the United Kingdom and Colonies) elsewhere unlawfully and maliciously—
> (a) does any act with intent to cause, or conspires to cause, by an explosive substance an explosion of a nature likely to endanger life, or cause serious injury to property, whether in the United Kingdom or the Republic of Ireland, or
> (b) makes or has in his possession or under his control an explosive substance with intent by means thereof to endanger life, or cause serious injury to property, whether in the United Kingdom or the Republic of Ireland, or to enable any other person so to do, shall, whether any explosion does or does not take place, and whether any injury to person or property is actually caused or not, be guilty of an offence."

(2) MODE OF TRIAL AND PUNISHMENT

This offence if triable only on indictment, and carries a maximum penalty   3–135
of life imprisonment. Where any explosive substance is recovered, section 3(1)
provides that it "shall" be forfeited.

(3) RESTRICTIONS ON PROSECUTION

No proceedings for this offence may be instituted without the Attorney-   3–136
General's consent.[39]

---

[38] See n. 32 above.
[39] s.7 of the Explosive Substances Act 1883 as substituted by s.63(1) of the Administration of Justice Act 1982. For the timing of the consent, see n. 32 above.

(4) UNLAWFULLY

3–137   See paragraphs 1–024 to 1–083 above.

(5) MALICIOUSLY

3–138   See paragraphs 1–098 to 1–107 above.

(6) WITH INTENT

3–139   See paragraphs 1–090 to 1–097 above and 4–069 to 4–082 below.

(7) EXPLOSIVE SUBSTANCE

3–140   See paragraphs 3–095 and 3–127 to 3–128 above.

(8) ENDANGER LIFE

3–141   See paragraph 3–062 above.

(9) EXTENDED JURISDICTION

3–142   Section 3 deals with explosions taking place or intended to take place in the United Kingdom or the Republic of Ireland. The acts constituting the offence must take place in the United Kingdom or a dependency, unless the defendant is a citizen of the United Kingdom and Colonies, in which case the act can take place anywhere. So if a United Kingdom citizen does acts, *e.g.* on the Continent with intent to cause an explosion in the Republic of Ireland that would be triable in the United Kingdom, even though no overt act took place anywhere in the United Kingdom. Conversely, an act done by a person who was not a United Kingdom citizen with intent to cause an explosion in the United Kingdom or the Republic of Ireland, is only triable in the United Kingdom if that act occurred in the United Kingdom or dependencies. The "United Kingdom" means Great Britain and Northern Ireland, and excludes the Republic of Ireland.[40] "Dependency" is defined in section 3(2) as "the Channel Islands, the Isle of Man, and any colony other than a colony for whose external relations a country other than the United Kingdom is responsible".

3–143   The provisions of section 4(1) and (2) of the Suppression of Terrorism Act 1978[41] apply to this offence. Neither the Internationally Protected Persons Act 1978,[42] nor the Aviation Security Act 1982[43] apply.

---

[40] Sched. 1 to the Interpretation Act 1978.
[41] See para. 3–100 above.
[42] See paras. 1–087 to 1–089 above.
[43] See para. 3–027 above.

(10) Accessories

See paragraph 3–133 above. 3–144

XV. MAKING OR POSSESSING EXPLOSIVES UNDER SUSPICIOUS CIRCUMSTANCES

(1) Definition

Section 4(1) of the Explosive Substances Act 1883 provides: 3–145

"Any person who makes or knowingly has in his possession or under his control any explosive substance, under such circumstance as to give rise to a reasonable suspicion that he is not making it or does not have it in his possession or under his control for a lawful object, shall, unless he can show that he made it or had it in his possession or under his control for a lawful object, be guilty"

of an offence.

(2) Mode of Trial and Punishment

This offence is triable only on indictment and carries a maximum penalty 3–146 of 14 years' imprisonment. In addition, section 4 provides that the explosive substance "shall be forfeited".

(3) Restrictions on Prosecution

No proceedings may be instituted without the Attorney-General's consent.[44] 3–147

(4) Indictment

Section 4(1) creates two offences; one of making and the other of possessing 3–148 or having control. Knowledge is an ingredient of the offence of possessing or having control of an explosive substance, and the word "knowingly" should be included in the particulars of the offence.[45] If the allegation is that the defendant made the explosive substance, there seems no need to allege that he did so knowingly. It is conceivable but unlikely that a person could unwittingly make an explosive substance, but see paragraph 3–151 below.

(5) Burden of Proof

This is an unusual offence in that the prosecution must prove the defendant 3–149 made or knowingly possessed or had control over an explosive substance in suspicious circumstances. Once that is established, the burden is then on the defendant to prove that he was acting with a lawful purpose. The standard

---

[44] See n. 32 above.
[45] *R. v. Stewart* (1959) 44 Cr.App.R. 29.

of proof that the defendant must discharge is the balance of probabilities.[46] When the Explosive Substances Act was passed, an accused did not have the right to give evidence, and so section 4(2) specifically gave the accused the right to give evidence and call his or her spouse. Now that an accused is always competent to give evidence on his or her own behalf, and a spouse is compellable unless standing trial together with the accused,[47] section 4(2) has been repealed.[48]

(6) INGREDIENTS OF OFFENCE

3–150   In *R. v. Berry*[49] the defendant manufactured timers for export to the Middle East. The prosecution alleged they were for use by terrorists in making time bombs. The case was argued before the House of Lords principally on the issue of whether the unlawful object suspected from the defendant's conduct had to be an object which was contrary to *English* law. The House of Lords regarded this issue as beside the point. They held that the question of jurisdiction did not arise, and it was irrelevant whether the explosive device were to be used in circumstances in which the courts of the United Kingdom would have no jurisdiction. What had to be considered was, firstly, whether the defendant's acts were within the jurisdiction, and, secondly, whether those acts provoked the requisite suspicion.

The questions which arose, their Lordships thought, were:
(i) what did the prosecution have to prove on a charge brought under section 4(1), and, if that were proved;
(ii) what then did the defendant have to prove.

They held that section 4(1) creates a "conduct" crime, of which the *actus reus* is making an explosive substance, and the *mens rea* is making it under circumstances giving rise to a reasonable suspicion that it does not have a lawful purpose. If the prosecution proves those elements, then the burden of proving that he did make the explosive substance for a lawful purpose falls to the defendant, including (if need be) that the object was lawful according to the law of the place in which the acts were, carried out or intended to be carried out.

3–151   This distinction between *actus reus* and *mens rea* for the first type of offence created by section 4(1) is unhelpful. How can an accused's mental state consist of someone else's suspicions? The House of Lords in *Berry* did not deal with the other limb of section 4(1) which is qualified by "knowingly", but which also requires proof that the defendants' possession or control was in circumstances such as to give rise to a reasonable suspicion of an unlawful object. During the argument in the House of Lords, Berry absconded. He was rearrested several years later and reinstated his appeal in the Court of Appeal on matters which had not been decided by that court and had not been part of the certified question before the House of Lords. The Court of Appeal

---

[46] *R. v. Carr-Briant* (1943) 29 Cr.App.R. 76.
[47] Police and Criminal Evidence Act 1984, s.80(2) and (4).
[48] By s.119 of and Sched. 7 pt. V to the Police and Criminal Evidence Act 1984.
[49] [1985] A.C. 246.

held[50] that "knowingly" refers to possession or control; and they further held that it qualifies the word "makes" in section 4(1) even though the wording of the section appears to distinguish between *mens rea* required for the two different forms of the offence. In the light of *Berry* it is probable that proof of the offence requires proof of the knowledge of the nature of the substance but not knowledge that someone else will form a reasonable suspicion that the explosive substance is possessed or controlled for an unlawful purpose.

In three cases, namely *R. v. Hallam*,[51] *R. v. Stewart*[52] and *R. v. McVitie*[53]   **3–152**
the Court of Appeal dealt with offences of possession of an explosive substance. In each case, the court held that before the burden of proof shifts, the prosecution must prove:

(i)   the defendant knew he had the substance in his possession or under his control;

(ii) he knew it to be an explosive substance; and

(iii) the circumstances were such as to give rise to a reasonable suspicion that it was not in his possession or under his control for a lawful object.

The court also held that it was proper for a jury to infer the defendant's knowledge that the substance was an explosive substance if they were satisfied the prosecution had proved (i) and (iii). This approach makes sense of section 4(1) and gives helpful guidance for both trial judge and jury.

(7) EXPLOSIVE SUBSTANCE

See paragraphs 3–095 and 3–127 to 3–128 above.   **3–153**

(8) LAWFUL OBJECT

See paragraphs 1–024 to 1–083 above. If the accused asserts that his acts   **3–154**
are lawful according to the law applying in the jurisdiction where the object is to be carried out, he bears the burden of proving that his object is lawful under that foreign law.[54] It is not clear whether the defendant can discharge the burden by relying on genuine error of fact which if true would have made the purpose lawful,[55] but as he bears the burden of proof, that would be the fairest interpretation. "Object" means purpose or intent.[56]

In appropriate cases, self-defence will amount to a lawful object. In *Attorney-General's Reference (No. 2 of 1983)*[57] a victim of an impending racial attack of extreme violence was entitled to arm himself with petrol bombs to ward off the attack.

---

[50] (1994) 99 Cr.App.R. 88.
[51] (1957) 41 Cr.App.R. 111.
[52] (1959) 44 Cr.App.R. 29.
[53] (1960) 44 Cr.App.R. 201.
[54] *R. v. Berry* [1985] A.C. 246.
[55] As is the case in self defence: see *R. v. Gladstone Williams* (1983) 78 Cr.App.R. 276, approved in *Beckford v. R.* [1988] A.C. 130 (P.C.).
[56] *R. v. Berry* [1985] A.C. 246 at 255 D.
[57] (1984) 78 Cr.App.R. 183.

(9) EXTENDED JURISDICTION

3–155   Section 4 is limited to acts within the United Kingdom, giving rise to a suspicion arising there. It does not matter that the explosion was to occur outside the United Kingdom.[58] The defendant is still liable to be convicted for this offence even if he is outside the jurisdiction at the time of an explosion provided the acts prohibited by this section take place within the jurisdiction of the United Kingdom.

(10) ACCESSORIES

3–156   See paragraph 3–133 above.

XVI. POSSESSION OF ARTICLES FOR SUSPECTED TERRORIST PURPOSES

(1) DEFINITION

3–157   Section 16A of the Prevention of Terrorism (Temporary Provisions) Act 1989[59] provides:

> "(1) A person is guilty of an offence if he has any article in his possession in circumstances giving rise to a reasonable suspicion that the article is in his possession for a purpose connected with the commission, preparation or instigation of acts of terrorism to which this section applies.
> (2) The acts of terrorism to which this section applies are—
> (a) acts of terrorism connected with the affairs of Northern Ireland; and
> (b) acts of terrorism of any other description except acts connected solely with the affairs of the United Kingdom or any part of the United Kingdom other than Northern Ireland."

(2) MODE OF TRIAL AND PUNISHMENT

3–158   This offence is triable summarily or on indictment. On indictment it carries a maximum penalty of 10 years' imprisonment or a fine or both; on summary conviction it carries a maximum penalty of six months' imprisonment or a fine not exceeding the statutory maximum, or both.[60]

(3) INGREDIENTS OF OFFENCES

3–159   In many ways this offence mirrors section 4(1) of the Explosive Substances Act 1883, and the principles set out in paragraphs 3–145 and 3–152 above will apply. However, this offence is limited to acts of terrorism connected with (and intended to have connection with) the affairs of Northern Ireland, or foreign countries.

---

[58] *R. v. Berry* [1985] A.C. 246.
[59] As inserted by Criminal Justice and Public Order Act 1994, s.82(1).
[60] s.16(A)(5).

Section 16A(4) provides: 3–160

> "(4) Where a person is charged with an offence under this section and it is
>   proved that at the time of the alleged offence—
>   (a) he and that article were both present in any vehicle; or
>   (b) the article was on premises of which he was the occupier or of which he
>   habitually used otherwise than as a member of the public,
>   the court may accept the fact proved as sufficient evidence of his possessing
>   that article at that time unless it is further proved that he did not at that
>   time know of its presence in the premises in question, or, if he did know,
>   that he had no control over it . . .
> (6) This section applies to vessels, aircraft and vehicles as it applies to prem-
>   ises."

This provision goes further than allowing an inference to be drawn—it
deems that proof of one fact is sufficient evidence to prove guilt of the offence.
In this respect if is more draconian than the provisions about inferences to be
drawn from silence in section 34 to 38 the Criminal Justice and Public Order
Act 1994. Once one of those facts is proved, then the burden shifts to the
defendant to prove lack of knowledge. The burden of proof will, in the first
instance, lie on the prosecution to prove the facts beyond reasonable doubt;
but if that is done, the defendant must discharge the burden on him on the
balance of probabilities.[61]

(4) DEFENCES

Section 16A(3) provides: 3–161

> "(3) It is a defence for a person charged with an offence under this section to
>   prove that at the time of the alleged offence the article in question was
>   not in his possession for such a purpose as is mentioned in subsection (1)
>   above."

As usual, when the burden lies on the defendant, it will be discharged on
the balance of probabilities.[62]

XVII. DESTROYING, DAMAGING OR ENDANGERING THE SAFETY OF AIRCRAFT

(1) DEFINITION

Section 2 of the Aviation Security Act 1982 provides: 3–162

> "(1) It shall, subject to subsection (4) below, be an offence for any person unlaw-
>   fully and intentionally—
>   (a) to destroy an aircraft in service or so to damage such an aircraft as to
>   render it incapable of flight or as to be likely to endanger its safety in
>   flight; or

---

[61] *R. v. Carr-Briant* (1943) 29 Cr.App.R. 76.
[62] *ibid.*

(b) to commit on board an aircraft in flight any act of violence which is likely to endanger the safety of the aircraft.

(2) It shall also, subject to subsection (4) below, be an offence for any person unlawfully and intentionally to place, or cause to be placed, on an aircraft in service, any device or substance which is likely to destroy the aircraft, or is likely so to damage it as to render it incapable of flight; but nothing in this subsection shall be construed as limiting the circumstances in which the commission of such an act—

(a) may constitute an offence under subsection (1) above, or

(b) may constitute attempting or conspiring to commit, or aiding, abetting, counselling or procuring . . . the commission of such an offence."

(2) MODE OF TRIAL AND PUNISHMENT

3–163   Any offence under this section is triable only on indictment, and carries a maximum penalty of life imprisonment.[63]

(3) INDICTMENT

3–164   Section 2 seems to create these different offences; one each by section 2(1)(a) and (b) and the third by section 2(2).[64]

(4) RESTRICTION ON PROSECUTIONS

3–165   Section 8 of the Aircraft Security Act 1982 provides that proceedings for an offence under section 2 may not be instituted without the consent of the Attorney-General.[65]

(5) UNLAWFULLY

3–166   Section 2(6) provides:

"In this section "unlawfully"—

(a) in relation to the commission of an act in the United Kingdom, means so as (apart from this Act) to constitute an offence under the law of the part of the United Kingdom in which the act is committed;

(b) in relation to the commission of an act outside the United Kingdom, means so that the commission of the act would (apart from this Act) have been an offence under the law of England and Wales if it had been committed in England or of Scotland if it had been committed in Scotland."

For the general principles about when an act is unlawful, see paragraphs 1–024 to 1–083 above.

---

[63] Aviation Security Act 1982, s.2.
[64] For the effects of this see para. 3–078 and n. 92 above.
[65] See n. 32 above.

(6) INTENTIONALLY

See paragraphs 1–090 to 1–097 above and 4–069 to 4–082 below. 3–167

(7) LIKELY TO ENDANGER ITS SAFETY

No actual danger need arise for an offence to be committed contrary to 3–168
section 2(1)(a).[66]

(8) IN FLIGHT

Section 38(3) of the Aviation Security Act 1982 provides: 3–169

"For the purposes of this Act—
(a) the period during which an aircraft is in flight shall be deemed to include
any period from the moment when all its external doors are closed following embarkation until the moment when any such door is opened for dis-
embarkation, and, in the case of a forced landing, any period until the
competent authorities take over responsibility for the aircraft and for persons and property on board."

(9) ANY ACT OF VIOLENCE

This term which appears in section 2(1)(b) is given a statutory definition 3–170
by section 7:

"In this section, "act of violence" means—
(a) any act done in the United Kingdom which constitutes the offence of
murder, attempted murder, manslaughter, . . . assault, or an offence under
section 18, 20, 21, 22, 23, 24, 28 or 29 of the Offences Against the Person
Act 1861 or under section 2 of the Explosive Substances Act 1883, and
(b) any act done outside the United Kingdom which, if done in the United
Kingdom, would constitute such an offence as is mentioned in paragraph
(a) above."

(10) EXTENDED JURISDICTION

Section 2(3) of the Aviation Security Act 1982 confers jurisdiction on the 3–171
English courts for an act contrary to section 2(1) or 2(2) committed by a
person of whatever nationality, wherever the act is committed (*i.e.* within the
United Kingdom or elsewhere), and whatever the state in which the aircraft
is registered. The only limitation on this extensive jurisdiction is provided by
section 2(4) which limits jurisdiction in any case where the act was "committed
in relation to an aircraft used in military, customs or police service" to (i) an
act committed in the United Kingdom by a person of any nationality; (ii) an
act committed outside the United Kingdom by a United Kingdom national.

---

[66] See para. 3–062 above.

(11) OTHER OFFENCES

3-172   Section 3 of the Aviation Security Act 1982 creates an offence, which also
carries a maximum sentence of life imprisonment, of unlawfully and intentionally destroying, damaging or interfering with any property used for the provision of air navigation facilities, where the destruction, damage or interference
is likely to endanger the safety of aircraft in flight. This is not specifically an
offence against the person, but may result in risk of injury. Section 3 also
applies to providing false information which endangers or is likely to endanger
aircraft in flight.

XVIII. POSSESSING DANGEROUS ARTICLES
IN AN AIRCRAFT, ETC.

(1) DEFINITION

3-173   By section 4 of the Aviation Security Act 1982:

> "(1) It shall be an offence for any person without lawful authority or reasonable
>   excuse (the proof of which shall lie on him) to have with him—
>   (a) in any aircraft registered in the United Kingdom, whether at a time when
>   the aircraft is in the United Kingdom or not, or
>   (b) in any other aircraft at a time when it is in or in flight over, the United
>   Kingdom, or
>   (c) in any part of an aerodrome in the United Kingdom, or
>   (d) in any air navigation installation in the United Kingdom which does not
>   form part of an aerodrome
>   any article to whch this section applies.
> (2) This section applies to the following articles, that is to say—
>   (a) any firearm, or any article having the appearance of being a firearm,
>   whether capable of being discharged or not;
>   (b) any explosive, any article manufactured or adapted (whether in the form
>   of a bomb or grenade or otherwise) so as to have the appearance of being
>   an explosive, whether it is capable of producing a practical affect by
>   explosion or not, or any article marked or labelled so as to indicate that it
>   is or contains an explosive; and
>   (c) any article (not falling within either of the preceding paragraphs) made or
>   adapted for use for causing injury to or incapacitating a person or
>   destroying, damaging property, or intended by the person having it with
>   him for such use, whether by him or any other person."

(2) MODE OF TRIAL AND PUNISHMENT

3-174   This offence is triable either way. On summary conviction it carries a maximum penalty of three months' imprisonment and/or a fine not exceeding
the statutory maximum, and on indictment a maximum penalty of five years'
imprisonment and/or a fine.[67]

---

[67] Aviation Security Act 1982, s.4(4).

(3) RESTRICTION ON PROSECUTION

There is no requirement that the Attorney-General gives his consent before   3–175
proceedings are instituted for this offence.[68]

(4) BURDEN OF PROOF

The prosecution must prove the ingredients of the offence, namely that the   3–176
accused had with him in a place falling within section 4(1) an article described
in section 4(2). The prosecution need not prove that the accused *intended* that
the article had the appearance of a firearm nor that the accused intended that
the article looked like an explosive if it was manufactured or adapted to do so;
nor that the accused intended that an article made or adapted for causing
injury, etc., should be used for that purpose. However in the case of an article
intended by the accused to cause injury or damage but not made or adapted
to do so (*e.g.* a pen knife) then the prosecution must prove this intent. If the
article is intended by the accused to be an explosive,[69] but it is not, the prosecution must prove that intent. Once the prosecution has proved these ingredients appropriate to the particular article, the defendant bears the burden of
proving on the balance of probabilities,[70] that he had lawful authority or
reasonable excuse[71] for having that article with him.

(5) HAVING THE ARTICLE WITH HIM

For the purposes of section 4, any article contained within a person's bag-   3–177
gage is treated as being "with him", but not if the article is carried by one
aircraft and he travels on another. Section 4(3) provides:

"For the purposes of this section a person who for the time being in an aircraft,
or in part of an aerodrome, shall be treated as having with him in the aircraft, or
in that part of the aerodrome as the case may be, an article to which this section
applies if—
  (a) where he is in an aircraft, the article, or an article in which it is contained,
      is in the aircraft and has been caused (whether by him or by any other
      person) to be brought there as being, or as forming part of, his baggage on
      a flight in the aircraft or has been caused by him to be brought there as
      being, or as forming part of, any other property to be carried on such a
      flight, or
  (b) where he is in part of an aerodrome (otherwise than in an aircraft), the
      article, or an article in which it is contained, is in that or any other part of
      the aerodrome and has been caused (whether by him or by any other
      person) to be brought into the aerodrome as being, or as forming part of,
      his baggage on a flight from that aerodrome or has been caused by him to

---

[68] *ibid.*, cf. the offence under s.2—see para. 3–165.
[69] See the definition of "explosive" for the purposes of this Act in para. 3–184 below.
[70] *R. v. Carr-Briant* (1943) 29 Cr.App.R. 76.
[71] Lawful authority or reasonable excuse would include carrying the article for self-defence, or
    under duress. See paras. 1–046 to 1–068 above. It is arguable that as duress operates to excuse
    the accused from his acts, the prosecution should bear the burden of disproving duress, if that
    defence is raised.

be brought there as being, or as forming part of, any other property to be
carried on such a flight on which he is able to be carried,

notwithstanding that the circumstances may be such that (apart from this
subsection) he would not be regarded as having the article with him in the aircraft
or in a part of the aerodrome as the case may be."

3-178   Although this definition is wide, it is not exhaustive, and does not limit the
circumstances in which a person would otherwise be regarded as having an
article with him.[72]

3-179   The circumstances covered by section 4(3) are as follows:

(i)   A person while in an aircraft, is deemed to have with him any article
       which forms part of his own baggage on that flight whether or not
       he is responsible for it being there. An article might be caused by
       someone else to be bought there as part of his baggage if the article
       was packed by someone else for him to take; or was carried (*e.g.* by
       an employee of a travel company or the airport authority) from
       outside the aircraft and loaded onto it; or an article or bag containing
       the article has been checked in by another as being part of the
       baggage of the person travelling on that flight.

(ii)   A person while in an aircraft is deemed to have with him any article
       which he caused to be carried on that flight, even though not part
       of his own baggage, *e.g.* placed in someone else's bag, or secreted
       among the catering supplies.

(iii) A person at an aerodrome, but not in an aircraft, is deemed to have
       with him any article which forms part of his baggage for a flight
       from that aerodrome whether he or someone else has caused it to
       be there.

(iv)   A person at an aerodrome, but not in an aircraft is deemed to have
       with him any article not included in his baggage which he has
       caused to be brought to the aerodrome and which is to be carried
       on the same flight from the aerodrome as himself.

3-180   This analysis reveals some anomalies. There is no requirement in section 4
that the person should have the article with him "knowingly". This means
that an innocent courier will be convicted of an offence under this section
unless he can show on the balance of probabilities that he had a reasonable
excuse, *i.e.* ignorance.

3-181   On the other hand, a terrorist who places a bomb or firearm in an innocent
person's luggage and who does not travel on the same flight as the article
commits no offence under section 4; and only commits an offence under section 2[73] if the article is likely to destroy or seriously damage the aircraft. If
that terrorist plants in an innocent passenger's baggage a firearm, or dis-
mantled bomb not likely to explode in flight, intending it to be used for terrorist activities after the aircraft has reached its destination, then he is not deemed
to have that article with him. He commits no offence under section 4 unless
he is at the aerodrome to ensure that the article is carried on a particular flight,

---

[72] s.4(5).
[73] See para. 3–162 above.

in which case he will have the article with him while it is under his control, and the limitations in the definition contained in section 4(3) will not help him.

Section 4(3) only applies to a flight being taken by that aircraft or about to   3–182
be taken by it; or to a flight from the aerodrome. It does not apply to articles placed in a passenger's baggage or otherwise on the aircraft after it has touched down at its destination and its doors opened—see paragraph 3–169 above.

Other offences will be appropriate to cover the limitations in section 4,   3–183
provided there is adequate proof of the necessary ingredients, *e.g.* section 4 of the Explosive Substances Act 1883.[74]

(a) Definitions

Section 38(1) of the Aviation Security Act 1982 contains definitions of the   3–184
principal terms used in section 4. The most important are:

" 'article' includes any substance, whether in solid or liquid form or in the form of a gas or vapour;"

" 'explosive' means any article manufactured for the purpose of producing a practical effect by explosion, or intended for that purpose by a person having the article with him".[75]

This definition will include normally innocuous items, such as an aerosol   3–185
can, if the defendant (who must for the purposes of this definition be the person who has the article with him) intends that the pressure in the container would cause it to explode at altitude in an unpressurised part of the aircraft.

XIX. ENDANGERING SAFETY AT AERODROMES

(1) DEFINITION

Section 1 of the Aviation and Maritime Security Act 1990 provides: 3–186

"(1) It is an offence for any person by means of any device, substance or weapon intentionally to commit at an aerodrome serving international civil aviation any act of violence which—
  (a) causes or is likely to cause death or serious personal injury, and
  (b) endangers or is likely to endanger the safe operation of the aerodrome or the safety of persons at the aerodrome.
(2) It is also, subject to subsection (4) below, an offence for any person by means of any device, substance or weapon unlawfully and intentionally—
  (a) to destroy or seriously to damage—
    (i) property used for the provision of any facilities at an aerodrome serving international civil aviation (including any apparatus or equipment so used), or,
    (ii) any aircraft which is at such an aerodrome but is not in service, or

---

[74] See para. 3–145. But note the territorial limitation of that offence.
[75] Compare the definition of "explosive substance" in the Explosives Act 1875, paras. 3–095 and 3–127 to 3–128 above.

        (b) to disrupt the services of such an aerodrome, in such a way as to endanger or be likely to endanger the safe operation of the aerodrome or the safety of persons at the aerodrome."

(2) MODE OF TRIAL AND PUNISHMENT

3-187   This offence if triable only on indictment, and carries a maximum penalty of imprisonment for life.[76]

(3) RESTRICTION ON PROSECUTION

3-188   Proceedings for an offence under this section require the consent of the Attorney-General.[77]

(4) ACT OF VIOLENCE

3-189   Section 1(9) of the Aviation and Maritime Security Act 1990 provides a definition of this term which is identical to that contained in section 2 of the Aviation Security Act 1982—see paragraph 3–170 above.

(5) INTENTIONALLY

3-190   See paragraphs 1–090 to 1–097 above, and 4–069 to 4–082 below.

(6) UNLAWFULLY

3-191   This term is given a statutory definition by section 1(9) of the Aviation and Maritime Security Act 1990:

> " 'unlawfully'—
>   (a) in relation to the commission of an act in the United Kingdom, means so as (apart from this section) to constitute an offence under the law of the part of the United Kingdom in which the act was committed, and
>   (b) in relation to the commission of an act outside the United Kingdom, means so that the commission of the act would (apart from this section) have been an offence under the law of England and Wales if it had been committed in England and Wales . . ."

Note that an offence under subsection (1) does not explicitly require the act to be unlawful. Nevertheless, a lawful act must amount to a defence even under subsection (1). If it does not an armed police officer firing at a terrorist in order to disable him from activating a bomb or using a weapon would have no defence; nor would a civilian who decided heroically to disable a terrorist and did so with something which came to hand as a weapon rather than resorting to bare hands. For the general principles about when an act is unlawful, see paragraphs 1–024 to 1–083 above.

---

[76] s.1(5).
[77] s.1(7) and see n. 32 above.

(7) Endanger

No actual danger need arise—see paragraph 3–062 above. **3–192**

(8) Extended Jurisdiction

Section 1(3) and (4) give these offences extraterritorial effect: **3–193**

> "(3) Except as provided by subsection (4) below, subsections (1) and (2) above apply whether any such act as is referred to in those subsections is committed in the United Kingdom or elsewhere and whatever the nationality of the person committing the act.
> (4) Subsection (2)(a)(ii) above does not apply to any act committed in relation to an aircraft used in military, customs or police service unless—
> (a) the act is committed in the United Kingdom, or
> (b) where the act is committed outside the United Kingdom, the person committing it is a United Kingdom national."

XX. ENDANGERING THE SAFETY OF SHIPS OR FIXED PLATFORMS

(1) Definition

Section 11 of the Aviation and Maritime Security Act 1990 provides: **3–194**

> "(1) Subject to subsection (5) below, a person commits an offence if he unlawfully and intentionally—
> (a) destroys a ship or a fixed platform,
> (b) damages a ship, its cargo or a fixed platform so as to endanger, or to be likely to endanger, the safe navigation of the ship, or as the case may be, the safety of the platform, or
> (c) commits on board a ship or fixed platform an act of violence which is likely to endanger the safe navigation of the ship, or as the case may be, the safety of the platform.
> (2) Subject to subsection (5) below, a person commits an offence if he unlawfully and intentionally places, or causes to be placed, on a ship or fixed platform any device or substance which—
> (a) in the case of a ship, is likely to destroy the ship or is likely so to damage it or its cargo as to endanger its safe navigation, or
> (b) in the case of a fixed platform, is likely to destroy the fixed platform or so to damage it as to endanger its safe navigation.
> (3) Nothing in subsection (2) above is to be construed as limiting the circumstances in which the commission of any act—
> (a) may constitute an offence under subsection (1) above, or
> (b) may constitute attempting, or conspiring to commit, or aiding, abetting, counselling, procuring or inciting . . . the commission of such an offence.
> (4) Except as provided by subsection (5) below, subsections (1) and (2) above apply whether any such act as is mentioned in those subsections is committed in the United Kingdom or elsewhere and whatever the nationality of the person committing the act.
> (5) Subsections (1) and (2) above do not apply in relation to any act committed in relation to a warship or any other ship used as a naval auxiliary or in customs or police service unless—

(a) the person is a United Kingdom national, or
(b) his act is committed in the United Kingdom, or
(c) the ship is used in the naval or customs service of the United Kingdom or in the service of any police force in the United Kingdom."

(2) MODE OF TRIAL AND PENALTY

3-195   This offence is triable only on indictment, and carries a maximum penalty of imprisonment for life.[78]

(3) INGREDIENTS OF OFFENCE

3-196   The principal terms are defined in exactly the same way as in section 1 of the Act—see paragraphs 3–198 to 3–192 above. A "fixed platform" is defined by section 17(1) as:

"(a) any offshore installation within the meaning of the Mineral Workings (Offshore Installations) Act 1971, which is not a ship, and
(b) any other artificial island, installation or structure which—
  (i) permanently rests on, or is permanently attached to, the seabed,
  (ii) is maintained for the purposes of the exploration or exploitation of resources or for other economic purposes, and
  (iii) is not connected with dry land by a permanent structure providing access at all times and for all purposes."

XXI. DEVELOPING OR POSSESSING A BIOLOGICAL WEAPON OR AGENT

3-197   The Biological Weapons Act 1974 makes it an offence to develop or possess a biological weapon, or any biological agent or toxin which has no peaceful purpose.

(1) DEFINITION

3-198   Section 1(1) of the Biological Weapons Act 1974 provides:

"No person shall develop, produce, stockpile, or retain—
(a) any biological agent or toxin of a type and in a quantity that has no justification for prophylactic, protective, or other peaceful purpose; or
(b) any weapon, equipment or means of delivery designed to use biological agents or toxins for hostile purposes or in armed conflict."

(2) MODE OF TRIAL AND PUNISHMENT

3-199   This offence is triable only on indictment and carries a maximum penalty of life imprisonment.[79]

---

[78] s.11(6).
[79] s.1(3).

(3) Restrictions on Prosecution

Proceedings for an offence under section 1 cannot be instituted without the   3–200
consent of the Attorney-General.[80]

(4) Offences by Bodies Corporate

Where an offence under section 1 is committed by a body corporate, any   3–201
director, manager, secretary or other similar officer or person purporting to act
in such a capacity shall be guilty of the offence as well as the body corporate if
he is proved to have consented to and connived at its commission; or its
commission by the body corporate was attributable to his negligence.[81]

(5) Biological Agent or Toxin

These terms are defined by section 1(2) as follows: 3–202

"In this section—
    'biological agent' means any microbial or biological agent; and
    'toxin' means any toxin, whatever its origin or method of production."

XXII. USING, DEVELOPING, POSSESSING OR
TRANSFERRING CHEMICAL WEAPONS

(1) Definition

The Chemical Weapons Act 1996 was enacted on April 3, 1996. It came   3–203
into force on September 16, 1996.[82] Section 2 of the Act provides:

"(1) No person shall—
    (a) use a chemical weapon;
    (b) develop or produce a chemical weapon;
    (c) have a chemical weapon in his possession;
    (d) participate in the transfer of a chemical weapon;
    (e) engage in military preparations, or in preparations of a military nature,
        intending to use a chemical weapon.
(4) For the purposes of subsection (1)(d) a person participates in the transfer
    of an object if—
    (a) he acquires or disposes of the object or enters into a contract to acquire or
        dispose of it, or
    (b) he makes arrangements under which another person acquires or disposes
        of the object or another person enters into a contract to acquire or dispose
        of it.
(5) For the purposes of subsection (4)—
    (a) to acquire an object is to buy it, hire it, borrow it or accept it as a gift;
    (b) to dispose of an object is to sell it, let it on hire, lend it or give it.
(6) In proceedings for an offence under subsection (1)(a), (c) or (d) relating to
    an object it is a defence for the accused to prove—

---

[80] See n. 32 above.
[81] s.3.
[82] Chemical Weapons Act 1996 (Commencement) Order 1996, S.I. 1996 No. 2054.

(a) that he neither knew nor suspected nor had reason to suspect that the object was a chemical weapon, or

(b) that he knew or suspected it to be a chemical weapon and as soon as reasonably practicable after he first knew or suspected he took all reasonable steps to inform the Secretary of State or a constable of his knowledge or suspicion.

(7) Nothing in subsection (6) prejudices any defence which it is open to a person charged with an offence under this section to raise apart from that subsection."

(2) Mode of Trial and Punishment

3-204   This offence is triable only on indictment and carries a maximum penalty of life imprisonment.[83]

(3) Indictment

3-205   It seems that section 2 creates five separate offences, and the indictment should therefore specify which offence is alleged.

(4) Restrictions on Prosecution

3-206   No proceedings under section 2 of this Act may be instituted without the consent of the Attorney-General.[84]

(5) Chemical Weapons

3-207   Section 1 of the Chemical Weapons Act contains a definition of this term. To understand the definition and the exclusions from the definition, section 1 and section 2(2) and (3) must be read together.

"1(1) Chemical weapons are—
(a) toxic chemicals and their precursors;
(b) munitions and other devices designed to cause death or harm through the toxic properties of toxic chemicals released by them;
(c) equipment designed for use in connection with munitions and devices falling within paragraph (b).
(2) Subsection (1) is subject to section 2(2) and (3) . . ."

Section 2(2) and (3) are as follows:

"(2) For the purposes of subsection (1)(a) an object is not a chemical weapon if the person uses the object only for permitted purposes; and in deciding whether permitted purposes are intended the types and quantities of objects shall be taken into account.
(3) For the purposes of subsections (1)(b), (c), (d) or (e) an object is not a chemical weapon if the person does the act there mentioned with the intention that the object will be used only for permitted purposes; and in deciding whether permitted purposes are intended the types and quantities of objects shall be taken into account."

---

[83] s.1(8).
[84] See n. 32 above.

We then return to section 1 for a definition of "permitted purposes":

"1(3) Permitted purposes are—
    (a) peaceful purposes;
    (b) purposes related to protection against toxic chemicals;
    (c) legitimate military purposes;
    (d) purposes of enforcing the law.
    (4) Legitimate military purposes are all military purposes except those which depend upon the use of the toxic properties of chemicals as a method of warfare in circumstances where the main object is to cause death, permanent harm or temporary incapacity to humans or animals.
    (5) A toxic chemical is a chemical which through its chemical action on life processes can cause death, permanent harm or temporary incapacity to humans or animals; and the origin, method of production and place of production are immaterial.
    (6) A precursor is a chemical reactant which takes part at any stage in the production (by whatever method) of a toxic chemical."

The definition of chemical weapons is wide enough to cover not only wea-   **3–208**
pons of mass destruction but also CS gas sprays, and small anti-attack aerosols.
The likely increased use by police forces of CS gas for crowd control might
lead to controversial prosecutions under this Act—either private prosecutions
of police officers on the basis that the use of the gas was not for "purposes of
enforcing law" within section 1(3)(d); or alternatively against persons against
whom CS gas canisters are fired who then throw them back at the police.

The definition of "legitimate military purposes" in section 1(4) excludes   **3–209**
only military activity which "depend" on the use of such weapons. This definition fails to consider the possible effect of chemical weapons being used as
an ancillary method of conducting warfare in breach of the Geneva Conventions of 1949 and, *e.g.* U.N. Resolution 2675 of 1970[85] which make specific
provision for protecting civilians during armed conflict:

"1. Fundamental human rights, as accepted in international law and laid down in
international instruments, continue to apply fully in situations of armed conflict.
    2. In the conduct of military operations during armed conflict, a distinction
must be made at all times between persons actively taking part in the hostilities
and civilian populations.
    3. In the conduct of military operations, every effort should be made to spare
civilian populations from the ravages of war, and all necessary precautions should
be taken to avoid injury, loss or damage to civilian populatioins.
    4. Civilian populations as such should not be the object of military operations.
    5. Dwellings and other installations that are used only by civilian populations
should not be the object of military operations.
    6. Places or areas designated for the sole protection of civilians, such as hospital
zones or similar refuges, should not be the object of military operations.
    7. Civilian populations, or individual members thereof, should not be the object
of reprisals, forcible transfers or other assaults on their integrity."

---

[85] G.A. Res. 2675, U.N. GAOR, 25th Sess., Supp. No. 28, at p. 76, U.N. Doc. A/8028 (1970).
See for a detailed judicial analysis of the application of international principles of human rights
protection in a time of armed conflict the judgment of the International Tribunal for the
Prosecution of Persons Responsible for Serious Violations of International Humanitarian Law
Committed in the Territory of the Former Yugoslavia since 1991, reported in *Criminal Law
Forum*, Vol. 7 No. 1 (1996) pp. 51–138.

(6) DESIGNED

3–210   The Act uses the word "designed" as well as the word "intended". Although the words often in law bear similar meanings, it seems that their close proximity in section 1 and the detailed provisions in section 2(2) and (3) indicate that the word "designed" must be construed as meaning that the object was created or manufactured with the purposes set out in section 1(1)(b).

(7) DEFENCES

3–211   Section 2 provides specific defences for proceedings under section 2(1)(a), (c), or (d), but not for proceedings under section 2(1)(b) or (e):

> "2(6) In proceedings for an offence under subsection (1)(a), (c), or (d) relating to an object it is a defence for the accused to prove—
> (a) that he neither knew nor suspected it to be a chemical weapon nor had reason to suspect that the object was a chemical weapon, or
> (b) that he knew or suspected it to be a chemical weapon and as soon as reasonably practicable after he first so knew or suspected he took all reasonable steps to inform the Secretary of State or a constable of his knowledge or suspicion."

This defence is without prejudice to any other defence which is open to a person.[86]

(8) BURDEN OF PROOF

3–212   The burden of proving the primary facts lies on the prosecution. Generally, where a statute provides an exception or excuse to the offence, the burden of proving that exception or excuse lies upon the defendant.[87] Section 2 of the Act provides for three different situations:

(i)   general defences by virtue of section 2(7);
(ii)   exceptions to the definition of "chemical weapon" provided by section 2(2) and (3) and section 1(3) and (4);
(iii)   the specific statutory defences provided by section 2(6).

As the exceptions to the meaning of "chemical weapon" go to the definition of the offence itself, the burden of proof remains on the prosecution throughout where that is the issue, though there is an evidential burden on the defence to raise the issue. Only when the specific statutory defence is invoked will the defence bear the burden of proof.[88]

(9) EXTENDED JURISDICTION

3–213   By section 3 of the Act, section 2 applies (i) to any acts done in the United Kingdom and (ii) to any acts outside the United Kingdom by United Kingdom

---

[86] s.2(7). For general defences see paras. 1–024 to 1–083 above.
[87] *R. v. Hunt* [1987] A.C. 352.
[88] The standard of proof born by the defence is the balance of probabilities—*R. v. Carr-Briant* (1943) 29 Cr.App.R. 76.

nationals, Scottish partnerships and bodies incorporated under the law of any part of the United Kingdom. Where jurisdiction exists for an offence committed outside the United Kingdom it may be tried as if it had occurred in any place in the United Kingdom.

XXIII. OFFENCES INVOLVING NUCLEAR MATERIAL

Section 1 of the Nuclear Material (Offences) Act 1983 extends jurisdiction to the United Kingdom courts in the case of any person, of whatever nationality, who does an act outside the United Kingdom involving nuclear material, which, if committed in the United Kingdom would amount to an offence of murder, manslaughter, or an offence contrary to sections 18 or 20 of the Offences Against the Person Act 1861. That person can be tried in any part of the United Kingdom as if the act were committed in that place.   3–214

By section 2 of the Nuclear Material (Offences) Act 1983, a person commits an offence under that section if in the United Kingdom or elsewhere he   3–215

"(2) receives, holds or deals with nuclear material—
(a) intending, or for the purpose of another, to do by means of nuclear material an act [amounting to an offence of murder, manslaughter, or an offence contrary to sections 18 or 20 of the Offences Against the Person Act 1861]; or
(b) being reckless as to whether another would do such an act.
(3) A person contravenes this subsection if he—
(a) makes to another person a threat that he or any other person will do by means of nuclear material such an act [amounting to murder, manslaughter, or an offence contrary to sections 18 or 20 of the Offences Against the Person act 1861]; and
(b) intends that the person to whom the threat is made shall fear that it will be carried out."

(1) MODE OF TRIAL AND PUNISHMENT

This offence is triable only on indictment and carries a maximum penalty of 14 years' imprisonment; subject to the maximum which the offence of violence itself would carry.[89]   3–216

(2) RESTRICTIONS ON PROSECUTION

Proceedings for an offence under section 2 shall not be begun (were the act not an offence but for this section—disregarding the effects of the Internationally Protected Person Act 1978[90] and the Suppression of Terrorism Act 1978[91]) without the consent of the Attorney-General.[92]   3–217

---

[89] s.2(5).
[90] See paras. 1–087 to 1–089 above.
[91] See para. 3–100 above.
[92] See n. 32 above.

(3) Nuclear Material

3–218   The definition appears in Schedule 1 to the Act and is taken from Article 1 of the Convention on the Physical Protection of Nuclear Material opened for signature at Vienna and New York on March 3, 1980[93]:

> "(a) 'nuclear material' means plutonium except that with isotopic concentration exceeding 80% in the plutonium–238; uranium0233; uranium enriched in the isotopes 235 or 233; uranium containing the mixture of isotopes as occurring in nature other than in the form of ore or ore-residue; any material containing one or more of the foregoing;
>
> (b) 'uranium enriched in the isotope 235 or 233' means uranium containing the isotopes 235 or 233 or both in an amount such that the abundance ratio of the sum of these isotopes to the isotope 238 is greater than the ratio of the isotope 235 to the isotope 238 occurring in nature."

XXIV. SETTING SPRING GUN WITH INTENT TO CAUSE GRIEVOUS BODILY HARM

3–219   This and the other remaining offences under the Offences Against the Person Act 1861 are not terrorist offences, but they may in some cases be appropriate to prosecute cases of sabotage.

(1) Definition

3–220   Section 31 of the Offences Against the Person act 1861 provides:

> "Whosoever shall set or place or cause to be set or placed, any spring gun, man trap, or other engine calculated to destroy human life or inflict grievous bodily harm, with the intent that the same or whereby the same may inflict grievous bodily harm upon a trespasser or other person coming in contact therewith, shall be guilty . . .; and whosoever shall knowingly and wilfully permit any such spring gun, man trap or other engine which may have been set or placed in any place then being in or afterwards coming into his possession or occupation by some other person to continue so set or placed, shall be deemed to have set or placed such gun, trap, or engine with such intent as aforesaid: Provided that nothing in this section contained shall extend to make it illegal to set or place any gun or trap such as may have been or may be usually set or placed with the intention of destroying vermin: Provided also, that nothing in this section shall be deemed to make it unlawful to set or place, or cause to be set or placed, or to be contained set or placed, from sunset to sunrise, any spring gun, man trap, or other engine which shall be set or placed, or caused or continued to be set or placed, in a dwelling-house for the protection thereof."

This is an offence aimed principally at those who over-zealously protect their land from other persons—whether they be poachers or people protesting about a new planning scheme.

---

[93] s.6(5).

(2) Mode of Trial and Punishment

This offence is triable only on indictment, and carries a maximum penalty   3–221
of five years' imprisonment.[94]

This offence may be committed either by the person who is responsible for   3–222
setting the trap, or by a person who owns or comes into possession of the
place where the trap is set and knowing what it is nevertheless allows it to
remain.

(3) Spring Gun, Man Trap or Other Engine

The devices contemplated by section 31 have to be constructed or intended   3–223
for causing severe injury to humans. They must be mechanical devices. The
words "or other engine" means that the categories of device must be homo-
geneous, and more sophisticated devices such as wires which could electrocute
a person coming into contact with them, *e.g.* a gate or fence or window is not
covered by section 31.[95]

(4) Inflict Grievous Bodily Harm

See paragraphs 3–017 to 3–020 above.   3–224

(5) Intent

See paragraphs 1–090 to 1–097 above and 4–069 to 4–082 below.   3–225

(6) Knowingly and Wilfully

See paragraphs 3–081 to 3–083 above.   3–226

(7) Defences

Section 31 does not contain the words "unlawfully" or "maliciously". An   3–227
intent to inflict grievous bodily harm is consistent with lawful self-defence. It
would be odd if a person genuinely fearing violent attack upon himself, his
family or his property could lawfully equip himself with explosive substances
(see paragraph 3–096 above), but could not claim lawful self-defence if he set
a mechanical device.

The two provisos create specific exemptions. The first seems to embrace   3–228
traps, etc., which are capable, and may even have been set with the intention
of, causing serious injury to the person, provided that it is a device set, or
usually set to destroy vermin. Although "man-traps" has an antiquated ring,
it is possible that a mechanical device could be used to cause injury, *e.g.* to
demonstrators or protesters, or visitors to a pop festival by an irate landowner.

---

[94] Penal Servitude Act 1891, s.1(1), and Criminal Justice Act 1948, s.1(1).
[95] *R. v. Munks* (1963) 48 Cr.App.R. 56.

Equally, such devices might be used by those with property in the country intent on deterring ramblers or huntsmen from entering their property.

3–229   The use of the expression "such as may have been or may be usually" is probably a recognition that when section 31 was enacted, the accused could not give evidence on his own behalf. The provisos must be disproved by the prosecution; they do not place a burden on the accused.

3–230   A defendant who is able to rely on the first proviso will not by virtue of that proviso alone have a defence to a charge of inflicting injury contrary to, *e.g.* section 20 if the ingredients of such an offence are made out.

3–231   The second proviso makes it clear that setting a spring gun, etc., in defence of property between the hours of sunset and sunrise does not give rise to an offence. Like the first proviso, it does not provide a defence to anything except a charge under this section, so that injury caused to a person by such a device set out to protect the property between sunset and sunrise would be an offence contrary, *e.g.* to section 47, unless it were reasonable for that person to have that device to protect that property from imminent attack.[96]

XXV. OFFENCES ENDANGERING THE SAFETY OF RAILWAY PASSENGERS OR OTHER PERSONS ON A RAILWAY

3–232   Sections 32 to 34 of the Offences Against the Person Act 1861 create specific offences of doing acts which endanger passengers or other persons (*e.g.*, the driver or ticket collector) carried on the railway. It is no doubt a reflection of the age of railway expansion in which the Offences Against the Person Act was enacted that there are three sections to cover such acts. It should be noted that the danger is restricted to those being carried on the railway, and not to others, *e.g.* those working on repairs, or people using a level crossing, or those who may be injured on an adjacent highway by the derailment of a train. Where an accident is caused and injury results, then if the act was unlawful, and done with the requisite *mens rea*, it would constitute one of the other offences under the Offences Against the Person Act; or murder or manslaughter[97] if death resulted.

XXVI. PLACING WOOD, ETC., ON A RAILWAY WITH INTENT TO ENDANGER PASSENGERS

(1) DEFINITION

3–233   Section 32 of the Offences Against the Person act 1861 provides:

"Whosoever shall unlawfully and maliciously put or throw upon or across any

---

[96] See paras. 1–046 to 1–055 above, and especially *Attorney-General's Reference (No. 2 of 1983)* (1984) 78 Cr.App.R. 183, and see *R. v. Gladstone Williams* (1984) 78 Cr.App.R. 276.

[97] For an example of manslaughter resulting from an offence contrary to s.23 see *D.P.P. v. Newbury* [1977] A.C. 500 (although no reference was made to the statutory offence in that

railway any wood, stone or other matter or thing, or shall maliciously take up, remove or displace any rail, sleeper or other matter or thing belonging to any railway, or shall unlawfully and maliciously turn, move, or divert any points or other machinery belonging to any railway, or shall unlawfully and maliciously make or show, hide or remove any signal or light upon or near any railway, or shall unlawfully and maliciously do or cause to be done any other matter or thing, with intent, in any of the cases aforesaid, to endanger the safety of any person travelling or being upon such railway, shall be guilty"

of an offence.

(2) Mode of Trial and Punishment

This offence is triable only on indictment, and carries a maximum penalty of life imprisonment. Section 17(2) of the Firearms Act 1968[98] applies to this offence.   **3-234**

(3) Indictment

Section 32 creates a single offence which may be committed in a variety of ways.[99]   **3-235**

(4) Unlawfully

See paragraphs 1–024 to 1–083 above.   **3-236**

(5) Maliciously

See paragraphs 1–098 to 1–107 above.   **3-237**

(6) With Intent

See paragraphs 1–090 to 1–097 above and 4–069 to 4–082 below.   **3-238**

(7) To Endanger the Safety of Any Person

This offence is concerned with intent rather than consequences. Even if no-one is endangered an act done unlawfully and maliciously with intent to endanger safety is an offence under this section; *e.g.* causing damage to a signal which is discovered and counteracted before any danger is caused to any particular person or persons as was the case in *R. v. Pearce*[1] in which the Court of Appeal held that a potential danger of lowering of standards of safety which would lead to an endangering of a person on the railway was sufficient to contribute "endangering".   **3-239**

---

decision); and for an example of murder in the analogous circumstances of dropping a lump of concrete onto a motorway see *R. v. Hancock* [1986] A.C. 455.

[98] See para. 3–004 above.

[99] See para. 3–078 and n. 92 above.

[1] (1967) 50 Cr.App.R. 305. This was a case under s.34, for which see para. 3–247 below.

XXVII. CASTING A STONE, ETC., UPON A RAILWAY CARRIAGE WITH INTENT TO ENDANGER THE SAFETY OF ANY PERSON THEREIN

(1) DEFINITION

3–240 Section 33 of the Offences Against the Person Act 1861 provides:

"Whosoever shall unlawfully and maliciously throw, or cause to fall or strike, at, against, into, or upon any engine, tender, carriage, or truck used upon any railway, any wood, stone, or other matter or thing, with intent to injure or endanger the safety of any person being in or upon such engine, tender, carriage or truck, or in or upon any other engine, tender, carriage or truck of any train of which such first mentioned engine, tender, carriage or truck shall form part, shall be guilty of"

an offence.

(2) MODE OF TRIAL AND PUNISHMENT

3–241 This offence is triable only on indictment and carries a maximum penalty of life imprisonment.

(3) INDICTMENT

3–242 Like section 32, this section creates a single offence which may be committed in a variety of ways.[2] Section 33 is confined to acts directed at or against any part of a train and done with the appropriate intent.

(4) UNLAWFULLY

3–243 See paragraphs 1–024 to 1–083 above.

(5) MALICIOUSLY

3–244 See paragraphs 1–098 to 1–107 above.

(6) WITH INTENT

3–245 See paragraphs 1–090 to 1–097 above and 4–069 to 4–082 below.

(7) TO ENDANGER THE SAFETY OF ANY PERSON

3–246 See paragraphs 3–239 above.

---

[2] See para. 3–078 and n. 92 above.

XXVIII. DOING OR OMITTING ANYTHING AS TO ENDANGER PASSENGERS BY RAILWAY

(1) DEFINITION

Section 34 of the Offences Against the Person Act 1861 provides: **3–247**

> "Whosoever by any unlawful act, or by any wilful omission or neglect, shall endanger or cause to be endangered the safety of any person conveyed or being in or upon a railway, or shall aid or assist therein, shall be guilty of",

an offence.

(2) MODE OF TRIAL AND PUNISHMENT

This offence is triable either way,[3] and on indictment carries a maximum   **3–248**
penalty of two years' imprisonment.

(3) UNLAWFUL

See paragraphs 1–024 to 1–083 above.   **3–249**

(4) WILFUL OMISSION OR NEGLECT

To be "wilful", the omission or neglect must be either deliberate, or else   **3–250**
reckless in the sense that the defendant foresaw the risk but nevertheless
omitted or neglected to do the act which would have averted the risk, or
failed to foresee the risk as a result of not caring whether anyone's safety was
endangered.[4] This section will apply to a variety of situations, *e.g.* a signalman
who wilfully omits or neglects to operate a signal. Causing a vehicle to stop
on a level crossing would not be an omission or neglect, but failing to move
it or notify the crossing keepers would be.[5]

(5) TO ENDANGER THE SAFETY OF ANY PERSON

See paragraphs 3–239 above.   **3–251**

---

[3] Magistrates' Courts Act 1980, s.17 and Sched. 1.
[4] *R. v. Sheppard* (1980) 72 Cr.App.R. 82 (H.L.) This was a case about "wilful neglect" in the context of s.1 of the Children and Young Persons Act 1933, but the principle applies wherever a statute prohibits a particular type of "wilful" conduct.
[5] By analogy with *Fagan v. Metropolitan Police Commissioner* (1968) 52 Cr.App.R. 700 and see para. 2–008 above.

XXIX. ENDANGERING THE SAFETY OF THE CHANNEL TUNNEL RAILWAY

3-252   The Channel Tunnel Act 1987 allows, by section 11, orders to be made to ensure the safety of the tunnel. Offences of engaging in acts of violence endangering the Channel Tunnel railway are provided by Article 6 of the Channel Tunnel (Security) Order 1994[6]:

> "6(1) A person commits an offence if he unlawfully and intentionally—
>> (a) destroys a Channel Tunnel train or the tunnel system, or destroys any goods on the train within the tunnel system so as to endanger or be likely to endanger, the safe operation of the train, or as the case may be, the safety of the tunnel system;
>> (b) damages a Channel Tunnel train or any goods on the train or the tunnel system or any goods within the system so as to endanger or be likely to endanger, the safe operation of the train, or as the case may be, the safety of the tunnel system; or
>> (c) commits on board a Channel Tunnel train or within the tunnel system an act of violence which is likely to endanger the safe operation of the train, or as the case may be, the safety of the tunnel system.
> (2) A person commits an offence if he unlawfully and intentionally places, or causes to be placed, on a Channel Tunnel train or in the tunnel system any device or substance which—
>> (a) in the case of the Channel Tunnel train is likely to destroy the train, or is likely so to damage it or any goods on it as to endanger its safe operation, or
>> (b) in the case of the tunnel system, is likely to destroy the tunnel system or so to damage it as to endanger its safety
> (3) Nothing in paragraph (2) above shall be construed as limiting the circumstances in which the commission of any act—
>> (a) may constitute an offence under paragraph (1) above, or
>> (b) may constitute attempting or conspiring to commit, or aiding, abetting, counselling or procuring or inciting . . . the commission of such an offence."

(1) MODE OF TRIAL AND PUNISHMENT

3-253   This offence is triable only on indictment and carries a maximum penalty of life imprisonment.[7]

(2) RESTRICTIONS ON PROSECUTION

3-254   No proceedings under this Article may be instituted without the consent of the Attorney-General.[8]

(3) EXTENDED JURISDICTION

3-255   The Channel Tunnel (International Arrangements) Order 1993 and the Channel Tunnel (Miscellaneous Provisions) Order 1994[9] make detailed pro-

---

[6] S.I. 1994 No. 570.
[7] Art. 6(4) of the Order.
[8] Art. 9, and see para. 3–124 and n. 32 above.
[9] S.I. 1993 No. 1813 and S.I. 1994 No. 1405 respectively.

vision for cross-Channel co-operation between the United Kingdom, France and Belgium and for jurisdiction in the United Kingdom courts for criminal acts taking place within the control zones.[10]

(4) ACT OF VIOLENCE

This expression, which features in Article 6(1)(c) of the Channel Tunnel **3–256** (Security) Order 1994 is defined in Article 6(5):

"In this article 'act of violence' means an act which constitutes—
(a) the offence of murder, attempted murder, manslaughter . . . or assault,
(b) an offence under section 18, 20, 21, 22, 23, 24, 28 or 29 of the Offences Against the Person act 1861 or
(c) an offence under section 2 of the Explosive Substances Act 1883,

or which, if committed in England, Wales . . . would constitute such an offence."

(5) UNLAWFULLY

Article 2(1) of the Channel Tunnel (Security) Order 1994 defines "unlaw- **3–257** fully" as:

"means so that the commission of the act is (apart from this Order) an offence under the law of England and Wales . . . or would be if committed there."

See paragraphs 1–024 to 1–083 above.

(6) INTENTIONALLY

See paragraphs 1–090 to 1–097 above and 4–069 to 4–082 below. As the **3–258** qualifying words of Article 6(1) "unlawfully *and* intentionally" apply to the provision of Article 6(1)(c), *i.e.* committing one of the specified offences under the Offences Against the Person Act 1861 the question will arise whether this Article supersedes the mental element of sections 20 to 24 and 28 to 29 of the 1861 Act so as to require a specific intent rather than malice.[11]

(7) ENDANGER

See paragraph 3–062 above.   **3–259**

(8) CHANNEL TUNNEL TRAIN

By Article 2(1) of the Channel Tunnel (Security) Order 1994:   **3–260**

" 'Channel Tunnel train' means a train or any part of a train (including a shuttle train) which has been assigned for use (whether in the United Kingdom or elsewhere) for conveying passengers or goods through the tunnel system."

[10] See the above statutory instruments for the detailed provisions relating to cross-border co-operation and extended jurisdiction, in particular Art. 38 of Sched. 2 to S.I. 1993 No. 1813.
[11] "Malice" is satisfied by a species of recklessness in which the defendant foresaw some injury as the possible consequences of his act but nevertheless continued—see para. 1–098 above.

(9) CHANNEL TUNNEL SYSTEM

3-261   By Article 2(1) of the Channel Tunnel (Security) Order 1994:

"references to the tunnel system include references to the tunnel system or any part of it (whether in England or France), except the inland clearance depot at Ashford in Kent, for the accommodation, in connection with the application to them of customs and other controls, of freight vehicles which have been or are being or are to be conveyed through the tunnel on shuttle services."

XXX. TORTURE

3-262   This represents the other side of terrorism—what is sometimes referred to as "state terrorism". The acts which amount to torture, and the injuries they cause, would be offences under sections 18, 20 or 47 of the Offences Against the Person act 1861 if committed in England and Wales by a person not exercising lawful authority. It would be hard to imagine a case in which acts amounting to torture could give rise to a defence of lawful authority, particularly as Article 3 of the European Convention for the Protection of Human Rights and Fundamental Freedoms prohibits any state which is a party to the Convention (as the United Kingdom is) derogating from its obligations in relation to torture.

(1) DEFINITION

3-263   The offence of torture was introduced into English law by section 134 of the Criminal Justice Act 1988, which provides:

"(1) A public official or person acting in an official capacity, whatever his nationality, commits the offence of torture if in the United Kingdom or elsewhere he intentionally inflicts severe pain or suffering on another in the performance or purported performance of his official duties.
(2) A person not falling within subsection (1) above commits the offence of torture, whatever his nationality, if—
(a) in the United Kingdom or elsewhere he intentionally inflicts severe pain and suffering on another at the instigation or with the consent or acquiescence—
(i) of a public official; or
(ii) of a person acting in an official capacity and
(b) the official or other person is performing or purporting to perform his official duties when he instigates the commission of the offence or consents to or acquiesces in it."

(2) MODE OF TRIAL AND PUNISHMENT

3-264   This offence is triable only on indictment, and carries a maximum penalty of life imprisonment.[12] It is a serious arrestable offence for the purpose of the Police and Criminal Evidence Act 1984.[13]

---

[12] Criminal Justice Act 1988, s.134.
[13] See s.117 and Sched. 5 of that Act as amended by Sched. 15 of the Criminal Justice Act 1988.

(3) RESTRICTIONS ON PROSECUTION

By section 135 of the Criminal Justice Act 1988, proceedings for an offence **3–265**
of torture can only be commenced by, or with the consent of, the Attorney-
General.[14]

(4) JURISDICTION

There is no limit on jurisdiction. An offence of torture committed anywhere **3–266**
in the world is triable in England, irrespective of the nationality of the defendant and the victim. So it would be possible for a prosecution to be brought
against a member of a torture squad in a foreign country who came to England,
e.g. as a visitor or as part of a delegation (not having diplomatic immunity).[15]
This situation is likely to arise given the presence in England of political
refugees. By section 136 of the Act, torture is an extraditable offence, so its
international effect is reinforced.

There will in some cases be potential conflicts of international law as to
which state has jurisdiction. The International Tribunal for the Prosecution
of Persons Responsible for Serious Violations of International Humanitarian
Law Committed in the Territory of Former Yugoslavia Since 1991 was set up
by the Statute of the International Tribunal.[16] This Tribunal has exclusive
jurisdiction over such serious breaches of international humanitarian law and
can therefore require states parties to the United Nations to cede jurisdiction
to the tribunal in cases falling within its remit.[17]

(5) TORTURE

Torture is defined in section 134(1) and (2) as inflicting "severe pain or **3–267**
suffering on another". Section 134(3) provides:

> "It is immaterial whether the pain and suffering is physical or mental and whether
> it is caused by an act or an omission."

This would be appropriate to include severe physical beatings, simulations
of executions, exposure to cold or heat or neglect as described by numerous
former victims[18]; or the psychological suffering experienced by the victims'
families.

This offence incorporates in effect the European Convention on Human **3–268**
Rights, which by Article 3 prohibits torture:

---

[14] See para. 3–124 and n. 32 above.

[15] See for an American example, albeit a tort case, *Filartiga v. Pena-Irala* 630 F. (2nd) 876.

[16] Published as an annex to the Report of the Secretary-General Pursuant to Paragraph 2 of
Security Council Resolution 808, U.N. Doc. S/25704 (1993) and adopted pursuant to Security
Council Resolution 827 on May 25, 1993.

[17] See the judgment of the Tribunal on a preliminary point of jurisdiction, reported in *Criminal
Law Forum*, Vol. 7 No. 1 (1996) 51 at 109. If the proposed permanent international court to
hear cases of serious breaches of human rights law wherever perpetrated is established, then
that too will inevitably acquire preferential jurisdiction.

[18] See, *e.g.* Jacobo Timerman, *Prisoner Without a Name, Cell Without a Number* (Penguin); or
Irina Ratushinskaya *No, I'm Not Afraid* (Bloodaxe).

> "No one shall be subjected to torture or to inhuman or degrading treatment or punishment."

The jurisprudence on the European Convention on Human Rights distinguishes between "torture" on the one hand and "inhuman or degrading treatment" on the other. In *Ireland v. U.K.*[19] the European Court of Human Rights by a majority decided that interrogation techniques which involved forcing detainees to stand for long periods spread-eagled against a wall, putting hoods over their heads, subjecting them to noise, and depriving them of sleep, food and drink amounted to inhuman or degrading treatment, but not to torture. In the judgment of the court:

> "This distinction derives principally from a difference in the intensity of the suffering inflicted. The Court considers in fact that, whilst there exists on the one hand violence which is to be condemned both on moral grounds and also in most cases under the domestic law of the Contracting State but which does not fall within Article 3 of the Convention, it appears on the other hand that it was the intention that the Convention, with its distinction between "torture" and "inhuman or degrading treatment", should by the first of these terms attach a special stigma to deliberate inhuman treatment causing very serious and cruel suffering. Moreover, this seems to be the thinking lying behind Article 1 in fine of Resolution 3452 adopted by the General Assembly of the United Nations on the 9th December, 1975, which declares: "Torture constitutes an aggravated and deliberate form of cruel, inhuman or degrading treatment or punishment." Although the five techniques, as applied in combination, undoubtedly amounted to inhuman and degrading treatment . . . they did not occasion suffering of the particular intensity and cruelty implied by the word torture or so understood".[20]

This was held to be so, even though "they caused, if not actual bodily injury, at least intense physical and mental suffering to the persons subjected thereto and also led to acute psychiatric disturbance during interrogation."[21]

3–269   On this basis, the victims of those techniques may well have suffered "severe pain or suffering" as required by section 134 of the Criminal Justice Act 1988. If so, it would mean that the European Court of Human Rights placed a more restrictive interpretation on the meaning of "torture" than that created by section 134. Indeed, Judge O'Donoghue, in a dissenting judgment said[22]:

> "It must remain for any judicial body to say if the facts before it amount to torture, inhuman or degrading treatment, having regard to the entire circumstances of the case under investigation. One is not bound to regard torture as only present in a medieval dungeon where the appliances of rack and thumbscrew or similar devices were employed. Indeed in the present-day world there can be little doubt that torture may be inflicted in the mental sphere. Torture is, of course, a more severe type of inhuman treatment. No amount of careful consideration can alter my opinion that the approach of the Commission[23] was the correct one."

3–270   In *The Greek Case*[24] the European Commission of Human Rights decided

---

[19] (1978) 2 E.H.R.R. 25.
[20] *ibid.* at p. 80.
[21] *ibid.* at pp. 79–80.
[22] *ibid.* at p. 116.
[23] The European Commission of Human Rights had concluded that the five interrogation techniques together amounted to torture:—see (1976) 19 Y.B. 794.
[24] (1969) 12 Y.B.

that persistent severe beatings of prisoners amounted to torture, as did administering electric shocks to prisoners. It was said in that case that torture is generally used to extract information or confessions or inflict punishment. This definition was adopted by the Court of Appeal of Northern Ireland in *R. v. McCormick*[25]:

> " 'inhuman treatment' which is 'at least such treatment as deliberately causes severe suffering, mental or physical'; torture 'often used to describe inhuman treatment, which has a purpose, such as the obtaining of information or confession, or the infliction of punishment, and it is generally an aggravated form of inhuman treatment' it includes non-physical torture, namely the infliction of mental suffering by creating a state of anxiety and stress by means other than bodily assault . . . Torture is an aggravated form of inhuman treatment."

The definition of torture contained within section 134 of the Criminal Justice Act 1988 does not require proof of any purpose behind the infliction of severe pain or suffering; and on the basis of *The Greek Case*[26] and *McCormick*[27] will include acts categorised as "inhuman treatment" by the European Court of Human Rights as well as treatment which that court describes as torture.[28] The extent to which decisions of the European Court of Human Rights are persuasive in courts in England and Wales is a developing area. In *R. v. Home Secretary, ex p. Brind*[29] the House of Lords decided that the European Convention is not part of English law and can only have influence when a statute is ambiguous (on the basis that the legislature is presumed not to have enacted legislation contrary to its treaty obligations), or when the court is exercising a discretion.[30] **3-271**

(6) PUBLIC OFFICIAL OR PERSON ACTING IN AN OFFICIAL CAPACITY

Both section 134(1) and 134(2) of the Criminal Justice Act 1988 require proof that the severe pain or suffering was inflicted by or at the instigation or with the consent of a public official or person acting in an official capacity. Proof that the accused was a public official will be proof of his appointment as, *e.g.* a police or prison officer. It would include those responsible for investigating offences as well as those responsible for prisoners' welfare, and will include members of the armed forces.[31] This element of the offence distinguishes it from other offences causing injury, in that it requires that the pain **3-272**

---

[25] [1977] N.I. 105 at 110–111 *per* McGonigal L.J., citing passages from *The Greek Case*.
[26] (1969) 12 Y.B.
[27] [1977] N.I. 105.
[28] For further details of Art. 3 and the jurisprudence on it see *Digest of Strasbourg Case Law*, Vol. 1. paras. 3.0.1 to 3.0.3.3; and the late Paul Sieghart, *The International Law of Human Rights*, para. 14.3, and the reports in the *Human Rights Case Digest* (HRCD).
[29] [1991] A.C. 696.
[30] See also the decision of the House of Lords in *R. v. Khan (Sultan)* [1996] 3 W.L.R. 162 that regard can be had to Art. 6 in determining how the discretion under s.78 of the Police and Criminal Evidence Act 1984 should be exercised. A review of judicial and academic opinion appears in Beloff and Mountfield, "Unconventional Behaviour? Judicial Uses of the European Convention in England and Wales" in [1996] EHRLR 467.
[31] See, *e.g. The Greek Case* (1969) 12 Y.B.; *R. v. McCormick* [1977] N.I. 105, and *Ireland v. U.K.* (1978) 2 E.H.R.R. 25.

be inflicted or permitted, *etc.*, by someone who had an official status. For the purposes of section 134(1) the official who instigated the torture but did not himself inflict it himself would be guilty on the basis of liability for acts carried out as a part of a joint enterprise. It is therefore appropriate in such a case to indict the public official or person acting in an official capacity as committing an offence contrary to section 134(1), and to indict the person who had no official status and who physically inflicted the severe pain or suffering with an offence contrary to section 134(2).

3–273   It is sufficient that the public official or person acting in an official capacity is acting in "purported" performance of his official duties. So it is not necessary to prove that, *e.g.* a secret torture centre had the official approval of the government concerned if it had all the trappings of officialdom and those instigating or administering the torture were acting in purported performance of their official duties.

(7) MENTAL ELEMENT

3–274   The severe pain or suffering must be inflicted "intentionally". As drafted, it is not clear whether the intention is confined to "inflicts" or extends to the severity of the pain or suffering. It is possible that severe pain or suffering could be caused to a victim as a result or a pre-existing injury or illness unknown to his tormentor. Bearing in mind the gravity of the offence, it must be understood to mean that "severe pain or suffering" must be intended by the offender before he commits this offence. For "intent" generally see paragraphs 1–090 to 1–097 above and 4–069 to 4–082 below. An offence contrary to section 134 may be committed without proof of any ulterior motive.

(8) DEFENCES

3–275   A special defence is provided by section 134(4) of the Criminal Justice Act 1988:

> "It shall be a defence for a person charged with an offence under this section in respect of any conduct of his to prove that he had lawful authority, justification or excuse for that conduct."

The burden of proving this defence lies upon the accused.[32]

3–276   What constitutes "lawful authority, justification or excuse" is set out in section 134(5):

> "For the purposes of this section "lawful authority, justification or excuse" means—
>   (a) in relation to pain and suffering inflicted in the United Kingdom, lawful authority, justification or excuse under the law of the part of the United Kingdom where it was inflicted;
>   (b) in relation to pain and suffering inflicted outside the United Kingdom—
>   (i) if it was inflicted by a United Kingdom official acting under the law of

---

[32] The standard of proof is the balance of probabilities—*R. v. Carr-Briant* (1943) 29 Cr.App.R. 76.

the United Kingdom or by a person acting in an official capacity under that law, lawful authority, justification or excuse under that law;
(ii) if it was inflicted by a United Kingdom official acting under the law of any part of the United Kingdom, or by a person acting in an official capacity under such law, lawful athority, justification or excuse under the law of the part of the United Kingdom under whose law he was acting; and
(iii) in any other case, lawful authority, justification or excuse under the law of the place where it was inflicted."

This envisages a number of situations:
(1) torture committed in the United Kingdom by a person of whatever nationality, deriving his official status from whatever source—the domestic law of the appropriate part of the United Kingdom applies;
(2) torture committed by a person of whatever nationality who derives his official status from, and is acting under, United Kingdom law (*e.g.*, a member of a British Embassy or Consulate, or a member of the British armed forces)—the law of the United Kingdom applies;
(3) similar to (2) but where the official status derives from the law of a part of the United Kingdom (*e.g.*, a police officer or civil servant whose authority derives from a law applying to part of the United Kingdom)—the law of the appropriate part of the United Kingdom applies; and
(4) torture inflicted abroad by a person of whatever nationality who derives his official status from a foreign state—the law of the place where the torture was inflicted will apply.

In practice, number (4) will create some problems. It is a comparatively **3–277** easy matter to determine whether the particular circumstances justified inflicting severe pain or suffering according to the law of the United Kingdom or one of its constituent parts. It will be more difficult to establish (and it will be for the defence to prove) that the law of the foreign state where the torture occurred provided lawful authority, justification or excuse. Even states with bad human rights records do not allow torture to be inflicted as a matter of law. However, the fact that this defence exists at all deviates from the European Convention on Human Rights. The prohibition on torture imposed by Article 3[33] is absolute, and allows of no excuse or exception.[34]

XXXI. OFFENCES AGAINST GENEVA CONVENTIONS

(1) DEFINITION

The Geneva Conventions Act 1957[35] provides: **3–278**

"Any person, whatever his nationality, who, whether in or outside the United

---

[33] See para. 3–268.
[34] *Ireland v. U.K.* (1978) 2 E.H.R.R. 25.
[35] As amended by the Geneva Conventions (Amendment) Act 1995.

Kingdom, commits, or aids, abets or procures the commission by any other person of a grave breach of any of the scheduled conventions or the first protocol shall be guilty of an offence . . ."

(2) MODE OF TRIAL AND PUNISHMENT

3–279   These offences are triable only on indictment. Where the grave breach results in death of a person protected by one of the scheduled conventions or the protocol, then the penalty is a mandatory term of life imprisonment; in any other case the penalty is imprisonment for a maximum of 14 years.[36]

(3) GRAVE BREACH OF CONVENTION OR PROTOCOL

3–280   The provisions breach of which give rise to an offence under this Act are:
  (i) Article 50 of the Geneva Convention for the Amelioration of the Condition of the Wounded and Sick in Armed Forces in the Field;
  (ii) Article 51 of the Geneva Convention for the Amelioration of the Condition of the Wounded, Sick and Shipwrecked Members of the Armed Forces at Sea;
  (iii) Article 130 of the Geneva Convention Relative to the Treatment of Prisoners of War;
  (iv) Article 147 of the Geneva Convention Relative to the Protection of Civilian Persons in Time of War; and
  (v) Articles 11 (paragraphs 4) and 85 (paragraphs 2 to 4) of the Protocol Additional to the Geneva Conventions of 12th August 1949 and Relating to the Protection of Victims of International Armed Conflict.[37]

XXXII. CIRCUMCISION OF A FEMALE

3–281   In 1985, the Prohibition of Female Circumcision Act was passed, prohibiting acts of female circumcision whether or not the victim consented, or (in the case of a female child) her parent or guardian consented. Although there is a saving for vaginal operations which are necessary for physical or mental health of the patient, compliance with the ritual of any religion is not an excuse or justification. Whether or not the victim consents to the unlawful circumcision, then it would be possible to charge an offence under one or more of sections 18, 20 or 47 of the Offences Against the Person Act 1861.

[36] s.1(1)(a) and (b).
[37] s.1(1A) of and Scheds. 1 to 5 of the Act.

(1) DEFINITION

Section 1 of the Prohibition of Female Circumcision Act 1985[38] provides: 3–282

"Subject to section 2 below, it shall be an offence for any person—
(a) to excise, infibulate, or otherwise mutilate the whole or any part of the labia majora or labia minora or clitoris of another person; or
(b) to aid, abet, counsel or procure the performance by another person of any of those acts on that other person's own body."

(2) MODE OF TRIAL AND PUNISHMENT

This offence is triable either way. On conviction on indictment, it carries a   3–283
maximum penalty of five years' imprisonment and/or a fine; and on summary
conviction a maximum penalty of six months' imprisonment and/or a fine not
exceeding the statutory maximum.[39]

(3) INDICTMENT

Section 1(1) creates two offences; the first consists of doing the excision,   3–284
etc., to another body and the second consists of assisting a woman to do it
herself.

(4) EVIDENCE

Whether what has been done falls within the terms set out in section 1(1)(a)   3–285
will be a matter of medical evidence, as will be the question of whether the
act was done as part of a necessary surgical operation for the purposes of
section 2 (which is set out in the next paragraph).

(5) SAVINGS FOR NECESSARY SURGICAL OPERATIONS

Section 2 provides: 3–286

"(1) Subsection (1)(a) of section 1 shall not render unlawful the performance of a surgical operation if that operation—
(a) is necessary for the physical or mental health of the person on whom it is performed and is performed by a registered medical practitioner;
(b) is performed on a person who is in any stage of labour or who has just given birth and is so performed for purposes connected with that labour or birth by—
(i) a registered medical practitioner or a registered midwife; or
(ii) a person undergoing a course of training with a view to becoming a registered medical practitioner or a registered midwife.
(2) In determining for the purpose of this section whether an operation is necessary for the mental health of a person, no account shall be taken of

---

[38] As amended by the Statute Law (Repeals) Act 1993.
[39] s.1(2).

the effect on that person of any belief on the part of that or any other person that the operation is required as a matter of custom or ritual."

3–287   Section 2 only affords an exception to section 1(1)(a). It would not apply to an operation performed by the woman upon herself even if she and/or her aider and abettor were medically qualified.

CHAPTER 4

MURDER

I. DEFINITION

"Murder is when a man of sound memory, and the age of discretion, unlawfully   **4–001**
killeth within any county of the realm, any reasonable creature in rerum natura
under the Queen's peace, with malice aforethought, either expressed by the party
or implied by law, so as the party wounded, or hurt, etc. die of the wound or
hurt, etc. (within a year and a day after the same)."

This is the common law definition as set out in Coke's Institutes.[1]

There are three situations in which a defendant will be convicted of man-   **4–002**
slaughter even though all of the elements of the charge of murder are made
out by the prosecution. These are: (a) where the defendant was provoked; (b)
where the defendant was suffering from diminished responsibility; (c) where
the killing was in pursuance of a suicide pact.[2]

II. MODE OF TRIAL AND PUNISHMENT

(1) MODE OF TRIAL

Murder is a Class 1 offence, triable only on indictment.   **4–003**

(2) PUNISHMENT

The penalty for murder is a mandatory sentence of life imprisonment.[3] This   **4–004**
also applies to a person under 21 and over 18.[4] A person under 18 at the time

---

[1] 3 Inst. 47. Matter in brackets now deleted by statute—see para 4.060 below.
[2] See para. 5–002 below.
[3] Murder (Abolition of Death Penalty) Act 1965, s.1(1).
[4] Criminal Justice Act 1982, s.8(1).

of the offence is to be detained during Her Majesty's pleasure.[5] The trial judge
has the power to recommend a minimum period of imprisonment before the
person convicted can be released on licence.[6] No appeal can be taken from
this recommendation.[7] The period of any such recommendation should not be
less than 12 years.[8] Prisoners may be released by the Home Secretary, subject
to Parole Board recommendation, and consultation with the Lord Chief Justice
and the trial judge, if available.[9] The judge may write to the Home Secretary
and give his views on special features of the case which the judge feels relevant
to the conditions of imprisonment or suitability for release on licence. As a
result of developments in the European Court of Human Rights[10] new procedures were adopted in section 34 of the Criminal Justice Act 1991 for
discretionary life prisoners. These provisions do not apply to those convicted
of murder. However, the decision in *R. v. Secretary of State for the Home
Department, ex p. Doody*[11] shows some attempt by way of judicial review to
encourage the administrative processes to afford mandatory lifers similar rights
to those serving discretionary terms.

(3) ATTEMPT

4-005   An attempt to commit murder is also a Class 1 offence triable only on
indictment.

4-006   The maximum penalty for attempted murder is life imprisonment, but this
is not a mandatory sentence.[12]

III. INDICTMENT

4-007   The date of the offence is the date when the death occurred. It is acceptable
to join other counts with the murder count in an indictment.[13] Two or more
charges of murder may be joined in one indictment and tried together if they
are founded on the same facts or form or are part of a series of offences of the
same or a similar character.[14] Murder is no exception to this rule.[15]

---

[5] Children and Young Persons Act 1933, s.53(1), as substituted by Children and Young Persons
Act 1965, s.1(5).
[6] Murder (Abolition of Death Penalty) Act 1965, s.1(2).
[7] *R. v. Aitken* [1966] 2 All E.R. 453; *R. v. Bowden and Begley* (1983) 77 Cr.App.R. 66.
[8] *R. v. Flemming* (1973) 57 Cr.App.R. 524.
[9] Murder (Abolition of Death Penalty) Act 1965, s.2; Criminal Justice Act 1967, s.61.
[10] *Thynne, Wilson and Gunnell v. The United Kingdom* (1991) 13 ECHRR 666.
[11] [1994] 1 A.C. 531; see too, Practice Direction (1993) 96 Cr.App.R. 397.
[12] Criminal Attempts Act 1981, s.4(1)(b).
[13] *Connelly v. Director of Public Prosecutions* [1964] A.C. 1254; Practice Direction [1964] 1 W.L.R.
1244.
[14] Indictment Rules 1971, r.9.
[15] *R. v. Kray* [1970] 1 Q.B. 125.

IV. ALTERNATIVE VERDICTS

The defendant may be convicted of attempt to murder if the acts are more **4-008** than merely preparatory and the defendant is shown to have intended to kill.[16] Where on a charge of murder the evidence relating to the mental element appears inconclusive, it has been held that the judge should direct the jury on manslaughter.[17] Infanticide is an alternative verdict,[18] as is child destruction.[19] Section 18 of the Offences Against the Person Act 1861 (causing grievous bodily harm with intent) is an alternative verdict,[20] as, by section 2(2) of the Suicide Act 1961, is aiding and abetting a suicide.[21] In *R. v. Saunders*[22] the House of Lords held that at common law a conviction of manslaughter could be returned even though the defendant had not first been acquitted of murder. This is in addition to section 6(2) of the Criminal Law Act 1967 which applies where the defendant has first been acquitted of murder. Section 6(2) is as follows:

> "On indictment for murder a person found not guilty of murder may be found guilty—
> (a) of manslaughter, or of causing grievous bodily harm with intent to do so,
> (b) of any offence of which he may be found guilty under an enactment specifically so providing, or under section 4(2) of this Act, or
> (c) of any attempt to commit murder, or an attempt to commit any other offence of which he might be found guilty;
>
> but may not be found guilty of any offence not included above."

V. ELEMENTS OF THE OFFENCE

(1) "OF SOUND MEMORY AND OF THE AGE OF DISCRETION"

(a) Capacity

The words from Coke's definition contain references to insanity and **4-009** infancy. Insanity can be raised as a defence in all offences. However, as it is closely connected with the special defence of diminished responsibility, which is only available on a charge of murder, it is discussed in the section on diminished responsibility in Chapter 5 below.

Infancy may also be a defence to charges of other crimes. A child cannot **4-010** be prosecuted if under 10 years of age.[23] If over 10 and under 14, he must be

---

[16] See para. 4-084.
[17] *Daley v. Director of Public Prosecutions* [1980] A.C. 237.
[18] See chap. 7.
[19] See chap. 7.
[20] See para. 3-045 and *R. v. Baker* [1994] Crim. L.R. 444.
[21] See para. 6-004.
[22] [1987] 2 A.E.R. 973.
[23] Children and Young Persons Act 1933, s.50, as amended by Children and Young Persons Act 1963, s.16.

shown to have a mischievous discretion.[24] In *R. v. Michael*[25] the defendant, intending to kill her child, gave her child's nurse a bottle of poison, stating that it was medicine to be given to the child. The nurse put the poison on a shelf in her room. While the nurse was absent, one of her children, aged five, took the bottle, gave the poison to the defendant's child, and thereby caused the child's death. The court found the defendant guilty of murder as principal. This doctrine of "innocent agency" can be applied in other situations of incapacity, *e.g.* where the person who is the immediate cause of death is insane.

4-011   A corporation, having legal personality, is capable of being found guilty of criminal offences.[26] It cannot be found guilty of murder, because the offence must be one punishable by fine, but a conviction for manslaughter is a possibility.

4-012   In *H. L. Bolton (Engineering) Co. Ltd. v. T. J. Graham and Sons Ltd.*[27] Lord Denning drew an analogy between a company and the human body. The directors and managers represent the directing mind and will of the company and control what it does. The state of mind of those directors is the company's state of mind. The company also has "mere servants and agents" who represent the hands to carry out its work.

4-013   In a case concerning the Trade Descriptions Act 1968, *Tesco Supermarkets Ltd. v. Nattrass*,[28] the House of Lords examined the question of the identification of those directors who were to be regarded as the directing mind and will. Most of the members of the House felt that the company's memorandum and articles of association were important in determining this question, although the members of the House expressed themselves differently. It is a question of law whether an individual is to be identified as the company, or regarded simply as its servant.

4-014   In *R. v. ICR Haulage Ltd.*,[29] a case concerning conspiracy to defraud, the Court of Appeal indicated that companies might be found liable for offences of violence. In *R. v. Robert Millar (Contractors) Ltd.*[30] a company was considered to be capable of prosecution for abetting manslaughter by its employees. In 1965 at Glamorgan Assizes, the Northern Strip Mining Construction Company Limited was acquitted of manslaughter.[31]

4-015   In *R. v. H. M. Coroner for East Kent, ex p. Spooner*,[32] on an application for judicial review of the decision of the coroner in the inquest on the loss of life in the Zeebrugge ferry disaster, the Divisional Court saw no reason in principle why a company could not be successfully prosecuted for manslaughter.

---

[24] *R. v. Gorrie* (1919) 83 J.P. 136; *J.M. (A Minor) v. Runeckles* (1984) 79 Cr.App.R. 255; see also *R. v. Coulburn* (1988) 87 Cr.App.R. 309; *T. v. D.P.P.* [1989] Crim. L.R. 498; *C. (A Minor) v. D.P.P.* [1966] 1 A.C. 1; *CC. (A Minor) v. D.P.P.* [1996] 1 Cr.App.R. 375.

[25] (1840) 9 C. & P. 356.

[26] See for discussion of the issues, Law Commission "Legislating the Criminal Code: Involuntary Manslaughter" Law Com. No. 237, Pt. VI.

[27] [1957] 1 Q.B. 159.

[28] [1972] A.C. 153. See also, *Meridian Global Funds Management Asia Limited v. The Securities Commission* [1995] 2 A.C. 500.

[29] [1944] K.B. 551; *contra, R. v. Cory Bros and Corp.* [1927] 1 K.B. 810.

[30] [1970] 2 Q.B. 54.

[31] Unrep., February 1, 1965, Glamorgan Assizes.

[32] (1989) 88 Cr.App.R. 10.

However, it would be necessary to show that those identified as the company had the requisite *mens rea*. It would not be possible to aggregate evidence against other persons in the company. However, it is not necessary to show that each of the directors is guilty. On the facts of the case, the court felt that there was no case of manslaughter to be left to the jury.

In *R. v. P & O European Ferries (Dover) Ltd*,[33] the company and seven   **4-016**
employees were prosecuted for manslaughter. At the Central Criminal Court Turner J., in a detailed ruling which fully reviewed the existing case law, confirmed the principle that a corporation could be properly indictable for manslaughter but concluded that, on the evidence before him, there was no case to answer and withdrew the case from the jury. The judge ruled out the possibility of aggregation when he held that, on the issue of the mental element, it was necessary to show that at least one of the controlling officers had the appropriate mental element for the offence. Such an analysis is only applicable to corporations because they have independent legal personality, and would not apply to unincorporated associations.

(2) "Unlawfully"

The considerations detailed in para. 1-028 *et seq.* are also relevant here.   **4-017**
However, there are some specific points which are of importance in cases of murder. A killing in execution of a sentence of the court is not murder.[34]

(a) Self-defence

It will not be murder if the killing is in the course of preventing a crime or   **4-018**
arresting offenders,[35] nor if it is done in self-defence (see paragraphs 1–046 to 1–055). It should be noted that the use of excessive force in the course of preventing a crime or arresting an offender or self-defence does not reduce murder to manslaughter. The defendant is still guilty of murder. The force used must be reasonable for the defence to succeed. In *Palmer v. R.*[36] a group of men, including the defendant, went to buy drugs. After a dispute the men left with the drugs, but without paying. They were pursued and a man was shot by the defendant, who had been carrying a gun. The defendant was charged with murder and raised the defence of self-defence. He was convicted of murder. His appeal to the Privy Council was rejected. The Privy Council refused to accept that excessive force used in self-defence would reduce a conviction from murder to manslaughter. Where there is evidence of self-defence this must be put to the jury and it is for the prosecution to prove that the defendant was not acting in self-defence.[37] In *R. v. Ferrari*[38] the defendant

---

[33] (1991) 93 Cr.App.R. 72.
[34] 1 Hale 496.
[35] Criminal Law Act 1967, s.3 applies.
[36] [1971] A.C. 814: see, too, *R. v. McInnes* (1971) 55 Cr.App.R. 551.
[37] *Palmer* (supra); *R. v. Abraham* (1973) 57 Cr.App.R. 799. On the judge raising the defence, see *D.P.P. v. Bailey* [1995] 1 Cr.App.R. 257.
[38] [1992] Crim. L.R. 747.

stabbed the deceased during a struggle outside a public house. The Court of Appeal considered the judge's ruling was adequate but expressed the view that it might have been better to use Lord Morris's words in *Palmer* which constituted the classic direction on self-defence.

4-019   The approach of the Privy Council has been followed by the House of Lords in *R. v. Clegg.*[39] The defendant was a soldier on patrol in Northern Ireland. As a speeding car drove at him he fired three shots, and a fourth, which killed one of the passengers, as the car had passed. The House of Lords made no distinction between the use of excessive force in self-defence and in the prevention of crime or arresting an offender. Furthermore, it made no difference whether the person using the force was a soldier or police officer acting in the course of his duty. Any alteration in the law to reduce what would otherwise be murder to manslaughter in a particular class of case could not be carried out by the judiciary but was for the legislature. In *R. v. Scarlett*[40] the deceased died when he struck his head after being ejected from a public house by the licensee. On a charge of manslaughter, it was held that, the accused is entitled to an acquittal unless the jury are satisfied that the degree of force used was plainly more than was called for by the circumstances as he believed them to be. Provided he believed the circumstances called for the degree of force used, he is not to be convicted even if his belief was unreasonable. This decision has been explained in *R. v. Owino*[41] to the effect that it was not meant to depart from *R. v. Williams.*[42] The mistaken belief in the need for force is to be judged subjectively, but the jury is to decide whether the response was reasonable.

(b) Duress

4-020   Duress is considered at paragraphs 1–056 to 1–068. It is no defence to a charge of murder, whether the defendant is charged as principal offender or as accomplice. In *R. v. Howe*[43] the defendant had met a man called Murray. On a number of occasions he was involved with others in attacks on young men. On one count Howe was charged with murder as a principal offender, on a second as an accomplice and on a third as a party to a conspiracy to murder. All killings were done in fear for his life as result of threats by Murray. In *Lynch v. Director of Public Prosecutions,*[44] the defendant had been forced to drive an IRA group to a place where they killed a police officer. The House of Lords, by a majority, allowed the defendant to plead the defence of duress, since he was charged only as an accomplice to murder. The House in *Howe* not only refused to extend this principle to principal offenders, but, indeed, decided to overrule *Lynch*. It is not now possible for any participant to use the defence of duress on a charge of murder. It was said, obiter, by

[39] [1995] 1 A.C. 482.
[40] [1993] 4 A.E.R. 629 and *R. v. Oatridge* (1991) 94 Cr.App.R. 367.
[41] [1996] 2 Cr.App.R. 128.
[42] (1983) 78 Cr.App.R. 276.
[43] [1987] A.C. 417.
[44] [1975] A.C. 653.

Lord Griffiths that the defence would be allowed to attempted murder, but the question was left open by Lord Hailsham. On the charge of conspiracy to murder, the trial judge had left the defence to the jury, but the House did not comment about this, so the issue remains open.

The House of Lords has now established that not only is duress not a **4-021** defence to murder, either as a principal or accessory, but also it is no defence on a charge of attempted murder. In *R. v. Gotts*,[45] a boy of 16 stabbed his mother. On a charge of attempted murder the defence was put forward that his father had ordered him to kill his mother under the threat that the boy would be shot if he did not comply. The House of Lords held, by a majority, Lords Keith and Lowry dissenting, that the defence of duress was not available. The House, in deciding how to apply the decision in *Howe*, having reviewed the authorities and concluded that the decision was one of policy, appears to have preferred the arguments that concentrated on the gravity of the mental element required in attempted murder (*i.e.* intent to kill) rather than the, often fortitious, result (*i.e.* survival of the victim). Necessity is not a defence which can be raised on a charge of murder.[46]

(c) Intoxication

Intoxication by drink or drugs,[47] whether involuntary or self-induced, can **4-022** be a defence to a charge of murder (though not manslaughter) because murder is a crime of specific intent. The intoxication must deprive the defendant of the necessary intent,[48] for, as Lord Birkenhead said in *Director of Public Prosecutions v. Beard*[49] "a drunken intent can nevertheless be a sufficient intent". The terms "specific" and "basic" intent are not clearly defined. In particular, the term "specific" intent has been given different meanings by different judges in different contexts. The law on intoxication appears settled since the decision of the House in *Commissioner of Police of the Metropolis v. Caldwell*.[50] In *Caldwell* Lord Diplock said that[51]:

> ". . . classification into offences of specific and basic intent is irrelevant where being reckless whether a particular harmful consequence will result from one's act is sufficient mens rea."

As a result of that decision it has been clear that the determining factor is whether the crime can be committed recklessly.

Voluntary, that is, self-induced, intoxication due to drink or drugs known **4-023** to have dangerous effects[52] can be no defence to manslaughter because it is a basic intent crime. However, the involuntary consumption of these substances

---

[45] [1992] 2 A.C. 412.
[46] *R. v. Dudley and Stephens* (1884) 14 Q.B.D. 152.
[47] *R. v. Lipman* [1970] 1 Q.B. 152.
[48] See *R. v. O'Connor* [1991] Crim. L.R. 135; *R. v. Cole* [1993] Crim. L.R. 300; *R. v. McKinley* [1994] Crim. L.R. 944.
[49] [1920] A.C. 479 at 501.
[50] [1982] A.C. 341.
[51] *R. v. Caldwell* [1982] A.C. 341 at 356A.
[52] *R. v. Bailey* [1983] 2 A.E.R. 503; *R. v. Hardie* [1984] 3 A.E.R. 848.

was considered by the House of Lords in *R. v. Kingston*[53] in a case of indecent assault. The view was expressed that in a case where the defendant has not formed the intent for the crime, he could be acquitted. Whether the courts will allow this as a defence to murder remains to be seen.

4-024 There is one exception to the statement that self-induced intoxication is a defence to murder. If a person takes alcohol to give himself "Dutch courage" to commit a crime, then his prior fault will be taken together with his later commission of the *actus reus* of the offence, and thus he can be convicted of the offence. This principle derives from the case of *Attorney-General for Northern Ireland v. Gallagher*,[54] where the defendant, intending to kill his wife, consumed the best part of a bottle of whisky in order to give himself the courage to carry out the offence.

(3) "Within any County of the Realm"

4-025 There are some situations in which murder or manslaughter committed outside England can be tried in England. These are: (i) an offence committed on land anywhere outside England by a British citizen[55]; (ii) an offence committed by anyone, British citizen or not, on a British ship[56] or aircraft[57]; (iii) an offence on a foreign ship within British territorial waters,[58] whether by a British citizen or not. Attempt and conspiracy to murder are both now covered by statutory definitions in section 1 of the Criminal Attempts Act 1981 and section 1 of the Criminal Law Act 1977 respectively. It is unlikely that these will be interpreted to extend extra-territorially to make indictable in England attempts or conspiracies by British citizens to kill outside the jurisdiction.

4-026 A number of situations may occur which involve problems of jurisdiction. Take, for example, the posting in England of a letter bomb addressed to an intended victim resident abroad. There is authority[59] for the proposition that an offence is committed where the conduct of the crime is committed. Where the crime is defined to require the occurrence of a consequence, this may not apply. If, however, substantial conduct occurred in England, *e.g.* fatal injury, and the consequence, *e.g.* death, occurred abroad then, it is submitted, this could come within the proposition stated. An attempt in England by a British citizen to commit a murder abroad is also triable in England, the attempt being the substantive offence. An attempt by an alien would not come within this principle because the English courts only have jurisdiction where a British citizen commits murder abroad. A conspiracy (including persons who are aliens) in England to murder abroad is an offence triable in England if the offence would be murder if carried out here.[60]

---

[53] [1995] 2 A.C. 355.
[54] [1963] A.C. 349.
[55] Offences Against the Person Act 1861, s.9; British Nationality Act 1948, s.3.
[56] This includes the case where the ship is in the tidal parts of foreign rivers: *R. v. Anderson* (1868) L.R. 1 C.C.R. 161; Merchant Shipping Act 1894, s.686(1).
[57] Civil Aviation Act 1949, s.62; see Tokyo Convention Act 1967 for aircraft flying over the U.K.
[58] Territorial Waters Jurisdiction Act 1878, s.2; Continental Shelf Act 1964, s.3.
[59] *Treacy v. D.P.P.* [1971] A.C. 537.
[60] Criminal Law Act 1977, s.1(4).

Where the conduct, *e.g.* posting the bomb, occurs abroad but the conse- **4-027** quence, *e.g.* death, occurs in England, then the occurrence of the consequence here would give the English courts jurisdiction.[61] It is doubtful whether this would apply to give jurisdiction over foreign nationals acting abroad.[62] It is unclear if an attempt (*e.g.* the bomb fails to explode) would be indictable. If it is intended that the act should have some effect in England then *Director of Public Prosecutions v. Stonehouse* would support the proposition that the attempt is indictable in England. A conspiracy abroad to commit an offence in England is indictable if the parties act in England in pursuance of the conspiracy.[63]

The War Crimes Act 1991 affects the jurisdiction to try offences of murder **4-028** or manslaughter in very limited circumstances. Section 1 of the Act provides:

> "(1) Subject to the provisions of this section, proceedings for murder, manslaughter or culpable homicide may be brought against any person in the United Kingdom irrespective of his nationality at the time of the alleged offence if that offence—
> (a) was committed during the period beginning with 1st September 1939 and ending with 5th June 1945 in a place which at the time was part of Germany or under German occupation; and
> (b) constituted a violation of the laws and customs of war.
> (2) No proceedings shall by virtue of this section be brought against any person unless he was on 8th March 1990, or has subsequently become, a British citizen or resident in the United Kingdom, the Isle of Man or any of the Channel Islands.
> (3) No proceedings shall by virtue of this section be brought in England and Wales or in Northern Ireland except by or with the consent of the Attorney General or, as the case may be, the Attorney General for Northern Ireland.
> (4) The Schedule to this Act provides a procedure for use instead of committal proceedings where a person is charged in England, Wales or Northern Ireland with an offence to which this section applies."

The alternative procedure referred to in subsection (4) and set out in Sched- **4-029** ule 1(1) is a transfer procedure which applies in a case where, in the opinion of either the Attorney-General or the D.P.P. (or an officer acting on their behalf), there is sufficient evidence for the defendant to be committed for trial and the case is of such complexity that it should be taken over without delay by the Crown Court.

(4) "ANY REASONABLE CREATURE IN BEING"

This is not a question of mental ability but relates to physical characteristics. **4-030** For the crimes of murder and manslaughter to apply the victim must be "alive". The law has sought to establish the point at which the newly born come within the protection of these offences. If still in the womb, or in the

---

[61] This includes attempt—*D.P.P. v. Stonehouse* [1978] A.C. 55 and Criminal Law Act 1977, s.1(4).
[62] *R. v. Keyn* (1876) 2 Ex. D. 63.
[63] *D.P.P. v. Doot* [1973] A.C. 807.

process of being born, the offence against the unborn child is either abortion[64] or child destruction.[65]

4–031   The whole child must be completely outside the mother's body.[66] There is no need for the umbilical cord to have been cut.[67] The child must also be born alive.[68] This requires proof of an independent existence. This can be established by either independent circulation[69] or breathing after birth.[70] However, proof of its having breathed may not be a conclusive[71] nor even a necessary test.[72] It should be noted that if a child is being born, is injured in the process, is born alive and then dies because of this injury, this can be murder.[73] This may also extend back to injury or poisoning in the womb. Provided that the child is then born alive and death occurs afterwards as a result of the earlier injury, then this can be murder or manslaughter.[74] A recent authority confirming this is *Attorney-General's Reference (No. 3 of 1994)*.[75] This does not extend to pre-natal injury caused by neglect by the mother, only to injuries caused by her acts.[76]

4–032   It has been held that a threat directed to a pregnant woman to cause her to miscarry is not a threat to kill another person within the offence under section 16 of the Offences Against the Person Act 1861.[77] The foetus "in utero" was not "another person" for the purpose of section 16. This may be contrasted with the situation where the defendant solicits a pregnant woman to kill a child at birth. This case will come within the offence of solicitation to murder.[78] In such circumstances the child will have been "born alive" before being killed, so the offence of murder could be committed.

4–033   The law of homicide does not have its own test of death. In *R. v. Malcherek and Steel*[79] the victims had been caused serious injuries which had led to them being placed on life support machines. In both cases the doctors took decisions to switch off the machines after carrying out medical tests to ascertain whether the victims were dead. The question arose as to when the death took place. The Court of Appeal espoused the view that the current state of medical knowledge was such that the law should not adopt a rigid test of what consti-

---

[64] Offences Against the Person Act 1861, s.58 (see chap. 7).

[65] Infant Life Preservation Act 1929, s.1 (see chap. 7).

[66] *R. v. Poulton* (1834) 5 C. & P. 329; see chap. 7.

[67] *R. v. Crutchley* (1837) 7 C. & P. 814; *R. v. Reeves* (1839) 9 C. & P. 25; *R. v. Trilloe* (1842) 2 Moo. 260.

[68] *R. v. Pritchard* (1901) 17 T.L.R. 310; *R. v. Sellis* (1837) 7 C. & P. 850.

[69] *R. v. Enoch* (1833) 5 C. & P. 539; *R. v. Wright* (1841) 9 C. & P. 754; *Crutchley* (1837) 7 C. & P. 814.

[70] *R. v. Handley* (1874) 13 Cox C.C. 79.

[71] *R. v. Sellis* (1837) 7 C. & P. 850; *Crutchley* (1837) 7 C. & P. 814.

[72] *R. v. Brain* (1834) 6 C. & P. 349.

[73] *R. v. Senior* (1832) 1 Moo. C.C. 346 (gross negligence by midwife).

[74] *R. v. West* (1848) 2 Cox C.C. 500 (unlawful abortion): see, too, *Kwok Chak Ming* [1963] H.K.L.R. 349, and *R. v. Cannon* [1963] Crim. L.R. 748.

[75] *Att.-Gen.'s Reference No. 3 of 1994* [1996] 2 W.L.R. 412.

[76] *R. v. Knights* (1860) 2 F. & F. 46; *R. v. Izod* (1904) 20 Cox C.C. 690; *R. v. Middleship* (1850) 5 Cox C.C. 275; but, to the contrary, if she is negligent at the time of the birth, *R. v. Pritchard* (1901) 17 T.L.R. 310.

[77] *R. v. Tait* [1989] Crim. L.R. 834; see para. 2–111.

[78] *R. v. Shephard* [1919] 2 K.B. 125.

[79] (1981) 73 Cr.App.R. 173.

tuted death in law. Instead, the court endorsed the medical practitioners' test, which is commonly called the brain death test[80]:

> "This is not the occasion for any decision as to what constitutes death. Modern techniques have undoubtedly resulted in the blurring of many of the conventional and traditional concepts of death. . . . There is, it seems, a body of opinion in the medical profession that there is only one true test of death and that is the irreversible death of the brain stem, which controls the basic functions of the body such as breathing. When that occurs it is said the body has died, even though by mechanical means the lungs are being caused to operate and some circulation of blood is taking place."

(5) "UNDER THE QUEEN'S PEACE"

This includes alien enemies, but not in the heat of war and in the exercise thereof.[81] It excludes killings in war or possibly rebellion. The Queen's peace includes people under sentence of death, unless they are killed by someone other than the lawful executioner or by some unauthorised method.[82] If an alien enemy kills a British subject, it is murder unless the heat of war rule applies[83] and if committed in England, it is no defence that the alien did not know English law.[84] Shooting prisoners of war is murder.[85]   **4-034**

(6) "KILLETH"

The conduct of the defendant which causes the death may be either a positive act or an omission.[86] The law relating to omissions is set out in Chapter 5 as it is more usual for a charge of manslaughter to follow than a charge of murder. The following rules of causation are generally applicable in the criminal law, but are explained in detail here since it is often in the context of charges of murder or manslaughter that such issues are encountered.[87]   **4-035**

(a) Causation principles

The defendant's act must accelerate death. Thus, the defendant can be responsible, even if the victim is already suffering from a fatal disease.[88] This would apply to the administration of pain killing drugs which it is known will shorten life. However, doctors need not calculate the effects in minutes or hours.[89]   **4-036**

---

[80] Adopted by the Conference of Royal Medical Colleges in 1976—see (1976) 2 Brit. Med. Jl. 1187.
[81] Hale 1 PC 433; 3 Co. Inst. 50.
[82] *R. v. Page* [1954] 1 Q.B. 170.
[83] *R. v. Depardo* (1807) R. & R. 134.
[84] *R. v. Esop* (1836) 7 C. & P. 456.
[85] *Maria v. Hall* (1807) 1 Taunt. 33.
[86] *R. v. Gibbons and Proctor* (1918) 13 Cr.App.R. 134.
[87] See Hart and Honore, *Causation in the Law* (2nd ed., 1985).
[88] *R. v. Martin* (1832) 5 C. & P. 128; *R. v. Fletcher* (1841) 1 Russ. 417: *R. v. Murton* (1862) 3 F. & F. 492; *R. v. Dyson* (1908) 1 Cr.App.R. 13: *R. v. Cato* (1976) 62 Cr.App.R. 41 (*contra*, *R. v. Johnson* (1827) 1 Lew. C.C. 164).
[89] *R. v. Adams* [1957] Crim. L.R. 365.

4–037   The defendant's action must be one of the factual causes of death. This question of fact is for the jury to decide. In *R. v. White*[90] the defendant put poison in a drink for his mother. The mother died of a heart attack, not the poison. The defendant's act was not, therefore, the cause of death, but he was found guilty of attempt.

4–038   It has been said that the defendant's act need not be the only, or main, cause of death, so long as it is a "substantial" cause. In *R. v. Smith*[91] the Court of Appeal said:

> "If at the time of death the original wound is still an operating cause and a substantial cause, then the death can properly be said to be the result of the wound, albeit that some other cause of death is also operating. Only if it can be said that the original wounding is merely the setting in which another cause operates can it be said that the death did not result from the wound. Putting it another way, only if the second cause is so overwhelming as to make the original wound merely part of the history can it be said that the death does not flow from the wound."

This has been explained as meaning that the defendant's act will not be ignored unless it is of minimal significance,[92] even though there are other causes. It is wrong to say that the defendant is not the cause if less than one fifth to blame.[93] It may also be unnecessary to add that the defendant's act must be "substantial".[94]

4–039   The prosecution must prove that what the defendant did, caused the death. In *R. v. Dalloway*[95] the defendant was driving a cart, but was not holding the reins. A child ran in front of the cart and was killed by it. The court held that to convict the defendant it must be shown that his negligence in not holding the reins affected whether the child died. The defendant was acquitted of manslaughter. In *R. v. Dyos*[96] two injuries were caused to the deceased, each potentially fatal, but there was no indication which came first. Equally, it was possible that the victim could have recovered from the first injury. There was evidence that the defendant struck one blow, but it could not be shown that that would necessarily have caused death. As there was no evidence of a joint enterprise with whoever struck the other wound, the defendant was acquitted. This case should be compared with *Attorney-General's Reference No. 4 of 1980* discussed at 4–083.

4–040   There may be negligence by the victim which contributes to the death, but this is ignored.[97] In *R. v. Swindall and Osborne*[98] an old man was run over by a carriage driven by the defendants. The court held that the negligence of the victim was not relevant to the issue of causation, unlike civil proceedings. The

---

[90] [1910] 2 K.B. 124; *R. .v. Pankotai* [1961] Crim. L.R. 546.
[91] [1959] 2 Q.B. 35.
[92] *R. v. Cato* (1976) 62 Cr.App.R. 41.
[93] *R. v. Hennigan* (1971) 55 Cr.App.R. 262; *R. v. Notman* [1994] Crim. L.R. 518; *R. v. Kimsey* [1996] Crim. L.R. 35.
[94] *R. v. Malcherek* (1981) 73 Cr.App.R. 173.
[95] (1847) 2 Cox C.C. 273.
[96] [1979] Crim. L.R. 660.
[97] *R. v. Martin* (1827) 3 C. & P. 211; *R. v. Longbottom* (1849) 3 Cox C.C. 439.
[98] (1846) 2 C. & K. 230; *R. v. Walker* (1824) 1 C. & P. 320.

contributory negligence of third parties is also ignored, as in *R. v. Benge.*[99] The defendant was a foreman platelayer on a railway. He was working on the rails and failed to put a flagman sufficiently far up the track to warn oncoming trains. He also failed to place fog signals. It was held that any negligence of a third party such as the train driver or the flagman was irrelevant to the issue of the defendant's liability for the death of some of the passengers.

(b) Novus actus interveniens

Where there is a second event contributing to the death, there may be a problem in determining whether the defendant's act is still to be regarded as the legal cause of death, or whether the intervening event is the legal cause. This is often expressed as the issue of whether the later act "breaks the chain of causation". The phrase *"novus actus interveniens"* has been said to be:

4–041

> "a term of art which conveys to lawyers the crucial feature that there has not merely been an intervening act of another person, but that that act was so independent of the act of the accused that it should be regarded in law as the cause of the victim's death, to the exclusion of the act of the accused."[1]

If the defendant's act is still an operating cause and the later injury is minor, though in combination with the defendant's act causes death, then the defendant is still guilty. Events which are foreseeable results of the defendant's act do not break the chain. This would include foreseeable acts of defence by the victim, such as trying to escape.[2] Particular rules have been developed for the situation where the victim is frightened into escape and dies in the flight.

4–042

The authorities suggest that if the victim is put in such fear arising from a threat of, or actual physical violence that he tries to escape, and in the course of that escape he dies, provided the fear was reasonable, and the mode of escape reasonable, then the defendant's conduct will be held to be the cause of the death. In *Director of Public Prosecutions v. Daley and McGie*[3] the Privy Council set out the following tests:

4–043

> "(1) That the victim immediately before he sustained the injuries was in fear of being hurt physically;
> (2) that this fear was such that it caused him to try to escape;
> (3) that whilst he was trying to escape, and because he was trying to escape, he met his death;
> (4) that his fear of being hurt there and then was reasonable and was caused by the conduct of the defendant."

As to whether fear of the defendant caused the death, the case of *R. v.*

---

[99] (1865) 4 F. & F. 504; *cf. R. v. Ledger* (1862) 2 F. & F. 857 (these cases date from a time when contributory negligence and common employment were complete defences in a civil case).

[1] *R. v. Pagett* (1983) 76 Cr.App.R. 279 at 288.

[2] *R. v. Roberts* (1971) 56 Cr.App.R. 95; see para. 3–014 above.

[3] [1973] Crim. L.R. 307; *cf. R. v. Evans* (1812) 1 Russ. 12th 414; *R. v. Beech* (1912) 77 Cr.App.R. 197; *R. v. Coleman* (1920) 84 J.P. 112; *R. v. Pitts* (1842) Car. & M. 284; *R. v. Curley* (1909) 2 Cr.App.R. 96; *R. v. Halliday* (1889) 61 L.T. 79: *R. v. Lewis* (1970) Crim. L.R. 647; *R. v. Mackie* (1973) 57 Cr.App.R. 453; *R. v. Boswell*; see the much criticised case of *Cartledge v. Allen* [1973] Crim. L.R. 530; *R. v. Williams and Davis* (1992) 95 Cr.App.R. 1; *R. v. Corbett* [1996] Crim. L.R. 594.

Evans[4] should be considered. The deceased died from a fall from a window but the prosecution were unable to establish any unlawful act by the defendant which might have caused the death.

4-044   In *R. v. Roberts*[5] the defendant molested a young woman who was a passenger in his car. To escape she opened the door and jumped out while the car was in motion. She suffered grazing and concussion. The defendant was convicted of an offence under section 47 of the Offences Against the Person Act 1861. On appeal the Court of Appeal said the question to ask about the victim's act was as follows:

> "Was it the natural result of what the alleged assailant said and did, in the sense that it was something that could reasonably have been foreseen as the consequence of what he was saying or doing?"

4-045   This approach has been applied to foreseeable acts of self-defence by third parties. The act of the third party is seen as an involuntary act caused by the defendant's conduct. In *R. v. Pagett*[6] the defendant held a young girl hostage in front of himself to shield himself from armed policemen, who were pursuing him. The defendant fired at the police, who returned his fire and killed the girl. The defendant's conviction for manslaughter was upheld by the Court of Appeal. The court held that an act, caused by the defendant's act, which is done in execution of a legal duty, cannot be regarded as a voluntary act, and does not affect the chain of causation.

4-046   In *R. v. Armstrong*[7] the defendant supplied heroin to the victim. The victim had already consumed a large, possibly lethal, quantity of alcohol. The victim injected himself with the heroin and died shortly after. The medical experts were unsure whether or not the heroin had been a contributory cause of death. In the light of that evidence the court upheld the submission that there was insufficient evidence that the heroin had been a substantial cause of death. Since the experts could not be sure of this then, it was held, the jury could not be. The court also held well-founded a second submission, namely, that if the heroin did cause the death, the victim's self-injection was a *novus actus interveniens* breaking the chain of causation which started with the defendant's acts of supply.

4-047   This is to be contrasted with *R. v. Dalby*[8] where the defendant's supply of drugs to the self-injecting victim was said not to have been an act "aimed at" the victim (see paragraph 5–083). This case was re-examined by the Court of Appeal in *R. v. Goodfellow*[9] and said to turn on causation principles, not any "aimed at" doctrine.

4-048   In *R. v. Cato*[10] the defendant actually injected the victim with illegal drugs, so no question of *novus actus* arose. In *R. v. Ball*[11] the appellant sold a vehicle

---

[4] [1992] Crim. L.R. 659.
[5] (1971) 56 Cr.App.R. 95; see also *R. v. Dear* [1996] Crim. L.R. 595.
[6] (1983) 76 Cr.App.R. 279.
[7] [1989] Crim. L.R. 149.
[8] [1982] 1 W.L.R. 621.
[9] (1986) 83 Cr.App.R. 23.
[10] (1975) 62 Cr.App.R. 41.
[11] [1989] Crim. L.R. 730.

belonging to the victim which he had stored on his land with her consent. When the victim called on the appellant to see the vehicle, the appellant followed her and her companion into the garden. He was carrying a gun and behaving aggressively. The appellant and the victim started to argue and the victim ran towards a wall. As she tried to climb over it the appellant shot her. He asserted in his defence that he believed the gun to contain blank cartridges and that he did not intend to kill or cause grievous bodily harm. The court held that the defendant's act of firing at the victim was an assault directed at the victim with no intervening cause between the act and death. In this the court followed *Dalby*, as explained by Lord Lane in *R. v. Goodfellow*. Since there was no intervening act here, the point was not material. The case does, however, emphasise that the *Goodfellow* explanation of *Dalby* is being followed.

(c) Medical treatment

Where the victim dies during medical treatment after the injury inflicted   **4-049** by the defendant, for example, by choking while swallowing medicine, or if he dies in the course of an operation,[12] this does not affect the chain of causation.[13]

The most recent statement by the courts is in *Malcherek*[14] where it was   **4-050** held that treatment given by careful medical practitioners does not break the chain. The Court of Appeal said:

> "In the ordinary case if treatment is given bona fide by competent and careful medical practitioners, then evidence will not be admissible to show that the treatment would not have been administered in the same way by other medical practitioners."

This case approved the approach taken in *R. v. Smith*.[15] In this case the   **4-051** defendant stabbed a fellow soldier in a fight in a barrack room. The victim was taken to the medical station, but he was dropped twice on the way. The doctors, who had several other casualties to attend to, failed to realise that one wound had pierced the victim's lung and caused haemorrhaging. It was held that the subsequent events did not affect the chain of causation, and the defendant was found guilty of murder.

If, however, the treatment is not normal, or is grossly negligent, then the   **4-052** medical treatment will be the legal cause of death. In *R. v. Jordan*[16] the victim, who had been stabbed in the stomach, was taken to hospital. At the hospital he was given an antibiotic to which, unknown to the doctors, he was intolerant, and large quantities of water were given intravenously. He died a few days later. It was found that at the time of the death the stab wound had mainly healed, but the lungs were waterlogged and he had a pulmonary oedema, which medical evidence suggested was the cause of death. The Court of Appeal allowed the defendant's appeal against conviction.

---

[12] *R. v. Pym* (1846) 1 Cox C.C. 339; *R. v. Davis and Wagstaffe* (1883) 15 Cox C.C. 174.
[13] *R. v. McIntyre* (1847) 2 Cox C.C. 379.
[14] (1981) 73 Cr.App.R. 173.
[15] [1959] 2 Q.B. 35.
[16] (1956) 40 Cr.App.R. 152, approved on its facts in *Smith*, and in *R. v. Blaue* [1975] 3 All E.R. 446.

4-053   These principles can be illustrated by the following cases. In *R. v. Cheshire*[17] the Court of Appeal confirmed that the emphasis is on the question whether the defendant's act is the substantial (not necessarily sole or main) cause of death, not the blameworthiness of the doctor's conduct. The deceased was wounded by a gun in a fight in a chip shop. At the hospital he underwent an operation which included the insertion of a tracheotomy tube. He died two months later from complications arising out of the operation. The court said that it is likely only to be in the most extraordinary and unusual case that the medical treatment will break the chain of causation. In *R. v. McKechnie*[18] it was said that these principles apply equally where the death results from the inability to provide medical treatment due to the defendant's actions. In this case the defendants entered the deceased's flat and assaulted him. He was not operated on for a pre-existing medical condition because of the head injuries, and in fact died five weeks after the attack when his ulcer burst. The appeal was dismissed.

4-054   If the victim refuses medical treatment this will not break the chain of causation.[19] In *R. v. Holland*[20] the victim of an assault refused amputation of his finger, and died of lockjaw. The defendant was found guilty of his death. This rule will apply even if the refusal is unreasonable. In *R. v. Blaue*[21] the victim had been stabbed several times by the defendant and her lung had been pierced. She refused a blood transfusion because of her religious beliefs, and died as a result. The defendant sought to argue that this decision had broken the chain of causation. Dismissing the appeal, the Court of Appeal said:

> "It has long been the policy of the law that those who use violence on other people must take their victims as they find them. This in our judgment means the whole man, not just the physical man. It does not lie in the mouth of the assailant to say that his victim's religious beliefs which inhibited him from accepting certain kinds of treatment were unreasonable."

4-055   In *R. v. Hayward*[22] the defendant chased his wife from the house, threatening her. She fell into the road where the defendant kicked her arm. Evidence showed that she suffered from a medical condition described as a persistent thyrus gland. Evidence further showed that she died as result of the effects of fright and exertion on her medical condition. The defendant's knowledge, or lack of it, of his wife's condition (which made her more likely to suffer in these circumstances) was irrelevant on the charge of manslaughter. In *R. v. Dawson, Nolan and Walmsley*[23] and *R. v. Watson*,[24] the defendant's knowledge of the victim's age or physical condition were not taken into account in assessing the issue of causation.

[17] (1991) 93 Cr.App.R. 251; *R. v. Mellor* [1996] Crim. L.R. 743.
[18] (1991) 94 Cr.App.R. 51.
[19] *R. v. Wall* (1802) 28 St. Tr. 51.
[20] (1841) 2 Moo. & R. 351.
[21] [1975] 3 A.E.R. 446; see, too, *R. v. Martin* (1832) 5 C. & P. 128 and *R. v. Plummer* (1844) 1 C. & K. 600.
[22] (1908) 21 Cox C.C. 692.
[23] (1985) 81 Cr.App.R. 150.
[24] [1989] 1 W.L.R. 684.

(d) Roles of the judge and jury

In *R. v. Pagett*[25] the Court of Appeal explained that in the rare case where   **4-056**
a judge found it necessary to direct a jury on causation it was usually enough
to say that the defendant's act need not be the sole or main cause of death,
provided it contributed significantly to it. Where a specific issue of causation
arises, then the judge should direct the jury on the specific legal principles
applicable to the issue. It is for the jury to decide if the causal link is established. It has been suggested that if the facts are admitted and there is no
conflict of evidence the judge can rule on the question of causation.[26] Where
medical evidence is given the word of the doctors is not regarded as final; it
is still for the court to decide the legal cause of death.[27]

If the defendant's act causes shock from which the victim dies then the   **4-057**
chain of causation may be established. In *R. v. Hayward*[28] death from a threat
of violence was attributed to the defendant, and there was no need for proof
of physical violence. In *R. v. Towers*[29] the defendant's assault on a girl caused
her to scream. These screams frightened the child she was holding and made
it cry. Later the child suffered convulsions and died. The defendant was found
guilty. It is unlikely that this would apply to adult victims.

R. v. McDaniel[30] can be said to suggest that if perjury by witnesses causes   **4-058**
the defendant to be hanged, then this is neither murder nor manslaughter by
the witness. Blackstone[31] suggests this is because it is a policy not to deter
witnesses from giving evidence.

(e) Absence of a body

If the fact of death can be proved by circumstantial evidence, then this will   **4-059**
be acceptable to the court, even if the body cannot be found.[32]

(f) Time limit for death

Formerly, the death had to occur within a year and a day. In *R. v. Dyson*[33]   **4-060**
the evidence showed that the defendant severely beat his child in November,
1906 causing a fractured skull. He beat the child again in December, 1907. In
February, 1908 the child developed meningitis and died in March, 1908.

---

[25] (1983) 76 Cr.App.R. 279.
[26] *R. v. Blaue* [1975] 3 All E.R. 446 at 450 but in *D.P.P. v. Stonehouse* [1978] A.C. 55 it was
stated that the judge must leave all questions of fact to the jury even if there is only one
reasonable conclusion: see, too, *R. v. Pagett* (1983) 76 Cr.App.R. 279.
[27] *Cato* (1976) 62 Cr.App.R. 41; *R. v. Jordan* (1956) 40 Cr.App.R. 152, criticised for allowing
medical experts to state medical treatment caused death.
[28] (1908) 21 Cox C.C. 692.
[29] (1874) 12 Cox C.C. 530.
[30] (1756) 1 Leach 44.
[31] Comm. iv. 196; see also 1 East PC 333.
[32] *R. v. Davidson* (1934) 25 Cr.App.R. 21; *R. v. Onufrejczyk* [1955] 1 Q.B. 388; *R. v. Cheverton*
(1862) 2 F. & F. 833; *R. v. Burton* (1854) Dears C.C. 282; *R. v. Kersey* (1908) 1 Cr.App.R.
260.
[33] [1908] 2 K.B. 454.

Medical evidence showed that although the fractured skull was the main cause of death, the later assaults would have accelerated death. The defendant was convicted of manslaughter. The Court of Appeal upheld his appeal. The court held that it was a misdirection to allow the jury to consider whether the death was caused by the injuries in 1906, since the death must be shown to have occurred within a year and a day after the injury was inflicted. It would have been a proper question to consider whether the injuries in 1907 accelerated the child's death. This rule has been abolished (with transitional provisions) by the Law Reform (Year and a Day Rule) Act 1996, which also makes provision for the consent of the Attorney-General for proceedings where the injury causing death was sustained more than three years before the death occurred or the person has been previously convicted of any offences in connection with the death.

VI. MENTAL ELEMENT

(1) "MALICE AFORETHOUGHT"

4-061   The distinction between murder and involuntary manslaughter lies in the mental element. It has been said that:

> "Murder is unlawful homicide with malice aforethought. Manslaughter is unlawful homicide without malice aforethought."[34]

Lord Diplock has said:

> "What distinguishes murder from manslaughter is that murder falls within the class of crime in which the mental element or mens rea necessary to constitute the offence in English law includes the attitude of mind of the accused not only towards his physical act itself, which is the actus reus of the offence, as is the case with manslaughter, but also towards a particular evil consequence of that act."[35]

4-062   The phrase "malice aforethought" has acquired, despite its criticism as anachronistic, wholly inappropriate and ripe for abolition,[36] a specific legal meaning. As Lord Hailsham said in *R. v. Cunningham*[37]:

> "The expression 'malice aforethought' in whatever tongue expressed, is unfortunate since neither the word 'malice' nor the word 'aforethought' is construed in its ordinary sense."

The killing need not have been premeditated, nor need the person who kills be motivated by "malice" in the popular sense of the word.

4-063   Before examining the current definition of malice aforethought, it is worth noting something of the history of the concept. Malice aforethought was formerly recognised as taking one of three forms, express, implied or constructive.[38] Constructive malice was established either where the defendant killed

---

[34] *R. v. Doherty* (1887) 16 Cox C.C. 304 at 307.
[35] *Hyam v. D.P.P.* [1975] A.C. 55 at 86C.
[36] *Hyam* at p. 66H *per* Lord Hailsham; *R. v. Moloney* [1985] A.C. 905 at 920H *per* Lord Bridge.
[37] [1982] A.C. 566.
[38] *R. .v. Cunningham* [1982] A.C. 566 at 576, *per* Lord Hailsham.

in the course of a felony (the felony-murder rule)[39] or the killing occurred in the course of or for the purpose of the defendant resisting an officer of justice or resisting or avoiding or preventing a lawful arrest or effecting or assisting an escape or rescue from legal custody (the arrest-murder rule).[40]

Constructive malice was abolished by section 1 of the Homicide Act 1957:   **4-064**

> "(1) Where a person kills another in the course or furtherance of some other offence, the killing shall not amount to murder unless done with the same malice aforethought (express or implied) as is required for a killing to amount to murder when not done in the course or furtherance of another offence.
>
> (2) For the purposes of the foregoing subsection, a killing done in the course or for the purpose of resisting an officer of justice, or of resisting or avoiding or preventing a lawful arrest, or of effecting or assisting an escape or rescue from legal custody, shall be treated as a killing in the course of furtherance of an offence."

This section left untouched the other forms of malice, namely, express and   **4-065** implied. In *R. v. Vickers*[41] it was stated by the Court of Appeal that the *mens rea* of murder was now satisfied by either an intention to kill ("express malice") or an intention to do grievous bodily harm ("implied malice"). This left two outstanding questions for the law to settle. The first was whether or not an intention to do grievous bodily harm *simpliciter* was enough, or whether the harm had to be such as to endanger life. The second was the meaning of intention.

(a) What must be intended

In *Vickers* the defendant entered a shop to steal money. He was seen by the   **4-066** elderly shopkeeper, who lived in a flat on the premises. As she entered the cellar to confront the defendant, he attacked her, striking her with his fists and kicking her, as a result of which she died. The defendant was convicted or murder. Lord Goddard, dismissing the appeal, held that, although section 1 of the Homicide Act 1957 abolished constructive malice, it specifically preserved implied malice. If a defendant intends to inflict grievous bodily harm, this is sufficient to imply the necessary malice aforethought for murder. He rejected the suggestion that grievous bodily harm was the "other offence" referred to in section 1, in the course of commission of which the victim was killed. Logically the section must mean the offence which the defendant was committing when the killing occurred.

The decision was approved, *obiter*, in *Director of Public Prosecutions v.*   **4-067** *Smith.*[42] The defendant was driving a car containing stolen property. When stopped by a policeman and asked to draw into the kerb, the defendant accelerated and drove off. The policeman clung to the side of the car, which travelled some distance before he fell off in front of another car and was killed. The

---

[39] *R. v. Jarmain* [1946] K.B. 74; *R. v. Beard* [1920] A.C. 479.
[40] *R. v. Porter* (1873) 12 Cox C.C. 444.
[41] [1957] 2 Q.B. 664.
[42] [1961] A.C. 290.

defendant was convicted of murder. On appeal to the Court of Criminal Appeal, his conviction was quashed and a conviction of manslaughter substituted. The Crown appealed to the House of Lords. The House upheld the murder conviction. Viscount Kilmuir L.C. explained that grievous bodily harm was to be interpreted in its ordinary and natural meaning:

> " 'Bodily harm' needs no explanation and 'grievous' means no more and no less than 'really serious'."[43]

4-068 The trial judge had referred to the definition given in *R. v. Ashman*,[44] "seriously interfere with health and comfort" (once described as the "murder by pinprick" doctrine[45]). This was not endorsed by the House of Lords. A suggestion was put to the House that in murder a narrower view of grievous bodily harm should be taken, such as "obviously dangerous to life", or "likely to kill". This was also rejected by the House.

4-069 In *Hyam v. Director of Public Prosecutions*,[46] Lord Diplock raised the question again. In this case the defendant, being suspicious of her lover's relationship with another woman, and wishing to frighten the woman into leaving the neighbourhood, poured petrol through the letterbox of the woman's house. The defendant then set light to the petrol, and two children in the house were killed in the ensuing fire. The defendant was convicted of murder, and her appeals to the Court of Appeal and House of Lords were dismissed. Lord Diplock was of the view that the definition of grievous bodily harm in murder should not be tied to the definition of the statutory offence, as suggested in *Smith*.[47] He conceded that the intent to do harm less than death was an aspect of malice aforethought, but that it required an intent to do harm which endangered life. Intent to do grievous bodily harm had only been sufficient while constructive malice existed. This view formed the basis of his dissent, in which he was joined by Lord Kilbrandon. However, Lord Hailsham stated his support for *Vickers* and confirmed the definition used in *Smith*. Viscount Dilhorne agreed, although Lord Cross was unsure on the point. He "effectively sat on the fence",[48] but was prepared to accept that *Vickers* was rightly decided.

4-070 The matter was resolved by the House of Lords decision in *R. v. Cunningham*.[49] In this case the defendant attacked the victim with a chair in a public house. He was convicted of murder and his appeal to the Court of Appeal was dismissed. On appeal to the House of Lords, Lord Hailsham, speaking for the House, stated that *Vickers* was correct. He also expressed the view that there should be no change in the law to require intent to endanger life.

4-071 The decision in Cunningham was approved in *R. v. Moloney*.[50] For an

[43] [1961] A.C. 290 at 334.
[44] (1858) 1 F. & F. 88.
[45] *Cunningham* [1985] A.C. 566 *per* Lord Hailsham.
[46] [1975] A.C. 55.
[47] [1961] A.C. 290.
[48] As described in *R. v. Moloney* [1985] A.C. 905 at 924G *per* Lord Bridge.
[49] [1982] A.C. 566.
[50] [1985] A.C. 905.

explanation of the case law on grievous bodily harm in the statutory offences under section 18 and section 20 of the Offences Against the Person Act 1861, see Chapter 3.

(b) Proof of intent

The second question referred to above was the meaning of the word intention. The House of Lords considered this in *Moloney*.[51] The defendant was in a room with his stepfather. Both men had been drinking. They got into an argument over who was quicker to load and fire a gun. At the deceased's suggestion Moloney found two guns and some cartridges. Moloney loaded first and the deceased said "I didn't think you'd got the guts but if you have pull the trigger". Moloney did so but without taking aim. The gun went off killing the other man. Moloney was convicted of murder. Allowing his appeal, Lord Bridge stated that: **4–072**

> "The golden rule should be that, when directing a jury on the mental element necessary in a crime of specific intent, the judge should avoid any elaboration or paraphrase of what is meant by intent, and leave it to the jury's good sense to decide whether the accused acted with the necessary intent, unless the judge is convinced that, on the facts and having regard to the way the case has been presented to the jury in evidence and argument, some further explanation or elaboration is strictly necessary to avoid misunderstanding."[52]

It is, therefore, necessary to consider the legal meaning of intention in order to be able to direct juries in those cases in which some further explanation is required. There are authorities which favour a narrow interpretation of intention, confining it to the defendant's purpose or desire.[53] This approach has not, however, been taken in the case law on murder. The difficulty has been to define the exact scope of any extended definition of intent. In particular, the courts have had to deal with the question of the extent to which the foreseeability of a consequence is relevant to intention.   **4–073**

In *Moloney* Lord Bridge, giving the leading speech and speaking for the House, said that frequently it was necessary to explain to a jury that intention was different from motive or desire. However, as to whether foresight of a given degree of probability of a consequence occurring is equivalent or alternative to intent, he said: **4–074**

> "I am firmly of the opinion that foresight of consequences as an element bearing on the issue of intention in murder, or indeed, any other crime of specific intent, belongs, not to the substantive, but to the law of evidence."[54]

In support Lord Bridge cites Lord Hailsham's view in *Hyam*[55] and thereby

---

[51] [1985] A.C. 905.

[52] *Moloney* at p. 926A. This had formerly been advocated by Lawton L.J. in *R. v. Beer* (1976) 63 Cr.App.R. 222 at 225 and see *Leung Kam Kwok* (1985) 81 Cr.App.R. 83.

[53] *R. v. Steane* [1947] K.B. 997; *R. v. Ahlers* [1915] 1 K.B. 616; *Thorne v. Motor Trade Assoc.* [1937] A.C. 797; *Sinnasamy Selvanayagam v. R.* [1951] A.C. 83.

[54] [1985] A.C. 905 at 928.

[55] *Moloney* at p. 928a, citing Lord Hailsham in *Hyam* [1975] A.C. 55 at 75 and 77; in fact, in that case the House had considered the same question and, although Lord Hailsham had rejected the equation of foresight with intent, Viscount Dilhorne had accepted that foresight of high prob-

rejects the other views expressed therein. The House did not, however, expressly overrule *Hyam*.

4-075 Should any direction be given to the jury on how they should approach the way in which this evidence of foresight is to be used? Lord Bridge felt it would be rare in murder trials to need to give any elaboration to the jury, although Lord Scarman doubted this in *R. v. Hancock*.[56] Where it is necessary, Lord Bridge said that the judge should invite the jury to consider two questions[57]:

> "First, was death or really serious injury in a murder case (or whatever relevant consequence must be proved to have been intended in any other case) a natural consequence of the defendant's voluntary act? Secondly, did the defendant foresee that consequence as being a natural consequence of his act? The jury should then be told that if they answer yes to both questions it is a proper inference for them to draw that he intended that consequence."

4-076 Thus it is made clear that, although foresight of consequences is not the same thing in law as intending those consequences, nonetheless it is sufficient evidence from which a jury may infer intention. The degree of likelihood of the consequence occurring required to make this a proper inference is expressed in the word "natural". Unfortunately Lord Bridge did not make crystal clear his definition of that word. He said that the word "conveys the idea that in the ordinary course of events a certain act will lead to a certain consequence unless something unexpected supervenes to prevent it".[58] He said he thought that in murder cases "the probability must be little short of overwhelming" to suffice to establish the necessary intent.[59] Furthermore, he gives an example of a man seeking to evade pursuers, who boards a plane bound for Manchester. Although this may be the last place the man wants to go, he intends to go there because it is a "moral certainty" he will arrive there.[60] It would seem that he was trying to convey the idea that intention may be inferred from foresight of consequences which are morally certain to occur.[61]

4-077 The expression "natural and probable" consequence had been used in the earlier case law. In *Smith* the House of Lords had decided that it must be presumed that a person intends all those consequences which are the natural and probable consequences of his action.[62] This was described by Lord Bridge

---

ability did equate with intent (p. 82), Lord Cross had considered the possibility (p. 95), and Lord Diplock was certainly of the view that the two were equivalent (p. 86). Indeed, Lord Diplock reiterated his views in *R. v. Lemon* [1979] A.C. 638, and *R. v. Sheppard* [1981] A.C. 405, in the context of other offences. Doubts about this view had been expressed by the Court of Appeal in *R. v. Mohan* [1975] 2 W.L.R. 859 (charge of attempt) and *R. v. Belfon* [1976] 3 A.E.R. 46 (charge of s. 18 of the Offences Against the Person Act 1861). In *Hyam*, Viscount Dilhorne and Lord Cross had suggested that, notwithstanding whether foresight was equivalent to intent, it was a suitable alternative formulation for the meaning of malice aforethought.

[56] [1986] A.C. 455 at 468F.
[57] [1985] A.C. 905 at 929.
[58] [1985] A.C. 905 at 929.
[59] [1985] A.C. 905 at 925.
[60] [1985] A.C. 90 at 926.
[61] See on this Lord Hailsham in *Hyam v. D.P.P.* [1975] A.C. 55 at 74.
[62] See also *R. v. Ward* [1956] 1 Q.B. 351.

as treating the presumption as an irrebuttable one, and effectively making it a rule of law.[63] This aspect of *Smith*[64] had already been severely criticised both in the case law and by commentators and the reform bodies.[65] It was said to have been effectively reversed by section 8 of the Criminal Justice Act 1967.[66] Section 8 states as follows:

> "A court or jury, in determining whether a person has committed an offence,—
>
> (a) shall not be bound in law to infer that he intended or foresaw a result of his actions by reason only of its being a natural and probable consequence of those actions; but
>
> (b) shall decide whether he did intend or foresee that result by reference to all the evidence, drawing such inferences from the evidence as appear proper in the circumstances."

In *Frankland v. The Queen*[67] the Privy Council considered two consolidated appeals from the Isle of Man. The cases had been tried in 1980 and 1982, prior to the Isle of Man Evidence Act 1983, in which section 6 incorporated section 8 of the Criminal Justice Act 1967 into Isle of Man law. In both cases trial court directions were given which included the objective test expounded in *Smith*. The Privy Council held that *Smith* did not accurately represent English law, drawing on the criticisms noted above. Thus, even before the change in Isle of Man law, directions based on the *Smith* formula were erroneous. Thus, it can be said that section 8 did not change the law of murder at all as the principle in *Smith* was wrong.   **4-078**

In *R. v. Hancock*[68] the House of Lords had the opportunity to reconsider Lord Bridge's view. In this case two men dropped a piece of concrete block from a motorway bridge into the path of an oncoming car. The block hit the car and killed the driver. The two men stated that they had intended only to frighten the passenger in the car. Lord Scarman approved Lord Bridge's views in *Moloney*, but felt that the word "natural" may not be sufficient to draw the jury's attention to the need to look closely at the degree of probability. Any direction would need to refer more closely to probability: **4-079**

> "They [*i.e.* the jury] require an explanation that the greater the probability of a consequence the more likely it is that the consequence was foreseen and that if that consequence was foreseen the greater the probability is that the consequence was also intended."[69]

Probability is, therefore, a factor to be considered with all the other evidence.[70]

Lord Scarman also criticised the Court of Appeal for creating in their judgment in *Hancock* elaborately structured guidelines for use by trial judges. He felt that guidelines should be given sparingly and juries should be encouraged   **4-080**

---

[63] *Moloney* at 928G.
[64] [1961] A.C. 290.
[65] In *Hyam* at p. 70; Law Com. No. 10 (1967) *Imputed Criminal Intent*.
[66] *Moloney* at pp. 928H and 929C, *per* Lord Bridge.
[67] [1987] A.C. 576.
[68] [1986] A.C. 455.
[69] [1986] A.C. 455 at 473.
[70] *ibid.*

to use their common sense.[71] Despite this, the Court of Appeal has considered the issue again in *R. v. Nedrick*[72] and given further guidance to trial court judges. In this case the defendant poured paraffin through the letter box of a house and set it alight. In the ensuing fire a child was killed. The defendant said all he wanted to do was to frighten the child's mother, who was in the house. The Court of Appeal reiterated that in the majority of cases there would be no need for a direction to the jury. Where it was necessary, the judge should first explain that a person may intend a result even if it is not desired. If the defendant did not appreciate that death or serious harm was likely to follow, then he cannot have intended it. If he did appreciate but thought the risk was slight, then the jury may find it easy to conclude that he did not intend it. But if he sees it as virtually certain to occur, then they may find it easy to infer intent.

> "Where the charge is murder and in the rare cases where the simple direction is not enough, the jury should be directed that they are not entitled to infer the necessary intention unless they feel sure that death or serious bodily harm was a virtual certainty (barring some unforeseen intervention) as a result of the defendant's actions and that the defendant appreciated that such was the case. Where a man realises that it is for all practical purposes inevitable that his actions will result in death or serious harm, the inference may be irresistible that he intended that result, however little he may have desired or wished it to happen. The decision is one for the jury to be reached on a consideration of all the evidence."[73]

This has been followed in *R. v. O'Connor*.[74]

4-081   The above decisions clearly assert that foresight of consequence is only evidence of intention.[75] Nowhere does the case law define intention. Clearly desire is an aspect of intention, but it is not the definition of intention, since the judiciary believe that intention is wider than desire. If a person desires a consequence, however unlikely it is to occur, then he intends that consequence. The more unlikely it is to occur, the less likely it is that a jury will believe that he desired it. The decision in *Nedrick*, it is submitted, comes close to establishing a rule of law that in cases where desire is not an issue, the jury may only decide that the defendant intended the consequence if he foresaw it as virtually certain to occur. This would be to define intention as desire or foresight of virtual certainty. This is indeed the view of the Law Commission, but the House of Lords was at pains in *Moloney* to emphasise the evidential role of the foresight issue. Furthermore, the House of Lords in *Hancock* appeared to allow the jury greater flexibility in inferring intent (and thus, the defendant's liability to conviction for murder or manslaughter). In the absence of a rule of law that intention may only be established where there is proof of foresight of the virtual certainty of the consequence occurring conviction will be for the jury's own opinion. Furthermore, even if it is now the rule that juries may only infer intent from proof of foresight of virtual certainty, this

---

[71] *ibid.*
[72] [1986] 1 W.L.R. 1025.
[73] [1986] 1 W.L.R. 102 at 108.
[74] [1991] Crim. L.R. 135, and para. 4–070 above.
[75] As reiterated in *R. v. Scalley* [1995] Crim. L.R. 504; *R. v. Gregory and Mott* [1995] Crim. L.R. 507. See also *R. v. Woollin* [1997] Crim. L.R. 519.

does not say that they must so infer. The power of inference is still the jury's.

Some other aspects of the mental element in murder need to be discussed.   **4-082**
In *Hyam*[76] Lord Hailsham expressed the view that the action which kills must
be aimed at the victim. He drew on statements in *Smith*.[77] This view has been
rejected by Lord Bridge in *Moloney*[78] and no longer has currency.

In *Hyam* Lord Hailsham had suggested that it was sufficient to establish   **4-083**
malice aforethought if it were shown that the defendant intentionally exposed
the victim to a serious risk of death or grievous bodily harm.[79] This view
was also rejected in *Moloney*,[80] because of potential confusion with reckless
manslaughter.

(2) Attempt

The mental element for attempted murder is intent to kill.[81] Intent to do   **4-084**
grievous bodily harm is not enough.[82] In *R. v. Walker and Hayles*[83] the victim
was in a fight with the defendants. His head was banged against a wall and he
was threatened by one of the defendants with a knife. As he escaped he was
pursued by them. They caught him and dropped him over a third-floor bal-
cony. Dismissing their appeal against convictions for attempted murder, the
Court of Appeal reiterated that the mental element of attempt to murder is
intent to kill, not merely to do grievous bodily harm. In rare cases would it
be necessary for a trial judge to enter into a "foresight" direction.[84] Where
such directions were necessary *Nedrick*[85] was to be followed and the phrase
"virtual certainty" best summed up the degree of foresight. However, it would
not be a misdirection to use "a very high degree of probability".

(3) Transferred Malice

If the defendant causes the death of the victim, even though he intended   **4-085**
another to die, the defendant will be guilty of murder, or manslaughter. This
is commonly called the doctrine of transferred malice.[86] In *R. v. Gore*[87] the
defendant mixed poison with her husband's medicine as a result of which he
died. The apothecary who had made the medicine drank it, in order to show

[76] [1975] A.C. 55.
[77] [1961] A.C. 290 at 327.
[78] [1985] A.C. 905 at 927B.
[79] [1975] A.C. 55 at 79.
[80] [1985] A.C. 905 at 927F.
[81] *R. v. Whybrow* (1951) 35 Cr.App.R. 141; *R. v. Donovan* (1850) 4 Cox C.C. 399; compare *R. v. Grimwood* [1962] 2 Q.B. 621.
[82] *R. v. O'Toole* [1987] Crim. L.R. 759.
[83] [1990] Crim. L.R. 44.
[84] *R. v. Fallon* [1994] Crim. L.R. 519.
[85] [1986] 1 W.L.R. 1025.
[86] On transferred malice, see *R. v. Latimer* (1886) 17 Q.B.D. 359.
[87] (1611) Co. Rep. 81; see also *R. v. Saunders and Archer* (1575) 75 E.R. 706; *R. v. Salisbury* (1533) 1 Plowd. 1000.

that it was, as he believed, safe. The defendant was found guilty of his murder.[88]

(4) KILLING A SUPPOSED CORPSE

4-086   If the defendant does an act or omission with *mens rea*, but this does not kill the victim, and then, thinking the victim to be dead, the defendant does another act which is in fact the cause of death, the defendant may still be liable for murder. This is so even though when he does the act which actually kills he does not have malice aforethought. The courts have achieved this by applying various devices, such as regarding all the acts as part of a preconceived plan,[89] or regarding them as a series of acts.[90]

4-087   The defendant may be liable for murder even if there has been an appreciable interval of time between the application of force and the eventual act causing death. In *R. v. LeBrun*[91] the defendant struck his wife but without intent to do really serious harm. He dragged her away to avoid detection but she died from bruising of the brain caused by a fracture of the skull when her head hit the pavement. The appellant was convicted of manslaughter and the appeal was dismissed.

4-088   In *Attorney-General's Reference No. 4 of 1980*[92] it was impossible to say which of two acts done by the defendant was the cause of death. Both acts could have caused death. The Court of Appeal held that only if the defendant had the mental element for manslaughter when he did both acts could he be guilty.

(5) JOINT ENTERPRISE

4-089   Where a person aids, abets, counsels or procures the death of another person, he may be charged with murder as if he were the principal offender (*i.e.* the actual killer).[93] It is not intended to discuss here all the rules on secondary participation, but to examine the particular problem of the mental element required to be proven to make the accomplice guilty of murder. Although it be argued that the accomplice should have to be shown to have the same state of mind as the principal, the few authorities which have taken this line (*R. v. Smith*[94] and *R. v. Barr*[95]) are against the weight of authority.[96]

4-090   The first point to establish is whether or not the defendants were acting

---

[88] For constructive manslaughter see *R. v. Mitchell* [1983] Q.B. 741; see also, for provocation, *R. v. Gross* (1913) 23 Cox C.C. 455. See also, *Att.-Gen.'s Reference No. 3 of 1994* [1996] 2 W.L.R. 412.
[89] *Meli v. R.* [1954] 1 W.L.R. 228; *R. v. Moore and Dorn* [1975] Crim. L.R. 229.
[90] *R. v. Church* [1966] 1 Q.B. 59.
[91] [1992] Q.B. 61.
[92] [1981] 1 W.L.R. 705.
[93] Accessories and Abetters Act 1861, s.8.
[94] [1988] Crim. L.R. 616.
[95] (1986) 88 Cr.App.R. 362.
[96] *R. v. Barr* was criticised and not followed in *R. v. Slack* [1989] 3 A.E.R. 90.

together, rather than independently. In that case they would be charged as joint principals.[97] This is most commonly established by showing that the defendants acted in a joint enterprise. Despite a few unconvincing analyses (*R. v. Wan and Chan*[98] and *R. v. Stewart and Schofield*[99]) it is now clear to the Court of Appeal that a joint enterprise is not a separate form of accessorial liability, but one way of establishing aiding and abetting.[1] Once the common purpose is established the next question to ask is whether the principal's act was within the scope of the agreement. The accomplice can be charged with any offence committed by the principal if that is within the range of offences contemplated by the accomplice.[2] That the accomplice is not liable for the consequences of any unauthorised act by the principal that goes beyond what is tacitly agreed was established by *R. v. Anderson and Morris*.[3] The authorisation may be express as well as implied,[4] although these may in some cases be practically indistinguishable.[5]

Must the accomplice have contemplated, or foreseen, the principal's offence as certain to occur? As indicated above, the answer is no. The accomplice may be guilty of the offence if he foresaw the killing as a possible result of the criminal enterprise. This was established by the Privy Council in *Chan Wing-Siu v. R.*[6] Three men armed with knives burst into a prostitute's flat intent on robbery. When her husband appeared from another room one of the men stabbed him. On appeal from the Hong Kong Court of Appeal, the Privy Council, dismissing the appeals, held that an accomplice may be guilty of murder even if he does not necessarily intend it, provided that he foresees the killing as a possible incident of the joint venture. If there is evidence that he did not contemplate the risk or that the risk of murder was too remote then the accomplice will not be guilty. **4-091**

The Court of Appeal has followed the Privy Council in a number of decisions. In *R. v. Ward*[7] the defendant, armed with scissors, participated in an assault on the victim. His co-accused held a knife which he used to kill the victim. The defendant argued that he had no intent to injure and did not know that the principal had a knife. On appeal against his conviction for murder, the Court of Appeal held that the decisions in *Moloney* and *Hancock* had not altered the law on joint enterprise. The decisions in *Anderson and Morris* and *Chan Wing-Siu* were approved. **4-092**

In *R. v. Slack*[8] the defendant went with another man to the flat of an elderly woman with intent to rob her. During the robbery his co-accused **4-093**

---

[97] *R. v. O'Rourke* [1994] Crim. L.R. 688; *R. v. Labbie* [1995] Crim. L.R. 317; *R. v. Petters and Parfitt* [1995] Crim. L.R. 501.
[98] [1995] Crim. L.R. 256.
[99] [1995] 1 Cr.App.R. 441.
[1] *R. v. Powell and Daniels* [1996] 1 Cr.App.R. 14.
[2] *D.P.P. for Northern Ireland v. Maxwell* [1978] 3 A.E.R. 1140; [1966] 2 Q.B. 110; *R. v. Mahmood* [1994] RTR 48; *R. v. Carberry* [1994] Crim. L.R. 446; *R. v. Pearman* [1996] 1 Cr.App.R. 24.
[3] [1966] 2 Q.B. 110.
[4] *Chan Wing-Siu v. R.* [1985] A.C. 168; see also *R. v. Bamborough* [1996] Crim. L.R. 745.
[5] *R. v. Wakely, Symonds and Holly* [1990] Crim. L.R. 119.
[6] [1985] A.C. 168.
[7] (1986) 85 Cr.App.R. 71.
[8] [1989] 3 A.E.R. 90.

told him to fetch a knife which he wanted to use to frighten the woman. In fact he used it to cut her throat. The defendant's appeal against conviction for murder was dismissed. Following *Ward* and approving *Chan Wing-Siu*, the Court of Appeal held that in a joint enterprise, if it was understood expressly or tacitly between the parties that if necessary one of them would kill or do serious harm as part of the enterprise, the accomplice can be guilty of murder.

4-094   The case which now provides the approved direction in *R. v. Hyde, Sussex and Collins*.[9] The deceased died in a brawl outside a public house. The case turned on the part played by the various defendants and their respective responsibilities within the joint enterprise. It was said by the Court of Appeal that there are two main types of joint enterprise: those where the object of the participants is to do some kind of physical injury and the other where the primary object is some other offence but where the victim is injured during the course of it. It is enough to affix the secondary party with responsibility that he realised that the person who commits the fatal assault might kill or intentionally inflict serious bodily harm, but the secondary party nonetheless continues to participate.

4-095   The Court of Appeal has followed this principle in *R. v. Roberts*[10] where the co-defendants went to the house of an old man with intent to rob, and during the struggle the victim died. It was held that *Hyde* was of general application and applied whether or not weapons are carried and whether the object of the enterprise is to cause physical injury or to do some other unlawful act. In *R. v. Rook*[11] the acts of one who gave assistance and encouragement to two others to kill a woman were held to be judged on the same principles as set out above.

4-096   The Privy Council has followed *Chan Wing Siu* in *Hui Chi-Ming v. R.*[12] In this case five men attacked and killed another. Two years after the trial of the first three defendants Hui Chi-Ming and another were tried and found guilty. However, in the unusual case of *R. v. McKechnie*[13] the Court of Appeal held that where the principal is provoked into killing, the joint enterprise is deemed to be at an end. This case was distinguished without reasons being given in *R. v. Pearson*.[14] The Court of Appeal has applied these principles to attempted murder.[15] The Court of Appeal reviewed the authorities and reiterated its view in *Hyde* in *R. v. Powell and Daniels*.[16]

[9] [1991] 1 Q.B. 134.
[10] (1993) 96 Cr.App.R. 291.
[11] (1993) 97 Cr.App.R. 327; followed in *R. v. Wan and Chan* [1995] Crim. L.R. 256; see also *R. v. Baker* [1994] Crim. L.R. 444.
[12] [1992] 1 A.C. 34.
[13] (1991) 94 Cr.App.R. 51.
[14] [1992] Crim. L.R. 193.
[15] *R. v. O'Brien* [1995] 2 Cr.App.R. 649.
[16] [1996] 1 Cr.App.R. 14.

VII. SOLICITATION TO MURDER

(1) DEFINITION

Section 4 of the Offences Against the Person Act 1861, as amended by   4–097
section 5(10) of the Criminal Law Act 1977 provides that:

> "Whosoever shall solicit, encourage, persuade or endeavour to persuade, or shall
> propose to any person, to murder any other person, whether he be a subject of
> her Majesty or not, and whether he be within the Queen's dominions or not,
> shall be guilty of a misdemeanour, and being convicted thereof shall be liable to
> imprisonment for life."

(2) MODE OF TRIAL AND PUNISHMENT

The maximum penalty for this offence is life imprisonment.   4–098

(3) ELEMENT OF THE OFFENCE

Publication of an article in a newspaper may be within the offence even it   4–099
if is not addressed to any particular persons.[17]

However, it must be shown that the mind of the person alleged to be sol-   4–100
icited has been reached, though not necessarily affected.[18]

Various factors including the language used, occasion of use, persons to   4–101
whom and circumstances in which said, are of importance.[19]

The person to be murdered need not be named by the defendant, provided   4–102
the class is sufficiently well-defined.[20] This person need not be a British citizen, nor be in the United Kingdom or its dominions. The defendant may be
a British citizen or an alien.

Where a pregnant woman was solicited to murder her child at birth, and it   4–103
was subsequently born alive, this was held to be conduct within the scope of
section 4.[21]

Incitement to commit the offence of solicitation to murder was recently   4–104
considered in *R. v. Evans*.[22]

---

[17] *R. v. Most* (1881) 7 Q.B.D. 244.
[18] *R. v. Krause* (1902) 66 J.P. 121.
[19] *R. v. Diamond* (1920) 84 J.P. 211.
[20] *R. v. Antonelli* (1905) 70 J.P. 4.
[21] *R. v. Shephard* [1919] 2 K.B. 125.
[22] [1986] Crim. L.R. 470.

CHAPTER 5

MANSLAUGHTER

I. INTRODUCTION

There is only one crime of manslaughter in law, but it is commonly   **5–001**
regarded as being divided into two categories—voluntary and involuntary.

Voluntary manslaughter is where all of the elements of murder, including   **5–002**
the mental element, are present, but the conviction is reduced to manslaughter
for one of the following reasons:
  (a) provocation;
  (b) diminished responsibility;
  (c) the killing was carried out in pursuance of a suicide pact.

Provocation and diminished responsibility are considered in this chapter;   **5–003**
killing in pursuance of a suicide pact is dealt with in Chapter 6.

Involuntary manslaughter can itself be sub-divided into two categories—   **5–004**
constructive (or unlawful act) manslaughter and reckless manslaughter. The
difference between involuntary manslaughter and murder lies in the mental
element, *i.e.* the absence of malice aforethought in involuntary manslaughter.[1]
The *actus reus* of the two offences is, however, the same and this is fully
covered in Chapter 4. This chapter will concentrate on the mental element.

II. MODE OF TRIAL AND PUNISHMENT

(1) MODE OF TRIAL

Manslaughter is a Class 2 common law offence triable only on indictment.   **5–005**
For the extended jurisdiction to try offences of homicide which amount to
war crimes, see Chapter 4.

---

[1] *R. v. Taylor* (1834) 2 Lew. 215.

185

(2) PUNISHMENT

5-006   Manslaughter carries a maximum sentence of life imprisonment.[2] A fine may be imposed in addition to or in lieu of the sentence of imprisonment.[3] It should be noted that the judge cannot recommend a minimum period to be served in prison.[4]

(3) ALTERNATIVE VERDICT

5-007   Child destruction is an alternative verdict in appropriate cases on a charge of manslaughter.[5]

III. VOLUNTARY MANSLAUGHTER: PROVOCATION

(1) DEFINITION

5-008   The classic common law definition of provocation is that given by Devlin J. in *R. v. Duffy*[6]:

> "Provocation is some act, or series of acts, done by the dead man to the accused which would cause in any reasonable person, and actually causes in the accused, a sudden and temporary loss of self-control, rendering the accused so subject to passion as to make him or her for the moment not the master of his mind."

This definition has been altered, but not completely superseded, by section 3 of the Homicide Act 1957, which provides as follows:

> "Where on a charge of murder there is evidence on which the jury can find that the person charged was provoked (whether by things done or by things said or by both together) to lose his self-control, the question whether the provocation was enough to make a reasonable man do as he did shall be left to be determined by the jury; and in determining that question the jury shall take into account everything both done and said according to the effect which, in their opinion, it would have on a reasonable man."

5-009   It has been suggested by the Court of Appeal that section 3 lays down the precise test for provocation[7] but contrary authority holds that the common law test is still applicable.[8] The decision of the House of Lords in *R. v. Camplin*[9] accepts the latter view. In *R. v. Brown*[10] the Court of Appeal stated that there should be a two-stage approach to the provocation issue: it must be asked (a) whether the defendant was in fact provoked and (b) whether the

---

[2] s.5 of the Offences Against the Person Act 1861 as modified by s.1(1) of the Criminal Justice Act 1948.
[3] Powers of Criminal Courts Act 1973, s.30(1).
[4] *R. v. Flemming* (1973) 57 Cr.App.R. 524.
[5] Infant Life Preservation Act 1929.
[6] [1949] 1 A.E.R. 932n.
[7] *R. v. Brown* (1972) 56 Cr.App.R. 564.
[8] *R. v. Whitfield* (1976) 63 Cr.App.R. 39.
[9] [1978] A.C. 705.
[10] n. 7 above; see also *R. v. Phillips* [1969] A.C. 137.

provocation might have provoked a reasonable man to act as the defendant did.

(2) AVAILABILITY OF THE DEFENCE

The defence of provocation is only available on a charge of murder.[11] The effect of a successful defence is to reduce the conviction from murder to manslaughter.[12] In *Holmes v. Director of Public Prosecutions*,[13] the House of Lords explained that: 5–010

> "In the case of lesser crimes, provocation does not alter the nature of the offence at all, but it is allowed for in the sentence. In the case of felonious homicide, the law has to reconcile respect for the sanctity of human life with recognition of the effect of provocation on human frailty."

Although cases from the nineteenth century[14] are to the effect that provocation was a defence to attempted murder, doubts have been expressed whether the defence can be used on such a charge. In *R. v. Bruzas*[15] the Court of Appeal rejected the availability of the defence on a charge of attempt to murder. It is arguable that, as the defendant would be convicted of manslaughter if he completed the act, it would be logical that his attempt to kill should be described as attempted manslaughter.   5–011

However, it should be noted that even if the defendant were to be convicted of attempted murder, the mandatory penalty of life imprisonment for the full offence would not apply. Thus, if, as may be argued, one of the purposes of the defence of provocation is to release the judge from the mandatory requirement of imposing a sentence of life imprisonment, then no injustice is suffered by the defendant.   5–012

The judge must explain to the jury that the issue of provocation should be considered only when the jury is sure that all the elements of murder, including the mental element, have been made out by the prosecution.[16]   5–013

Where the doctrine of transferred malice applies on a murder charge, the defence of provocation may still be available; in other words, the defence is transferred, as well as the "malice".[17]   5–014

---

[11] *R. v. Cunningham* (1959) 43 Cr.App.R. 79 (charge of malicious wounding).

[12] *R. v. Camplin* [1978] A.C. 705 at 713D.

[13] [1946] A.C. 588 at 601.

[14] *R. v. Thompson* (1825) 1 Moo. 80; *R. v. Bourne* (1831) 5 C. & P. 120; *R. v. Beeson* (1835) 7 C. & P. 142; *R. v. Thomas* (1835) 7 C. & P. 817; *R. v. Hagan* (1837) 8 C. & P. 167.

[15] [1972] Crim. L.R. 367.

[16] *Lee Chun Chuen v. R.* [1963] A.C. 220 at 227 (followed in *R. v. Martindale* (1965) 50 Cr.App.R. 273) explaining the error of dicta in *Holmes v. D.P.P.* [1946] A.C. 588 to the effect that provocation negatives malice. See, too, *R. v. Ali* [1989] Crim. L.R. 736. Evidence of provocation is, of course, relevant at the earlier stage when the jury must decide whether the defendant had the mental element for murder—Criminal Justice Act 1967, s.8 and *R. v. Ives* (1969) 53 Cr.App.R. 474. The text assumes that the defendant has been found to have the requisite mental element but is now using the defence of provocation to reduce his conviction.

[17] *R. v. Gross* (1913) 23 Cox C.C. 455; *R. v. Porritt* (1961) 45 Cr.App.R. 348 (D aimed at his stepfather's attacker and killed his stepfather).

(3) BURDEN OF PROOF

5-015   The burden of proof is on the prosecution to show the absence of provocation[18]; the defendant carries only an evidential burden.[19] This is to be contrasted with diminished responsibility where the defendant carries the legal
burden of proof. It is necessary, therefore, for the defendant to point to material of relevance in the prosecution case, or to adduce evidence of his own, in
order to discharge the evidential burden.

(4) RAISING THE PLEA

5-016   Section 3 states that where there is evidence on which the jury can find that
the defendant was provoked to lose his self-control, the question whether this
was enough to make a reasonable man do as he did shall be left to be determined by the jury. Thus, the judge must leave the issue of provocation to the
jury if there is some evidence to support the defence,[20] however slight this
might appear to be to the judge.[21] This does not require the judge to put
before the jury strained or implausible inferences for the purpose of creating
a defence for which there is no basis.[22]

5-017   The issue of provocation must be left to the opinion of the jury even if, in
the opinion of the judge, it is unlikely that a reasonable person would have
lost his self-control.[23] If the issue is not left to the jury, then it was unusual
for the proviso to be applied on appeal.[24] In the direction the judge must deal
with all the requirements of provocation.[25]

5-018   The judge is under a duty to raise the issue even where the defence prefers
not to on the grounds that to do so would be inconsistent with the primary
defence. This will be the case where, for example, the defendant is relying on
self-defence,[26] accident or diminished responsibility,[27] alibi or a general denial
that the defence had caused the death or had the requisite intent.[28] Although

---

[18] *R. v. McPherson* (1957) 41 Cr.App.R. 213.
[19] *Lee Chun Chuen* [1963] A.C. 220; *R. v. Ibrams* (1982) 74 Cr.App.R. 154.
[20] *Camplin* [1978] A.C. 705 at 716D; *R. v. Rossiter* (1992) 95 Cr.App.R. 326; *R. v. Cambridge*
(1994) 99 Cr.App.R. 142; *R. v. Stewart* [1996] 1 Cr.App.R. 229; *R. v. Dhillan* [1997] Crim.
L.R. 295.
[21] *R. v. Newell* [1989] Crim. L.R. 906; *R. v. Johnson* (1989) 89 Cr.App.R. 148; *R. v. Acott* (H.L.)
[1997] Crim. L.R. 515.
[22] *R. v. Walch* [1993] Crim. L.R. 714; *R. v. Wellington* [1993] Crim. L.R. 616; generally on the
judge leaving manslaughter to the jury see *R. v. Williams* (1993) 99 Cr.App.R. 163.
[23] *R. v. Gilbert* (1978) 66 Cr.App.R. 237 (on the facts, held that it should not have been left).
See also *Holmes*; *Lee Chun Chuen* and *R. v. Coker* (1989) Crim. L.R. 740.
[24] *R. v. Whitfield* (1976) 63 Cr.App.R. 39; *R. v. Burgess and McLean* [1995] Crim.L.R. 425.
[25] *R. v. Jones* [1987] Crim. L.R. 701; *R. v. Stewart* [1996] 1 Cr.App.R. 229; *R. v. Cox* [1995] 2
Cr.App.R. 513.
[26] *Mancini v. D.P.P.* [1942] A.C. 1; *Porritt* (1961) 45 Cr.App.R. 348; *R. v. Cascoe* (1970) 54
Cr.App.R. 401; *R. v. Johnson* (1989) 89 Cr.App.R. 148; *R. v. Sawyer* [1989] Crim. L.R. 831;
R. v. Baille [1995] 2 Cr.App.R. 31.
[27] *R. v. Hopper* [1915] 2 K.B. 435; *R. v. Rossiter* (1992) 95 Cr.App.R. 326; *R. v. Stewart* [1996]
1 Cr.App.R. 229; *R. v. Thornton (No. 2)* [1996] 2 All E.R. 1023.
[28] *R. v. Burke* [1987] Crim. L.R. 336; *R. v. Cambridge* (1994) 99 Cr.App.R. 142; *R. v. Burgess
and McLean* [1995] Crim. L.R. 425.

the defence may express the opinion that a direction would be inappropriate, the decision rests with the judge.[29]

Where the defendant relies on self-defence, there will often be evidence   5-019
which justifies consideration of provocation. The defendant will encounter
tactical problems when deciding whether or not to use the defence as an
alternative to provocation.[30] The issue must be put to the jury, even if the
defendant has not raised it. In *R. v. Cox*[31] the Court of Appeal spelt out the
new duties of counsel in such a case. Both have an obligation to the court to
point out to the judge any evidence which might raise the issue of provocation
and invite him to consider whether there could be such a finding on the facts,
and, if so, that it is his duty to direct the jury accordingly.

Where the defendant pleads diminished responsibility, the psychiatric evi-   5-020
dence used on that plea can be admitted to show that the defendant was more
likely to lose his self-control than others. However it cannot be used when the
jury assesses the objective test. It should be noted that, although the judge
can leave provocation to the jury if not raised by the defence, the defendant
must himself plead diminished responsibility if he wishes this issue to be put
to the jury.[32]

(5) LOSS OF SELF-CONTROL DUE TO PROVOCATION

The first question, as part of the two-stage approach, as posed in *Brown*,[33]   5-021
asks whether the defendant was provoked into losing his self-control. It is a
question of fact whether the causal relationship is established between the
provocation and the defendant's response.

If there is evidence that the killing was premeditated this will show that the   5-022
response was not sudden and temporary as would evidence of a desire for
revenge. In *R. v. Ibrams and Gregory*[34] the two defendants and a young woman
had, over a period of time, suffered provocation by the victim. Three days
after the last incident of provocation, and fearing a repetition in a week's time,
the three agreed a plan. The victim was to be lured into a room by the woman
and the two men were then to enter the room and attack the man. Four days
later the plan was carried out, the victim dying in the attack. The defendants
were convicted of murder. The Court of Appeal held that the trial judge had
acted correctly in not leaving the defence of provocation to the jury. The court
emphasised that it was necessary to show the "sudden and temporary loss of
self-control" referred to by Devlin J. in *Duffy*.[35]

---

[29] *Burgess and McLean* [1995] Crim. L.R. 425.
[30] *Bullard v. R.* [1957] A.C. 635; *Lee Chun Chuen* [1963] A.C. 220; *Rolle v. R.* [1965] 1 W.L.R.
1341.
[31] *R. v. Cox* [1995] 2 Cr.App.R. 513.
[32] *R. v. Campbell* (1987) 84 Cr.App.R. 255.
[33] (1972) 56 Cr.App.R. 564; see para. 5–009 above.
[34] (1982) 74 Cr.App.R. 154; *R. v. Duffy* [1949] 1 All E.R. 932n (para. 5–008 above) and see the
trial judge's decision in *R. v. Davies* (1975) 60 Cr.App.R. 253 described by the Court of Appeal
as "over lenient".
[35] See para. 5–008 above and *R. v. Cocker* [1989] Crim. L.R. 740.

5–023   It is clear from *R. v. Ahluwalia*[36] that lapse of time—the so-called "slow-burn" factor—does not necessarily prevent use of the defence of provocation, but the longer the delay, the more likely it is that prosecution would be able to negative the plea. Lack of immediacy of reaction may be illustrated by evidence that the defendant went to fetch a weapon.[37] If, however, the defendant is carrying a weapon but it can be established that he had no intent to use it before the incident of provocation, then the defence of provocation can still be raised.[38] Formerly this immediacy of reaction was expressed in the supposed test of whether there had been any "cooling time" between the provocation and the killing.[39]

5–024   The final incident which triggers the defendant's response may, although minor in itself, re-open previous provocation. In *R. v. Davies*[40] the defendant's wife had been having an adulterous affair with another man. The defendant and his wife had been apart for three months when, on the day in question, he saw her coming out of a building to meet her lover. The defendant shot and killed his wife. Although the defendant's conviction for murder was upheld by the Court of Appeal, it was clear that the incident of the wife meeting her lover could revive the provocation constituted by the earlier acts of adultery. However, in this case the actual meeting between his wife and the lover could itself have been provocation when it was observed by the defendant. Cumulative acts, that is to say, acts carried out over a period of time, may be taken together and constitute the provocation.[41]

5–025   Cases of family killings involving often extensive periods of domestic violence have brought into focus the difficulty in applying the traditional test of loss of self-control. The case of *R. v. Ahluwalia*[42] should be contrasted with *R. v. Thornton*,[43] where the defendant went to the kitchen, sharpened a knife and returned to stab her husband who was lying on the couch. The court emphasized that, although past conduct in relation to the appellant was relevant, it was still essential to establish that, at the time of the killing, there had been a sudden loss of self-control. The cases had not changed the principle established by section 3 of the Homicide Act 1957. In this case the defence had been based on diminished responsibility, but the judge left the question of provocation to the jury as an alternative. In *R. v. Pearson*[44] two brothers killed their father. The younger brother lived mainly with the father and had

---

[36] *R. v. Ahluwalia* (1993) 96 Cr.App.R. 133.
[37] *R. v. Hayward* (1833) 6 C. & P. 157; *R. v. Lynch* (1832) 5 C. & P. 324; *R. v. Eagle* (1862) 2 F. & F. 827; *cf. R. v. Fisher* (1837) 8 C. & P. 182.
[38] *R. v. Fantle* [1958] Crim. L.R. 782.
[39] *R. v. Albis* (1913) 9 Cr.App.R. 158; *R. v. Hall* (1928) 21 Cr.App.R. 48; *Kwaku Mensah* [1946] A.C. 93; *R. v. Hayward* (1833) 6 C. & P. 157; *R. v. Thomas* (1837) 7 C. & P. 211; *R. v. Jervis* (1833) 6 C. & P. 156.
[40] [1975] Q.B. 691; see also *Duffy* [1949] 1 All E.R. 932n; *R. v. Simpson* [1957] Crim. L.R. 815; *R. v. Fantle* [1959] Crim. L.R. 584; note that in *Ibrams* the court suggested that even in a series of incidents the last act must constitute provocation.
[41] See M. Wasik's article [1982] Crim. L.R. 29.
[42] *R. v. Ahluwalia* (1993) 96 Cr.App.R. 133.
[43] *R. v. Thornton* (1993) 96 Cr.App.R. 112; reiterated in *R. v. Thornton (No. 2)* [1996] 2 All E.R. 1023.
[44] *R. v. Pearson* [1992] Crim. L.R. 193.

been subjected to violence and abuse over many years. The court held that events over the previous eight years were relevant to the issue of provocation.

The defendant cannot, in the absence of mental illness, adduce psychiatric evidence that he was a person who was likely to have been provoked.[45] The decision in *R. v. Roberts*[46] suggests that although medical evidence may assist on this issue, the jury would need to exclude that evidence of excitability when examining the second, objective, stage of the provocation test.

5-026

(6) SELF-INDUCED PROVOCATION

In *Edwards v. R.*[47] the Privy Council held that self-induced provocation cannot be taken into account, unless the victim's response to the defendant's conduct is excessive. The defendant arranged to meet a man with the intention of blackmailing him. The man attacked the defendant who, in the ensuing struggle, removed the knife from the attacker's grasp and killed him. The Privy Council held that the blackmailer could not argue that the predictable, even though violent, response of the victim constituted provocation. However, as the victim's response was extreme, then the defendant could use this reaction as the basis of the defence of provocation. The defendant's appeal was allowed and his conviction for murder reduced to manslaughter.

5-027

The Court of Appeal had the opportunity to consider this aspect of provocation in *R. v. Whitfield*.[48] The defendant had pestered his wife causing her to insult him. The court confirmed that the trial judge had been justified in withdrawing the issue of provocation from the jury on the ground that the victim's response was not excessive.

5-028

In *R. v. Johnson*[49] the defendant had been drinking in a club. He threatened the deceased and his girlfriend. The defendant had been called a "white nigger" by a woman in the club. The deceased poured beer over the defendant and held him against a wall. The woman started to pull at the defendant's hair. As the deceased dropped the glass which he was holding, the defendant produced a knife and stabbed the deceased. In his defence at his trial for murder, the defendant said that he had acted in fear of being "glassed", that is, struck by the deceased with the glass he was holding. This had happened to the defendant before. The defence of self-defence was clearly rejected by the jury as a verdict of murder was returned.

5-029

The Court of Appeal allowed the defendant's appeal, in which he submitted that the issue of provocation should have been left to the jury. There was sufficient evidence of provocation, the court decided, to be left to the jury. Whether or not there were elements in the appellant's conduct which justified the conclusion that he had induced the deceased to react in the way he did made no difference to this point. This approach is clearly consistent with

5-030

---

[45] *R. v. Turner* [1975] Q.B. 834.
[46] [1989] Crim. L.R. 122.
[47] [1973] A.C. 648; see also *Leung Ping Fat* [1973] H.K.L.J. 342.
[48] (1976) 63 Cr.App.R. 39.
[49] [1989] 2 A.E.R. 839; see also *R. v. Richens* (1993) 98 Cr.App.R. 43; *R. v. Baille* [1995] Crim. L.R. 39; *R. v. Morhall* [1996] 1 A.C. 90.

section 3 of the Homicide Act, as interpreted in *Camplin*.[50] The approach of the Privy Council in *Edwards*, which was referred to by the Court of Appeal, cannot stand in the light of this decision, although the court could not, of course, overrule it. All the evidence of provocation, including the predictable results of the defendant's conduct, must be put before the jury. It is suggested that if the defendant deliberately set out to provoke a response from the victim in order to obtain provocation, the "Dutch courage" principle of *Attorney-General v. Gallagher*[51] could be adopted to prevent the defence being raised.

(7) THE REASONABLE MAN

5-031   The second question posed in *Brown* is whether the provocation was enough to make a reasonable man do as the defendant did. This is a question for the jury to answer.[52] The judge must remind the jury of the qualities of the reasonable man, as they were explained in *Camplin*[53]:

"[The reasonable man is] an ordinary person of either sex, not exceptionally excitable or pugnacious, but possessed of such powers of self-control as everyone is entitled to expect that his fellow citizens will exercise in society as it is today."

5-032   Lord Diplock set out a model direction to the jury in the following terms[54]:

"A proper direction to a jury on the question left to their exclusive determination by section 3 of the Homicide Act 1957 would be on the following lines. The judge should state what the question is using the very words of the section. He then explains to them that the reasonable man referred to in the question is a person having the power of self-control to be expected of an ordinary person of the sex and age of the accused, but in other respects sharing such of the accused's characteristics as they think would affect the gravity of the provocation to him; and that the question is not merely whether such a person would in like circumstances be provoked to lose his self-control but would also react to the provocation as the accused did."

5-033   The judge will need to remind the jury of any material characteristics, although it is for the jury to decide which characteristics to take into account. The judge does not have to repeat the model direction in its exact terms.[55] The defendant may not adduce evidence of how reasonable people would behave.[56]

5-034   The level of self-control required is that of an ordinary person of the same

---

[50] [1978] A.C. 705.
[51] [1963] A.C. 349. See para. 4–022 above.
[52] *R. v. Phillips* [1969] 2 A.C. 130; *R. v. Ives* [1970] 1 Q.B. 208; in *R. v. Cook* [1982] Crim. L.R. 670 the pathologist's evidence was treated as expert opinion on the question of provocation and was held to be a material irregularity.
[53] [1978] A.C. 705 at 717A. The reasonable man appeared in *R. v. Welsh* (1869) 11 Cox C.C. 336 and received the approval of the Court of Appeal in *R. v. Lesbini* [1914] 3 K.B. 116 *cf.* the reasonable man in duress, *R. v. Graham* [1982] 1 W.L.R. 294 and *R. v. Bowen* [1996] Crim. L.R. 577.
[54] [1978] A.C. 705 at 718E.
[55] *R. v. Burke* [1987] Crim. L.R. 336.
[56] *R. v. Camplin* [1978] A.C. 705 at 716E.

sex and age[57] as the defendant. It is the level of self-control to be expected of such a person when sober.[58] This requirement works against those defendants who are exceptionally excitable, pugnacious or ill-tempered.[59] Lord Simon has said that it matters not whether the characteristics are idiosyncratic, environmental or ethnic.[60]

Other characteristics of the defendant may be relevant and the reasonable man will be endowed with them in so far as they affect the gravity of the provocation to the defendant.[61] In *Camplin* the defendant was a 15-year-old boy. He went to the flat of a middle-aged Pakistani man. The defendant gave evidence that the man had buggered him, despite his resistance, and had then laughed at him. The defendant lost his self-control, picked up a chapati pan, struck and killed his assailant. The boy was convicted of murder, but appealed successfully to the Court of Appeal. The House of Lords rejected the prosecutor's appeal. The House gave examples of relevant characteristics: race,[62] physical disability,[63] impotence,[64] some shameful incident in the defendant's past,[65] ethnic origin,[66] sex.[67] These can be illustrated by reference to the facts of cases decided before *Camplin*, though it should be noted that the cases are not necessarily still authority on the law of provocation. In *R. v. Raney*[68] a one-legged man had his crutch knocked away. This physical disability would now be a relevant characteristic. In *Bedder v. Director of Public Prosecutions*[69] the defendant killed a prostitute who taunted him about his sexual impotence when he failed in his efforts to have intercourse with her. The fact of impotence would not be considered a relevant characteristic.

5-035

The initial approach to the classification of the types of characteristic which could be relevant was set out in the Court of Appeal decision in *R. v. Newell*.[70] The defendant, a chronic alcoholic, killed the deceased by striking him repeatedly with a glass ashtray after the deceased had made rude remarks about the defendant's former girlfriend. The trial judge did not make any reference to the question of chronic alcoholism in his summing up. The Court of Appeal approved this omission because in this case the alcoholism had no connection with the provocation. It was not decided whether or not alcoholism could constitute a characteristic in an appropriate case. Transient states, such as depression, grief, and drug overdoses, were held to be irrelevant. It was held

5-036

---

[57] *R. v. Raven* [1982] Crim. L.R. 51; see, pre-Homicide Act, to the contrary *R. v. Alexander* (1913) 9 Cr.App.R.139. The limits of this are seen in *R. v. Ali* [1989] Crim. L.R. 736.
[58] *R. v. McCarthy* [1954] 2 Q.B. 105, approved in *Camplin*.
[59] *Mancini v. D.P.P.* [1942] A.C. 1 approved in *Camplin*.
[60] [1978] A.C. 705 at 726F.
[61] The judge must not direct the jury on the relevant characteristics—*Bedder v. D.P.P.* (1954) 38 Cr.App.R. 133 is wrong on this point.
[62] [1978] A.C. 705 at 717D, 726C.
[63] *ibid.* at pp. 717D, 726D.
[64] *ibid.* at p. 720H.
[65] *ibid.* at p. 717D.
[66] *ibid.* at p. 721D.
[67] *ibid.* at pp. 721F, 724E.
[68] (1942) 29 Cr.App.R. 14.
[69] (1954) 38 Cr.App.R. 133.
[70] (1980) 71 Cr.App.R. 331.

that there must be some connection between the provoking words or conduct and the characteristic which is claimed to be relevant[71]:

> "The characteristic must be something definite and of sufficient significance to make the offender a different person from the ordinary run of mankind, and have also a sufficient degree of permanence to warrant its being regarded as constituting part of the individual's character or personality . . .Moreover, there must be some real connection between the nature of the provocation and the particular characteristic of the offender by which it is sought to modify the ordinary man test."

This statement was based on New Zealand authority which required that the characteristic have a degree of permanence. Since that authority has now changed, this requirement should not now be considered to be part of the test.[72]

5-037   The House of Lords has now considered the issue of those characteristics of the defendant which should be attributed to the reasonable man in *R. v. Morhall*.[73] The defendant had spent the day sniffing glue. The deceased had on several occasions during the day chided the defendant about his glue-sniffing habit. A fight ensued in which the deceased was fatally stabbed. Lord Goff explained that the function of the reasonable (Lord Goff preferred "ordinary") man test is to introduce as a matter of policy a standard of self-control which has to be complied with if provocation is to be established in law. This cannot be modified to take account of intoxication through alcohol or drugs. However, the English cases are not clear on the question of the relevance of other mental or emotional characteristics such as immaturity or eccentricity, some cases permitting their inclusion.[74] In *Luc Thiet-thuan v. R.*[75] the Privy Council has held there is no basis for mental infirmity which reduces self-control to be included as a characteristic, except in where taunts or abuse constitute the provocative act.

5-038   There will be cases where it is necessary to direct the jury as to the relevance of characteristics of the defendant or even circumstances in which he is placed at the relevant time, such as his past history, including his relationship with the deceased. Although it has been held that battered woman syndrome might now be recognised as a relevant characteristic (when established on the evidence),[76] it is suggested that this can only be the case if the provocation is aimed at that characteristic. A better plea in such circumstances would be diminished responsibility. It should be noted that the characteristic can be a discreditable one, *e.g.* a convicted sex offender taunted in relation to the offence. Thus Morhall's addiction to glue sniffing should have been taken into account as the taunt was aimed at that characteristic.

---

[71] (1980) 71 Cr.App.R. 33.
[72] Lord Goff in *R. v. Morhall* [1996] 1 A.C. 90 referring to *R. v. McCarthy* [1992] 2 N.Z.L.R. 550 and previously *R. v. McGregor* (1962) N.Z.L.R. 1069.
[73] [1996] 1 A.C. 90.
[74] *R. v. Humphreys* [1995] 4 A.E.R. 1008; *R. v. Dryden* [1995] 4 A.E.R. 987.
[75] *Luc Thiet-thuan v. R.* [1996] 2 A.E.R. 1033; for Court of Appeal reaction see *R. v. Campbell (No. 2)* [1997] Crim. L.R. 227.
[76] *R. v. Ahluwalia* (1993) 96 Cr.App.R. 133; *R. v. Thornton (No. 2)* [1996] 2 A.E.R. 1023.

(8) What Constitutes Provocation?

It is no longer for the judge to explain what constitutes provocation.[77] **5–039**
Provocation can be anything said or done by either the victim or a third
party, to either the defendant or a third party, including acts provoked by the
defendant's own conduct. Formerly, adultery would only be provocation if it
were seen by the aggrieved spouse. However, in *Holmes v. Director of Public
Prosecutions*[78] it was said *obiter* that, although mere words, such as an insult,
would not be provocation, words of "a most extreme and exceptional character" could constitute provocation where, for example, they were of a violently
provocative character. That words could be provocation was made clear in the
Homicide Act. Thus, for example, confessions of adultery can now constitute
provocation.[79]

The act of provocation need not be unlawful. This is illustrated by *R. v.* **5–040**
Doughty.[80] The defendant covered his 17-day-old child with a cushion and
knelt on him to stop him screaming. The child died as a result. The Court of
Appeal allowed the defendant's appeal against his conviction for murder and
substituted a conviction for manslaughter. The crying of the baby was held to
be capable of being provocation.

Mere circumstances caused by nature would not be enough, since the sec- **5–041**
tion impliedly requires something said or done by another human being. If
the circumstances are caused by a human being, then they could come within
the proposition that provocation can be given by a third party. Thus, loss of
self-control at finding one's house flooded by rainwater would not excuse a
killing, but finding the property damaged by vandals might.

A third party may offer the provocation as in the case of *R. v. Davies*.[81] The **5–042**
object of the provocative incident need not be the defendant, but may be some
third party.[82]

(9) Relationship Between the Provocation and the Response

There was formerly a rule of law in *Mancini v. Director of Public Pros-* **5–043**
ecutions[83] that the relationship between the provocation and the defendant's
response must be reasonable:

---

[77] [1978] A.C. 705 at 716G.
[78] [1946] A.C. 588.
[79] [1978] A.C. 705 at 716C.
[80] (1986) 83 Cr.App.R. 319; formerly in *Mawgridge* (1707) 84 E.R. 1107 it had been said that
lawful blows could not be provocation.
[81] [1975] Q.B. 691; *cf. R. v. Twine* [1967] Crim. L.R. 710, and see *R. v. Pearson* [1992] Crim.
L.R. 193.
[82] Pre–Homicide Act cases where exceptions were made include *Mawgridge* (1707) 84 E.R. 1107
(sight of a friend being beaten or a citizen being unlawfully deprived of his liberty); *R. v. Fisher*
(1837) 8 C. & P. 132 (rape of wife): *R. v. Harrington* (1886) 10 Cox C.C. 370; *R. v. Porritt*
(1961) 45 Cr.App.R. 348 (provocation aimed at stepfather).
[83] [1942] A.C. 1.

> "The mode of resentment must bear a reasonable relationship to the provocation if the offence is to be reduced to manslaughter."

In *Phillips v. R.*[84] the Privy Council stated:

> "That there is no intermediate stage between icy detachment and going berserk is false."

However, the rule in *Mancini* is now abrogated by section 3 and it is for the jury[85] to decide whether the reasonable man would have retaliated in the same way as the defendant did.

(10) MISTAKE OF FACT

5-044   Where the defendant has made a mistake as to the facts which constitute the provocation, it has been held that the mistake must be reasonable.[86] However, recent developments in the law of mistake suggest that now such mistakes need only be honestly made.[87] Mistakes caused by self-induced intoxication were once held to be relevant even if unreasonable.[88] It is now clear that drunken mistakes cannot be relied on by the defendant.[89]

IV. DIMINISHED RESPONSIBILITY

(1) DEFINITION

5-045   The Homicide Act 1957 introduced the concept of diminished responsibility into English law.[90] The definition of diminished responsibility is set out in section 2(1) of the Act:

> "Where a person kills or is a party to the killing of another, he shall not be convicted of murder if he was suffering from such abnormality of mind (whether arising from a condition of arrested or retarded development of mind or any inherent causes or induced by disease or injury) as substantially impaired his mental responsibility for his acts and omissions in doing or being a party to the killing."

(2) AVAILABILITY OF THE DEFENCE

5-046   It is only possible to plead diminished responsibility on a charge of murder.[91] If the plea is successful the defendant will only be convicted of

---

[84] [1969] 2 A.C. 130; in *R. v. Walker* [1969] 1 W.L.R. 311 it was suggested, *obiter* that the rule was abolished by s.3.
[85] [1978] A.C. 705 at 718. See *R. v. Clarke* [1991] Crim. L.R. 383.
[86] *R. v. Brown* (1776) 1 Leach. 148.
[87] *Beckford v. The Queen* [1988] A.C. 130.
[88] *R. v. Letenock* (1917) 12 Cr.App.R. 221; see also *R. v. Wardrope* [1960] Crim. L.R. 770; *R. v. Raney* (1942) 29 Cr.App.R. 14.
[89] *R. v. O'Grady* [1987] 3 W.L.R. 221.
[90] The defence originated in Scotland in the decision of *H.M. Advocate v. Dingwall* (1867) 5 Irv. 466.
[91] Homicide Act 1957, s.2(1).

manslaughter.[92] By section 2(4) of the Homicide Act 1957 the verdict of not guilty of murder but guilty of manslaughter by reason of diminished responsibility does not affect the liability of the co-accused to be convicted of murder if that co-accused participated with the requisite intent (including realisation that really serious injury might be inflicted). If, for example, the defendant who kills in the course of an attack is found to be suffering from diminished responsibility, his co-accused could be convicted of murder even though he did not inflict the fatal injury.

(3) BURDEN OF PROOF

Unlike provocation, the burden of proof of diminished responsibility is on the defendant[93] and the defence must, as usual, be established on the balance of probabilities.[94] As with provocation, the defendant will have been found to have the requisite intent for murder before diminished responsibility is considered by the jury. "A man may know what he is doing and intend to do it and yet suffer from such abnormality of mind as substantially impairs his mental responsibility."[95]

5-047

(4) RAISING THE PLEA

Although it will usually be the defendant who raises the plea, it is possible for the prosecution to do so where the defendant raises the defence of insanity. Conversely, if the defendant raises diminished responsibility this risks the possibility that the prosecution may choose to raise the issue of insanity. These seemingly illogical positions, whereby the prosecution is raising matters technically of acquittal, are the result of section 6 of the Criminal Procedure (Insanity) Act 1964. The text of the section is as follows:

5-048

"Where on a trial for murder the accused contends—
  (a) that at the time of the alleged offence he was insane so as not to be responsible according to law for his actions; or
  (b) that at the time he was suffering from such abnormality of mind as is specified in subsection (1) of section 2 of the Homicide Act 1957 (diminished responsibility),

the court shall allow the prosecution to adduce or elicit evidence tending to prove the other of those contentions, and may give directions as to the stage of the proceedings at which the prosecution may adduce such evidence."

In both situations the prosecution must prove its case beyond reasonable doubt.[96]

Could the prosecution raise diminished responsibility, or insanity, if the defendant puts his state of mind in issue in some other way, for example, when raising the question of automatism? It has been held that where the

5-049

---

[92] Homicide Act 1957, s.2(3).
[93] Homicide Act 1957, s.2(2).
[94] *R. v. Dunbar* [1958] 1 Q.B. 1.
[95] *Rose v. R.* [1961] A.C. 496.
[96] *R. v. Grant* [1960] Crim. L.R. 424.

defendant raises automatism, the prosecution can lead evidence of insanity.[97] The defendant's abnormality of mind must have been put in issue before the prosecution can take this course of action.[98] If the prosecution does choose to take this line of argument, then the prosecutor must show any medical reports to the defendant's counsel and make the doctor available as a defence witness.[99]

5-050   Can the judge raise the questions of diminished responsibility or insanity? In *R. v. Campbell*[1] the Court of Appeal said that the judge could raise the question of diminished responsibility if evidence came to light during the trial (*e.g.* from evidence of provocation adduced by the defendant). If the judge decides to do so, he should first put the issue to the defendant's counsel for the defendant to decide whether it should be put to the jury. This contrasts with the rules on provocation and self-defence, where the judge must raise the defence if there is any evidence for its foundation. With regard to insanity, in *R. v. Dickie*[2] it was held that the judge has the power to raise the issue of his own motion, but he must allow both the prosecution and the defence to call evidence before he puts the issue to the jury. In *R. v. Straw*[3] it was held that where a properly advised defendant has decided not to raise the defence, an appeal based on fresh evidence of medical incapacity is unlikely to succeed, except in highly unusual circumstances.

(5) ACCEPTING A PLEA OF GUILTY OF MANSLAUGHTER

5-051   A plea of guilty to manslaughter was held unacceptable in *R. v. Matheson*[4] but it may now be accepted at the discretion of the trial judge,[5] if medical evidence is clear on the elements of the defence.[6] In the trial of Peter Sutcliffe, the so-called "Yorkshire Ripper", the plea was left to the jury, who found Sutcliffe guilty of murder.[7] It is only in exceptional circumstances that the plea should be accepted by the prosecution, because the burden of proof is on the defence and often the plea depends upon a factual situation which may be disputed.

(6) MEDICAL EVIDENCE

5-052   The defendant must prove the facts which are the basis of his defence by admissible evidence.[8] This means he will have to lay a foundation of fact, and although medical evidence is not required by the section, it is in practice a

[97] *R. v. Kemp* [1964] 2 Q.B. 341; see also *Bratty v. Att.-Gen. for Northern Ireland* [1963] A.C. 386.
[98] *R. v. Dixon* [1961] 1 W.L.R. 337.
[99] *R. v. Casey* (1947) 32 Cr.App.R. 91.
[1] (1987) 84 Cr.App.R. 255; *R. v. Kooken* (1982) 74 Cr.App.R. 30.
[2] [1984] 3 A.E.R. 173; *R. v. Thomas* [1995] Crim. L.R. 314.
[3] [1995] 1 A.E.R. 187 and *R. v. Ahluwalia* (1993) 96 Cr.App.R. 133.
[4] [1958] 42 Cr.App.R. 145.
[5] *R. v. Vinagre* (1979) 69 Cr.App.R. 104.
[6] *R. v. Cox* (1968) 52 Cr.App.R. 130.
[7] See (1983) 23 *Medicine Science and Law* 17; *The Times,* May 23, 1981.
[8] *R. v. Ahmed Din* (1962) 46 Cr.App.R. 239, considered in *R. v. Bathurst* [1968] 2 Q.B. 99; *R. v. Vinagre* (1979) 69 Cr.App.R. 104; *R. v. Bradshaw* (1985) 82 Cr.App.R. 79.

necessity.[9] The jury should not be given a transcript of the medical evidence.[10] In *R. v. Spratt*,[11] where the prosecution medical evidence was found to be defective, a verdict of manslaughter was substituted. The source of the abnormality is a medical question.[12]

The task of the jury in deciding whether the defendant suffered from   5–053
diminished responsibility can involve the rejection of the medical evidence. However, any such rejection will only be upheld on appeal where there is other evidence on which the jury could have decided the issue.[13] In *R. v. Sanders*,[14] although the defendant was said by the medical evidence to suffer from a reactive depression, there was other evidence of premeditation. It was held that the medical evidence should be assessed in the light of the other circumstances. The jury cannot decide that there was diminished responsibility where there is no medical evidence to bring the case within the section.[15] If the medical experts differ, the jury must decide the question.[16]

(7) The Judge's Duty

The judge must explain the section to the jury[17] but they do not need to   5–054
be directed to consider the elements of the defence in the order in which they are set out in the section.[18] It is not enough merely to read the section to the jury, as was formerly held in *R. v. Spriggs*.[19] In *R. v. Terry* the Court of Appeal held that the explanation to be given should be in the form set out in *R. v. Byrne*. It would be a rare case where the judge could comment on the defence not giving evidence,[20] but it is unlikely to be conclusive even if he does.[21]

(8) "Abnormality of Mind"

It is for the jury to decide on all the relevant evidence whether there is an   5–055
abnormality of mind.[22] The judge should not say that the state is very near insanity,[23] because it is only so in the sense that laymen use the term, "the broad popular sense".[24] If the defendant is using the argument of irresistible

---

[9] *R. v. Dix* (1982) 72 Cr.App.R. 306.
[10] *R. v. Terry* [1961] 2 Q.B. 314.
[11] (1980) 71 Cr.App.R. 125.
[12] *R. v. Byrne* [1960] 2 Q.B. 396.
[13] *R. v. Matheson* (1958) 42 Cr.App.R. 145; *R. v. Bailey* (1978) 66 Cr.App.R. 31; *R. v. Walton* [1978] 1 A.E.R. 542; *R. v. Kisko* (1979) 68 Cr.App.R. 62; *R. v. Cascoe* [1970] 2 A.E.R. 833; *R. v. Vernege* [1982] 1 W.L.R. 293.
[14] (1991) 93 Cr.App.R. 245. *R. v. Campbell* [1997] Crim. L.R. 495.
[15] *R. v. Byrne* [1960] 2 Q.B. 396; *R. v. Dix* (1981) 74 Cr.App.R. 306.
[16] *R. v. Jennion* (1962) 46 Cr.App.R. 212.
[17] *Terry* [1961] 2 Q.B. 314.
[18] *R. v. Mitchell* [1995] Crim. L.R. 506.
[19] [1958] 1 Q.B. 270; see *R. v. Walden* [1959] 3 A.E.R. 203.
[20] *Bathurst* [1968] 2 Q.B. 99.
[21] *Bradshaw* (1985) 82 Cr.App.R. 79.
[22] *R. v. Byrne* [1960] 2 Q.B. 396.
[23] *R. v. Seers* (1984) 79 Cr.App.R. 261.
[24] *Rose v. R.* [1961] A.C. 496.

impulse then the jury must approach it in a common sense way.[25] The problem with the defence is that "abnormality of mind" is not a concept familiar to psychiatrists who will inevitably be giving evidence on the subject. The expression used by psychiatrists is "mental disorder" which in effect is likely to mean the same as "abnormality" but causes problems of definition. *R. v. Brown*[26] illustrates that judges should supplement the statutory definition along the line set out in *Byrne* and especially where there is medical evidence.[27]

5-056   In *Byrne* the Court of Appeal said[28]:

> "Abnormality of mind, which has to be contrasted with the time-honoured expression in the M'Naghten Rules 'defect of reason' means a state of mind so different from that of ordinary human beings that the reasonable man would term it abnormal."

The defendant had strangled a young woman at a hostel and mutilated her body. The Court of Criminal Appeal upheld the defendant's appeal and quashed the conviction for murder. It was said in this case that "abnormality" covered the mind in all its aspects, including a rational judgment as to whether an act was right or wrong, and the ability to exercise will power to control physical acts in accordance with that rational judgment. The defence under section 2 was said to be available when either (i) the defendant was incapable of exercising will-power to control his physical acts, or (ii) he had such difficulty in controlling his physical acts as to amount to substantial impairment, provided in each case that it resulted from one of the causes specified in section 2.

(9) REASONS FOR ABNORMALITY

5-057   These are set out in section 2 of the Homicide Act 1957 (paragraph 5-045 above). The cause need not have existed from birth.[29] In *Byrne* it was said that "the aetiology of the abnormality of mind . . . does, however, seem to be a matter to be determined by expert evidence".[30]

5-058   The transitory effects of alcohol are to be ignored.[31] Where alcoholism is a disease, however, this may be relevant.[32] The drinking must have become involuntary to the extent that the defendant cannot resist the first drink. In *Tandy* this was not the case on the facts. The effect of alcohol or drugs is to be disregarded because abnormality due to these is not a result of inherent causes. As the Court of Appeal said in *R. v. Egan*,[33] the question is whether

---

[25] *R. v. Byrne* [1960] 2 Q.B. 314 at 404; followed in *R. v. Walton* [1978] 1 W.L.R. 542.

[26] [1993] Crim. L.R. 961.

[27] *R. v. Sanderson* (1994) 98 Cr.App.R. 325.

[28] At p. 403.

[29] *R. v. Gomez* (1964) 48 Cr.App.R. 310.

[30] *R. v. Byrne* [1960] 2 Q.B. 396 at 403.

[31] *R. v. Di Duca* (1959) 43 Cr.App.R. 167; *R. v. Fenton* (1975) 61 Cr.App.R. 261, approved in *R. v. Gittens* [1984] Q.B. 698, which disapproved *R. v. Turnbull* (1977) 65 Cr.App.R. 242; *R. v. Atkinson* {1985] Crim. L.R. 314.

[32] *R. v. Tandy* (1988) 87 Cr.App.R. 45; followed in *R. v. Inseal* [1992] Crim. L.R. 35.

[33] *R. v. Egan* (1992) 95 Cr.App.R. 278.

the defendant's abnormality of mind was such that he would have been under diminished responsibility, drink or no drink.

(10) "SUBSTANTIAL IMPAIRMENT OF MENTAL RESPONSIBILITY"

Where the case turns on the defendant's difficulty in controlling his behaviour, the impairment of responsibility will be shown if his inability to exercise control was substantially greater than that of the reasonable man. In *Byrne* it was said that "consideration of the extent to which the accused's mind is answerable for his physical acts which must include a consideration of the extent of his ability to exercise will-power to control his physical acts" was a question for the jury. The impairment must be more than minimal.[34] In *R. v. Egan*[35] it was said that the jury must adopt a broad common sense approach to the question whether the defendant's responsibility was substantially impaired, *i.e.* whether his ability to control himself was impaired to more than a trivial degree.

5–059

(11) INSANITY

If the defendant does not specifically plead either insanity or diminished responsibility, it is unlikely that psychiatric evidence will be admitted on the question of the defendant's intent.[36] The legal test of insanity is set out in *M'Naghten's case*[37]:

5–060

> "To establish a defence on the ground of insanity, it must be clearly proved that, at the time of committing the act, the party was labouring under such a defect of reason, from disease of the mind, as not to know the nature and quality of the act he was doing, or, if he did know it, that he did not know he was doing what was wrong."

Where the defect of reason does not arise from disease, the defendant can raise the issue of automatism.[38] The Court of Appeal has neatly summed this up in *R. v. Hennessy*[39]:

5–061

> "If the defendant did not know the nature and quality of his act because of something which did not amount to defect of reason from disease of the mind, then he will probably be entitled to be acquitted on the basis that the necessary criminal intent which the prosecution has to prove is not proved. But, if on the other hand, his failure to realise the nature and quality of his act was due to a defect of reason from disease of the mind, then in the eyes of the law he is suffering from insanity, albeit M'Naghten insanity."

[34] *R. v. Simcox* [1964] Crim. L.R. 402; *R. v. Lloyd* [1967] 1 Q.B. 575 approved in *Gittens* [1984] Q.B. 698; *R. v. Campbell* (1987) 84 Cr.App.R. 255, and see *R. v. Campbell (No. 2)* [1997] Crim. L.R. 227.
[35] (1992) 95 Cr.App.R. 278; *R. v. Mitchell* [1995] Crim. L.R. 506.
[36] *R. v. Reynolds* (1989) Crim. L.R. 220; *R. v. Masih* (1986) Crim. L.R. 395; see also *R. v. Turner* (1975) 60 Cr.App.R. 80; *R. v. Lowery* [1974] A.C. 85.
[37] (1843) 10 Cl. & F. 200.
[38] *R. v. Clarke* (1972) 1 A.E.R. 219.
[39] [1989] 2 A.E.R. 9.

The first part of this passage must not be taken too literally as there are times when automatism does not lead to an acquittal.[40]

5-062 It is for the judge to rule on the question whether the condition of the defendant constitutes a defect of reason arising from a disease of the mind. The test for disease of the mind was examined by the House of Lords in *R. v. Sullivan*.[41] The defendant suffered an epileptic fit when visiting an elderly man. During the fit he assaulted the man. The defendant preferred to plead guilty to the charge rather than face the problems of the insanity plea. The House of Lords criticised the procedures which had led to the case being taken on appeal to the House, but accepted that the defendant was faced with a real dilemma. Nonetheless, the definition of "disease" which they endorsed clearly covered epilepsy:

> " 'Mind' in the M'Naghten rules is used in the ordinary sense of the mental faculties of reason, memory and understanding. If the effect of disease is to impair these faculties so severely as to have either of the consequences referred to in the latter part of the rules, it matters not whether the aetiology of the impairment is organic, as in epilepsy, or functional, or whether the impairment itself is permanent or is transient and intermittent, provided that it subsisted at the time of the commission of the act."

5-063 This definition approved the Court of Appeal's decision in *R. v. Quick*.[42] This case drew clearly the distinction between internal factors (*e.g.* bodily disorders such as arteriosclerosis, brain tumour, epilepsy, diabetes) and external factors (*e.g.* violence, drugs including anaesthetics, alcohol,[43] hypnotic influences). The former constitute insanity, the latter automatism.[44] Sleepwalking was considered in *R. v. Burgess*[45] and classed as insanity on the basis of the principles developed in the case law. In *Hennessy*[46] the diabetic defendant suffered hyperglycaemia (high blood sugar level) as a result of not taking insulin. On charges of taking and driving a car and driving while disqualified, the trial judge held that the defendant's disability constituted M'Naghten insanity, whereupon the defendant, like Mr Sullivan, pleaded guilty to the charges. His appeal was dismissed by the Court of Appeal. If the diabetic suffered from hypoglycaemia (too little sugar) this would be regarded as automatism.[47]

5-064 The defendant must be shown either not to know the nature and quality of his physical act[48] or, if he did know what he was doing, that he did not know it was legally wrong.[49]

---

[40] See paras. 2–047–2–051.
[41] [1984] A.C. 156.
[42] (1973) 3 A.E.R. 347.
[43] If alcohol leads to delirium tremens it will be insanity: *Davis* (1881) 14 Cox C.C. 563; *cf. R. v. Tandy* (1988) 87 Cr.App.R. 45.
[44] But not necessarily PMT (pre-menstrual tension): *R. v. Smith* (1982) Crim. L.R. 531.
[45] [1991] 2 Q.B. 92.
[46] [1989] 2 A.E.R. 9.
[47] *R. v. Bingham* [1991] Crim. L.R. 433.
[48] *R. v. Codere* (1916) 12 Cr.App.R. 21.
[49] *R. v. Windle* (1982) 2 Q.B. 826.

(12) EFFECT OF A FINDING OF INSANITY

If the insanity defence is made out, the defendant is found "not guilty by   **5–065**
reason of insanity"[50] and will be ordered to be detained in hospital.[51] The
defendant may appeal against this finding.[52]

V. INVOLUNTARY MANSLAUGHTER

Involuntary manslaughter is a crime which covers such a diversity of situ-   **5–066**
ations that it is difficult to define its exact boundaries.[53] In *Director of Public
Prosecutions v. Newbury*[54] Lord Salmon pointed out that cases of manslaughter
can amount to "little more than pure inadvertence and sometimes to little less
than murder".

A. *CONSTRUCTIVE MANSLAUGHTER*

(1) DEFINITION

Although constructive murder was abolished by the Homicide Act 1957,   **5–067**
the doctrine of constructive manslaughter continued. In *Newbury* the House
of Lords approved this definition given by Humphreys J. in *R. v. Larkin*[55]:

> "Where the act which a person is engaged in performing is unlawful, then if at
> the same time it is a dangerous act, that is, an act which is likely to injure another
> person, and quite inadvertently he causes the death of that other person by that
> act, then he is guilty of manslaughter."

The House stated that the practice of directing juries other than in accord-   **5–068**
ance with these principles should cease. Lord Salmon said that it was manslaughter if the defendant "intentionally did an act which was unlawful and
dangerous and that act caused death". He said it was "unnecessary to prove
that the accused knew that the act was unlawful or dangerous".

In *R. v. Pagett*[56] the Court of Appeal said that it was sufficient that the   **5–069**
defendant "intentionally did an act which was both unlawful and, objectively
considered, dangerous, and which in fact caused the victim's death". More
recently, in *R. v. Goodfellow*[57] the Court of Appeal has listed the questions
which a jury must decide. These are:

---

[50] Criminal Procedure (Insanity) Act 1964, s.1.
[51] Criminal Procedure (Insanity) Act 1964, s.5 as substituted by s.3 of the Criminal Procedure
(Insanity and Unfitness to Plead) Act 1991.
[52] Criminal Appeal Act 1968, s.12.
[53] *Andrews v. D.P.P.* [1937] A.C. 576 at 581 *per* Lord Atkin.
[54] [1977] A.C. 500.
[55] (1944) 29 Cr.App.R. 18.
[56] (1983) 76 Cr.App.R. 279.
[57] (1986) 83 Cr.App.R. 23 at 27.

"(1) Was the act intentional? (2) Was it unlawful? (3) Was it an act which any reasonable person would realise was bound to subject some other human being to the risk of physical harm albeit not necessarily serious harm? (4) Was that act the cause of death?"

(2) "UNLAWFUL ACT"

5–070　　In *R. v. Lowe*[58] the Court of Appeal suggested that there was a "clear distinction between an act of omission and an act of commission likely to cause harm". Where there was an omission this would need to be considered as gross negligence or reckless manslaughter. Where, however, the negligence comes within a defined offence, such as child neglect, constructive manslaughter will apply.[59]

5–071　　There is authority for the proposition that a tortious act is sufficient for manslaughter. In *R. v. Fenton*[60] stones were thrown down a mineshaft causing the wooden scaffolding to break. A man descending the shaft in a basket was killed. It was held by Tindal C.J. that this could be manslaughter, based on the unlawful act of trespass. However, in the later case of *R. v. Franklin*[61] the court did not follow this decision. *Fenton* was distinguished on its facts, and a civil wrong was held to be insufficient as the basis of manslaughter. The case proceeded on the basis of negligence. In *Franklin* the defendant picked up a box and threw it over the edge of a pier, causing the death of a swimmer in the sea below.

5–072　　*Franklin* was approved in *R. v. Lamb*,[62] where the Court of Appeal reiterated that a criminal wrong was needed. The act in that case was said not to have been "unlawful in the criminal sense of the word".[63] However, the decision of the House of Lords in *Newbury*[64] casts some doubt on this proposition. Two boys dropped a piece of paving stone from a bridge onto an oncoming train. The stone went through the window of the driver's cab and killed the guard. The House of Lords upheld the boys' convictions for manslaughter, but failed to identify the exact wrong committed by the boys. The House said that the judge need not direct a jury that the defendant must have foreseen harm to someone. This would suggest that the defendant is not required to have assessed whether the act is dangerous or not. The House stated that it was not possible to maintain that the defendant's acts were lawful. What, therefore, was the unlawful act which they had committed? If it was unnecessary to show that the defendants' foresaw harm, then it could not have been the offence of assault. Other possibilities are the tort of trespass, the crimes

---

[58] (1973) Q.B. 702.
[59] See para. 5–074.
[60] (1830) 1 Lew. C.C. 179.
[61] (1883) 15 Cox C.C. 163.
[62] [1967] 2 Q.B. 981.
[63] "It is perhaps as well to mention that when using the phrase 'unlawful in the criminal sense of that word' the court has in mind that it is long settled that it is not in point to consider whether an act is unlawful merely from the angle of civil liabilities." *ibid.* at 988D.
[64] [1977] A.C. 500.

of negligently endangering the safety of railway passengers[65] and criminal damage.[66] These possibilities are considered below.

If it was the trespass which was the unlawful act, then *Newbury* may be 5–073 suggested to resurrect the principle in *Fenton*. It is submitted that despite the ambiguity of the phrase "unlawful act", proof of a criminal offence will be required. Does the law place any restriction on the type of criminal offence upon which a charge of manslaughter can be founded? In *Andrews*[67] Lord Atkin said that it was not enough that the activity was criminal because of the negligent manner of performance. That case concerned charges of manslaughter arising out of offences of dangerous driving contrary to section 11 of the Road Traffic Act 1930.

A possible conflict with this principle would be offences defined to cover 5–074 neglect. A number of cases involving child neglect illustrate the approach. In *R. v. Senior*[68] it was held that death resulting from the offence of wilful neglect of a child could be manslaughter. However, in *R. v. Lowe*[69] the defendant was charged with the offence under section 1(1) of the Children and Young Persons Act 1933 and the offence of manslaughter. The manslaughter conviction was quashed. Although the case was later disapproved on another ground,[70] *Lowe* remains authority on this point.

If the offences of neglect were purely offences of negligence then Lord 5–075 Atkin's statement in *Andrews* would apply. However, since the offence of wilful neglect can be committed intentionally, this is not really a crime of negligence. The conviction in *Lowe* was also quashed on the point, noted above, that offences committed by omission cannot be manslaughter. On this question of offences of negligence, *Newbury* is again relevant. Could the unlawful act have been an offence of negligence, such as negligently endangering the safety of railway passengers contrary to section 34 of the Offences Against the Person Act 1861? If so, this would contradict the *Andrews* principle.

Although the unlawful act which leads to death will usually be some form 5–076 of assault, this is not a prerequisite for constructive manslaughter. In *Newbury* it is possible that the offence was criminal damage to the train. In *Goodfellow*[71] the offence was arson. In *R. v. Dalby*[72] the supply of drugs was considered sufficient. Indeed, in *R. v. Cato*[73] the Court of Appeal appear to have been prepared to create an offence in order to support a conviction. In this case the victim had prepared a mixture of heroin and water and requested the defendant to inject it into him. This the defendant did on several occasions over the course of the evening. As a result the victim died. The Court of Appeal suggested that "injecting the victim with a mix of heroin and water which at the

---

[65] See para. 3–264.
[66] Criminal Damage Act 1971, s.1.
[67] [1937] A.C. 576.
[68] [1899] 1 Q.B. 283.
[69] [1973] Q.B. 702.
[70] In *R. v. Sheppard* [1981] A.C. 394.
[71] (1986) 83 Cr.App.R. 23.
[72] [1982] 1 A.E.R. 916.
[73] [1976] 1 A.E.R. 260.

time of injury Cato had unlawfully taken into his possession" was sufficient unlawfulness for manslaughter. This was despite the facts that Cato had committed no offence under the Misuse of Drugs Act 1971, that he had been given the syringe by the victim with the heroin in it, and that he had injected the victim at the victim's express request. However, the Court of Appeal's suggestion was *obiter*, since the court was satisfied that, on the facts, Cato had committed an offence under section 23 of the Offences Against the Person Act 1861 of administering a noxious thing.[74] An interesting illustration of the need to establish that the acts which caused death were unlawful is the Crown Court case of *R. v. Slingsby*[75] where the injuries were held to be an accidental consequence of lawful, consensual activity. In *R. v. Jennings*[76] where the prosecution relied on the offence of carrying an offensive weapon, the defendant's intent with regard to the weapon (it not being an offensive weapon, per se) was relevant.

5-077   Death caused in the course of an illegal abortion can also be manslaughter.[77]

(3) "DANGEROUS"

5-078   In *R. v. Larkin*[78] the defendant found a woman of his acquaintance drinking with another man. He held out an open razor at the man, intending to frighten him. The woman, who was drunk, fell against the defendant, cut her throat on the razor and died. It was held that the unlawful act must be such as was "likely to injure" another. This decision was followed in *R. v. Church*[79] where it was stated that the act must be such "as all sober and reasonable people would inevitably recognise must subject the other person to at least the risk of some harm resulting therefrom, albeit not serious harm". Church had taken his victim to a van to have sexual intercourse. When he proved unable to satisfy her, she slapped his face. In the ensuing fight he knocked her out. Being unsuccessful in his attempt to revive her, he took her from the van and threw her into the river where she drowned. The form of words used in *Church* was approved by the House of Lords in *Newbury*, and was confirmed more recently in *Goodfellow*.[80] In *Newbury* the House referred to *Gray v. Barr*[81] where Lord Denning had suggested that the defendant must have realised the likelihood of harm, *i.e.* a subjective test. The House rejected this view and confirmed the objective test:

> "In judging whether the act was dangerous, the test is not did the accused recognise that it was dangerous, but would all sober and reasonable people recognise its danger."[82]

---

[74] See also the unusual case of *R. v. Pike* [1961] Crim. L.R. 114.
[75] [1995] Crim. L.R. 570.
[76] [1990] Crim. L.R. 588.
[77] *Buck v. Buck* (1960) 44 Cr.App.R. 213: *R. v. Creamer* [1966] 1 Q.B. 72.
[78] [1943] 1 A.E.R. 217.
[79] [1966] 1 Q.B. 59.
[80] (1986) 83 Cr.App.R. 23 at 26; see also *R. v. Mahal* [1991] Crim. L.R. 632.
[81] [1971] 2 Q.B. 554.
[82] [1977] A.C. 500 at 507D.

It is submitted that this is the aspect of manslaughter which was being referred to when the House said in *Newbury* that the defendant need not have any foresight of the risk of harm occurring as a result of his actions.[83] It should be noted that *Larkin* speaks of "injury" and *Church* of "some harm". This may not be a material difference.

There must be some activity which constitutes an unlawful act. Where the **5-079** defendant was shown to have been walking along a station platform apparently looking for the victim, this was not enough to constitute an assault and, therefore, not manslaughter when the victim was killed crossing the track in order to escape.[84] A minor touching will not be enough, but a battery likely to cause harm will be.[85]

If the unlawful act is only likely to frighten a person, this is not sufficient, **5-080** unless the act is likely to cause physical harm as a result of the fright. So, if an assault is likely to cause harm, it is sufficient; but if it is likely only to cause fear then it is not. In *R. v. Reid*[86] the Court of Appeal felt that if offensive weapons, such as knives or firearms, are used to frighten people, then this would lead to a likelihood that they might be used in some way to cause injury. In this case, it is reasonable to conclude that physical harm might occur and thus is sufficient for manslaughter. However, in *R. v. Dawson, Nolan and Walmsley*[87] the defendants attempted to rob the attendant at a filling station. They used a replica gun and a pickaxe handle to frighten the attendant, a 60-year-old man with a heart condition. He pressed the alarm button to summon the police. Soon after the men had fled and the police arrived, the attendant collapsed and died of a heart attack. Allowing the appeals, the Court of Appeal held that an unlawful act causing emotional disturbance, even terror, was not enough. However, if the act caused shock, which itself caused physical injury, then a manslaughter conviction could be maintained.

What is foreseeable by the reasonable man is assessed on the facts known **5-081** to the defendant at the time of the offence.[88] In *R. v. Watson*[89] the defendant and another broke a window and entered the home of an 87-year-old man, who suffered from a heart condition and lived alone. The two men verbally abused the victim before making off without stealing anything. An hour and a half later the old man died of a heart attack. The unlawful act alleged was the burglary contrary to section 9(1)(a) of the Theft Act 1968, that is to say, the unlawful entry. In the defendant's appeal he contended that the reasonable man could only be taken to know the facts as at the time of entry. The Court of Appeal rejected this, and held that the unlawful act comprised the whole of the burglarious intrusion and knowledge of the victim's frailty acquired

---

[83] See para. 5–072 above.
[84] *R. v. Arobieke* [1988] Crim. L.R. 314.
[85] *R. v. Alabaster* (1912) 47 L.J.N. 397; *R. v. Woods* (1921) J.P. 272; *R. v. Garforth* [1954] Crim. L.R. 936.
[86] (1976) 62 Cr.App.R. 109; see *R. v. Conner* (1835) 7 C. & P. 438 and *R. v. Larkin* [1943] 1 A.E.R. 217.
[87] (1985) 81 Cr.App.R. 150; see also *R. v. Edmonds* [1963] 2 Q.B. 142; see also para. 4–051.
[88] (1985) 81 Cr.App.R. 150 at 157.
[89] [1989] 1 W.L.R. 684; see also para. 4–051.

during the time the defendant was on the premises could be attributed to the reasonable man.

5-082   In *R. v. Ball*[90] the Court of Appeal said that *Dawson* only went as far saying that the sober and reasonable man must look at the unlawful act and decide if it were dangerous. He should not look at the victim's peculiarities. However, in that case, the characteristics of the victim were not known. In *Watson* they were known to the defendant and were, therefore, known to the sober and reasonable man.

(4) "AIMED AT"

5-083   In *R. v. Dalby*[91] the Court of Appeal suggested that it was a requirement of manslaughter that the unlawful act be "aimed at" the victim. In that case the defendant lawfully obtained drugs which he unlawfully supplied to the victim. The victim took the drugs, and other drugs, and died as a result. The defendant's conviction of manslaughter was quashed on the ground that the supply of drugs was not an act directed at the person of the victim and did not cause any direct injury to him.

5-084   The requirement identified in *Dalby* was considered in *R. v. Mitchell*[92] where the defendant had pushed an elderly man in a queue at a post office. The man fell against an elderly woman, who suffered injuries and later died. The Court of Appeal found that there was a causal link between the defendant's act and the death and decided that it was the direct and immediate cause. The defendant's conviction was upheld and *Dalby* was not applied. In *R. v. Pagett*[93] the defendant held a girl hostage in front of himself and fired at police officers. The officers returned his fire and killed the girl. His act was clearly not "aimed at" the victim, but the court upheld the conviction of manslaughter as Pagett's act was the cause of death. Again, a causal link was established by the court. Finally, in *Goodfellow*[94] the Court of Appeal stated that the court in *Dalby* had been wrong to introduce another requirement into the offence and that the case could be explained as a decision on causation. The cases of *Pagett* and *Mitchell* were used to support this conclusion. In the light of the recent rejection of the "aimed at" requirement in the law of murder,[95] it is unlikely to continue to figure in constructive manslaughter. However, in *Ball* the Court of Appeal cited Waller L.J. in *Dalby* in support of the point that the defendant's act was an assault directed at the victim. The point is still moot.

5-085   In *Newbury*[96] the House held that the defendant must be shown to have intentionally done an act which was unlawful. In *Goodfellow* the Court of Appeal said that one of the questions for the jury is whether the act was

---

[90] [1989] Crim. L.R. 730 and see para. 4–046.
[91] (1982) 1 A.E.R. 916.
[92] [1983] 1 Q.B. 741.
[93] (1983) 76 Cr.App.R. 279 and see para. 4–043.
[94] (1986) 83 Cr.App.R. 23.
[95] *R. v. Moloney* [1985] A.C. 905; see paras. 4–078–4–079, and 4–081.
[96] [1977] A.C. 500; see para. 5–072.

intentional. These statements could be read to restrict constructive manslaughter to crimes of intention. It is submitted that this is not correct. Indeed,
the acceptance of assault and criminal damage as "unlawful acts" demonstrates
that crimes of recklessness will suffice. The statements in *Newbury* and *Goodfellow* could also be read to suggest that the defendant need only have the
intention to act (*i.e.* he must not have been in a state of automatism). This
would also be contrary to authority, as it would suggest that strict liability
offences would be sufficient. The only sensible interpretation is one which
reads the statements as requiring that the defendant has the *mens rea* of the
relevant offence.[97] The reference in *Newbury* to the fact that the defendant
need not know that his act is unlawful cannot be intended to negate the need
for *mens rea*, but must rather be a reiteration of the rule that ignorance of the
law is no excuse. It has already been shown that the defendant need not
himself be aware of the dangerousness of his act, that is, need not be aware
that his unlawful act may cause harm.

(5) "UNLAWFUL"

There may be several reasons why the act is not unlawful, apart from the   **5–086**
fact that the activity is not contrary to the criminal law. For example, on facts
which would otherwise disclose an offence, the defendant may have made a
material mistake of fact, or the defendant may not have the mental element
required for the offence. In *R. v. Lamb*[98] the defendant pointed a loaded
firearm as a joke at his friend. Not realising how revolvers worked, and thinking there was no danger because the chamber opposite the barrel was empty,
the defendant pulled the trigger. His friend, who equally thought there was
no danger, was killed. Since the defendant neither wanted nor realised that
fear or harm would result, he lacked the mental element for the crimes of
battery or assault.

If the reason why the defendant lacks *mens rea* for the offence is self induced   **5–087**
intoxication, this is no defence, as manslaughter is a crime of basic intent.[99]

B. *RECKLESS MANSLAUGHTER*

(1) LAWFUL ACT OR OMISSION

In *R. v. Larkin*[1] the Court of Criminal Appeal said that it might be man-   **5–088**
slaughter "If a person is engaged in doing a lawful act and in the course of
doing that lawful act behaves so negligently as to cause the death of some
other person."

---

[97] See *R. v. Jennings* [1990] Crim. L.R. 588.
[98] *R. v. Lamb* [1967] 2 Q.B. 981.
[99] *R. v. Lipman* [1970] 1 Q.B. 152.
[1] [1943] 1 A.E.R. 217 at 219.

(2) OMISSIONS AS A BASIS OF LIABILITY

5-089   It is the case that an omission to perform a legal duty may lead to criminal liability under this head of manslaughter. This is so despite any argument advanced earlier at paragraph 5–070 concerning the position under constructive manslaughter.

5-090   Although statute imposes duties to act in various situations, it is with the common law on omissions that this section is primarily concerned. The cases offer many examples of killing by omission, but develop few clear principles. The following text suggests categories into which the cases could be divided.

(3) DUTY ARISING FROM A RELATIONSHIP BETWEEN THE PARTIES

5-091   The only decided case in which relationship alone imposed a duty is *R. v. Gibbons and Proctor*.[2] Gibbons lived with Proctor, who was not his wife, in premises together with several children, including the victim, who was Gibbons' daughter by a previous relationship. Proctor kept the girl in a room without food. Gibbons was aware of this but did nothing to help. The girl died as a result. Both Gibbons and Proctor were charged and convicted of murder. The court held that a natural father has a duty to a child to look after the child's welfare. No duty was imposed on Proctor as a result of the relationship, but a duty was imposed on the basis of implied contract (see paragraph 5–094).

5-092   The extent of this duty on parents may be questioned. Does the parent have to be living with the child? Is the child's age or ability to care for itself of any relevance? Is the duty on natural parents only, or on legal parents, *e.g.* adoptive parents or foster parents? Why are de facto parents, such as cohabitees not under the same duty?

5-093   There are no decided cases supporting the duty on a child towards a parent. Other relationships have been mentioned in the case law, but none of them appears to be sufficient alone to impose a duty. In *R. v. Instan*[3] a girl lived with her elderly aunt. The girl was given money by the aunt to buy food. She did not give any food to the aunt, who developed gangrene and could not move. The girl did not seek the help of a doctor and the aunt died. The girl was charged and convicted of manslaughter, but it was held that the basis of her duty was not merely that of her relationship (see paragraph 5–094). Likewise, in *R. v. Stone and Dobinson*[4] the defendant Stone was the brother of the deceased. This relationship, however, was not sufficient to impose a duty on Stone as is shown below at paragraph 5–096. In *R. v. Smith*[5] the defendant's wife fell ill after childbirth. Consistent with her wishes, the defendant did not call for a doctor. When the wife become so ill that the defendant felt he had to call in medical assistance, it was too late and the woman died. The court

---

[2] (1918) 13 Cr.App.R. 134; see also *R. v. Russell and Russell* [1987] Crim. L.R. 494.
[3] (1893) 1 Q.B. 450; see *R. v. Nicholls* (1874) 13 Cox C.C. 75 (grandmother).
[4] [1977] 2 A.E.R. 341; see para. 5–078.
[5] [1979] Crim. L.R. 251.

did not seek to put any duty on the husband by virtue solely of his relationship with the woman.

(4) DUTY ARISING OUT OF CONTRACT

A contract, express or implied, may impose a duty on one individual towards another. An express contract was the basis of the decision in *R. v. Pittwood*.[6] The defendant was a gatekeeper of a level crossing. He opened the gate to allow a cart to pass over the line, left the gate open and went away. While he was absent the victims were killed in their cart as they crossed the line in the path of an oncoming train. The defendant was charged with manslaughter. The contract here was between the defendant and the railway company, but was for the benefit of the victims. In *Instan*[7] a contract was implied from the provision of funds to the niece for the purchase of necessaries. It may, however, be questioned whether there was any intention to create legal relations in this context. In this context, it may be that the criminal law is not as precise as the civil law in its requirements for the formation of a contract.

5–094

(5) DUTY GRATUITOUSLY UNDERTAKEN

The case law supports a proposition that there is a duty upon one who gratuitously undertakes responsibility for another who is, or becomes, dependant by virtue of infirmity or age.

5–095

That this covers the care of the infirm is supported by the decisions in *Instan* and *Stone and Dobinson*. In *Stone and Dobinson*[8] Stone, 67 years old, partially deaf, and blind, lived with Dobinson who was 43 years old and described by the court as "ineffectual and inadequate". Stone's sister, Fanny, came to live with them in the front room of their house. Fanny took ill, refused to leave her bed, eat or wash. She developed anorexia nervosa. Dobinson and a neighbour once gave Fanny a wash, since, being confined to bed, she was covered in her own excrement. A social worker called from time to time to see Stone's subnormal son, but was not told of Fanny's condition. Stone tried unsuccessfully to get a doctor to visit, despite the fact that Fanny would not give him the name of her doctor. Fanny died and Stone and Dobinson were both charged with manslaughter. Dismissing their appeal against conviction, the Court of Appeal held that the jury was entitled to find that a duty had been assumed. Once Fanny became helplessly infirm, the appellants were obliged to summon help or to care for Fanny themselves. The important factors appeared to be that Fanny was a blood relation of Stone, occupied a room in his house, Dobinson had undertaken the duty of trying to wash Fanny, and Stone had tried to get a doctor.

5–096

---

[6] (1902) 19 T.L.R. 37; see *contra R. v. Smith* (1869) 11 Cox C.C. 210.
[7] (1893) 1 Q.B. 450; see also the defendant Proctor in *R. v. Gibbons and Proctor* [1990] Crim. L.R. 588.
[8] [1977] 2 A.E.R. 341; see also *R. v. Marriott* (1838) 8 C. & P. 425; *Nicholls* (1874) 13 Cox C.C. 75.

5–097   In *Smith*[9] the court stated that the husband had a duty towards his wife
once she became so infirm that she could not make decisions for herself. Both
this case and *Stone and Dobinson* suggest that while the other person is sufficiently *compos mentis* to be able to make rational decisions about his or her
treatment, the law will respect this and will not expect others to impose treatment on them.

(6) CREATING A DANGEROUS SITUATION

5–098   In *R. v. Miller*[10] a squatter, who was smoking a cigarette, fell asleep inside
a building. He awoke to find the mattress smouldering. He realised this but
did nothing about it. The man went into the adjoining room and fell asleep
again. When he woke up he found the building was on fire. He was charged
with the offence of criminal damage under the Criminal Damage Act 1971,
section 1. The House of Lords held that "failing to take measures that lie
within one's power to counteract a danger that one has oneself created" could
give rise to liability for this offence. If this duty is regarded as a general duty,
then it could widen the applicability of the manslaughter offence. The duty
does, however, presuppose that the defendant has a capacity to rectify the
situation, and appears to apply when the defendant himself has created the
dangerous situation.

5–099   If, then, the defendant fails to perform a duty which he is legally obliged
to carry out, and the death of another results, he may be found guilty of
manslaughter. As stated earlier at paragraph 4–031, a failure to act may, if
accompanied by the intention to kill or do grievous bodily harm, lead to a
conviction for murder.

(7) ACTS AND OMISSIONS

5–100   The distinction between act and omission is not an easy one to make. This
problem has been highlighted in various situations concerning medical practice, *e.g.* turning off life support machines, and the non-feeding of handicapped babies.[11] It can be argued that to withhold treatment is to omit to treat.
This omission can only be culpable if the actor has a duty to act. In the case
of Doctor Arthur[12] it was said that the doctor need not treat the patient at all.
However, it could further be argued that the doctor has a contractual duty to
act for the patient.

5–101   If, however, the doctor has begun to treat a patient and then terminates the
treatment, this could be classified as an act. To avoid culpability the wilful, or
even negligent, practitioner would need to persuade the court to classify the
ending of the treatment as an omission in a context where there was no duty
imposed. In the *Arthur* case the defendant ordered nursing care only for a
newly born handicapped child. Drugs were administered which inhibited the

---

[9] [1979] Crim. L.R. 251.
[10] [1983] 2 A.C. 161.
[11] Skegg (1978) 41 M.L.R. 423.
[12] [1985] Crim. L.R. 70; [1986] Crim. L.R. 383, 390, 760.

child's desire for food. The defendant was charged with, and acquitted of, attempted murder. In *Re B*[13] a child's parents refused consent to surgery. The child was made a ward of court and the court gave its consent to the operation. However, the court did not criticise the parents' decision. Indeed, the parents were said to have acted entirely responsibly, which would suggest that the court did not feel that they had infringed any duty which they might have.

(8) THE FAULT ELEMENT

What is the precise fault element in this form of manslaughter? The issue here has been subject to a long and tortured history of the judicial definitions of two concepts—recklessness and gross negligence. **5–102**

(9) HISTORY

Early cases of manslaughter employed a test of gross negligence. In *R. v. Finney*[14] the defendant, an attendant at a lunatic asylum, was bathing an inmate. He told the man to get out of the bath. While his attention was drawn away he turned on the hot water tap. The inmate who was still in the bath was scalded and died. The trial judge directed the jury that the degree of culpability for manslaughter must amount to gross negligence. The defendant was found not guilty of manslaughter. **5–103**

The classic test of criminal negligence was set out in *R. v. Bateman*[15]: **5–104**

> "In explaining to juries the test which they should apply to determine whether the negligence, in the particular case, amounted or did not amount to a crime, the Judges have used many epithets, such as 'culpable', 'criminal', 'gross', 'wicked', 'clear', 'complete'. But, whatever epithet be used and whether an epithet be used or not, in order to establish criminal liability the facts must be such that, in the opinion of the jury, the negligence of the accused went beyond a mere matter of compensation between subjects and showed such disregard for the life and safety of others as to amount to a crime against the State and conduct deserving punishment."

This excluded simple negligence. The circularity of the test (criminal negligence was negligence sufficiently serious to be criminal) was criticised by the House of Lords in *Andrews v. Director of Public Prosecutions*.[16] However, the House did approve the test and reiterated the point that: **5–105**

> "Simple lack of care such as will constitute civil liability is not enough."[17]

Subsequent cases have repeated this. For example, in *R. v. Stone and Dobinson*[18] the Court of Appeal said:

> "Mere inadvertence is not enough."

---

[13] [1981] 1 W.L.R. 141; see also *Re C.*, *The Times*, April 21, 1989.
[14] (1874) Cox C.C. 625; *R. v. Jones* (1874) 12 Cox C.C. 628.
[15] (1925) 19 Cr.App.R. 8.
[16] [1937] A.C. 576.
[17] *ibid.* at p. 583.
[18] [1977] 2 A.E.R. 341.

5–106 In *Andrews* the House introduced the idea that recklessness was the appropriate expression of the mental element for manslaughter:

> "Simple lack of care is not enough. For the purposes of the criminal law there are degrees of negligence, and a very high degree of negligence is required to be proved before the felony is established. Probably of all the epithets that can be applied, 'recklessness' most nearly covers the case. It is difficult to visualise a case of death by dangerous driving caused by 'reckless' driving in the connotation of that term in ordinary speech which would not justify a conviction for manslaughter. But it is probably not all embracing, for 'reckless' suggests an indifference to risk, whereas the accused may have appreciated the risk and endeavoured to avoid it and yet shown such a high degree of negligence in the means adopted to avoid the risk as would justify a conviction."

5–107 In *R. v. Larkin*[19] in explaining the direction on manslaughter, the Court of Appeal said:

> "It is the duty of the presiding judge to tell them that it will not amount to manslaughter unless the negligence is of a very high degree: the expression most commonly used is unless it shows the accused to have been reckless as to the consequence of the act."

The passage in *Andrews* suggests that there can be liability where, although the defendant has realised the risk, his steps to avoid the event occurring are taken in a highly negligent way.

5–108 In *R. v. Lamb*[20] the defendant pointed a revolver at a friend, believing that, the bullets in the chamber not being opposite the barrel, the gun would not go off. The friend was killed. The Court of Appeal said that when criminal negligence "often referred to as recklessness"[21] was being considered, reference should be made to the defendant's state of mind and whether he thought that what he was doing was safe. The court, allowing Lamb's appeal, said:

> "In the present case it would have been fully open to a jury, if properly directed, to find the accused guilty because they considered that his view of there being no danger was formed in a criminally negligent way; but he was entitled to a direction that the jury should take into account the fact that he had undisputedly formed this view and that there was expert evidence of this being an understandable view."

5–109 In *R. v. Lowe*[22] the Court of Appeal said that:

> "It seems strange that an omission which is wilful solely in the sense that it is not inadvertent, the consequences of which are not in fact foreseen by the person who is neglectful should, if death results, automatically give rise to an indeterminate sentence."

5–110 In *Stone and Dobinson*[23] the Court of Appeal rejected the proposition that this statement supported a purely subjective test for recklessness and cited *Andrews* as the authority. The court went on to say that:

---

[19] [1943] 1 A.E.R. 217.
[20] [1967] 2 A.E.R. 1282.
[21] *ibid.* at 1285G.
[22] [1973] Q.B. 702.
[23] [1977] 2 A.E.R. 341.

"Mere inadvertence is not enough. The defendant must have been proved to have been indifferent to an obvious risk of injury to health, or actually to have foreseen the risk but to have determined nevertheless to run it."

In *R. v. Cato*[24] the Court of Appeal suggested that as recklessness was an ordinary English word it would not require definition. Although the court did accept the trial judge's view that gross negligence was the same as recklessness, they spoke of the defendant needing to know the consequences of his action.   5–111

In *R. v. Smith*[25] the Court of Appeal said that the defendant was guilty if it was shown that he was in reckless disregard of his duty. This was defined to mean appreciation of risk and either not acting because of indifference, or deliberately running an unjustified and unreasonable risk.   5–112

In summary, the above cases suggest that recklessness covers not only the state of mind of one who knowingly takes a risk, but also of one who is indifferent to a risk. Indifference to risk is seen as the failure to consider a risk, though this is qualified in that the failure to consider must be gross. Recklessness also seems to cover one who considers a risk and rules out the existence of the risk in a grossly negligent way.   5–113

(10) IMPACT OF THE DECISION IN R. V. CALDWELL

The use in the above cases of the expression "reckless" meant that the courts would be faced with arguments based on the use of the same expression in other offences, usually statutory offences where it had become the legislative style to adopt intention and recklessness as the words to express the fault element, forsaking, by and large, words such as wilfully or maliciously. The jurisprudence on the concept of recklessness as used in the criminal law was substantially changed with the House of Lords' decision in *R. v. Caldwell*[26] and *R. v. Lawrence*.[27] Although stated in a case concerning criminal damage, Lord Diplock referred to the definition he advanced in *Caldwell* as being valid for all statutory offences.[28]   5–114

In *Caldwell* the defendant, when drunk, set fire to a hotel. Fortunately none of the occupants were killed in the blaze. The defendant was charged with causing criminal damage with the intention of being reckless as to endangering the life of another. His appeals to the Court of Appeal and House of Lords were rejected. Lord Diplock proposed a model direction for use when defining recklessness in both cases concerning criminal damage and any statutory offences (except those where the mental element is malice or maliciously). A person is: 5–115

"reckless as to whether or not any property would be destroyed or damaged if (1) he does an act which in fact creates an obvious risk that property will be destroyed or damaged and (2) when he does the act he either has not given any thought to

---

[24] [1976] 62 Cr.App.R. 41 at 48.
[25] [1979] Crim. L.R. 251.
[26] [1982] A.C. 341.
[27] [1982] A.C. 510.
[28] *R. v. Lawrence* [1982] A.C. 510 at 525C.

the possibility of there being any such risk or has recognised that there was some risk involved and has nevertheless gone on to do it."

5-116   In *R. v. Lawrence*[29] the House used this definition in a case concerning reckless driving. The direction was, however, modified as follows:

"In my view, an appropriate instruction to the jury on what is meant by driving recklessly would be that they must be satisfied of two things:

     First, that the defendant was in fact driving the vehicle in such a manner as to create an obvious and serious risk of causing physical injury to some other person who might happen to be using the road or of doing substantial damage to property; and

     Second, that in driving in that manner the defendant did so without having given any thought to the possibility of there being any such risk or, having recognised that there was some risk involved, had nonetheless gone on to take it.

It is for the jury to decide whether the risk created by the manner in which the vehicle was being driven was both obvious and serious and, in deciding this, they may apply the standard of the ordinary prudent motorist as represented by themselves.

     If satisfied that an obvious and serious risk was created by the manner of the defendant's driving, the jury are entitled to infer that he was in one or other of the states of mind required to constitute the offence and will probably do so; but regard must be given to any explanation he gives as to his state of mind which may displace the inference."[30]

5-117   Two particular issues arising from this definition were examined by the Court of Appeal. In *Elliott v. C.*[31] a 14-year-old girl of low intelligence set fire to some white spirit and damaged a garden shed. It was held that where the defendant is alleged not to have considered the existence of a risk, although such risk must be one which would have been obvious to a reasonable man, it need not be proved to have been obvious to the defendant. Particular characteristics, *e.g.* age, mental ability, of the defendant which might affect his or her ability to see the risk are not relevant. The test is purely objective.

5-118   What of the person who may have considered the existence of a risk, but ruled it out? In *Chief Constable of Avon v. Shimmen*[32] the question was raised whether a person who thought about and ruled out a risk was to be held to be reckless. The defendant aimed a kick at a plate glass window. Believing that his skills in martial arts would mean that he could control his kick so as not the cause damage, the defendant put out his leg. Unfortunately he struck the window and broke it. The court said, *obiter* that although ruling out a risk might not be recklessness, in this case the defendant was reckless as he had realised there was a risk, albeit a small one, and had gone on to run the risk of damage occurring. In *R. v. Merrick*[33] it was accepted that in order to establish a defence on these lines, the defendant must take steps to prevent the risk, not merely to remedy the effects after he has created the risk.

[29] [1982] A.C. 510.
[30] *ibid.* at 526H.
[31] (1983) 77 Cr.App.R. 103; *R. v. Stephen* (1984) 79 Cr.App.R. 334.
[32] (1987) 84 Cr.App.R. 7.
[33] [1996] 1 Cr.App.R. 130.

The approach taken in *Caldwell* and *Lawrence* was approved by the House   **5–119**
of Lords in *R. v. Reid*.[34] Meanwhile, the courts took steps to apply this line
of reasoning to manslaughter. In *R. v. Seymour*[35] the vehicles of the defendant
and the victim were in a collision. The victim got out of her car and
approached the defendant. The defendant drove his lorry at the victim,
intending, he said, to push her out of the way, but in fact he crushed her
between the vehicles and killed her. The House of Lords reiterated their view
expressed in *Government of the U.S.A. v. Jennings*[36] that manslaughter arising
out of reckless driving of a motor vehicle was still a common law offence
separate from the statutory offence of causing death by reckless driving in
section 1 of the Road Traffic Act 1972 and required separate indictments, and
applied the test set out in *R. v. Lawrence*.[37]

(11) GROSS NEGLIGENCE

The House of Lords in *R. v. Adomako*[38] has now made clear that, in man-   **5–120**
slaughter, this approach is no longer relevant, whatever the position in relation
to other offences.[39] The appellant, an anaethetist, had failed to notice during
an operation the disconnection of the endotrachael tube, as a result of which
the supply of oxygen to the patient ceased and this led to cardiac arrest. There
was no question about the existence of the duty of care, nor that there had
been a breach of that duty. In the opinion of the House, the ordinary principles
of the law of negligence apply to ascertain whether or not the defendant has
been in breach of a duty of care towards the victim who has died. If such a
breach is established, the next question is whether that breach caused the
death of the victim. Finally, the jury must consider whether that breach of
duty should be characterised as gross negligence and therefore as a crime. As
the Lord Chancellor said, "The essence of the matter, which is supremely a
jury question, is whether, having regard to the risk of death involved, the
conduct of the defendant was so bad in all the circumstances as to amount in
their judgment to a criminal act or omission".[40] The House, reasserted the
test of gross negligence by specifically approving the cases of *Bateman*[41] and
Andrews,[42] and the use of the word "reckless" in cases of involuntary manslaughter, in the "ordinary connotation of that word", as Lord Atkin put it,
was approved. The House went on to hold that, as a result of changes to the
statute law on reckless driving, *Seymour*[43] no longer applied, and it was not
necessary to follow *Lawrence*. The appeal was not allowed. The path to consideration of the issues and authorities had been eased for the House of Lords

---

[34] [1992] 1 W.L.R. 793.
[35] [1983] 2 A.C. 493.
[36] [1983] A.C. 624.
[37] [1982] A.C. 510.
[38] [1995] 1 A.C. 171.
[39] *R. v. Coles* [1995] 1 Cr.App.R. 157 (reckless in criminal damage).
[40] [1995] 1 A.C. 171.
[41] (1925) 19 Cr.App.R. 8.
[42] [1937] A.C. 576.
[43] [1983] 2 A.C. 493.

by the Court of Appeal when hearing this case with two similar appeals (both of which were successful).[44]

5-121   It is to be noted that the House of Lords referred to the risk of death. Earlier cases, it is to be noted, toyed with the possibility of culpability based on a risk of something less than death. In *Kong Cheuk Kwan*[45] the Privy Council accepted a ruling couched in terms of an obvious and serious risk of physical damage to the ship, a risk closely linked with risk of injury to the person on the facts. In *R. v. Goodfellow*[46] the Court of Appeal referred to a risk only of physical injury. Previously the court in *Bateman*[47] had spoken of a disregard for the life and safety of others and in *Stone and Dobinson* the Court of Appeal used a formulation wider still—"disregard for the health and welfare of the victim".[48]

(12) Causing Death by Dangerous Driving

5-122   The offence of causing death by dangerous driving is set out in section 2A(1) of the Road Traffice Act 1988, as substituted by section 1 of the Road Traffic Act 1991. It is triable only on indictment. The offence carries a maximum penalty of five years' imprisonment and obligatory disqualification of twelve months (unless there are special reasons). It is not intended to discuss this offence in detail, but is included for the sake of completeness. The previous offence of causing death by reckless driving in section 1 of the Road Traffic Act 1988 was the subject of much judicial discussion in the context of the debate on recklessness.

(13) Ancillary Points

5-123   For transferred malice see 4–080. For the killing of a supposed corpse see 4–082–4–083. For joint enterprise see 4–084–4–087.

---

[44] *Sub nom. Prentice* [1993] 3 W.L.R. 931.
[45] (1986) 82 Cr.App.R. 18.
[46] (1986) 83 Cr.App.R. 23.
[47] (1925) 19 Cr.App.R. 8 at 11.
[48] [1977] Q.B. 354 at 363.

CHAPTER 6

SUICIDE

I. INTRODUCTION

Suicide used to be a felony at common law.[1] It was regarded as self-murder **6–001** and required proof of an intent on the deceased's part to kill himself, or that he had killed himself while trying to kill another.

Suicide is no longer an offence, although it is still available as a verdict in **6–002** a coroner's court.[2] It was abolished by section 1(1) of the Suicide Act 1961[3]:

"The rule of law whereby it is a crime for a person to commit suicide is hereby abrogated."

The attempt to commit suicide was a misdemeanour at common law. This is also no longer an offence.[4]

As the *mens rea* of suicide was the *mens rea* of murder, if the defendant **6–003** failed to kill himself but did kill another person during the attempted suicide, then the defendant could be guilty of murder. This was achieved by the use of the doctrine of transferred malice.[5] This can no longer apply. However, in such a situation the defendant could be guilty of the death of the other if he has the *mens rea* or murder, or, perhaps, more likely, reckless manslaughter, with regard to the victim.

---

[1] Hawkins 1 P.C. 77; 1 Hale P.C. 411–419—"Felo de se or suicide is, where a man of the age of discretion, and *compos mentis*, voluntarily kills himself by stabbing, poison or any other way."

[2] *R. v. Cardiff Crown Court, ex p. Thomas* [1970] 3 All E.R. 469.

[3] See 2nd Report, Criminal Law Revision Committee (1960) Cmnd. 1187.

[4] Held not to be attempted murder under s.15 of the Offences Against the Person Act 1861 (repealed in the Criminal Law Act 1977) in *R. v. Burgess* (1862) 9 Cox C.C. 247; *R. v. Mann* (1914) 2 K.B. 107.

[5] *R. v. Hopwood* (1913) 8 Cr.App.R. 143; *R. v. Spence* (1957) 41 Cr.App.R. 80; *R. v. French* (1955) 39 Cr.App.R. 192.

II. AIDING AND ABETTING SUICIDE

(1) DEFINITION

6–004   The offence is set out in section 2(1) of the Suicide Act 1961:

> "A person who aids, abets, counsels or procures the suicide of another, or an attempt by another to commit suicide shall be liable on conviction on indictment to . . ."

(2) MODE OF TRIAL AND PUNISHMENT

6–005   The offence under section 2(1) is triable on indictment only, and is a Class 3 offence. The maximum sentence is fourteen years' imprisonment.[6]

(3) RESTRICTIONS ON PROSECUTION

6–006   Proceedings may only be commenced by or with the consent of the Director of Public Prosecutions.[7]

(4) ALTERNATIVE VERDICT

6–007   If the defendant is charged with an offence under section 2(1) and it is found that he did the killing, then it is not possible to find an alternative verdict of murder or manslaughter, and the defendant will be acquitted.

(5) "AIDS, ABETS, COUNSELS OR PROCURES"

6–008   It will be noted that these are the words used to describe secondary acts of participation in section 8 of the Accessories and Abettors Act 1861. However, in section 2(1) the acts of participation are themselves the substantive offence. It has been suggested that the words should bear the same meaning as they do in the Accessories and Abettors Act.[8]

6–009   In *Attorney-General v. Able*,[9] Woolf J. said that the words should be "seen as a whole".[10] It was not necessary to allege that the defendant had done any particular one of the four activities. He further distinguished aiding and procuring, requiring a causal link where procuring is relied on, but not where there is only an act of assistance.[11]

It would seem, then, that the actions required to constitute the offence under section 2(1) are the same as in the general law of secondary participation. Woolf J. stated the elements required for this offence in the context

---

[6] Suicide Act 1961, s.2(1).
[7] Suicide Act 1961, s.2(2).
[8] *R. v. Reed* [1982] Crim. L.R. 819; see too Magistrates' Courts Act 1980, s.4.
[9] [1984] 1 All E.R. 277; see article by K. Smith in [1983] Crim. L.R. 579.
[10] *ibid.* at p. 285.
[11] *ibid.* at p. 288.

of a case involving a booklet entitled "A Guide to Self-Deliverance", published by the Voluntary Euthanasia Society:

"Before an offence can be established to have been committed, it must at least be proved (a) that the alleged offender had the necessary intent, that is, he intended the booklet to be used by someone contemplating suicide and intended that that person would be assisted by the booklet's contents, or otherwise encouraged to take or to attempt to take his own life; (b) that while he still had that intention he distributed the booklet to such a person who read it; and, (c) in addition, if an offence under section 2 of the 1961 Act is to be proved, that such a person was assisted or encouraged by so reading the booklet to take or to attempt to take his own life."[12]

If inaction by the deceased led to death, then it is submitted this is not **6–010** suicide, as the offence requires an act. Hence, there can be no liability under section 2 for those whose acts assist, *e.g.* doctors assisting patients to die if the patient refuses treatment. There is some doubt whether the offence covers an omission to prevent suicide. If the defendant fails to act to prevent a suicide, then it is further submitted that there is no offence under section 2. At the very least, this could only lead to liability if the defendant were under some duty towards the deceased, which the defendant failed to perform intending to assist the suicide.

It should be noted that section 2(1) covers both aiding and abetting suicide, **6–011** and aiding and abetting attempted suicide. There are two forms of the offence. Suicide or an attempt must be established.

(a) Mental element

It was said in *Attorney-General v. Able* that it was not necessary for the **6–012** supplier of the booklet to know the state of mind of the actual recipient of the booklet.[13] An intention to assist need not, however, involve a desire that the suicide should be committed or attempted.[14] The case does not resolve a difficult issue on the mental element. Does the mental element of the offence follow the rules in the general law of participation, or, since the acts of participation here constitute the main offence, is the mental element to be defined in a way independent of those general rules?

(b) Attempt to aid and abet

Since the substantive offence in section 2 is the act of participation, it is **6–013** possible for a defendant to be charged with an attempt to commit the offence.[15] The restriction in the Criminal Attempts Act 1981 does not apply.[16] It is not necessary for this form of the offence to show that the other person has com-

---

[12] *ibid.* at p. 288C.
[13] *ibid.* at p. 287.
[14] *ibid.* at p. 287; for further discussion see the article by Smith cited in n. 9 above.
[15] *McShane* (1977) 66 Cr.App.R. 97.
[16] See s.1(4)(b) of the Criminal Attempts Act 1981; note s.3 of the Criminal Attempts Act 1981 (see para. 3–068).

mitted or attempted to commit suicide.[17] The law on attempt set out in the Criminal Attempts Act 1981 applies to the attempt under section 2(1).

(c) Aids and abets suicide by a child

6-014   For this see section 2(3) of the Suicide Act 1961 and Schedule I.

III. KILLING BY THE SURVIVOR OF A SUICIDE PACT

(1) DEFINITION

6-015   The following provision is made by section 4(1) of the Homicide Act 1957:

> "It shall be manslaughter and shall not be murder, for a person acting in pursuance of a suicide pact between him and another to kill the other or be a party to the other being killed by a third person."

6-016   If one person by his act intentionally kills another, even though the other has requested this, it is murder. If, however, the killer has himself agreed to die, then section 4(1) will apply.

Section 4(1) covers the situation where the defendant carries out the killing of the deceased, or is a party to the killing of the deceased by another member of the pact. If the deceased had taken his own life, a charge would lie under section 2(1). That offence is an alternative verdict on a manslaughter charge.[18]

6-017   It is presumably the case that if the defendant attempts to kill the other and fails, then it will be attempted manslaughter, not attempted murder. There is doubt about this in the context of the other forms of voluntary manslaughter (see Chapter 5). The defendant could always be charged with some other offence, such as section 18 of the Offences Against the Person Act 1861, if the requisite degree of injury is caused.

(2) BURDEN OF PROOF

6-018   The burden of proof is on the defendant to prove that he was acting pursuant to the pact on a balance of probabilities.[19]

(3) MODE OF TRIAL AND PUNISHMENT

6-019   The maximum sentence is life imprisonment.

(4) "SUICIDE PACT"

6-020   "Suicide pact" is defined by section 4(1) of the Homicide Act 1957:

> "For the purposes of this section "suicide pact" means a common agreement

---

[17] *McShane* (1977) 66 Cr.App.R. 97.
[18] *R. v. Robey* (1979) 1 Cr.App.R. (S.) 127.
[19] Homicide Act 1957, s.4(2).

between two or more persons having for its object the death of all of them, whether or not each is to take his own life, but nothing done by a person who enters into a suicide pact shall be treated as done by him in pursuance of the pact unless it is done while he has the settled intention of dying in pursuance of the pact."

It must be noted that the defendant must have a settled intent to die himself, at the time of the killing, in order to bring himself within the section. If two parties both agree to commit suicide, this is not a suicide pact, but concurrent suicides.

(a) Year and a day rule

The year and a day rule no longer applies to either manslaughter under   **6–021**
section 4(1) or suicide as referred to in section 2(1).[20]

IV. GENOCIDE

(1) INTRODUCTION

Genocide is made a crime under English law by section 1(1) of the Genocide   **6–022**
Act 1969. This Act defines "genocide" by reference to Article II of the Convention on the Prevention and Punishment of the Crime of Genocide, approved by the General Assembly of the United Nations on December 9, 1948.[21]

(2) DEFINITION OF "GENOCIDE"

The definition of "genocide" is contained in the Schedule to the Act, which   **6–023**
reproduces Article II of the Convention:

"In the present Convention, genocide means any of the following acts committed with intent to destroy, in whole or in part, a national, ethnical, racial or religious group, as such:
(a) killing members of the group;
(b) causing serious bodily harm or mental harm to members of the group;
(c) deliberately inflicting on the group conditions of life calculated to bring about its physical destruction in whole or in part;
(d) imposing measures intended to prevent births within the group;
(e) forcibly transferring children of the group to another group."

(3) MODE OF TRIAL AND PUNISHMENT

The offence of genocide is triable on indictment and falls in Class 1. The   **6–024**
maximum punishment is life imprisonment if any person is killed,[22] and 14 years' imprisonment in any other case.[23]

---

[20] Law Reform (Year and a Day Rule) Act 1996.
[21] s.1(1) and Sched.
[22] s.1(2)(a).
[23] s.1(2)(b).

(4) RESTRICTIONS ON PROSECUTION

6–025   Prosecutions may only be brought by or with the consent of the Attorney-General.[24]

(5) TERRITORIAL APPLICATION

6–026   The Act provides for its extension by Order in Council with exception, adaptation, or modification to the Channel Islands, Isle of Man or any colony, other than a colony for whose external relations the United Kingdom is not responsible.[25] Orders have been made extending the Act to Guernsey,[26] Overseas Territories,[27] and the Isle of Man and Jersey.[28]

---

[24] s.1(3).
[25] s.3(2).
[26] Genocide Act 1969 (Guernsey) Order 1969 (S.I. 1969 No. 739).
[27] Genocide Act 1969 (Overseas Territories) Order 1970 (S.I. 1970 No. 146).
[28] Genocide Act 1969 (Isle of Man and Jersey) Order 1974 (S.I. 1974 No. 1113).

CHAPTER 7

ABORTION, CHILD DESTRUCTION AND INFANTICIDE

I. ABORTION

To kill a child in the womb or in the process of being born is not murder. **7–001**
At common law the killing of a child in the womb after quickening[1] was a
misdemeanour. In 1803[2] it became a felony punishable by death to administer
a poison with intent to procure the miscarriage of a woman quick with child
and a felony punishable with imprisonment or transportation, to administer a
poison with like intent where the woman was not proved to be quick with
child. In 1837[3] the distinction between a foetus which had quickened and one
which had not quickened was abolished.[4]

Abortion is now covered by section 58 of the Offences Against the Person **7–002**
Act 1861, which makes it an offence to attempt to procure a miscarriage from
any time after the conception of a child until its birth (subject to the Abortion
Act 1967). The offence overlaps with that created by section 1 of the Infant
Life (Preservation) Act 1929, which was enacted to fill the gap in the law
which existed where a child was killed during the process of birth. Where the
infant victim has been wholly expelled from the mother's body and is alive
the law of murder applies,[5] except where the mother is entitled to the defence
in section 1(1) of the Infanticide Act 1938.

(1) ATTEMPTING TO PROCURE A MISCARRIAGE

Section 58 of the Offences Against the Person Act 1861 provides: **7–003**

"Every woman being with child who, with intent to procure her own miscarriage,
shall unlawfully administer to herself any poison or other noxious thing or shall
unlawfully use any instrument of other means whatsoever with the like intent,

---

[1] 3 Co. Inst. 50; Hale 1 P.C. 433.
[2] 43 Geo.II c.58.
[3] Offences Against the Person Act 1837 (7 Will. IV & 1 Vic. c.85).
[4] *Rance v. Mid-Downs Health Authority*, *The Times*, February 15, 1990.
[5] *R. v. O'Donoghue* (1927) 20 Cr.App.R. 132.

and whosoever, with intent to procure the miscarriage of any woman, whether she be or be not with child, shall unlawfully administer to her or cause to be taken by her any poison or other noxious thing, or shall unlawfully use any instrument or other means whatsoever with the like intent, shall be guilty of an offence, and being convicted thereof shall be liable . . . to imprisonment for life . . .".

It is a Class 2 offence, triable only on indictment.

7-004　　The important distinction in the section is that against the woman herself it must be proved that she was in fact pregnant, but this is not necessary where the accused is anyone other than the mother. However, a woman who is not pregnant may be convicted of conspiracy with another to procure her own abortion[6] or of aiding and abetting another to commit the offence.[7] "Similar facts" evidence that the defendant had performed the same operation on other women with the effect that miscarriage followed is admissible to establish intent.[8]

(2) "KNOWINGLY SUPPLYING OR PROCURING POISON, ETC."

7-005　　Section 59 of the 1861 Act makes it a substantive offence to do certain acts preparatory to an abortion. It provides:

"Whosoever shall unlawfully supply or procure any poison or other noxious thing, or any instrument or thing whatsoever, knowing that the same is intended to be unlawfully used or employed with intent to procure the miscarriage of any woman, whether she be or be not with child shall be guilty of [an offence] and being convicted thereof shall be liable . . . to imprisonment . . . for any term not exceeding five years . . .".

This is a Class 3 offence, triable only on indictment.

7-006　　Only someone who has not already got possession of something can "procure" it, so in *R. v. Mills*[9] where the prosecution evidence was that instruments which could be used for the purpose of procuring an abortion were in the defendant's flat but there was no evidence as to how they came into his possession, the conviction was quashed. The phrase "knowing that the same is intended to be unlawfully used" has been construed as meaning believing that it is to be unlawfully used and it is no defence to show that the person to whom the poison, etc., was supplied did not intend to use it,[10] or that the identity of the potential user was unknown to the supplier.[11]

(3) PROCURING A MISCARRIAGE

7-007　　"Miscarriage" and "abortion" would seem to be synonymous: for example, the 1967 Act refers to sections 58 and 59 as "the law relating to abortion". The word "miscarriage" describes the termination of pregnancy by natural or

[6] *R. v. Whitchurch* [1890] 2 Q.B.D. 420.
[7] *R. v. Sockett* (1908) 72 J.P. 428.
[8] *R. v. Bond* [1906] 2 K.B. 389; 21 Cox C.C. 252.
[9] [1963] 1 Q.B. 522; following *Scully* (1903) 23 N.Z.L.R. 380.
[10] *R. v. Hillman* (1863) 9 Cox C.C. 386.
[11] *R. v. Titley* (1880) 14 Cox C.C. 502.

artificial means and would normally involve the expulsion of the entire contents of the womb. However the Supreme Court of Australia in *Trim*,[12] a case on the equivalent of section 58, held that the section required only:

> "an intent to cause the event of birth, carriage or bearing which would take place in the ordinary course of nature to go amiss—go wrong or fail".[13]

It is unclear whether expulsion of the foetus is necessary for a miscarriage to have occurred. Recent advances in medical techniques have made that difficult issue very much a live one.[14]

(4) "UNLAWFULLY"

Prior to the enactment of the 1967 Act (see below) the law was as laid down   **7–008**
in *R. v. Bourne*[15] Section 5(2) of the Abortion Act, as amended by section 37(5) of the Human Fertilisation and Embryology Act 1990 provides:

> "(2) For the purposes of the law relating to abortion, anything done with intent to procure a woman's miscarriage (or, in the case of a woman carrying more than one foetus, her miscarriage of any foetus) is unlawfully done unless authorised by section 1 of this Act and, in the case of a woman carrying more than one foetus, anything done with intent to procure her miscarriage of any foetus is authorised by that section if:
> (a) the ground for termination of the pregnancy specified in subsection (1)(d) of that section applies in relation to any foetus and the thing is done for the purpose of procuring the miscarriage of that foetus, or
> (b) any of the other grounds for termination of the pregnancy specified in that section applies."

The amendment was designed to cope with the problem of selective reduction and selective feticide which is discussed in detail in paragraphs 7–024 and 7–025. The aim is to bring the procedures within the scope of the Abortion act 1967.

It is not clear whether this section is intended to exclude the general defences to crime, for example, the defence of necessity which might protect a doctor who did not fall within the terms of section 1(4) of the 1967 Act.

(5) "POISON, OTHER NOXIOUS THING . . . INSTRUMENT OR OTHER MEANS"

"Poison" is defined as "that which when administered is injurious to health   **7–009**
or life".[16] Administration of a recognised poison amounts to the *actus reus* of the offence under section 58 even though the quantity given is so small as to be incapable of doing harm.[17] Noxiousness is a question of degree. A "noxious thing" is something other than a "recognised poison" and must be adminis-

---

[12] [1943] V.L.R. 109.
[13] *ibid.* at p. 112.
[14] See paras. 7–023 *et seq.* below on particular problems.
[15] [1939] 1 K.B. 687.
[16] *R. v. Cramp* (1880) 5 Q.B.D. 307 at 309.
[17] *ibid.* at p. 307.

tered in such quantity as to be actually harmful, although not necessarily capable of causing an abortion.[18]

7-010   In *R. v. Cramp*[19] the noxious thing alleged was half an ounce of oil of juniper and the evidence was that oil of juniper was commonly used in much smaller quantities as a diuretic without any bad effects, but that a dose of that size would produce violent purging and vomiting which would have a tendency to procure miscarriage. It was argued on behalf of the defendant that there was no evidence that it was a noxious thing, since the evidence showed only that it would be noxious when taken in excess. Lord Coleridge C.J. rejected the argument, saying:

> "Some things administered in small quantities are useful, which, when administered in larger quantities, are noxious".[20]

In *R. v. Perry*[21] Wilde C.J. held that there was no evidence that a substance was noxious when there was evidence that it might cause a little disturbance in the stomach for a time but no further injury. A substance, which was harmless in itself but which the woman who took it believed to be an abortifacient and who suffered adverse physical effects induced by that belief, was held not to be noxious in *R. v. Issacs*.[22] In *R. v. Weatherall*[23] the thing administered was a sleeping tablet and the quantity was sufficient to have the effect only of mild sedation. It was held not to be noxious. It is not a defence that the supplier gave no instructions as to the quantity to take if a large quantity would be harmful.

7-011   "Other means" include manual manipulation. In *R. v. Spicer*[24] expert evidence was given to the effect that manual manipulation had not caused the miscarriage which the woman suffered 10 days later and that such acts could not cause a miscarriage at that stage of pregnancy. The Court of Appeal held that if done with the intention of procuring a miscarriage it was irrelevant whether the method adopted could or could not procure a miscarriage.

(6) THE ABORTION ACT 1967

7-012   The situations in which an abortion may be lawfully performed are set out in section 1(1) of the Abortion Act 1967 as amended by section 37 of the Human Fertilisation and Embryology Act 1990:

> "(1) Subject to the provisions of this section, a person shall not be guilty of an offence under the law relating to abortion when a pregnancy is terminated by a registered medical practitioner if two registered medical practitioners are of the opinion, formed in good faith—
>   (a) that the pregnancy has not exceeded its twenty-fourth week and that the

---

[18] *R. v. Marlow* (1964) 49 Cr.App.R. 49; *R. v. Douglas* [1966] N.Z.L.R. 45; *cf. R. v. Marcus* [1981] 1 All E.R. 833.
[19] (1880) 5 Q.B.D. 307.
[20] *ibid*. at 309.
[21] (1883) 15 Cox C.C. 169.
[22] (1862) 32 L.J. (M.C.) 52.
[23] [1968] Crim. L.R. 115.
[24] [1955] Crim. L.R. 772.

continuance of the pregnancy would involve risk, greater than if the pregnancy were terminated, of injury to the physical or mental health of the pregnant woman or any existing children of her family; or

(b) that the termination is necessary to prevent grave permanent injury to the physical or mental health of the pregnant woman; or

(c) that the continuance of the pregnancy would involve risk to the life of the pregnant woman, greater than if the pregnancy were terminated; or

(d) that there is a substantial risk that if the child were born it would suffer from such physical or mental abnormalities as to be seriously handicapped".

The ground which was formerly subsection 1(1)(a) of the 1967 Act is now separated into the two grounds set out in (a) and (c). The provision in the new 1(1)(a) contains a time limit of 24 weeks. The other grounds do not have such a time limit. It is also to be noted that the "maternal medical" ground now comprises two situations where the mother's well being is at risk, namely 1(1)(b) and 1(1)(c). The grounds in 1(1)(a) and 1(1)(b) require certification by two medical practitioners (see s.1(2) of the Abortion Act 1967).

The above changes do not alter the substance of the grounds for abortion which were set down in the Abortion Act 1967.

The question of good faith is one for the jury to determine on the totality 7-013 of the evidence and does not depend on the views of expert witnesses.[25] Provided that two medical practitioners are of the opinion that one of the statutory risks is present, no offence under sections 58 or 59 of the Offences Against the Person Act 1861 is committed if the abortion is carried out by a registered medical practitioner, whether or not he is one of those whose opinion has been obtained and, subject to certain limitations, the termination takes place in a hospital vested in the Secretary of State for Health or a place currently approved by him. Provided a doctor prescribes the treatment for termination of the pregnancy, remains in charge and accepts responsibility throughout, and the treatment is in fact carried out in accordance with his direction, the pregnancy is "terminated by a registered medical practitioner" for the purposes of the Act and any person taking part in the termination is entitled to the protection offered by section 1(1).

(7) THE ENVIRONMENT TEST

Section 1(2) provides that: 7-014

"in determining whether the continuance of a pregnancy would involve such risk of injury to health as is mentioned in paragraph (a) of subsection (1) of this section, account may be taken of the pregnant woman's actual or reasonably foreseeable environment."

Although there is no definition of "environment", the term clearly has the 7-015 effect of permitting consideration of a wide range of factors other than her pregnancy affecting the health of a woman. It has been argued[26] that those

---

[25] *R. v. Bourne* [1939] 1 K.B. 687 at 689. See Morgan, "Abortion: the Unexamined Ground" [1990] Crim. L.R. 687.

[26] Glanville Williams, *Textbook of Criminal Law* (2nd ed.) p. 301.

include a threat to her physical or mental well-being by virtue of the fact of the hostility which the birth will occasion, for example, because it has been established that the foetus is female.

II. CHILD DESTRUCTION

7–016   Section 1(1) of the Infant Life (Preservation) Act 1929 provides that:

"... any person, who, with intent to destroy the life of a child capable of being born alive, by any wilful act causes a child to die before it has an existence independent of its mother, shall be guilty of felony, to wit, of child destruction ...".

A proviso to this section excludes cases of medical necessity:

"Provided that no person shall be found guilty of an offence under this section unless it is proved that the act which caused the death of the child was not done in good faith for the purpose only of preserving the life of the mother".

(1) MODE OF TRIAL AND PUNISHMENT

7–017   The jury may convict of this offence on an indictment for murder, manslaughter, infanticide or an offence under section 58 of the 1861 Act, and on an indictment for child destruction they may convict of a section 58 offence. The maximum penalty is life imprisonment. It is triable only on indictment, and is a class 2 offence.

7–018   The Abortion Act 1967 expressly provides[27] that it shall not affect the offence of child destruction unless carried out in accordance with the 1967 Act:

"(1) No offence under the Infant Life (Preservation) Act 1929 shall be committed by a registered medical practitioner who terminates a pregnancy in accordance with the provisions of this Act."

(2) "CAPABLE OF BEING BORN ALIVE"

7–019   Section 1(2) of the 1929 Act states that:

"... evidence that a woman had ... been pregnant for ... twenty-eight weeks or more shall be prima facie proof that she was at that time pregnant of a child capable of being born alive".

The act does not provide that a child cannot be born alive before the 28 weeks has passed nor does it expressly say that "capable of being born alive" means "capable of survival". Babies of as little as 23 weeks' gestation have survived and foetuses of such age are clearly protected by the Act if they are capable of being born alive. What about foetuses who may be born alive but who do not have the capacity to survive? Academic writers were divided on

---

[27] In s.5(1), as amended by s.37(4) of the Human Fertilisation and Embryology Act 1990.

this issue,[28] but the Court of Appeal considered it in *C. v. S.*[29] on the application by a father, on his own behalf and as next friend of the unborn child, to prevent the mother terminating her pregnancy. Sir John Donaldson M.R., with whom Stephen Brown and Russell L.JJ. agreed, rejected the father's argument that although a foetus of 18 to 21 weeks' gestation would be "dying" when it was born, it would be "alive" until it showed no further signs of life, whereupon it would be dead. The medical experts had disagreed as to whether the foetus, which would not be capable of breathing either naturally or with the aid of a ventilator, was capable of being born alive and the court held that it was a matter of interpretation of the statute. Later the same day the House of Lords Appeal Committee unanimously agreed with the Court of Appeal decision and refused leave to appeal.[30]

The decision was a sensible one and in accordance with the purpose of the **7–020** Act. The wording of section 1 pre-supposes that the baby would have been capable of independent existence if it had not been destroyed before or during birth. However the Court of Appeal, which unfortunately decided not to give reasons for its judgment, did not lay down any general guidance as to what guidelines would be necessary for a baby capable of being born alive, and there could clearly be very difficult problems of fact with babies of 23 to 25 weeks' gestation as to whether they are capable of being born alive and maintaining an existence independent of their mothers, or whether, though not necessarily born dead, they would be born in the process of death. It seems unlikely that the courts will have to wrestle often with such difficult factual questions. Sir John Donaldson expressly agreed with the views of Sir George Baker in *Paton v. BPAS Trustees*[31] that:

> "it would be a bold and brave judge who would seek to interfere with the discretion of doctors acting under the Abortion Act 1967, but I think he would be a foolish judge who would try to do any such thing, unless possibly where there is clear bad faith and an obvious attempt to perpetuate a criminal offence. Even then, of course, the question if whether that is a matter which should be left to the Director of Public Prosecutions and the Attorney-General."[32]

In *Rance v. Mid-Downs Health Authority and another*[33] Brooke J. (following **7–021** *R. v. Handley*[34]) held that the words "a child capable of being born alive" meant capable of existing as a live child, breathing and living by reason of its breathing through its own lungs alone, without deriving any of its living or power of living by or through any connection with its mother. The court was there considering whether there could have been a lawful abortion at 27 weeks when a foetal abnormality was discovered. The evidence was that if the child had been born at 27 weeks' gestation he could have breathed unaided "for at

---

[28] Glanville Williams, *op. cit.* 290, 305; "Protecting the Life of the Unborn Child" (1987) L.Q.R. 341.
[29] [1987] 2 W.L.R. 1108.
[30] *ibid.* at p. 1124.
[31] [1979] Q.B. 276.
[32] At p. 282.
[33] *The Times*, February 15, 1990.
[34] (1874) 13 Cox C.C. 79.

least two or three hours and probably longer" and he was thus capable of being born alive.

(3) "Preserving the Life of the Mother"

7–022   These words are to be given a wide meaning. In *Bourne*[35] McNaughton J., having ruled that the exception in the 1929 Act was available to a defendant charged under the 1861 Act because of the use of the word "unlawfully" in sections 58 and 59, commented on the difficulty of deciding exactly what constituted "preservation of life" and in particular how it was to be distinguished from preservation of health, and told the jury that:

> "those words ought to be construed in a reasonable sense, and if the doctor is of the opinion, on reasonable grounds and with adequate knowledge, that the probable consequence of the continuance of a pregnancy will be to make the woman a physical or mental wreck, the jury are quite entitled to take the view that the doctor who, under those circumstances and in that honest belief, operates, is operating for the purpose of preserving the life of the mother".[36]

(4) Particular Problems

(a) Post-coital contraception

7–023   When is a woman "with child"? Post-coital contraceptive methods such as I.U.D.'s and the "morning-after pill" are widely used and generally regarded as methods of contraception rather than abortion.[37] This approach is founded on the view that a woman is not pregnant until the fertilised egg is implanted in the womb. However, the offences in the 1861 Act are defined without reference to "pregnancy" or "conception" and there is no definition of a "woman being with child". In many cases, of course, the use of such drugs and procedures would be within the provisions of the 1967 Act but it cannot be said with any certainty that no offence is committed where the statutory defence is not available.

(b) Selective foeticide

7–024   See now the amended section 5(2) of the Abortion Act 1967, set out at paragraph 7–008, above. Multiple pregnancies have become much more common in recent years because of the administration of so-called fertility drugs and techniques of in vitro fertilisation. It is possible, and quite common, to kill one or more of the foetuses in such multiple pregnancies without causing premature expulsion of the whole contents of the uterus. This is done sometimes to give a greater chance of survival to the remaining foetuses, sometimes to avoid the distress to parents who view with horror the prospect of

---

[35] [1939] 1 K.B. 687.
[36] *ibid.* at p. 689.
[37] Colin Brewer, 11 *World Medicine* 33; G.W. Duncan and R.G. Wheeler, 12 *Biology of Reproduction* 143.

the sudden arrival of a number of children and sometimes because of the risk which would otherwise exist to the health of the mother, or that the child would be born handicapped. The implications of selective reduction for the criminal law have been considered by a number of academic writers,[38] although the courts have yet to deal with the problem. The consensus of opinion is that selective foeticide probably amounts to a "miscarriage" within the meaning of sections 58 and 59, even if the purpose of such reduction is to enable the remaining foetus or foetuses to survive. There is no such consensus as to whether the 1967 Act can afford a defence in such a situation. In 1967 the techniques involved in a selective foeticide were unknown and any act which contravened sections 58 or 59 must inevitably have had the effect (if the woman was pregnant) of terminating the pregnancy by the evacuation of the contents of the womb. In referring to termination of pregnancy in the 1967 Act, Parliament must have believed it was referring to abortion or miscarriage, which are synonymous. The Act speaks both of "continuance of a pregnancy" and of "continuance of the pregnancy". It may be argued that where there is a selective reduction, pregnancy would not be terminated because the woman would continue to be pregnant. The alternative (and better) argument involves focusing on the individual foetus. When a foetus is destroyed, the pregnancy in relation to that child is terminated. This construction would appear to be consistent with the purpose of the 1967 Act, which was intended to cover not only the case where to continue to carry the child would in itself endanger the mother's health, but also the case where to have a particular child would be undesirable, either because the child would be handicapped or because the mother would be unable to cope with the child if it were born.

However, with such an approach one anomaly would remain. One reason 7–025
for selective foeticide is to reduce the numbers of a multiple pregnancy to give the survivors a better, or even any, chance of survival. But it is clear that the 1967 Act does not regard the protection of the remaining foetuses in itself as relevant consideration, since section 1(1) refers only to "any existing children of her family". It may of course be arguable in any particular case that a medical practitioner is entitled under the 1967 Act to have regard to the effect on the health of a woman and her family of the birth of a large number of children, particularly since her environment is a relevant consideration,[39] or to take the view that, if she gives birth to such a number of children, none are likely to survive, and her health is likely to suffer.

(c) Non-consensual foetal destruction

Most abortions will be consensual. However, an assault on a pregnant 7–026
woman may have the side effect of causing an unintended abortion and this was an offence at common law apart from the assault on the woman herself. According to Coke:

---

[38] See, *e.g.* Diana Braham, "Selective Reduction of Pregnancy" (1988) L.S. Gaz. 6 January; John Keown, "Selective Reduction of Multiple Pregnancy" (1987) N.L.J. 11 December.
[39] Abortion Act 1967, s.1(2).

> "If a woman be quick with childe, and by a poison or otherwise killeth it in the wombe; or if a man beat her whereby the childe dieth in her body, and she is delivered of a dead childe, this is a great misprision and no murder."[40]

In 1987, a man was convicted of child destruction after he had attacked his pregnant girlfriend, the attack resulting in the death of the eight-month-old foetus she was carrying. It does not follow that there would have been a conviction under the differently defined offence under section 58 if the foetus had not been capable of being born alive.

7-027   A reckless assault resulting in foetal death would not amount to either abortion or child destruction. However, at common law an assault on a pregnant woman which was followed by the birth of a live child which later died as a result of the injuries inflicted, apparently amounted to murder, even if neither death nor grievous bodily harm was intended to any living person. Coke continued the definition cited above as follows:

> ". . . but if the childe be born alive, and dieth of the poison, battery, or other cause, this is murder: for in law its accounted a reasonable creature, in rerum natura, when it is born alive."

The same approach seems to have been adopted under the 1837 Offences against the Person Act and since the felony murder rule was abolished by section 1 of the Homicide Act 1957, the better view is probably that Coke's interpretation no longer prevails.[41]

III. INFANTICIDE

7-028   The killing of an infant by a person other than its mother is murder, whatever the child's age. There is, however, an exception if the infant is killed by its mother while the balance of her mind is disabled. This defence was originally contained in a statement of 1922 which compared it to a "newly born" child and is now contained in the Infanticide Act 1938 section 1(1), which is differently worded. It reads:

> "Where a woman by any wilful act or omission causes the death of her child being a child under the age of twelve months, but at the time of the act or omission the balance of her mind was disabled by reason of her not having fully recovered from the effect of giving birth to the child or by reason of the effect of lactation consequent upon the birth of the child, then, notwithstanding that the circumstances were such that but for this Act the offence would have amounted to murder, she shall be guilty of [an offence], to wit of infanticide, and may for such offence be dealt with and punished as if she had been guilty of the offence of manslaughter of the child."[42]

7-029   Section 1(2) provides that a woman indicted for the murder of her infant may be acquitted of murder and convicted of infanticide if the conditions of

---

[40] 3 Co. Inst. 50.
[41] *Att.-Gen.'s Reference No. 3 of 1994* [1996] 2 W.L.R. 412.
[42] See paras. 5–005 to 5–007 for manslaughter.

section 1(1) are satisfied. Although most, if not all, cases would be covered by the defence of diminished responsibility which was not available when the Act was passed, infanticide avoids the necessity of indicting the mother for murder.

CHAPTER 8

OFFENCES AGAINST THE YOUNG

I. INTRODUCTION

Offences of assault committed on young people, particularly children, stir strong emotions and cause distress. As the Education (No. 2) Act 1986 shows, the Victorian adage "spare the rod and spoil the child" is not in accordance with the criminal law's present attitude to children. The principal statute providing criminal offences for mistreatment of the young is the Children and Young Persons Act 1933. It is inevitable that standards of child care vary from age to age, and application of the various authorities on that Act and its predecessors must be subject to such changing standards.

8–001

Reforms in the laws of evidence have been designed to reduce the pressures on young people giving evidence. When the person in the dock is the father or mother, the difficulties for a child giving evidence in strange and intimidating surroundings about events which took place in private is obvious. Before turning to the specific offences of assault on the young, we therefore consider some general matters of evidence.

8–002

II. PROBLEMS OF EVIDENCE

In cases where a child is the principal witness for the prosecution, the question whether the child should give sworn or unsworn evidence once assumed critical importance. If the evidence was unsworn, and there was no corroboration (*e.g.*, because all the evidence against the accused came from witnesses who were unsworn), then, however compelling the evidence appeared to be, the accused had to be discharged as there was no sufficient evidence to go before the jury. The spectacle of children answering questions about their belief in a divine being before they can be sworn was often viewed

8–003

as absurd—particularly when no such questions are put to adults who may have equal difficulty giving a satisfactory answer.[1]

8–004   The Criminal Justice Act 1988 introduced a number of measures to enable children to give evidence more easily and these have been developed by amendments made by the Criminal Justice Act 1991 and the Criminal Justice and Public Order Act 1994. Section 33A of the Criminal Justice Act 1988 reads (as amended):

> "(1) A child's evidence in criminal proceedings shall be given unsworn.
> (2) A deposition of a child's unsworn evidence may be taken for the purposes of criminal proceedings as if that evidence had been given on oath.
> (2A) A child's evidence shall be received unless it appears to the court that the child is incapable of giving intelligible testimony.
> (3) In this section "child" means a person under fourteen years of age."

Note that by section 33A(2A) there is a presumption that the child's evidence is admissible. The exception is when it appears to the court that the child is incapable of giving intelligible (not honest or accurate) evidence. The judge will have to determine this by a series of questions if the issue seems to arise. The Court of Appeal in *R. v. Hampshire*[2] suggested that, even though it was no longer necessary for the judge to ascertain the child's understanding of the need to tell the truth, a gentle reminder to that effect may be appropriate. If there is real reason for thinking that the child is perfectly capable of giving intelligible evidence, but is wholly unreliable for other reasons (*e.g.* has told a series of provable lies either in relation to the case being tried, or on other occasions; or is suffering from some mental illness which substantially affects the child's memory or awareness of the truth) then it will be open to the other party to invite the trial judge either to rule that the evidence should not be given (under section 78 of the Police and Criminal Evidence Act 1984), or to direct the jury that they should approach the child's evidence with special care. In *R. v. Makanjuola*[3] the Court of Appeal said that the abolition of the requirement for corroboration meant that in most cases no warning of any kind to the jury would be appropriate. Lord Taylor C.J. went on to say:

> "Where, however, the witness has been shown to be unreliable, he or she may consider it necessary to urge caution. In a more extreme case, if the witness is shown to have lied, to have made previous false complaints, or to bear the defendant some grudge, a stronger warning may be thought appropriate and the judge may suggest it would be wise to look for some supporting material before acting on the impugned witness's evidence. We stress that these observations are merely illustrative of some, not all, of the factors which judges may take into account in measuring where a witness stands in the scale of reliability and what response they should make at that level in their directions to the jury. We also stress that judges are not required to conform to any formula and this court would be slow to interfere in the exercise of discretion by a trial judge who has the advantage of assessing the manner of a witness's evidence as well as its content."[4]

---

[1] For a discussion of some of the problems, see McEwan, "Child evidence: more proposals for reform" [1988] Crim. L.R. 813; and Spencer, "Child witnesses, corroboration and expert evidence" [1987] Crim. L.R. 239.
[2] [1995] 2 Cr.App.R. 319.
[3] [1995] 2 Cr.App.R. 469.
[4] At p. 472.

A defendant may now be convicted solely on the uncorroborated and unsworn evidence of a child. Section 34 of the Criminal Justice Act 1988 abolished the rule that a child's unsworn evidence required corroboration; and also abolished the rule that a judge should warn a jury about convicting on a child's evidence alone. If there is some other reason for the child's evidence requiring corroboration (in the very few cases where it is now necessary, *e.g.* perjury), then the warning will have to be given. The effect is that a child's unsworn evidence is treated on a par with the sworn evidence of any other witness.

It is often the case when children are the principal victims that the pros- **8–005** ecution rely upon the evidence of a number of child witnesses. Often these cases involve allegations of similar fact evidence where it is said that the defendant behaved in a similar way towards a number of different children. Normally these cases are allegations of sexual abuse, but the principles of evidence apply equally to cases of non-sexual assault. Where child witnesses are known to each other, there is a possibility that they may have colluded before complaining to their parents or to someone in authority. Except in the most extreme cases, this is no longer a ground for ruling that the children's evidence is inadmissible, either at all, or in support of each other's allegation. The House of Lords in *R. v. H. (Evidence: Corroboration)*[5] held that the credibility of the child or children is a matter for the jury to assess having heard all the evidence, and the possibility of collusion is but one of the pieces of evidence for them to consider.

(1) Evidence Through Live Television Links

Section 32(1)(a) of the Criminal Justice Act 1988 enables a witness aged less **8–006** than 14, other than the accused, to give evidence through a live television link. This provision is confined to trials on indictment, proceedings in youth courts and appeals from such courts to the Crown Court or proceedings before the Criminal Division of the Court of Appeal. Evidence may only be given in this way with the leave of the court, and by section 32(2), only in cases involving the offences set out in that subsection, namely offences involving the killing of any person, assault or injury or threat of injury; offences contrary to section 1 of the Children and Young Persons Act 1933; various sexual offences; and inchoate forms of such offence.[6]

Rules of court[7] provide that notice must be given in writing to the court of an application for leave to call evidence through a live television link within 28 days of committal for trial or leave to prefer a bill of indictment. In the case of an appeal, the application must accompany the application to call witnesses, but in any event be made at least 14 days before the hearing unless

---

[5] [1995] 2 Cr.App.R. 437.
[6] Criminal Justice Act 1988 as amended by the Criminal Justice Act 1991, s.55 and Public Order Act 1994, Sched. 9.
[7] The Crown Court Rules 1982, r. 23A, as amended by the Crown Court (Amendment) Rules 1992 (S.I. 1992 No. 1847).

the court otherwise gives leave. Once leave has been given, then the child's evidence must be given by that means unless the court rules otherwise.[8]

(2) VIDEO RECORDINGS

8–007   The Criminal Justice Act 1991 made further changes in procedure. Further protection for a child is provided by section 54 (introducing a new section 32A into the 1988 Act). This allows a video recording of an interview with a child witness to be given in evidence, with the leave of the court, as part or the whole of that witness' evidence in chief.[9]

Section 32A continues:

"(2) In any proceedings a video recording of an interview which—
(a) is conducted between an adult and a child who is not the accused or one of the accused "the child witness"; and
(b) relates to any matter in the proceedings,
may, with the leave of the court, be given in evidence in so far as it is not excluded by the court under subsection (3) below.
(3) Where a video record is tendered in evidence under this section, the court shall (subject to the exercise of any power of the court to exclude evidence which is otherwise admissible) give leave under subsection (2) above unless—
(a) it appears that the child witness will not be available for cross- examination;
(b) any rules of court requiring disclosure of the circumstances in which the recording was made have not been complied with to the satisfaction of the court; or
(c) the court is of opinion, having regard to all the circumstances of the case, that in the interests of justice the recording ought not to be admitted;
and where the court gives such leave it may, if it is of the opinion that in the interests of justice any part of the recording ought not to be admitted, direct that that part shall be excluded.
(4) In considering whether any part of a recording ought to be excluded under subsection (3) above, the court shall consider whether any prejudice to the accused, or one of the accused, which might result from the admission of that part is outweighed by the desirability of showing the whole or substantially the whole, of the recorded interview.
(5) Where a video recording is admitted under this section—
(a) the child witness shall be called by the party who tendered it in evidence;
(b) that witness shall not be examined in chief on any matter which, in the opinion of the court, has been dealt with in his recorded testimony.
(6) Where a video recording is given in evidence under this section, any statement made by the child witness which is disclosed by the recording shall be treated as if given by that witness in direct oral testimony; and accordingly—
(a) any such statement shall be admissible evidence of any fact of which such testimony from him would be admissible;
(b) no such statement shall be capable of corroborating any evidence given by him;
and in estimating the weight, if any, to be attached to such a statement,

---

[8] Criminal Justice Act 1988, ss.3C to 3E as inserted by s.62(1) of the Criminal Procedure and Investigations Act 1996.
[9] s.32A(2).

regard shall be had to all the circumstances from which any inference can reasonably be drawn (as to its accuracy or otherwise).

(6A) Where the court gives leave under subsection (2) above the child witness shall not give relevant evidence (within the meaning given by subsection (6D) below) otherwise than by means of the video recording; but this is subject to subsection (6B) below.

(6B) In a case falling within subsection (6A) above the court may give permission for the child witness to give relevant evidence (within the meaning given by subsection (6D) below) otherwise than by means of the video recording if it appears to the court to be in the interests of justice to give such permission.

(6C) Permission may be given under subsection (6B) above—
  (a) on an application by a party to the case, or
  (b) on the court's own motion;
  but no application may be made under paragraph (a) above unless there has been a material change of circumstances since the leave was given under subsection (2) above.

(6D) For the purposes of subsections (6A) and (6B) above evidence is relevant evidence if—
  (a) it is evidence in chief on behalf of the party who tendered the video recording, and
  (b) it relates to matters which, in the opinion of the court, is dealt with in the recording and which the court has not directed to be excluded under subsection (3) above.[10]

(7) In this section "child" means a person who—
  (a) in the case of an offence falling within section 32(2)(a) or (b) above [an offence which involves an assault on, or injury or a threat of injury to, a person; and an offence of cruelty to a person under the age of 16 under section 1 of the Children & Young Persons Act 1933] is under fourteen years of age or, if he was under that age when the video recording was made, is under fifteen years of age; or
  (b) in the case of an offence falling within section 32(2)(c) above [an offence under the Sexual Offences Act 1956, the Indecency With Children Act 1960, the Sexual Offences Act 1967, section 54 of the Criminal Law Act 1977 or the Protection of Children Act 1978] is under seventeen years of age or, if he was under that age when the video recording was made, is under eighteen years of age.

(8) Any reference in subsection (7) above to an offence falling within paragraph (a), (b), or (c) of section 32(2) above includes a reference to an offence which consists of attempting or conspiring to commit, or of aiding, abetting, counselling, procuring or inciting the commission of, an offence falling within that paragraph . . .

(12) Nothing in this section shall prejudice the admissibility of any video recording which would be admissible apart from this section."

Section 32A(11) makes provision for rules of court to be made. Rule 23C **8–008** of the Crown Court Rules 1982 (as amended) provides that where the criteria in section 32A are satisfied any party may apply in writing for leave to tender a video recording of a child's testimony in evidence. The application must provide details of the witness' name, age, that he is willing to attend for cross-examination, and setting out in detail the circumstances of the recording; and where it is proposed to rely on only part of the recording, identifying which

---

[10] Subs. (6A) to (6D) were inserted by s.62(2) of the Criminal Procedure and Investigations Act 1996.

part. The notice of application must be made within 28 days of the committal or transfer. That period may be extended by the court. The notice must be served on the court and on all other parties.

In *Practice Direction (Crime: Child's Video Evidence)*[11] directions were given, including the following:

> "2. Where a court grants leave to admit a video recording in evidence under section 32A(2) of the Criminal Justice Act 1988 it may direct that any part of the recording be excluded: section 32A(3). When such a direction is given, the party who made the application to admit the video recording must edit the recording in accordance with the judge's directions and send a copy of the edited recording to the appropriate officer of the Crown Court and to every other party to the proceedings.
>
> 3. Where a video recording is to be adduced during proceedings before a Crown Court, it should be produced and proved by the interviewer, or any other person who was present at the interview with the child at which the recording was made. The applicant should ensure that such a person will be available for this purpose, unless the parties have agreed to accept a written statement in lieu of attendance by that person.
>
> 4. It is for the person adducing the video recording to make arrangements for the operation of the video playing equipment in court during the trial.
>
> 5. Once a trial has begun, if by reason of faulty or inadequate preparation or for some other cause, the procedures set out above have not been properly complied with, and an application is made to edit the video recording, thereby making necessary an adjournment for the work to be carried out, the court may make at its discretion an appropriate award of costs."

A video recording is equivalent to a witness statement, or to oral evidence given in the conventional way. It is not therefore an exhibit which the jury can take with them when they retire.[12] If the jury require reminding of the child's evidence, in whole or in part, then the judge should find out whether it will be sufficient if he reminds them. If the jury require to see the video again, then (i) the video should be played in open court; (ii) the judge should warn the jury not to place disproportionate weight upon the video but should bear in mind all the other evidence; the judge should, after playing the video, remind the jury of cross-examination and re-examination of the witness.[13]

8-009   By section 55(7) of the 1991 Act, a new section 34A is added to the 1988 Act which prohibits the accused in an offence of violence, a sexual offence, or an offence of cruelty to a child, from cross-examining in person a child witness or a witness in whose case the judge has given leave for the admission of a video of that witness' interview.

(3) Committal Proceedings

8-010   A child need not give evidence in committal proceedings, and the statement of that child may be read. This is provided by section 103 in the Magistrates' Courts Act 1980.[14] That provision applies to the same list of offences as is set

[11] [1992] 1 W.L.R. 839.
[12] *R. v. Coshall, The Times,* February 17, 1995.
[13] *R. v. Rawlings & Broadbent* [1995] 2 Cr.App.R. 222; *R. v. B.* [1996] 4 C.L. 161.
[14] As amended by Criminal Justice Act 1988, s.33, Criminal Justice Act 1991, s.55 and Criminal Procedure and Investigations Act 1996, s.47.

out in paragraph 8–006 above. In addition, if a video interview of the child is to be used at trial, that may be used as the child's evidence at committal. Section 32A(10) of the Criminal Justice Act 1988 provides:

> "(10) A magistrates' court inquiring into an offence as examining justices under section 6 of the Magistrates' Courts Act 1980 may consider any video recording as respects which leave under subsection (2) above is to be sought at the trial, notwithstanding that the child witness is not called at the committal proceedings."

Committal proceedings can be avoided by use of section 53 of the 1991 Act **8–011** in cases of violence, cruelty and sexual offences where the Director of Public Prosecutions is of the opinion that there is sufficient evidence to justify committal, and that a child is alleged to be the victim or has witnessed the offence and will be called to give evidence, and that to avoid any prejudice to the welfare of the child the case should be taken over and proceeded with without delay by the Crown Court (*i.e.* transfer proceedings).

"Child" is defined for these purposes in exactly the same way as in section 32(7) at paragraph 8–007 above.

(4) EVIDENCE OF SPOUSE

Section 80 of the Police and Criminal Evidence Act 1984 provides that a **8–012** spouse is a competent witness for the prosecution or for a co-accused, and a compellable witness for the accused. A spouse of an accused is also compellable to give evidence for the prosecution or a co-accused in any proceedings only where (by section 80(3)(a)):

> "the offence charged involves an assault on, or injury or threat of injury to, the wife or husband of the accused or a person who was at the material time under the age of sixteen"

or any inchoate form of such an offence. Where age is in issue for these purposes section 80(6) provides that the person's age shall "be deemed to be or to have been that which appears to the court to be or to have been his age at the time." Where spouses are jointly charged, then these provisions do not apply unless, by reason of a plea of guilty for example, one spouse is no longer on trial for that offence.

See also paragraph 1–084 above.

III. WILFUL CRUELTY TO A PERSON UNDER SIXTEEN

(1) DEFINITION

Section 1(1) of the Children and Young Persons Act 1933 provides: **8–013**

> "If any person who has attained the age of sixteen years and has the custody, charge, or care of any child or young person under that age, wilfully assaults, ill-treats, neglects, abandons, or exposes him, or causes or procures him to be assaulted, ill-treated, neglected, abandoned or exposed, in a manner likely to cause

him unnecessary suffering or injury to health (including injury to or loss of sight, or hearing, or limb, or organ of the body, and any mental derangement), that person shall be guilty of [an offence]."

(2) Mode of Trial and Punishment

8-014   This offence is triable either way. An offence committed after September 29, 1988 carries a maximum sentence on indictment of 10 years' imprisonment.[15] An offence committed prior to that date carries a maximum sentence on indictment of two years' imprisonment unless it is proved that the offender was directly or indirectly interested in any sum of money accruing or payable on the death of the child or young person and knew that that sum would become due, in which case the maximum penalty on indictment is five years' imprisonment.[16]

(3) Other Offences

8-015   The increase in the penalty for this offence means that except in the cases of really serious injury inflicted on a child by the person or persons having care of that child, this offence can be charged instead of *e.g.* assault occasioning actual bodily harm. There is an offence under section 27 of the Offences Against the Person Act 1861[17] of abandoning a child under the age of two which is rarely if ever used.

(4) Indictment

8-016   It is important that in framing the indictment the prosecution chooses the most appropriate form of the offence set out in section 1(1), *i.e.* they should allege either "assault" or "ill-treatment", etc., as the case may be.[18] However, section 1(1) creates a single offence which may be committed in any of the ways set out in the subsection, and where an indictment alleges ill-treatment the jury can convict provided that ill-treatment is proved even if some other allegation (*e.g.* assault) would have been more appropriate.[19] Section 14 of the Children and Young Persons Act 1933 provides:

> "(1) Where a person is charged with committing any of the offences mentioned in the First Schedule to this Act [which includes an offence contrary to section 1 and "Any other offence involving bodily injury to the child or young person"] in respect of two or more children or young persons, the same information or summons may charge the offence in respect of all or any of them, but the person charged shall not, if he is summarily convicted, be liable to a separate penalty in respect of each child or young person except upon separate informations.
>
> (2) The same information or summons may also charge any person as having

---

[15] Children and Young Persons Act 1933, s.1(1) as amended by s.45 of the Criminal Justice Act 1988.
[16] *ibid.*, s.1(1) (unamended) and s.1(5).
[17] See para. 8–032 below.
[18] *R. v. Beard* (1987) 85 Cr.App.R. 395.
[19] *R. v. Hayles* (1969) 53 Cr.App.R. 36.

the custody, charge or care, alternatively or together, and may charge him with the offence of assault, ill-treatment, neglect, abandonment, or exposure, together or separately, and may charge him with committing all or any of those offences in a manner likely to cause unnecessary suffering or injury to health, alternatively or together, but when those offences are charged together the person charged shall not, if he is summarily convicted, be liable to a separate penalty for each . . .

(4) When any offence mentioned in the First Schedule to this Act charged against any person is a continuing offence, it shall not be necessary to specify in the information, summons, or indictment, the date of the acts constituting the offence."

Where the prosecution allege a number of incidents which might justify a conviction for cruelty to a child, there is no need for the jury to be directed that they must all agree about the facts giving rise to the finding of cruelty; it is sufficient for the jury to be satisfied that the defendant had been cruel for the reasons alleged by the prosecution. In *R. v. Young*[20] Latham J. said[21]:

"Provided that overall they are unanimous that cruelty in the sense alleged by the prosecution has been established, that is sufficient. It might well be wrong for the jury to be given the impression that they can convict of cruelty if some were satisfied that there had been neglect, but others were not satisfied as to the neglect but were satisfied there had been an assault or ill-treatment."

(5) PERSON HAVING RESPONSIBILITY FOR CHILD

By section 17 of the Children and Young Persons Act 1933[22]:   **8–017**

"(1) For the purposes of this Act, the following shall be presumed to have responsibility for a child or young person—
  (a) any person who—
    (i) has parental responsibility for him (within the meaning of the Children Act 1989), or
    (ii) is otherwise legally liable to maintain him; and
  (b) any other person who has care of him.

(2) A person who is presumed to be responsible for a child or young person by virtue of subsection (1)(a) shall not be taken to have ceased to be responsible for him by reason only of the fact that he does not have care of him."

The effect of subsection (2) is to make clear that, for example, a parent remains responsible for a child even while that child is in the care of a babysitter or childminder, or while the child is in hospital receiving treatment. Paragraph (a) of subsection (1) involved mixed issues of law and fact; paragraph (b) will often be a question of fact.[23]

(6) JOINT RESPONSIBILITY

Where more than one person is responsible for the child or young person   **8–018**
at the time the injury is caused, they may in certain circumstances be jointly

---

[20] (1993) 97 Cr.App.R. 280. *R. v. Brown* (above para. 3–078 and n. 92) was distinguished.
[21] At p. 287.
[22] As substituted by the Children Act 1989, s.108 and Sched. 13.
[23] *Liverpool Society for the Prevention of Cruelty to Children v. Jones* [1914] 3 K.B. 813.

liable and both convicted, even if the prosecution cannot prove which of them caused the injury. If the allegation is of a single act, then the prosecution must prove which person was responsible for it or that they were acting in a joint enterprise, as with any other type of offence.[24] Where a single act or series of acts capable of being committed by one person was the cause of the injuries to the child, then in a prosecution of the parents or persons in *loco parentis* the prosecution must show which person inflicted the injuries, and how the other assisted. In *R. v. Aston*[25] the Court of Appeal held that the case against each of two defendants should have been stopped at the close of the prosecution case. There was nothing to indicate that one rather than the other had inflicted the injuries, and no evidence that they had acted in concert.

8-019   Where it is alleged that the offence was committed by a course of conduct which must have been apparent even to the person who did not commit the acts, then both will be guilty in the absence of evidence that he or she took steps to protect the child or young person, or was acting under duress.[26] Where it is proved that an accused was present at the time or times that injury was inflicted, then failure to give any explanation for that injury can give rise to an inference that person was party to the offence. In *R. v. Russell*[27] the Court of Appeal dismissed the appeal against a conviction of manslaughter by the parents of a 15-month-old child who had died of a massive overdose of methadone. They had been in the habit of dipping her dummy in the drug to placate her. The amount which caused her death must have been administered deliberately. Both denied doing so. The Court of Appeal held that the jury was entitled to infer joint enterprise from their previous conduct in giving drugs to their child, and from the absence of any other explanation by them for the child's death. The court said that, generally speaking, parents were in no different position from any other person charged with a joint offence except that a parent may have a positive duty to intervene to protect a child. There was no evidence in *Russell* to prove that both defendants were present when the fatal dose was administered other than their past conduct, which the court held enabled the jury to infer participation by both in the offence. Where there is no evidence of earlier participation in the kind of conduct which is alleged to constitute the offence so as to give rise to such an inference, then the position is different. In *R. v. Lane and Lane*, Croom-Johnson L.J. said[28]:

> "Evidence of general custody and care does not establish presence; it is only a step towards proof. Failure to give an acceptable explanation of what happened does not fill the gap in the evidence."

8-020   In *R. v. S, R. v. C*[29] a child was subjected to a series of assaults. The defendants were the child's mother and the mother's boyfriend. The first count related to serious injuries inflicted on the child during a period of nine-

---

[24] *R. v. Abbott* (1955) 39 Cr.App.R. 141; *R. v. Lane and Lane* (1985) 82 Cr.App.R. 5; *R. v. Russell* (1987) 85 Cr.App.R. 388; and see paras. 1–015 and 1–016 above.
[25] (1992) 94 Cr.App.R. 180.
[26] See n. 24 above. For duress, see paras. 1–056 to 1–068 above.
[27] (1987) 85 Cr.App.R. 388.
[28] (1985) 82 Cr.App.R. 5 at 17.
[29] [1996] Crim. L.R. 346.

teen hours during which the mother was constantly present, but her boyfriend was not. The second count concerned injuries inflicted by assaults at times when the prosecution could not prove who committed them, nor who was present. Both defendants were convicted on count two, and the mother alone on count one. The convictions were quashed. The Court of Appeal held that the trial judge should have ruled at the end of the prosecution case that there was no evidence on count two (based upon *R. v. Abbott*[30]). The mother's conviction on count one was also quashed because the judge had failed to direct the jury properly to consider whether she was guilty by reason of joint enterprise, or whether the boyfriend alone had committed it, or whether she alone was responsible, or whether they could not be sure who had done it. There was no count in the indictment for an offence contrary to section 1 of the Children and Young Persons Act 1933—had there been then the issue of who actually assaulted the child would have been of less significance; the prosecution could have relied upon failure to take steps to protect the child in the care of either defendant from the acts of each other.

(7) PROOF OF AGE

Section 99(2) of the Children and Young Persons Act 1933 provides: **8–021**

"Where in any charge or indictment for any offence under this Act or any of the offences mentioned in the First Schedule to this Act except as provided in that Schedule, it is alleged that the person by or in respect of whom the offence was committed was a child or young person or was under or had attained any specified age, and he appears to the court to have been at the date of the alleged offence a child or young person or to have been under or to have attained a particular age, as the case may be, he shall for the purposes of this Act be presumed to have been under or to have attained that age, as the case may be, unless the contrary is proved."

For the offences mentioned in the First Schedule see paragraph 8–016 above.

Section 99(4) of the Children and Young Persons Act 1933 provides: **8–022**

"Where a person is charged with an offence under this Act in respect of a person apparently under a specified age it shall be a defence to prove that the person was actually over that age."

The burden of proof lies on the defendant on the balance of probabilities.[31]

(8) CUSTODY, CHARGE, OR CARE

See paragraph 8–017 above. One parent cannot divest himself of the   **8–023**
responsibility imposed by this section by agreement with the other parent.[32]

---

[30] See n. 24 above.
[31] *R. v. Carr-Briant* (1943) 29 Cr.App.R. 76.
[32] *Brooks v. Blount* [1923] 1 K.B. 257.

(9) Assaults

8-024   See paragraphs 2–002 to 2–013 above. In *R. v. Hatton*[33] it was held that an assault must be such as is likely to cause unnecessary suffering or injury to the health of the child if it is to be within section 1.

(10) Ill-Treats

8-025   The Act contains no definition of this word. It is apt to cover conduct consisting of a series of acts, none serious enough in themselves to amount to a specific alternative under section 1(1), *e.g.* a series of minor assaults, or psychological cruelty, or locking the child in a room.

(11) Neglects

8-026   Section 1(2) of the 1933 Act[34] provides:

> "(a) a parent or other person legally liable to maintain a child or young person shall be deemed to have neglected him in a manner likely to cause injury to his health if he has failed to provide adequate food, clothing, medical aid or lodging for him, or if, having been unable otherwise to provide such food, clothing, medical aid or lodging he has failed to take steps to procure it to be provided under the enactments applicable on that behalf;
>
> (b) where it is proved that the death of an infant under three years of age was caused by suffocation (not being suffocation caused by disease or the presence of any foreign body in the air or throat passages of the infant) while the infant was in bed with some other person who has attained the age of sixteen years, that other person shall, if he was, when he went to bed, under the influence of drink, be deemed to have neglected the infant in a manner likely to cause suffering to its health."

8-027   Lord Russell of Killowen C.J. in *R. v. Senior*[35] said:

> "Neglect is the want of reasonable care—that is the omission of such steps as a reasonable parent would take such as are usually taken in the ordinary experience of mankind—that is, in such a case as the present, provided the parent had such means as would enable him to take the necessary steps."

In that case the defendant belonged to a religious sect which objected to medical aid. He refused to call a doctor to his child who was dangerously ill and who died as a result. He was convicted of manslaughter and his conviction was upheld on appeal. The defendant in *Oakey v. Jackson*[36] refused to let his daughter, aged 13, undergo an operation to remove her adenoids, which were impairing her health. The operation was not a dangerous one. It was held that his refusal made him guilty of wilful neglect. However, the court did say that refusal to allow a child to have an operation would not amount to wilful neglect

---

[33] [1925] 2 K.B. 322.
[34] As amended by the Children Act 1989, Scheds. 12 and 13.
[35] [1899] 1 Q.B. 283 at 290–291, a decision of the Court of Crown Cases Reserved on s.1 of the Prevention of Cruelty to Children Act 1894, a predecessor of s.1 of the 1933 Act.
[36] [1914] 1 K.B. 216. This was a decision on s.1 of the Children Act 1908, a predecessor of s.1 of the 1933 Act.

in every case—it would depend on the circumstances. So it would not be an offence to refuse to allow a child to undergo an operation which was likely to be hazardous to health if the potential benefit of such an operation did not warrant the risk.

(12) ABANDONS OR EXPOSES

To abandon a child means to leave it to its fate.[37] In *R. v. Falkingham*[38] the **8–028** mother of a 5-week-old child put it in a hamper wrapped in a shawl and packed to keep the child warm. She took it to the railway station and paid for the hamper to be delivered unaccompanied to the father. She said nothing about the contents of the hamper other than telling the ticket clerk to be very careful of it. The hamper and child were safely delivered within an hour and the child suffered no ill-effects from the journey. The child died subsequently from causes which had nothing to do with the defendant's actions. She was convicted of abandoning and exposing her child under section 27 of the Offences Against the Person Act 1861[39] and her conviction was affirmed on appeal. In *R. v. White*[40] the mother of a child aged less than two years left her child at the door of her estranged husband and told him she had done so. He allowed the child to remain outside for several hours during the night until it was found by a police officer cold and stiff. The mother's conviction for abandoning and exposing her child was upheld. In *R. v. Boulden*[41] the defendant's wife left him after an argument. The defendant then also left the house, where his five children, aged between one and nine, remained alone with little food and in darkness. He telephoned the N.S.P.C.C. and asked them to send someone to look after the children but gave a false explanation of why it was necessary. He was convicted of abandoning his children contrary to section 1 of the 1933 Act.

(13) LIKELY TO CAUSE UNNECESSARY SUFFERING OR INJURY TO HEALTH

No actual harm need have befallen the child. Section 1(3) of the Children **8–029** and Young Persons Act 1933 provides:

"A person may be convicted of an offence under this section
(a) notwithstanding that actual suffering or injury to health, or the likelihood of actual suffering or injury to health, was obviated by the action of another person;
(b) notwithstanding the death of the child or young person in question."

In *R. v. Sheppard*[42] Lord Diplock said:

[37] *R. v. Boulden* (1957) 41 Cr.App.R. 105.
[38] (1870) L.R. 1 C.C.R. 222.
[39] See para. 8–032 below.
[40] (1871) L.R. 1 C.C.R. 31, another case on s.27 of the Offences Against the Person Act 1861.
[41] (1957) 41 Cr.App.R. 105.
[42] (1980) 72 Cr.App.R. 82 at 87. In *R. v. Wills* [1990] Crim. L.R. 714 the Court of Appeal adopted this dictum (which they described as *obiter*) and said that "likely" meant anything which could well happen. The decision is criticised in the commentary in [1990] Crim. L.R. 715.

"The section speaks of an act or omission that is "likely" to cause unnecessary suffering or injury to health. This word is imprecise. It is capable of covering a whole range of possibilities from "It's on the cards" to "It's more probable than not"; but having regard to the ordinary parent's lack of skill in diagnosis and to the very serious consequences which may result from failure to provide a child with timely medical attention, it should in my view be understood as excluding only what would fairly be described as highly unlikely."

(14) WILFULLY

8–030   The inclusion of this adverb qualifying all the acts covered by the section means that the defendant is only guilty of the offence if he acted deliberately, knowing that the child or young person might be at risk of unnecessary suffering or injury to health as a result of his actions, or not caring whether there was any risk. In *R. v. Senior*[43] Lord Russell of Killowen defined it as follows:

" 'Wilfully' means that the act is done deliberately and intentionally, not by inadvertence, but so that the mind of the person who does the act goes with it."

In *R. v. Sheppard*[44] the appellants were a young couple of low intelligence, living in deprived conditions. Their 16-month-old son died of hypothermia and malnutrition. They were charged with wilful neglect in that they had failed in the weeks preceding his death to provide him with medical attention. The appellant's case was that they had not realised the child was so ill as to require a doctor. At trial, the judge directed the jury that the offence was one of strict liability, and that the test was whether reasonable parents with the defendants' knowledge of the facts would have appreciated that failure to seek medical help was likely to cause the child unnecessary suffering or injury to health. The House of Lords decided that the judge had applied the wrong test. Their Lordships held that the mens rea of this offence is deliberately or recklessly failing to provide care (and recklessness in this context means appreciating the risk exists but nonetheless carrying on; or else failing to foresee the risk due to indifference or self-induced intoxication[45]). Lord Diplock said[46]:

"The presence of the word 'wilfully' qualifying all five verbs, 'assaults, ill-treats, neglects, abandons, or exposes' makes it clear that any offence under section 1 requires mens rea, a state of mind on the part of the offender directed to the particular act or failure to act that constitutes the actus reus and warrants the description 'wilful'."

Later in his speech[47] he said:

"The proper direction to be given to a jury on a charge of wilful neglect of a child under section 1 of the Children and Young Persons Act 1933 by failing to provide adequate medical aid is that the jury must be satisfied (1) that the child did in fact need medical aid at the time at which the parent is charged with failing

[43] [1899] 1 Q.B. 283 at 290.
[44] (1980) 72 Cr.App.R. 82.
[45] See *R. v. Majewski* at para. 1–103 above.
[46] (1980) 72 Cr.App.R. 82 at 86.
[47] *ibid.* at p. 90.

to provide it (the actus reus), and (2) either that the parent was aware at that time that the child's health might be at risk if it was not provided with medical aid, or that the parent's unawareness of this fact was due to his not caring whether his child's health was at risk or not (the mens rea)."

(15) DEFENCES

Two specific defences are highlighted by the Children and Young Persons   **8-031**
Act 1933, namely wilful chastisement, and proof that the victim was aged 16 or over. On the first, section 1(7) of the Act provides:

"Nothing in this section shall be construed as affecting the right of any parent, teacher, or other person having the lawful control or charge of a child or young person to administer punishment to him."

For the extent of this right see paragraphs 1–031 to 1–037 above.
On the second defence section 99(4) of the Act provides:

"Where a person is charged with an offence under this Act in respect of a person apparently under a specified age it shall be a defence to prove that the person was actually of or over that age."

The standard of proof borne by the defendant is on the balance of probabilities.[48]

IV. EXPOSING A CHILD

(1) DEFINITION

Section 27 of the Offences against the Person Act 1861 provides: **8-032**

"Whosoever shall unlawfully abandon or expose any child, being under the age of two years, whereby the life of such child shall be endangered, or the health of such child shall have been or shall be likely to be permanently injured, shall be guilty"

of an offence.

(2) MODE OF TRIAL AND PUNISHMENT

This offence is triable either way[49] and carries a maximum penalty on con-   **8-033**
viction on indictment of five years' imprisonment.
Unlike an offence under section 1 of the Children and Young Persons Act   **8-034**
1933, this offence is not confined to those who have the custody, charge or care of the child; and this offence can be committed by persons under the age of 16.

---

[48] *R. v. Carr-Briant* (1943) 29 Cr.App.R. 76.
[49] Magistrates' Courts Act 1980, s.17 and Sched. 1.

(3) Proof of Age

8–035   See paragraph 8–021 above, which applies equally to this offence by virtue of the First Schedule to the 1933 Act.

(4) Endangering Life or Health

8–036   See paragraph 8–029 above for the analogous but not identical provisions of the 1933 Act. Note that risk of injury to the health of the child is one of permanent injury, which is more restricted than the requirements in the 1933 Act as set out in paragraph 8–029 above.

(5) Abandon or Expose

8–037   See paragraph 8–028 above.

(6) Unlawfully

8–038   In contrast to section 1 of the 1933 Act, there is no requirement that the act should have been done wilfully. What is unlawful may depend upon the relationship of the defendant to the child, so that passive inactivity by a parent as in *R. v. White*[50] will be unlawful, whereas failure to act by *e.g.* a neighbour who realises that a child has been abandoned may not. The *mens rea* of this offence is probably a deliberate or reckless act, as for assault.[51] A defence of lawful chastisement is theoretically available to this offence, although in practice it is difficult to envisage circumstances in which it would be appropriate.

V. EXPOSING CHILDREN UNDER TWELVE TO RISK OF BURNING

(1) Definition

8–039   Section 11 of the Children and Young Persons Act 1933[52] provides:

> "If any person who has attained the age of 16 years, having the custody, charge or care of any child under the age of twelve years, allows the child to be in any room containing an open fire or any heating appliance liable to cause injury to a person by contact therewith not sufficiently protected to guard against the risk of his being burnt or scalded without taking reasonable precautions against that risk, and by reason thereof the child is killed or suffers serious injury," he is guilty of an offence.

---

[50] (1871) L.R. 1 C.C.R. 31. For the facts see para. 8–028 above.
[51] See para. 2–007 above.
[52] As amended by the Children and Young Persons Act (Amendment) Act 1952, ss. 8, 9 and Sched.

(2) MODE OF TRIAL AND PUNISHMENT

This offence is triable only summarily and carries a maximum penalty of a   8–040
fine not exceeding level one on the standard scale.[53]

(3) OTHER OFFENCES

Section 11 contains the following proviso: 8–041

"Provided that neither this section, nor any proceedings taken thereunder shall
affect any liability of any such person to be proceeded against by indictment for
any indictable offence."

(4) PROOF OF AGE

See paragraph 8–021 above.   8–042

(5) CUSTODY, CHARGE OR CARE

See paragraphs 8–017 and 8–023 above.   8–043

(6) ALLOWS

This verb indicates that the offence requires proof of the defendant's knowl-   8–044
edge that the child was in such a room as is described, but not that he appreciated the existence of any risk.

VI. TATTOOING OF MINORS

(1) DEFINITION

Section 1 of the Tattooing of Minors Act 1969 provides: 8–045

"It shall be an offence to tattoo a person under the age of eighteen except when
the tattoo is performed for medical reasons by a duly qualified medical practitioner
or by a person working under his direction, but it shall be a defence for a person
charged to show that at the time the tattoo was performed he had reasonable cause
to believe that the person tattooed was of or over the age of eighteen and did in
fact so believe."

(2) MODE OF TRIAL AND PUNISHMENT

This offence is triable only summarily, and on conviction carries a maxi-   8–046
mum penalty of a fine not exceeding level 3 on the standard scale.[54]

---

[53] s.11 as amended by s.37 of the Criminal Justice Act 1982.
[54] Tattooing of Minors Act 1969, s.2.

(3) OTHER OFFENCES

8–047   A tattoo is an injury, and if done without the consent of the person tattooed amounts to an assault occasioning actual bodily harm.[55] Where a child appears to consent but does not appreciate what he is doing, there is no real consent and so tattooing such a child is an assault. In *Burrell v. Harmer*,[56] a case decided before the Tattooing of Minors Act was enacted, the Court of Appeal upheld the conviction of assault occasioning actual bodily harm of a man who had tattooed the arms of two boys aged 12 and 13. The skin at the site of the tattoos subsequently became inflamed. The boys had consented to being tattooed, but the court held that they did not appreciate to what they were consenting and so there was no consent in law.

(4) PROOF OF AGE

8–048   As a tattoo involves some form of bodily injury, the presumption of apparent age set out in section 99(2) of the Children and Young Persons Act 1933 applies.[57]

(5) TATTOO

8–049   Section 3 of the Tattooing of Minors Act 1969 provides:

"For the purposes of this Act "tattoo" shall mean the insertion into the skin of any colouring material designed to leave a permanent mark."

This definition indicates that it is the nature of the colouring material rather than the intention of the tattooer which is important.

(6) IT SHALL BE A DEFENCE . . . TO SHOW

8–050   The burden of proof of this defence lies on the defendant, and the standard of proof is the balance of probabilities.[58] By way of contrast the defendant only bears the evidential burden of raising the issue of "medical reasons", which, once raised, the prosecution must disprove.

---

[55] See para. 3–002 to 3–014 above.
[56] [1967] Crim. L.R. 169.
[57] See para. 8–021 above.
[58] *R. v. Carr-Briant* (1943) 29 Cr.App.R. 76.

CHAPTER 9

FALSE IMPRISONMENT AND KIDNAPPING

I. FALSE IMPRISONMENT

(1) INTRODUCTION

False imprisonment is both a common law misdemeanour and a tort. In practice the civil remedy is more frequently invoked, although criminal proceedings do occasionally come before the courts. As a consequence most of the reported decisions concern civil actions.

9–001

(2) DEFINITION

False imprisonment consists in the unlawful and intentional or reckless restraint of a victim's freedom of movement from a particular place.[1]

9–002

(3) MODE OF TRIAL AND PUNISHMENT

False imprisonment is a class 3 offence and is triable only on indictment. The maximum penalty is life imprisonment.

9–003

(4) IMPRISONMENT

A false imprisonment is complete when the victim's freedom of movement is restrained. A physical assault is not a necessary ingredient of the offence,[2] although every false imprisonment is also an assault in law if the victim is caused to apprehend immediate and unlawful violence.

9–004

---

[1] *R. v. Rahman* (1985) 81 Cr.App.R. 349.
[2] *Grainger v. Hill* (1838) 4 Bing. N.C. 212; *R. v. Linsberg & Leies* (1905) 69 J.P. 107; *Warner v. Riddiford* (1858) E.B. & E. 942.

255

(5) DURATION

9–005   The offence is complete even though the restraint may be momentary only.[3]

(6) BOUNDARY

9–006   A false imprisonment may take place anywhere so long as the victim is prevented from moving from a particular place.[4] It is not necessary that the area of confinement has a physical boundary. It may be physical, *e.g.* a wall, or invisible, *e.g.* a city. There is, however, no reported authority on how large or small the area of confinement need be. No offence is committed where the victim is wrongfully prevented from moving in a particular direction if he is free to move in another direction.[5] In *Archibald Nugent Robinson v. Balmain New Ferry Company Ltd,*[6] a decision of the Privy Council, the plaintiff contracted to enter the defendant company's wharf and wait there until a boat came to take him across the harbour. Having entered the wharf the plaintiff changed his mind but refused to pay the one penny exit toll. As a consequence he was for a time forcibly prevented from leaving. In holding that there had been no false imprisonment, Lord Loreburn L.C. said:

> "The payment of a penny was quite a fair condition and if he did not choose to comply with it the defendants were not bound to let him through. He could proceed on the journey he had contracted for."

It would almost certainly be different if the victim could escape only by taking an unreasonable risk, *e.g.* sliding down a drainpipe to escape from a locked room.

(7) KNOWLEDGE

9–007   It is not necessary that the victim knows he has been falsely imprisoned, *e.g.* while he is asleep the door is locked and the key taken.[7]

(8) PRISON DETENTION

9–008   Where a person is in custody without lawful authority, then he is entitled to apply to the High Court for his release. There are two remedies potentially open—where there is no apparent justification for the detention, the prisoner

---

[3] *Simpson v. Hill* (1795) 1 Esp. 431; *Sandon v. Jervis* (1859) E.B. & E. 942.
[4] For examples of places of confinement see *Bird v. Jones* (1845) 7 Q.B. 742 (bridge); *Ludlow v. Burgess* [1971] Crim. L.R. 238 (street); *Warner v. Widdiford* (1858) 4 C.B.N.S. 180 (house); *Cobbett v. Grey* (1850) 4 Each. 729 (prison); *Heard v. Weardale Steel, Coal & Coke Ltd* [1915] A.C. 67 (mine); *Archibald Nugent Robinson v. Balmain New Ferry Company Ltd* [1910] A.C. 295 (wharf); *Otto v. J. Grant Wallace* [1988] 2 W.W.R. 728 (shop); *McDaniel v. State* [1942] Tex. Crim. R. (vehicle).
[5] *Bird v. Jones* (above); see also *Bristow v. Heywood* (1815) 1 Stark. 418; *Bridgett v. Coyney* (1827) 1 Man. & Ry. K.B. 211; *Innes v. Wylie* (1844) 1 Car. & Kir. 257.
[6] [1910] A.C. 295.
[7] *Meering v. Graham-White Aviation Co. Ltd.* (1919) 122 L.T. 44 *per* Atkin L.J. (Duke L.J. dissenting), approved by the House of Lords in *Murray v. Ministry of Defence* [1988] 1 W.L.R. 692; *cf. Alderson v. Booth* [1969] 2 Q.B. 216; *Herring v. Boyle* (1834) 1C.M. & R. 377, disapproved in *Murray* above.

is entitled to apply for a writ of *habeas corpus* which requires the person detaining him to show cause why he is in custody. This remedy takes precedence over all other court proceedings and must therefore be sparingly used. It is used when there is no justification for the prisoner's detention, *e.g.* because there was no warrant of commitment or else the prisoner's term of imprisonment had expired. The other alternative—where a decision of a court which issued the warrant of detention is challenged—is proceeding by way of judicial review.[8]

There are two possible circumstances in which it might seem that a person in prison (either on remand or serving a sentence of imprisonment) who has been lawfully committed to custody may claim to have been falsely imprisoned. The first is where the conditions of his detention fall below the minimum standards set out in the current Prison Rules under the Prison Act 1952 and the Criminal Justice Act 1991 (both as amended by the Criminal Justice and Public Order Act 1994 sections 93 to 101)[9] possibly to an extent that they may amount to "severe pain or suffering" so as to amount to a possible offence of torture.[10] Despite attempts to categorize such situations as false imprisonment, the House of Lords in *R. v. Deputy Governor of Parkhurst Prison, ex p. Hague*[11] said that a prisoner lawfully in prison could not claim that his liberty had been so curtailed that his detention had become unlawful. If a prisoner was ill-treated or subjected to intolerable conditions, then his remedy lay in an action for damages.

9-009

The second situation is where a prisoner, lawfully in custody, is detained by persons not acting under the purported authority of the prison legislation. An example is a prison riot where several serving prisoners are taken hostage by fellow prisoners. The House of Lords in *Hague* left that situation unresolved.

(9) DEFENCES

(a) Arrest

For the imprisonment to be "false" it must be unlawful. The vast majority of allegations arise in the exercise of police powers, and in particular those of arrest. These powers are discussed in Chapter 2, to which reference should be made. Where those powers are exceeded, a false imprisonment will occur on arrest by police officers.

9-010

(b) Parental discipline

In so far as an alleged "imprisonment" constitutes reasonable parental control, no offence is committed. For a full discussion of this topic see paragraph 9-020 below.

---

[8] *R. v. Oldham Justices, ex p. Cawley* [1996] 1 All E.R. 464 in which Simon Brown L.J. gave an analysis of the distinctions between cases when *habeas corpus* was appropriate and those when judicial review was the proper remedy.
[9] Prison Rules 1964, S.I. 1964 No. 388 as amended by Prison Rules 1994, S.I. 1994 No. 3195.
[10] See paras. 3–262 to 3–277 above.
[11] [1992] 1 A.C. 58.

(10) MENS REA

9–011   False imprisonment may be committed either intentionally or recklessly. There is no reported authority on the kind of recklessness required, although it has been argued that it must be *Cunningham* recklessness[12] on the basis that given that assault and false imprisonment are so clearly related, it would be inconceivable that different principles of *mens rea* should apply to each. For a full discussion of this topic see paragraphs 1–098 to 1–107 above.

II. KIDNAPPING

(1) INTRODUCTION

9–012   Kidnapping has been described as "the most aggravated species of false imprisonment"[13] but curiously until the abolition of the classification of criminal offences as felonies or misdemeanours it was classed as a misdemeanour only. In former days the offence required the removal of a person from the jurisdiction,[14] but that requirement has long since become obsolete and forms no part of the modern-day offence.[15] At one time too the offence could be committed not simply by taking or carrying a person away, but further or alternatively by secreting him, but this too is no longer an element of the offence, although it is present in the majority of cases.[16]

(2) DEFINITION

9–013   Kidnapping is an offence created by the common law. The modern-day definition is to be found in the speech of Lord Brandon of Oakbrook in *R. v. D.*[17]:

> "the offence contains four ingredients as follows:
> (1) the taking or carrying away of one person by another;
> (2) by force or by fraud;
> (3) without the consent of the person so taken or carried away; and
> (4) without lawful excuse."

The offence is complete when a person is taken or carried away without his consent. It is not to be regarded as a continuing offence involving the concealment of the person seized.[18]

---

[12] *R. v. Cunningham* (1957) 41 Cr.App.R. 155.
[13] *Earl's Pleas of the Crown* 1–429.
[14] *R. v. Hale* [1974] 1 Q.B. 819 at 821.
[15] *R. v. D.* [1984] A.C. 778 at 801 *per* Lord Brandon of Oakbrook.
[16] *R. v. Reid* [1973] 1 Q.B. 299 at 302; *R. v. D.* (above).
[17] See n. 15 above.
[18] *R. v. Wellard* [1978] 3 All E.R. 161; *R. v. Reid* (above).

(3) MODE OF TRIAL AND PUNISHMENT

Kidnapping is triable only on indictment.[19] The punishment for an attempt **9–014** is the same as for the full offence.[20]

(4) INDICTMENT

The consequences of failing to ensure that all four elements of the offence **9–015** are specified in the indictment were seen in *R. v. Hale*.[21] Hale was charged on an indictment containing two counts. Count one charged him with kidnap, stating that he had "unlawfully secreted (the victim) a girl aged 13 years, against the will of her parents and lawful guardians (named)." Lawson J. quashed the indictment on the grounds that count one did not allege that the named girl was taken or secreted by force against her will. It should also be noted that in the light of the decision in *R. v. D.*[22] if a similar count appeared in an indictment today it would also be bad on the ground that it alleges a lack of consent by a parent or guardian rather than by the child itself. (See paragraph 9–019 below). The offence frequently occurs in the context of an alleged kidnapping of a child by a parent or guardian, often in contravention of a court order. It appears from *obiter dicta* of the House of Lords in *R. v. D.* that prosecutors should be loath to indict for kidnapping in such cases. In general, as a matter of public policy, the conduct of such parents should be dealt with as contempt of court. In the view of their Lordships, a charge of kidnapping should be reserved for those exceptional cases where the parent's conduct was so bad that an ordinary right-thinking person would immediately and without hesitation regard it as criminal in nature. Their Lordships further felt that it was extremely undesirable in any circumstances that a private prosecution should be mounted for the kidnapping by a parent of his own child.[23]

(5) RESTRICTION ON PROSECUTION

No prosecution can be instituted for an offence of kidnapping except by or **9–016** with the consent of the Director of Public Prosecutions if it was committed against a child under the age of sixteen and by a person "connected" with the child within the meaning of that word in section 1 of the Child Abduction Act 1984.[24]

(6) PARTIES TO THE OFFENCE

The offence may be committed by any person against any person of any **9–017** age. A husband may kidnap his wife, or vice-versa, whether or not the couple

---

[19] Practice Direction (Crown Court Business Classification) (1988) 86 Cr.App.R. 142.
[20] Criminal Attempts Act 1981, s.4(1).
[21] [1974] 1 Q.B. 819.
[22] [1984] A.C. 778.
[23] *ibid.*, *per* Lord Brandon of Oakbrook at 816F-H. The Court of Appeal reiterated in *R. v. C.*, [1991] F.L.R. 252 that it is better to avoid a count of kidnapping in an indictment alleging child abduction (for which see paragraphs 9–022 to 9–031 below).
[24] Child Abduction Act 1984, s.5; for s.1 see para. 9–025 below.

are co-habiting.[25] As to the evidence of a spouse see paragraph 8–012 above. A parent may kidnap his child, whatever the age of the child. It has always been the case that a parent might kidnap his married child, even if under the age of majority. Until recently, however, the law in relation to unmarried offspring was unclear. A definitive account of the law is now to be found in the speech of Lord Brandon of Oakbrook in the leading case of *R. v. D.*[26] The accused stood trial on an indictment containing nine counts including, *inter alia*, two counts of kidnap of his daughter E, a ward of court, on two separate occasions when she was aged two and five years respectively. The accused was convicted, *inter alia*, on the second count of kidnap. On appeal the Court of Appeal quashed the conviction for kidnap, holding that there existed in English law no offence of kidnap of a child under the age of 14 years, and further that in any event the offence could not be committed by a parent against his own unmarried minor child.[27] On appeal by the Crown, Lord Brandon of Oakbrook, in giving the leading speech in the House of Lords, undertook a thorough review of the authorities before concluding[28]:

> "For these reasons I can find no support of any kind for the proposition laid down by the Court of Appeal in the present case that there is no common law offence of kidnapping a child who is under 14 years of age, and I wholly reject that proposition."

Lord Brandon then went on to consider whether or not a parent could kidnap his own unmarried minor child. His Lordship conceded that during the nineteenth century the conventions of society were such that a father was regarded as having absolute and paramount authority over any of his unmarried children who had yet to attain the age of majority, and it was therefore considered impossible for a father who took or carried away such a child, even by force or by fraud, to commit a criminal offence.[29] However, such conventions were out of place in a modern society:

> "I am of the opinion that, having regard to the changed social conditions and legal attitudes existing today, it is possible for a father to commit the common law offence of kidnapping his own minor child."[30]

(7) TAKING OR CARRYING AWAY

9–018   The offence is complete when the victim is carried from the place he wishes to be in to a place in which he does not wish to be. It is a matter for the jury whether or not the movement is sufficient to amount to a taking or carrying away. The offence does not require the concealment of the person seized. In *R. v. Wellard*[31] the accused spotted a couple together on a common. He

---

[25] *R. v. Reid* [1973] 1 Q.B. 299.
[26] [1984] A.C. 778.
[27] The reasoning appears to be based upon a somewhat strained interpretation of the now repealed Child Stealing Act 1814.
[28] At pp. 803H to 804A.
[29] See, *e.g. In re Agar-Ellis, Agar-Ellis v. Lascelles* (1883) 24 Ch.D. 317.
[30] At 805G. For a valuable discussion of this topic see Glanville Williams, "Can Babies be Kidnapped?" [1989] Crim. L.R. 473.
[31] (1978) 67 Cr.App.R. 364; see *R. v. Reid* (1973) 56 Cr.App.R. 703 on concealment.

approached them and told them falsely he was a police officer searching for drugs. He then said that he would escort the girl home. She accompanied him some 100 yards to his car and at the accused's request sat in the back. She was, however, helped out by her friend, who had become suspicious. He was convicted of kidnap. The Court of Appeal rejected submissions on his behalf that for the complete offence the victim had to be taken to the place which the accused intended ultimately to carry her, and that at the most the facts disclosed only an attempt. Lawton L.J., in upholding the conviction, held that the distance in question (100 yards) was "ample evidence" upon which a jury could convict of the full offence.

(8) By Force or by Fraud

This element of the offence must be viewed in the context of lack of con-   **9–019**
sent. The prosecution need only prove force sufficient to vitiate the consent of the person abducted.[32] A consent obtained by a fraudulent strategem is not a valid consent in law. In the Canadian case of *R. v. Metcalfe*[33] the victim, (named Molnar) entered the vehicle of the accused, a former acquaintance, in which a friend of the accused was also sitting. The victim was driven to a garage in the belief that he was either going to talk about "old times" or alternatively was going to be given drugs. In fact the accused and his friend were acting pursuant to a plan to lure the victim to the garage where he was to be confined and held to ransom. In refusing the appeal Nemets C.J.B.C. said:

> "In my opinion the offence of kidnapping for ransom was complete on Molnar's entry into the car. Molnar's agreement to go with the abductors was no consent of law. It was obtained by a fraudulent strategem. Fraud was used as a substitute for force."

(9) Without Consent

In all cases the relevant lack of consent is that of the person taken. In the   **9–020**
case of kidnap of a child it is the child's consent which is material and not that of the parent or guardian.[34] It appears from *R. v. D.* that a very young child will not possess the necessary intelligence or understanding to give consent. In such cases lack of consent will be a necessary inference from the child's age. In the case of older children it appears that there are two questions of fact to be decided by the jury. (a) Does the child concerned possess sufficient understanding and intelligence to give its consent? If yes, (b) has it been proved to the satisfaction of the jury that the child did not give its consent? As a guide, the House of Lords did not expect a jury to find at all

---

[32] It has been argued that in the case of kidnap of a young child, force or fraud will rarely feature, *e.g.* pushing away a pram from outside a supermarket. See Williams, [1989] Crim. L.R. 473.
[33] 10 Can. C.C. (3d) 114.
[34] *R. v. D.* [1984] A.C. 778.

frequently that a child under the age of 14 would have sufficient understanding and intelligence to give its consent.[35]

(10) WITHOUT LAWFUL EXCUSE

9–021   What amounts to a lawful excuse depends entirely upon the facts of each individual case. It was stated, *obiter*, in *R. v. D.* that in the case of kidnap of a minor, whilst the absence of consent of the parent or guardian was not material as far as the third ingredient of the offence was concerned, it may be highly relevant to the fourth element, and depending on all the circumstances may well support a claim of lawful excuse. It is to be noted that the burden remains on the Crown to prove absence of lawful excuse in all cases. It was held in *R. v. Rahman*[36] that in the circumstances of "parental kidnapping", a parent will very seldom be guilty of the offence in relation to his or her own child. The Lord Chief Justice observed that the sorts of restrictions imposed upon children are usually well within the realms of reasonable parental discipline and are therefore not unlawful. Whether or not reasonable parental discipline has been exceeded is a question of fact for the jury.[37] In *R. v. D.* Lord Bridge held that parental discipline included the situation where the parent acted in contravention of an order of a competent court. However, the question was left open whether or not kidnapping should extend to other circumstances where a parent is involved. It is clear however from *Rahman* that the proper test is whether or not the acts complained of constitute an excess of reasonable parental authority and not whether or not the offence extends to circumstances other than an abuse of an order of a competent court. In *R. v. Henman*[38] the accused was convicted of attempted kidnapping when he attempted to take by force an acquaintance whom he believed to be in moral and spiritual danger from a religious sect to which the victim belonged. The Court of Appeal held that the law does not recognise as a lawful excuse the conduct of anyone kidnapping another unless it can properly be said that there has arisen a necessity, recognised by the law as such, causing the would-be kidnapper to act in that way. As far as "parental kidnapping" is concerned this decision would appear to conflict with the decision of a differently constituted Court of Appeal in *Rahman*. Reasonable parental control continues to be the proper test in such cases, but where the facts extend beyond the family unit, as for example in *Henman*, a far stricter test is likely to be applied. Certainly *Henman* is an illustration of the unwillingness of the courts to define what does and what does not constitute a reasonable excuse. For what renders lawful an act which would otherwise be unlawful see paragraphs 1–024 to 1–083 above.

---

[35] *ibid.* at p. 806B–E.
[36] (1985) 81 Cr.App.R. 349. This will of course be subject to cases where there are orders made by a court in matrimonial or care cases, or where the child is a ward of court.
[37] For examples of parental discipline in other areas see *Cleary v. Booth* [1893] 1 Q.B. 465; *Mansell v. Griffin* [1908] 1 K.B. 180; *R. v. Newport* [1929] 2 K.B. 416; *In re Agar-Ellis, Agar-Ellis v. Lascelles* (1883) 24 Ch.D. 317 and paras. 1–031 to 1–037 above.
[38] [1987] Crim. L.R. 333.

III. CHILD ABDUCTION BY PARENT

(1) DEFINITION

The Child Abduction Act 1984 replaces section 56 of the Offences Against   **9–022**
the Person Act 1861. Section 1 of the 1984 Act provides:

> "Subject to subsections (5) and (8) below, a person connected with a child under
> the age of sixteen commits an offence if he takes or sends the child out of the
> United Kingdom without the appropriate consent."

(2) MODE OF TRIAL AND PUNISHMENT

The offence under section 1 is triable either way. Upon summary conviction   **9–023**
the maximum penalty is six months' imprisonment, or a fine not exceeding
the statutory maximum, or both. Upon conviction on indictment the maximum penalty is seven years' imprisonment.[39]

(3) RESTRICTION ON PROSECUTION

By section 4(2) of the 1984 Act no prosecution for an offence under section   **9–024**
1 shall be instituted except by or with the consent of the Director of Public
Prosecutions.[40]

(4) CONNECTED WITH

Section 1(2) of the 1984 Act[41] provides: **9–025**

> "(2) A person is connected with the child for the purposes of this section if—
> (a) he is the parent of the child; or
> (b) in the case of a child whose parents were not married to each other at the
>   time of his birth, there are reasonable grounds for believing that he is the
>   father of the child; or
> (c) he is a guardian of the child; or
> (d) he is a person in whose favour a residence order is in force with respect to
>   the child; or
> (e) he has custody of the child."

There is no reason why a person who is not connected with a child cannot,
in an appropriate case, be convicted of aiding and abetting, or conspiring with,
a connected person to commit an offence contrary to section 1 of the 1984
Act.[42]

---

[39] s.4.
[40] See para. 3–124 above.
[41] As amended by the Children Act 1989.
[42] R. v. Sherry, R. v. El Yamani [1993] Crim. L.R. 536.

(5) APPROPRIATE CONSENT

9–026   It is the question of consent which distinguishes the statutory offence from the common law offence of kidnapping. Whereas the common law requires an absence of consent on the part of the victim,[43] the statutory offence requires an absence of consent on the part of the person entitled to give the "appropriate consent". By section 1(3) of the Act[44] the persons or bodies able to give consent mirror those in subsection (2), above, except that a father can only give consent if he has parental responsibility for the child. In addition, the court can give leave—either under the provisions of Part II of the Children Act 1989, or the court which granted custody of the child to any person.

(6) DEFENCES

9–027   Section 1 of the 1984 Act provides a number of defences where the accused acts without the consent of the person whose consent is required under the Act.

> "(4) A person does not commit an offence under this section by taking or sending a child out of the United Kingdom without obtaining the appropriate consent if—
>   (a) he is a person in whose favour there is a residence order in force with respect to the child [see the Children Act 1989], and
>   (b) he takes or sends him out of the United Kingdom for a period of less than one month.
> (4A) Subsection (4) above does not apply if the person taking or sending the child out of the United Kingdom does so in breach of an order under Part II of the Children Act 1989.
>   (5) A person does not commit an offence under this section by doing anything without the consent of another person whose consent is required under the foregoing provisions if
>   (a) he does it in the belief that the other person—
>   (i) has consented; or
>   (ii) would consent if he was aware of all the relevant circumstances; or
>   (b) he has taken all reasonable steps to communicate with the other person but has been unable to communicate with him; or
>   (c) the other person has unreasonably refused to consent.
> (5A) Subsection (5)(c) above does not apply if—
>   (a) the person who refused to consent is a person—
>   (i) in whose favour there is a residence order in force with respect to the child; or
>   (ii) who has custody of the child; or
>   (b) the person taking or sending the child out of the United Kingdom is, by so acting, in breach of an order made by a court in the United Kingdom.
>   (6) Where, in proceedings for an offence under this section, there is sufficient evidence to raise an issue as to the application of subsection (5) above, it shall be for the prosecution to prove that that subsection does not apply."

There are special provisions concerning children who are in the care of a local authority detained in a place of safety, remanded to local authority

---

[43] See para. 9–020 above.
[44] As amended by the Children Act 1989.

accommodation or the subject of proceedings or an order relating to adoption. In these cases, the appropriate consent is that of the local authority; or in the case of a place of safety order or a remand in local authority accommodation the magistrates' court; or in the case of adoption the court or adoption agency.[45]

In *R. v. Griffin*[46] the defendant was the mother of two children who were in care. She bought single tickets to the Republic of Ireland for herself and the children and made preparations for travel. She then went to the children's school and told the teacher she had come to take them to the dentist. The headmistress questioned her, and she firstly denied being the children's mother, then admitted it. She left the school without the children. She was convicted of attempting to take the children out of the United Kingdom without the consent of the local authority. Her defence was that the acts were not sufficiently proximate to the removal of the children from the jurisdiction to amount to an attempt. The Court of Appeal held that on the facts of this case, her act in asking the teacher for the children was sufficiently proximate and her appeal was dismissed. The court pointed out that in cases such as this, the judge must identify for the jury what is capable of being sufficiently proximate, leaving it to them to decide whether as a matter of fact it is sufficient to amount to an attempt.

9–028

This offence is becoming alarmingly more common and increasingly problematical in terms of international enforcement.[47]

9–029

IV. CHILD ABDUCTION BY OTHER PERSONS

(1) DEFINITION

Section 2 of the 1984 Act[48] provides:

9–030

"2.(1) Subject to subsection (3) below, a person other than one mentioned in sub-

---

[45] See s.1(8) of and the Sched. to the Child Abduction Act 1984 as amended by the Children Act 1989.
[46] [1993] Crim. L.R. 515.
[47] This is shown in a study by Geraldine Van Bueren *The Best Interests of the Child—International Co-operation on Child Abduction*, published by the British Institute of Human Rights, King's College, London. This book is concerned principally with civil remedies to ensure the return of children who have been wrongfully taken from the countries where they live, and from the control of those who are legally responsible for their care. It includes (at p. 10) a table showing that applications to courts in respect of international child abduction increased almost fivefold in the years from 1987 to 1991. The book also sets out the texts of the Hague Convention on the Civil Aspects of International Child Abduction 1980, and the European Convention on Recognition and Enforcement of Decisions Concerning Custody of Children and on Restoration of Custody of Children 1980. The United Kingdom is a signatory to both these treaties. The former provides for international co-operation among the signatories in securing the return of any child under 16 who has been wrongfully removed from lawful custody in another contracting state. It therefore covers similar ground to that in ss. 1 and 2 of the Child Abduction Act 1984. The European Convention requires there to be in force a court order concerning custody; and it therefore enables enforcement in one contracting state of a decision by a court in another contracting state irrespective of the child's whereabouts; it is not therefore primarily concerned with abduction.
[48] As amended by the Children Act 1989.

section (2) below commits an offence if, without lawful authority or reasonable excuse, he takes or detains a child under the age of sixteen—

(a) so as to remove him from the lawful control of any person having lawful control of the child; or

(b) so as to keep him out of the lawful control of any person entitled to lawful control of the child.

(2) The persons are—

(a) where the father and mother of the child in question were married to each other at the time of his birth, the child's mother and father;

(b) where the father and mother of the child in question were not married to each other at the time of his birth, the child's mother; and

(c) any other person mentioned in section 1(2)(c) to (e) above.

(2) MODE OF TRIAL AND PUNISHMENT

9–031   As with the offence under section 1, this offence is triable either way. The maximum penalty upon summary conviction is six months' imprisonment and a fine not exceeding the statutory maximum or both, and following conviction on indictment, seven years' imprisonment.

(3) RESTRICTION ON PROSECUTION

9–032   Prosecution of this offence requires the consent of the Director of Public Prosecutions.[49]

(4) PARTIES TO THE OFFENCE

9–033   This offence may be committed by any person to whom section 1 of the Act does not apply, *i.e.* a person other than a parent, guardian or a person having custody under a court order.

(5) TAKING, SENDING AND DETAINING

9–034   By section 3 of the Act it is provided that "taking" includes the accused inducing or causing the child to accompany him or any other person; "sending" a child includes causing the child to be sent, and "detaining" includes causing the child to be detained or inducing the child to remain with the accused or any other person. It should be noted that, unlike the common law offence of kidnapping, there is no requirement of force or fraud. Equally the fact that the child readily consents is irrelevant. It was held in *R. v. Mousir*[50] that the phrase "so as to . . ." in section 2(1)(a) of the Act is concerned with the objective consequences of the taking or detaining, and not with the accused's subjective motives.

---

[49] Child Abduction Act 1984, s.4(2). See para. 3–124 above.
[50] [1987] Crim. L.R. 561.

(6) CONTROL

In *R. v. Leather*[51] the defendant was convicted of abduction contrary to   **9-035**
section 2 of the Child Abduction Act 1984. On three separate occasions he
approached children aged under 16 and asked them to help him look for a
stolen bicycle. On each occasion the children in question accompanied him. It
seems that nothing happened other than that they were with him for a period
of time. The defendant when questioned admitted speaking to the children
but denied the offences and said the children were free to go on their way.
He did not give evidence at his trial. He argued that there was no evidence
against him that the children had been removed from the "control" of their
parents or guardians. The Court of Appeal dismissed his appeal. The court
held that "control" did not have a spatial element, and did not necessarily
entail detaining as that was separately provided for in the section. The test
was whether they had been deflected by the defendant's actions from doing
something which they would otherwise have been doing with their parents'
consent. The trial judge's direction to the jury that they should consider
whether at the time the children were with the defendant was he rather than
the parents effectively in control of them was held to be a proper direction.

This decision leaves open the question of whether it is an offence for a
person, who has no lawful authority or reasonable excuse (lawful authority
includes removing a child who is at risk to a refuge—see section 51 of the
Children Act 1989, and reasonable excuse would no doubt include taking a
truanting child back to the school or home), to take on some frolic a child
who is, *e.g.* shoplifting or truanting from school. In such cases, it could not
be said that the child was being deflected from an activity which the child was
doing with parental consent. In such cases, a notional control would have to
be implied even for children disobeying the directions of their parents or
guardians—the "Little Red Riding Hood" type of case.

(7) DEFENCES

Section 2(3) of the 1984 Act provides: **9-036**

> (3) In proceedings against any person for an offence under this section, it shall
>   be a defence for that person to prove—
> (a) where the father and mother of the child in question were not married to
>   each other at the time of his birth—
>   (i) that he is the child's father; or
>   (ii) that, at the time of the alleged offence, he believed, on reasonable
>   grounds, that he was the child's father; or
> (b) that, at the time of the alleged offence, he believed that the child had
>   attained the age of sixteen."

Sections 1 and 2 of the 1984 Act are now fraught with various difficulties—
the burden of proving the defences being merely an evidential burden in section 1 but a legal burden in section 2(3); and in some instances the defence is

---

[51] (1993) 98 Cr.App.R. 179.

made out by actual belief, however unreasonable, whereas other cases require the belief to be reasonable. For example, in the case of proceedings under section 2, if the defendant asserts that he was the child's father he must prove it if he was not married to the child's mother at the date of birth; if he fails he must prove that he had reasonable grounds for so believing. On the other hand, a defendant is entitled to acquittal if he proves on the balance of probabilities to a jury that he believed that the child was over the age of sixteen— even though it is a totally unreasonable belief. As with other cases where genuine belief is a defence, the reasonableness of it will be a factor the jury will take into account—see, *e.g. Ryan*[52] at paragraph 1–052 above.

V. HIJACKING

(1) Definition

9–037   Section 1(1) of the Aviation Security Act 1982 provides:

"A person on board an aircraft in flight who unlawfully, by the use or force or by threats of any kind, seizes the aircraft or exercises control of it commits the offence of hijacking, whatever his nationality, whatever the state in which the aircraft is registered and whether the aircraft is in the United Kingdom or elsewhere."

(2) Mode of Trial and Punishment

9–038   Hijacking is triable only on indictment. By section 1(3) of the Act, the offence carries life imprisonment.

(3) Limitation on Prosecution

9–039   It is provided by section 1(2) of the Act that if the aircraft in question is used in military, or customs or police service, or both, and the place of take-off and the place of landing are in the territory of the state in which the aircraft is registered, section 1(1) shall not apply unless:

(a)   the person seizing or exercising control of the aircraft is a United Kingdom national; or

(b)   his act is committed in the United Kingdom; or

(c)   the aircraft is registered in the United Kingdom or is used in military, customs or police service in the United Kingdom.

9–040   It was held in *R. v. Membar*[53] that the offence would be committed even if the pilot was collaborating with the accused provided that the use of force or threats were made against other members of the crew.

---

[52] Unreported, February 19, 1993. See *Archbold News*, Issue 4, April 30, 1993.
[53] [1983] Crim. L.R. 618.

VI. HIJACKING OF SHIPS

(1) DEFINITION

Section 9 of the Aviation and Maritime Security Act 1990 provides: **9–041**

> "(1) A person who unlawfully, by the use of force or by threats of any kind, seizes a ship or exercises control of it, commits the offence of hijacking a ship, whatever his nationality and whether the ship is in the United Kingdom or elsewhere, but subject to subsection (2) below.
>
> (2) Subsection (1) above does not apply in relation to a warship or any other ship used as a naval auxiliary or in customs or police service unless—
>
> (a) the person seizing or exercising control of the ship is a United Kingdom national, or
>
> (b) his act is committed in the United Kingdom, or
>
> (c) the ship is used in the naval or customs service of the United Kingdom or in the service of any police force in the United Kingdom."

(2) MODE OF TRIAL AND PUNISHMENT

This offence is triable only on indictment and carries a maximum sentence **9–042** of imprisonment for life.[54]

(3) LIMITATION ON PROSECUTION

Prosecution of this offence requires the consent of the Attorney-General.[55]   **9–043**

(4) UNLAWFULLY

See paragraph 3–191 above.   **9–044**

(5) ACT OF VIOLENCE

See paragraphs 3–170 and 3–189 above.   **9–045**

VII. SEIZING OR EXERCISING CONTROL OF FIXED PLATFORMS

(1) DEFINITION

Section 10(1) of the Aviation and Maritime Security Act 1990 provides: **9–046**

> "A person who unlawfully, by the use of force or by threats of any kind, seizes a fixed platform or exercises control of it, commits an offence, whatever his nationality and whether the ship is in the United Kingdom or elsewhere."

---

[54] Aviation and Maritime Security Act 1990, s.9(3).
[55] s.16. See para. 3–124 above.

(2) MODE OF TRIAL AND PUNISHMENT

9–047   This offence is triable only on indictment and carries a maximum sentence of imprisonment for life.[56]

(3) LIMITATION ON PROSECUTION

9–048   Prosecution of this offence requires the consent of the Attorney-General.[57]

(4) UNLAWFULLY

9–049   See paragraph 3–191 above.

(5) ACT OF VIOLENCE

9–050   See paragraphs 3–170 and 3–189 above.

(6) FIXED PLATFORM

9–051   See paragraph 3–196 above.

(7) EXTENDED JURISDICTION

9–052   This offence is triable in a court in any part of the United Kingdom irrespective of where the offence occurred.

VIII. HIJACKING A CHANNEL TUNNEL TRAIN

(1) DEFINITION

9–053   By Article 4(1) of the Channel Tunnel (Security) Order 1994[58]:

> "A person who unlawfully, by the use of force or by threats of any kind, seizes a Channel Tunnel train or exercises control of it, commits the offence of hijacking a Channel Tunnel train."

(2) MODE OF TRIAL AND PUNISHMENT

9–054   This offence is triable only on indictment and carries a maximum sentence of imprisonment for life.[59]

---

[56] Aviation and Maritime Security Act 1990, s.10(2).
[57] s.16. See para. 3–124 above.
[58] S.I. 1994 No. 570, made pursuant to the Channel Tunnel Act 1987, s.11.
[59] *ibid.*, art. 4(2).

(3) Limitation on Prosecution

Prosecution of this offence requires the consent of the Attorney-General.[60]　　**9–055**

(4) Unlawfully

See paragraph 3–257 above.　　**9–056**

(5) Channel Tunnel Train

See paragraph 3–260 above.　　**9–057**

IX. SEIZING OR EXERCISING CONTROL OF THE CHANNEL TUNNEL SYSTEM

(1) Definition

By Article 5(1) of the Channel Tunnel (Security) Order 1994[61]:　　**9–058**

> "A person who unlawfully, by the use of force or by threats of any kind, seizes the tunnel system or exercises control of it, commits an offence."

(2) Mode of Trial and Punishment

This offence is triable only on indictment and carries a maximum sentence of imprisonment for life.[62]　　**9–059**

(3) Limitation on Prosecution

Prosecution of this offence requires the consent of the Attorney-General.[63]　　**9–060**

(4) Unlawfully

See paragraph 3–257 above.　　**9–061**

(5) Channel Tunnel System

See paragraph 3–261 above.　　**9–062**

X. TAKING OF HOSTAGES

(1) Definition

Section 1(1) of the Taking of Hostages Act 1982 provides:　　**9–063**

> "A person whatever his nationality who, in the United Kingdom or elsewhere—

---

[60] *ibid.*, art. 9.
[61] See n. 58 above.
[62] Art. 5(2).
[63] Art. 9.

(a) detains any other person ("the hostage"), and
(b) in order to compel a State, international governmental organisation or person to do or abstain from doing any act, threatens to kill, injure or continue to detain the hostage,

commits an offence."

(2) MODE OF TRIAL AND PUNISHMENT

9–064 This offence is triable only on indictment. By section 1(2) of the Act it carries a maximum sentence of life imprisonment.

(3) RESTRICTION ON PROSECUTION

9–065 By section 2(1) of the Act, proceedings must not be instituted in England and Wales except by or with the consent of the Attorney-General.

(4) INGREDIENTS OF OFFENCE

9–066 It is clear from the wording of section 1 that the Act creates an offence of extraordinary scope. The Act implements the International Convention against the Taking of Hostages, and came into force on November 26, 1982. It would appear from the detailed wording of the section that the offence is not committed until the accused threatens to kill, injure or continues to detain the hostage in the circumstances and for the ends described in the section. Until then the accused can only be guilty of false imprisonment or kidnapping. If he makes the threats against the hostage, but without the qualifying intent to compel a state to do or abstain from doing an act, then he would be guilty of assault or threat to kill[64] (if the threat were made in the United Kingdom). This offence has extraterritorial effect. This will be significant in cases where the accused claims he was acting lawfully,[65] since the offence contrary to section 1(1) is not expressed to provide a defence that the state, international governmental organisation or person was acting lawfully in carrying out the act (or refraining from doing what the accused demands it should do). This would mean that it is an offence triable in courts in the United Kingdom for a person overseas to take a hostage in the circumstances described in section 1(1) in order, for example, to put pressure on a foreign regime to stop torture.

XI. PIRACY

(1) DEFINITION

9–067 Section 4 of the Tokyo Convention Act 1967 provides:

"For the avoidance of doubt, it is hereby declared that for the purpose of any

---

[64] See paras. 2–002 and 2–091 above.
[65] See paras. 1–024 to 1–083 above.

proceedings before a court in the United Kingdom in respect of piracy, the provisions set out in the schedule to this Act of the Convention on the High Seas
signed at Geneva in April 1958 shall be treated as constituting part of the law of
nations."

Articles 15, 16 and 17 of that Geneva Convention provide:

"15. Piracy consists of any of the following acts:
  (1) Any illegal acts of violence, detention or any act of depredation, committed
      for private ends by the crew or the passengers of a pirate ship or a pirate
      aircraft, and directed:
  (a) on the high seas against another ship or aircraft, or against persons or
      property on board such ship or aircraft;
  (b) against a ship, aircraft, persons or property in a place outside the jurisdic-
      tion of any state;
  (2) Any act of voluntary participation in the operation of a ship or of an aircraft
      with knowledge of facts making it a pirate ship or aircraft;
  (3) Any act of inciting or of intentionally facilitating an act described in sub-
      paragraph (1) or sub-paragraph (2) of this article.

16. The acts of piracy as defined in article 15, committed by a warship, government ship or government aircraft whose crew has mutinied and taken control of
the ship or aircraft are assimilated to acts committed by a pirate ship.

17. A ship or aircraft is considered a pirate ship or aircraft if it is intended by the
persons in dominant control to be used for the purpose of committing one of the
acts referred to in article 15. The same applies if the ship or aircraft has been
used to commit any such act so long as it remains under the control of the persons
guilty of the act."

(2) MODE OF TRIAL AND PUNISHMENT

Piracy *jure gentium* is triable only on indictment. It is provided by the   **9–068**
Offences at Sea Act 1799 that offences committed at sea shall be liable for the
same penalty as if committed upon the shore. In addition, section 2 of the
Piracy Act 1837 provides:

"Whosoever, with intent to commit or at the time of or immediately before or
immediately after committing the crime of piracy in respect of any ship or vessel,
shall assault, with intent to murder, any person being on board of or belonging
to such ship or vessel, or shall stab, cut or wound any such person, or unlawfully
do any act, by which the life of such person may be endangered shall be guilty of
an offence, and being convicted thereof shall suffer death . . ."

In any case where the aggravated form of the offence is alleged, the indictment should specify the way in which it is alleged to fall within the aggravated
offence, *e.g.* "and at the time of committing piracy and with intent to do so
did stab [A]"

It should be noted that this is the only offence against the person which
carries the death penalty. For pragmatic reasons it is therefore not used as
other offences carrying life imprisonment are equally appropriate. By a con-
cession articulated by Sir Michael Havers as Attorney-General, the normal
practice that members of the Bar *must* appear in any case for which they are
briefed, available and are reasonably competent does not apply to cases which
carry the death penalty.

9-069   Until the passing of the 1967 Act the definition of piracy *jure gentium* was, to say the least, confused. In *Re Piracy Jure Gentium*[66] the Privy Council held that piracy was committed where an attempted robbery had been frustrated. Beyond this, the board was not prepared to offer a comprehensive definition of the offence. The question remains, however, whether the definition in the Geneva Convention is exhaustive. In *Cameron v. H.M. Advocate*[67] it was suggested that the relevant articles of the Convention merely supplemented existing law, since section 4 of the Tokyo Convention Act 1967 states that they "shall be treated as constituting part of the law of nations" rather than "part of the law of England and Wales." Essentially piracy is an offence "for private ends" against international law,[68] and is susceptible to the kind of arguments raised in *R. v. Berry*[69] on the lawfulness of acts to be carried out in different jurisdictions under the domestic law of that jurisdiction. Given that international law is derived from a variety of sources, the definition in Article 15 of the Geneva Convention can only be taken as a primary definition and may be subject to qualification by international law.

(3) PIRACY BY OR AGAINST AIRCRAFT

9-070   Section 5(1) of the Aviation Security Act 1982 provides:

> "Any court in the United Kingdom having jurisdiction in respect of piracy committed on the high seas shall have jurisdiction in respect of piracy committed by or against an aircraft, wherever that piracy is committed."

---

[66] [1934] A.C. 586.
[67] [1971] S.L.T. 333.
[68] The principles of international law specifically relating to hostilities between states (see, *e.g.* para. 3–209 and n. 85 to that paragraph) do not therefore apply.
[69] See para. 3–150 above.

SPECIMEN INDICTMENTS

1. Common assault (paragraph 2.002)

STATEMENT OF OFFENCE

Common assault, contrary to section 39 of the Criminal Justice Act 1988.

PARTICULARS OF OFFENCE

D on the . . . day of . . . assaulted A. [or did assault A by beating him]

2. Assault with intent to resist arrest (paragraph 2.084)

STATEMENT OF OFFENCE

Assault with intent to resist arrest, contrary to section 38 of the Offences Against the Person Act 1861.

PARTICULARS OF OFFENCE

D on the . . . day of . . . assaulted A with intent to resist the arrest or lawful apprehension or detention of himself [of another, namely . . .] for an offence, namely . . .

N.B. If the assault is with a firearm, this must be stated on the indictment, as by Firearms Act 1968 section 17(2) a much higher maximum penalty applies.)

3. Threats to kill (paragraph 2.091)

STATEMENT OF OFFENCE

Making a threat to kill, contrary to section 16 of the Offences Against the Person Act 1861.

PARTICULARS OF OFFENCE

D on the . . . day of . . . without lawful excuse made to A a threat that he would kill A [or another person, namely B] intending that A would fear that the said threat would be carried out.

4. Assault occasioning actual bodily harm (paragraph 3.002)

STATEMENT OF OFFENCE

Assault occasioning actual bodily harm, contrary to section 47 of the Offences Against the Person Act 1861.

PARTICULARS OF OFFENCE

D on the . . . day of . . . assaulted A thereby occasioning him actual bodily harm.

(*N.B.* See note to indictment no. 2.)

5. Unlawful wounding and inflicting grievous bodily harm
(paragraph 3.010)

STATEMENT OF OFFENCE

(1) Unlawful wounding, contrary to section 20 of the Offences Against the Person Act 1861.

PARTICULARS OF OFFENCES

D on the . . . day of . . . unlawfully and maliciously wounded A.

STATEMENT OF OFFENCE

(2) Inflicting grievous bodily harm, contrary to section 20 of the Offences Against the Person Act 1861.

PARTICULARS OF OFFENCE

D on the . . . day of . . . unlawfully and maliciously inflicted grievous bodily harm on A.

(*N.B. See note to indictment no. 2.*)

6. Wounding with intent (paragraph 3.028)

STATEMENT OF OFFENCE

Wounding [Inflicting grievous bodily harm] with intent to do grievous bodily harm [with intent to resist the lawful apprehension, etc.], contrary to section 18 of the Offences Against the Person Act 1861.

PARTICULARS OF OFFENCE

D on the . . . day of . . . unlawfully wounded [caused grievous bodily harm to] A [caused grievous bodily harm to A by assaulting him] with intent to do him [or another, namely . . .] grievous bodily harm [resist the lawful apprehension of himself or another, namely . . .]

7. Attempting to choke (paragraph 3.042)

STATEMENT OF OFFENCE

Attempting to choke, contrary to section 21 of the Offences Against the Person Act 1861.

PARTICULARS OF OFFENCE

D on the . . . day of . . . attempted to choke, suffocate or stifle A with intent to enable himself [another] to commit an indictable offence, namely . . .

8. Using chloroform to commit an indictable offence
(paragraph 3.047)

STATEMENT OF OFFENCE

Using chloroform [or some other stupefying drug] to commit an indictable offence, contrary to section 22 of the Offences Against the Person Act 1861.

PARTICULARS OF OFFENCE

D on the . . . day of . . . unlawfully applied or administered to [or caused to be taken by/attempted to apply or administer to/attempted to be administered to or taken by] A a stupefying [overpowering] drug [matter or thing], namely . . . with intent to enable himself [another] to commit an indictable offence, namely . . .

9. Maliciously administering poison so as to endanger life, etc.
(paragraph 3.053)

STATEMENT OF OFFENCE

Maliciously administering poison so as to endanger life or inflict grievous bodily harm, contrary to section 23 of the Offences Against the Person Act 1861.

PARTICULARS OF OFFENCE

D on the . . . day of . . . unlawfully and maliciously administered to [caused to be administered to or taken by] A some poison [other destructive or noxious thing] namely . . . so as thereby to endanger the life of A or inflict grievous bodily harm upon him.

10. Maliciously administering poison with intent to injure, aggrieve or annoy (paragraph 3.066)

STATEMENT OF OFFENCE

Maliciously administering poison with intent to injure, aggrieve or annoy, contrary to section 24 of the Offences Against the Person Act 1861.

PARTICULARS OF OFFENCE

D on the . . . day of . . . unlawfully and maliciously administered to [caused to be administered to or taken by] A a poison or other noxious thing, namely . . . , with intent to injure, aggrieve or annoy A [or another person]

11. Ill-treatment of mentally disordered persons (paragraph 3.075)

STATEMENT OF OFFENCE

(1) Ill-treating a mentally disordered patient, contrary to section 127(1)(a) of the Mental Health Act 1983.

PARTICULARS OF OFFENCE

D on the . . . day of . . . being an officer on the staff of [employed in/one of the managers of] a hospital [nursing home] namely . . ., ill-treated A, a patient then receiving treatment for mental disorder as an in-patient in that hospital [home].

STATEMENT OF OFFENCE

(2) Ill-treating a mentally disordered patient, contrary to section 127(1)(b) of the Mental Health Act 1983.

PARTICULARS OF OFFENCE

D on the . . . day of . . . being an officer on the staff [employed in/one of the managers of] a hospital [nursing home] namely . . . on the premises of the said hospital [home] ill-treated A, a patient then receiving treatment for mental disorder as an out-patient in that hospital [home].

STATEMENT OF OFFENCE

(3) Ill-treating a mentally disordered patient, contrary to section 127(2) of the Mental Health Act 1983.

PARTICULARS OF OFFENCE

D on the . . . day of . . . ill-treated A who was then a mentally disordered patient subject to his guardianship under the provisions of the Mental Health Act 1983 [in his custody/care].

STATEMENT OF OFFENCE

(4) Wilfully neglecting a mentally disordered patient, contrary to section 127(1)(a) of the Mental Health Act 1983.

PARTICULARS OF OFFENCE

D on the . . . day of . . . being an officer on the staff of [employed in/one of the managers of] a hospital [nursing home] namely . . ., wilfully neglected A, a patient then receiving treatment for mental disorder as an in-patient in that hospital [home].

STATEMENT OF OFFENCE

(5) Wilfully neglecting a mentally disordered patient, contrary to section 127(1)(b) of the Mental Health Act 1983.

PARTICULARS OF OFFENCE

D on the . . . day of . . . being an officer on the staff of [employed in/one of the managers of] a hospital [nursing home] namely . . . on the premises of the said hospital [home] wilfully neglected A, a patient then receiving treatment for mental disordeer as an out-patient at that hospital [home].

STATEMENT OF OFFENCE

(6) Wilfully neglecting a mentally disordered patient, contrary to section 127(2) of the Mental Health Act, 1983.

PARTICULARS OF OFFENCE

D on the . . . day of . . . wilfully neglected A who was then a mentally disordered patient subject to his guardianship under the provisions of the Mental Health Act 1983 [in his custody/care].

12. Causing bodily injury by explosive (paragraph 3.092)

STATEMENT OF OFFENCE

Causing bodily injury by explosive, contrary to section 28 of the Offences Against the Person act 1861.

PARTICULARS OF OFFENCE

D on the . . . day of . . . unlawfully and maliciously burned, maimed, disfigured, disabled or did grievous bodily harm to A by the explosion of gunpowder [or other explosive substance].

13. Causing an explosion, or sending or throwing an explosive substance (paragraph 3.101)

STATEMENT OF OFFENCE

Causing an explosion [sending/delivering to/causing to be taken or received by any person any explosive substance/dangerous or noxious thing] [putting or laying at any place/throwing at/applying to any person any corrosive fluid/destructive or explosive substance] with intent to do grievous bodily harm, etc., contrary to section 29 of the Offences Against the Person Act 1861.

PARTICULARS OF OFFENCE

D on the . . . day of . . . unlawfully and maliciously caused gunpowder [a corrosive substance] to explode [sent/delivered to/caused to be taken/received by A an explosive substance/a dangerous or noxious thing] [put or laid at any place/threw at/applied to A a corrosive fluid/destructive or explosive substance] [put or laid at . . ./threw at/applied to A a corrosive fluid/ destructive/explosive substance] with intent to burn, maim, disfigure, disable or do grievous bodily harm to A.

14. Placing gunpowder near a building with intent to do bodily injury (paragraph 3.112)

STATEMENT OF OFFENCE

Placing [throwing in/upon/against/near] a building [ship] an explosive substance with intent to do bodily injury, contrary to section 30 of the Offences Against the Person Act 1861.

PARTICULARS OF OFFENCE

D on the . . . day of . . . unlawfully and maliciously placed [threw] an explosive substance in [into/upon/against/near] a building [ship], namely . . . with intent to do grievous bodily injury to A.

15. Causing explosion likely to endanger life (paragraph 3.122)

STATEMENT OF OFFENCE

Causing an explosion likely to endanger life or property, contrary to section 2 of the Explosive Substances Act 1883.

PARTICULARS OF OFFENCE

D on the . . . day of . . . unlawfully and maliciously caused by an explosive substance an explosion at . . . of a nature likely to endanger life or to cause serious injury to property.

16. Attempting to cause an explosion (paragraph 3.134)

STATEMENT OF OFFENCE

Attempting to cause an explosion, contrary to section 3 of the Explosive Substances Act 1883.

PARTICULARS OF OFFENCE

D on the . . . day of . . . unlawfully and maliciously did an act, namely . . . with intent to cause [conspired to cause] by an explosive substance an explosion likely to endanger life or cause serious damage to property [or had in his possession or under his control an explosive substance with intent by means thereof to endanger life or cause serious damage to property or to enable another person to do so].

17. Making or possessing explosives under suspicious circumstances (paragraph 3.145)

STATEMENT OF OFFENCE

Making [Possessing] explosives, contrary to section 4 of the Explosive Substances Act 1883.

PARTICULARS OF OFFENCE

D on the . . . day of . . . knowingly made [had in his possession or under his control] a certain explosive substance, namely . . . under such circumstances as to give rise to a reasonable suspicion that he was not making it [did not have it in his possession or under his control] for a lawful object.

18. Possessing articles for suspected terrorist purposes
(paragraph 3.157)

STATEMENT OF OFFENCE
Possessing an article for the purposes of terrorism, contrary to section 16A of the Prevention of Terrorism (Temporary Provisions) Act 1989.
PARTICULARS OF OFFENCE
D on the . . . day of . . . knowingly had in his possession an article, namely . . . under such circumstances as to give rise to a reasonable suspicion that he had it for a purpose connected with the commission, preparation or instigation of an act of terrorism, namely acts of terrorism connected with Northern Ireland [acts of terrorism connected with . . .].

19. Destroying, damaging or endangering the safety of aircraft
(paragraph 3.162)

STATEMENT OF OFFENCE
Destroying an aircraft in service [Committing an act of violence on board an aircraft in flight/Placing an object on an aircraft likely to destroy of damage it], contrary to section 2 of the Aviation Security Act 1982.
PARTICULARS OF OFFENCE
D on the . . . day of . . . unlawfully and intentionally destroyed [damaged so as to render it incapable of flight or so as to be likely to endanger its safety in flight an aircraft in service/committed on board an aircraft in flight an act of violence, namely . . ., which was likely to endanger the safety of the aircraft] [placed or caused to be placed on an aircraft in service a device or substance, namely . . . which was likely to destroy the aircraft] [damaged an aircraft in service so as to render it incapable of flight or so as to be likely to endanger its safety in flight].

20. Possessing dangerous articles in an aircraft (paragraph 3.173)

STATEMENT OF OFFENCE
Having a dangerous article in an aircraft [aerodrome/air navigation installation], contrary to section 4 of the Aviation Security Act 1982.
PARTICULARS OF OFFENCE
D on the . . . day of . . . without lawful authority or reasonable excuse had with him (*e.g.* a firearm) in an aircraft registered in the United Kingdom [in an aircraft while it was in flight over the United Kingdom/in an aerodrome at . . ./in an air navigation installation at . . .]

21. Endangering safety at aerodromes (paragraph 3.186)

STATEMENT OF OFFENCE
(1) Endangering safety at aerodromes, contrary to section 1 of the Aviation Security Act 1990.

PARTICULARS OF OFFENCE

D on the . . . day of . . . at an aerodrome serving international civil aviation, namely, committed an act of violence, namely . . . likely to cause death or serious injury [likely to endanger the safe operation of the aerodrome or the safety of persons at the aerodrome].

STATEMENT OF OFFENCE

(2) Endangering safety at aerodromes, contrary to section 1 of the Aviation Security Act 1990.

PARTICULARS OF OFFENCE

D on the . . . day of . . . at an aerodrome serving international civil aviation, namely, unlawfully and deliberately destroyed [damaged] property used for the provision of facilities at the said aerodrome by means of a device, namely . . ., in such a way as to endanger the safety of passengers at the said aerodrome.

22. Endangering the safety of ships or fixed platforms
(paragraph 3.194)

STATEMENT OF OFFENCE

Endangering safety of a ship [fixed platform], contrary to section 11 of the Aviation and Maritime Security Act 1990.

PARTICULARS OF OFFENCE

D on the . . . day of . . . unlawfully and intentionally committed on board a ship, namely. . . [on a fixed platform, namely . . .] an act of violence, namely . . . likely to endanger the safe navigation of the ship [the safety of the platform].

N.B. Section 11 of the Aviation and Maritime Security Act 1990 creates several offences; only that specifically alleging an act of violence has been made the subject of this draft indictment.

23. Developing or possessing a biological weapon (paragraph 3.198)

STATEMENT OF OFFENCE

Developing [producing/stockpiling/retaining] a biological weapon, contrary to section 1(1) of the Biological Weapons Act 1974.

PARTICULARS OF OFFENCE

D on the . . . day of . . . developed [produced/stockpiled/retained] a biological agent [toxin], namely . . ., of a type and in a quantity that had no justification for prophylactic, protective, or other peaceful purposes a weapon/equipment/ means of delivery namely . . . designed to use biological agents or toxins for hostile purposes or in armed conflict.

24. Using, developing, possessing or transferring chemical weapons
(paragraph 3.203)

STATEMENT OF OFFENCE

Using [developing/possessing/transferring/engaging in military preparations intending to use] a chemical weapon, contrary to section 2 of the Chemical Weapons Act 1996.

PARTICULARS OF OFFENCE

D on the . . . day of . . . used [developed/possessed/transferred or engaged in military preparations intended to use] a chemical weapon, namely . . .

25. Receiving, holding or dealing with nuclear material, or threatening to use nuclear material to commit an offence against the person (paragraph 3.215)

STATEMENT OF OFFENCE

(1) Receiving [holding/dealing with] nuclear material, contrary to section 2(2) of the Nuclear Materials (Offences) Act 1983.

PARTICULARS OF OFFENCE

D on the . . . day of . . . received [held/dealt with] nuclear material, namely . . . intending thereby to commit murder [manslaughter/an offence contrary to section 18 or 20 of the Offences Against the Person Act 1861] or being reckless whether another would do such an act.

STATEMENT OF OFFENCE

(2) Making a threat to commit murder [manslaughter/an offence contrary to section 18 or 20 of the Offences Against the Person Act 1861] contrary to section 2(3) of the Nuclear Materials (Offences) Act 1983.

PARTICULARS OF OFFENCE

D on the . . . day of . . . made a threat to another, namely . . . that he or another would murder [commit manslaughter/an offence contrary to section 18 or 20 of the Offences Against the Person Act Act 1861 against] A . . . by means of nuclear material, namely . . . intending that [the person to whom the threat was made] would fear that the threat would be carried out.

26. Setting a spring gun or man trap (paragraph 3.220)

STATEMENT OF OFFENCE

Setting a spring gun [man-trap], contrary to section 31 of the Offences Against the Person Act 1861.

PARTICULARS OF OFFENCE

D on the . . . day of . . . set or placed a spring gun [man-trap/engine calculated to destroy human life or inflict grievous bodily harm] with intent that the same or whereby the same may inflict grievous bodily harm upon a person coming into contact with the said spring gun [etc.]

27. Endangering the safety of persons travelling on the railway (paragraph 3.232)

STATEMENT OF OFFENCE

Endangering the safety of persons travelling on the railway, contrary to section 32 of the Offences Against the Person Act 1861.

PARTICULARS OF OFFENCE

D on the . . . day of . . . unlawfully and maliciously put or threw on or across the railway line at . . . some wood [a stone/some object or matter namely . . .] [maliciously took up a sleeper/unlawfully and maliciously moved/concealed a signal, etc.] with intent to endanger the safety of a person [persons] travelling or being upon the railway.

28. Throwing a stone at a railway train (paragraph 3.240)

STATEMENT OF OFFENCE

Endangering the safety of persons travelling on the railway, contrary to section 33 of the Offences Against the Person Act 1861.

PARTICULARS OF OFFENCE

D on the . . . day of . . . unlawfully and maliciously threw or caused to fall or strike at, against, into or upon an engine [carriage/tender/truck] used upon the railway at . . . [*e.g.* a stone] with intent to injure any person therein or thereon.

29. Doing an act endangering the safety of persons travelling on the railway (paragraph 3.247)

STATEMENT OF OFFENCE

Endangering the safety of persons travelling on the railway, contrary to section 34 of the Offences Against the Person Act 1861.

PARTICULARS OF OFFENCE

D on the . . . day of . . . unlawfully and maliciously endangered [caused to be endangered] the safety of persons travelling or being in or on the railway at . . . by [here set out the act or omission].

30. Endangering the safety of the Channel Tunnel Railway (paragraph 3.252)

STATEMENT OF OFFENCE

Endangering the safety of the Channel Tunnel Railway, contrary to section 11 of the Channel Tunnel Act 1987 and article 6(1)(c) of the Channel Tunnel (Security) Order 1994.

PARTICULARS OF OFFENCE

D on the . . . day of . . . unlawfully and intentionally committed on board a Channel Tunnel train [within the Channel Tunnel system] an act of violence, namely . . . likely to endanger the safe operation of the train [the safety of the Tunnel system].

N.B. Section 11 of the Channel Tunnel Act and Order 6(1) of the Channel Tunnel (Security) Order 1994 create several offences; only that specifically alleging an act of violence has been made the subject of this draft indictment.

31. Torture (paragraph 3.263)

STATEMENT OF OFFENCE

Torture, contrary to section 134 of the Criminal Justice Act 1988.

PARTICULARS OF OFFENCE

D on the . . . day of . . . being a public official [person acting in a public capacity], namely . . . , at . . . intentionally inflicted severe pain or suffering on A in performance or purported performance of his official duties [intentionally inflicted severe pain or suffering on A at . . . at the instigation or with the consent or acquiescence of B who was a public official/acting in a public capacity, namely . . .]

32. Committing a grave breach of the Geneva Conventions (paragraph 3.278)

STATEMENT OF OFFENCE

Committing a grave breach of the Geneva Conventions, contrary to the Geneva Conventions Act 1957.

PARTICULARS OF OFFENCE

D on the . . . day of . . . committed [aided or abetted or procured the commission by another, namely . . . of] a grave breach of the Geneva Conventions, namely [here set out the convention and article breached] by [here set out the acts alleged].

33. Circumcision of a female (paragraph 3.281)

STATEMENT OF OFFENCE

Circumcision of a female, contrary to section 1(1) of the Prohibition of Female Circumcision Act 1985.

PARTICULARS OF OFFENCE

D on the . . . day of . . . unlawfully excised, infibulated, or otherwise mutilated the whole [part] of the labia major [labia minora/clitoris] of A. [unlawfully aided and abetted the excise, infibulation, or mutilation of the whole/part of the labia majora/labia minora/clitoris of A/herself].

34. Murder (paragraph 4.001)

STATEMENT OF OFFENCE

Murder.

PARTICULARS OF OFFENCE

D on the . . . day of . . . murdered A.

35. Solicitation to murder (paragraph 4.096)

STATEMENT OF OFFENCE

Solicitation to murder.

PARTICULARS OF OFFENCE

D on the . . . day of . . . solicited [persuaded, endeavoured to persuade or proposed to] B to murder A.

36. Manslaughter (paragraph 5.001)

STATEMENT OF OFFENCE

Manslaughter.

PARTICULARS OF OFFENCE

D on the . . . day of . . . unlawfully killed A.

37. Aiding and abetting suicide (paragraph 6.001)

STATEMENT OF OFFENCE

Aiding and abetting suicide, contrary to section 2 of the Suicide Act 1961.

PARTICULARS OF OFFENCE

D on the . . . day of . . . aided and abetted [counselled and procured] the suicide [attempted suicide] of A.

38. Genocide (paragraph 6.023)

STATEMENT OF OFFENCE

Genocide, contrary to section 1 of the Genocide Act 1969.

PARTICULARS OF OFFENCE

D on . . . with intent to destroy in whole or in part a national [ethnical/racial/religious] group, namely . . ., killed A and B [etc.] who were members of that group [caused serious bodily/mental harm to A and B, etc., who were members of that group [deliberately inflicted on the group conditions of life, namely . . ., calculated to bring about its physical destruction in whole or in part/imposed measures, namely . . . intended to prevent births within the group] [forcibly transferred children of the group, namely A and B [etc] to another group, namely . . .

39. Abortion (paragraph 7.001)

STATEMENT OF OFFENCE

(1) Attempting to procure [procuring] a miscarriage, contrary to section 58 of the Offences Against the Person Act 1861.

PARTICULARS OF OFFENCE

D on the . . . day of . . . being with child unlawfully administered to herself poison or other noxious thing [unlawfully used an instrument or other means] with intent to procure her own miscarriage.

STATEMENT OF OFFENCE

(2) Attempting to procure [procuring] a miscarriage, contrary to section 58 of the Offences Against the Person Act 1861.

PARTICULARS OF OFFENCE

D on the . . . unlawfully administered to A [caused A to take] poison or other noxious thing [unlawfully used an instrument or other means] with intent to procure the miscarriage of A.

40. Child destruction (paragraph 7.016)

STATEMENT OF OFFENCE

Child destruction, contrary to section 1 of the Infant Life (Preservation) Act 1929.

PARTICULARS OF OFFENCE

D on the . . . with intent to destroy the life of a child capable of being born alive, caused the death of the said child before it had an existence independent of A [herself] its mother by unlawfully . . . [e.g. using an instrument or administering a noxious substance].

41. Infanticide (paragraph 7.028)

STATEMENT OF OFFENCE

Infanticide, contrary to section 1 of the Infanticide Act 1938.

PARTICULARS OF OFFENCE

D on the . . . wilfully caused the death of her child under the age of twelve months by . . . [here set out the act or omission causing death].

42. Cruelty to a child (paragraph 8.013)

STATEMENT OF OFFENCE

Cruelty to a person under the age of sixteen, contrary to section 1(1) of the Children and Young Persons Act 1933.

PARTICULARS OF OFFENCE

D on the . . . day of . . . being a person over the age of sixteen years, wilfully ill-treated [neglected/abandoned/exposed] A, a child aged . . . of whom D had at the material time custody, charge or care, in a manner likely to cause unnecessary suffering to A or injury to his health.

43. Abandoning or exposing a child (paragraph 8.032)

STATEMENT OF OFFENCE

Abandoning [Exposing] a child, contrary to section 27 of the Offences Against the Person Act 1861.

PARTICULARS OF OFFENCE

D on the . . . day of . . . unlawfully abandoned [exposed] A, a child under the age of two years, whereby his life was endangered or his health was [was likely to be] permanently injured.

44. False imprisonment (paragraph 9.002)

STATEMENT OF OFFENCE

False imprisonment.

PARTICULARS OF OFFENCE

D on the . . . day of . . . [assaulted and] unlawfully imprisoned A and detained him against his will.

45. Kidnapping (paragraph 9.012)

STATEMENT OF OFFENCE

Kidnapping.

PARTICULARS OF OFFENCE

D on the . . . day of . . . unlawfully took or carried away A against his will.

46. Child abduction by a parent, etc. (paragraph 9.021)

STATEMENT OF OFFENCE

Abduction of a child, contrary to section 1 of the Child Abduction Act 1984.

PARTICULARS OF OFFENCE

D on the . . . day of . . . being the parent [guardian/the person to whom custody had been awarded] of A, a child under the age of 16 years, took the said A out of the United Kingdom without the appropriate consent.

47. Abduction of a child (paragraph 9.029)

STATEMENT OF OFFENCE

Abduction of a child, contrary to section 2 of the Child Abduction Act 1984.

PARTICULARS OF OFFENCE

D on the . . . day of . . . without lawful authority or reasonable excuse took or detained A, a child under the age of 16 years, so as to remove him from the lawful control of B [so as to keep him out of the lawful control of B].

48. Hijacking (paragraph 9.036)

STATEMENT OF OFFENCE

Hijacking, contrary to section 1(1) of the Aviation Security Act 1982.

PARTICULARS OF OFFENCE

D on the . . . day of . . . being a passenger on board an aircraft in flight, namely flight . . . between . . . and . . ., unlawfully by the use of force [by threats] seized or exercised control over the said aircracft.

49. Hijacking of ships (paragraph 9.040)

STATEMENT OF OFFENCE

Hijacking a ship, contrary to section 9 of the Aviation and Maritime Security Act 1990.

PARTICULARS OF OFFENCE

D on the . . . day of . . . unlawfully by the use of force [by threats] seized [exercised control of] a ship, namely . . .

50. Seizing or exercising control over fixed platforms (paragraph 9.045)

STATEMENT OF OFFENCE

Seizing [exercising control over] a fixed platform, contrary to section 10(1) of the Aviation and Maritime Security Act 1990.

PARTICULARS OF OFFENCE

D on the . . . day of . . . unlawfully by the use of force [by threats] seized [exercised control of] a fixed platform, namely . . .

51. Hijacking a Channel Tunnel train (paragraph 9.052)

STATEMENT OF OFFENCE

Hijacking a Channel Tunnel train, contrary to section 11 of the Channel Tunnel Act 1987 and article 4(1) of the Channel Tunnel (Security) Order 1994.

PARTICULARS OF OFFENCE

D on the . . . day of . . . unlawfully by the use of force [by threats] seized or exercised control of a Channel Tunnel train, namely . . .

52. Seizing control of the Channel Tunnel system (paragraph 9.057)

STATEMENT OF OFFENCE

Seizing [exercising control over] the Channel Tunnel system, contrary to section 11 of the Channel Tunnel Act 1987 and article 5(1) of the Channel Tunnel (Security) Order 1994.

PARTICULARS OF OFFENCE

D on the . . . day of . . . unlawfully by the use of force [by threats] seized [exercised control of] the Channel Tunnel system.

53. Taking hostages (paragraph 9.062)

STATEMENT OF OFFENCES

Taking hostages, contrary to section 1(1) of the Taking of Hostages Act 1982.

PARTICULARS OF OFFENCE

D on the . . . day of . . . detained A and in order to compel . . . [e.g. the United Kingdom government or the European Community] to do or abstain from doing an act, namely . . . , threatened to kill, injure, or continue to detain the said A.

54. Piracy (paragraphs 9.066, 9.067, and 9.039)

STATEMENT OF OFFENCE

(1) Piracy.

PARTICULARS OF OFFENCE

D on the . . . day of . . . upon the high seas assaulted and put in fear of their lives certain persons on board a ship [aircraft] namely . . . and unlawfully detained them [stole, etc., certain property thereon, namely . . .]

STATEMENT OF OFFENCE

(2) Piracy, contrary to section 2 of the Piracy Act 1837.

PARTICULARS OF OFFENCE

D on the . . . day of . . . upon the high seas with intent to commit [at the time of committing/after committing] an act of piracy namely . . ., against the passengers [crew] of a ship [aircraft] namely . . . assaulted A with intent to murder him [stabbed, cut or wounded A whereby his life might have been endangered] on board the said ship [aircraft].

Appendix 2

OFFENCES AGAINST THE PERSON ACT 1861

OFFENCES COVERED IN DETAIL IN THE TEXT
Section 16:

> "A person who without lawful excuse makes to another a threat, intending that that other would fear it would be carried out, to kill that other or a third person shall be guilty of an offence and liable on conviction on indictment to imprisonment for a term not exceeding ten years."

Section 16 in this form was substituted by section 65(4) and schedule 12 of the Criminal Law Act 1977.

Section 18:

> "Whosoever shall unlawfully and maliciously by any means whatsoever wound or cause any grievous bodily harm to any person . . . with intent . . . to do some grievous bodily harm to any person, or with intent to resist or prevent the lawful apprehension of any person, shall be guilty . . . [of an offence]".

Section 20:

> "Whoever shall unlawfully and maliciously wound or inflict any grievous bodily harm upon any other person either with or without any weapon or instrument, shall be guilty . . . [of an offence]".

Section 21:

> "Whosoever shall, by any means whatsoever, attempt to choke, suffocate, or strangle any other person, or shall by any means calculated to choke, suffocate, or strangle, attempt to render any other person insensible, unconscious, or incapable of resistance, with intent in any of such cases thereby to enable himself or any other person to commit, or with intent in any such case thereby to assist any other person in committing any indictable offence, shall be guilty . . . [of an offence]".

Section 22:

> "Whosoever shall unlawfully apply or administer or cause to be taken by, or attempt to apply or administer to or attempt to cause to be administered to or taken by, any person, any chloroform, laudanum, or other stupefying or over-powering drug, matter, or thing, with intent in any of such cases thereby to enable himself or any other person to commit, or with intent in any such case thereby to assist any other person in committing, any indictable offence, shall be guilty [of an offence]".

289

Section 23:

"Whosoever shall unlawfully and maliciously administer to or cause to be administered to or taken by any other person any poison or other destructive or noxious
thing, so as thereby to endanger the life of such person, or so as thereby to inflict
upon such person any grievous bodily harm shall be guilty [of an offence]".

Section 24:

"Whosoever shall unlawfully and maliciously administer to or cause to be administered to or taken by any other person any poison or other destructive or noxious
thing, with intent to injure, aggrieve, or annoy such person, shall be guilty [of an
offence]".

Section 28:

"Whosoever shall unlawfully and maliciously, by the explosion of gunpowder or
other explosive substance, burn, maim, disfigure, disable, or do any grievous
bodily harm to any person, shall be guilty [of an offence]".

Section 29:

"Whosoever shall unlawfully and maliciously cause any gunpowder or other corrosive substance to explode, or send or deliver to or cause to be taken or received
by any person any explosive substance or any other dangerous or noxious thing,
or put or lay at any place or cast or throw at or upon or otherwise apply to any
person, any corrosive fluid or any destructive or explosive substance, with intent
in any of the cases aforesaid to burn, maim, disfigure or disable any person, or to
do some grievous bodily harm to any person, shall, whether any bodily injury be
effected or not, be guilty [of an offence]".

Section 30:

"Whosoever shall unlawfully and maliciously place or throw in, into, upon,
against, or near any building, ship or vessel any gunpowder or other explosive
substance, with intent to do bodily injury to any person shall whether or not any
explosion takes place, and whether or not any bodily injury be effected, be guilty
[of an offence]".

Section 31:

"Whosoever shall set or place or cause to be set or placed, any spring gun, man
trap, or other engine calculated to destroy human life of inflict grievous bodily
harm, with the intent that the same or whereby the same may inflict grievous
bodily harm upon a trespasser or other person coming in contact therewith, shall
be guilty . . .; and whosoever shall knowingly and wilfully permit any such spring
gun, man trap or other engine which may have been set or placed in any place
then being in or afterwards coming into his possession or occupation by some
other person to continue so set or placed, shall be deemed to have set or placed
such gun, trap, or engine with such intent as aforesaid: Provided that nothing in
this section contained shall extend to make it illegal to set or place any gun or
trap such as may have been or may be usually set or placed with the intention of
destroying vermin: Provided also, that nothing in this section shall be deemed to
make it unlawful to set or place, or cause to be set or placed, or to be contained
set or placed, from sunset to sunrise, any spring gun, man trap, or other engine

which shall be set or placed, or caused or continued to be set or placed, in a dwelling-house for the protection thereof."

Section 32:

"Whosoever shall unlawfully and maliciously put or throw upon or across any railway any wood, stone or other matter or thing, or shall maliciously take up, remove or displace any rail, sleeper or other matter or thing belonging to any railway, or shall unlawfully and maliciously turn, move, or divert any points or other machinery belonging to any railway, or shall unlawfully and maliciously make or show, hide or remove any signal or light upon or near any railway, or shall unlawfully and maliciously do or cause to be done any other matter or thing, with intent, in any of the cases aforesaid, to endanger the safety of any person travelling or being upon such railway, shall be guilty [of an offence]".

Section 33:

"Whosoever shall unlawfully and maliciously throw, or cause to fall or strike, at, against, into, or upon any engine, tender, carriage, or truck used upon any railway, any wood, stone, or other matter or thing, with intent to injure or endanger the safety of any person being in or upon such engine, tender, carriage or truck, or in or upon any engine, tender, carriage or truck of any train of which such first mentioned engine, tender, carriage or truck shall form part, shall be guilty [of an offence]".

Section 34:

"Whosoever by any unlawful act, or by any wilful omission or neglect, shall endanger or cause to be endangered the safety of any person conveyed, or being in or upon a railway, or shall aid or assist therein, shall be guilty [of an offence]".

Section 38:

"Whoever shall assault any person with intent to resist or prevent the lawful apprehension or detainer of himself or any other person for any offence, shall be guilty.."

Section 47:

"Whoever shall be convicted upon an indictment of any assault occasioning actual bodily harm shall be liable . . .".

Section 58:

"Every woman being with child who, with intent to procure her own miscarriage, shall unlawfully administer to herself any poison or other noxious thing or shall unlawfully use any instrument or other means whatsoever with the like intent, and whosoever, with intent to procure the miscarriage of any woman, whether she be or be not with child, shall unlawfully administer to her or cause to be taken by her any poison or other noxious thing, or shall unlawfully use any instrument or other means whatsoever with the like intent, shall be guilty of an offence, and being convicted thereof shall be liable . . . to imprisonment for life . . .".

Section 59:

"Whosoever shall unlawfully supply or procure any poison or other noxious thing, or any instrument or thing whatsoever, knowing that the same is intended to be unlawfully used or employed with intent to procure the miscarriage of any woman, whether she be or be not with child shall be guilty of [an offence] and being convicted thereof shall be liable . . . to imprisonment . . . for any term not exceeding five years . . .".

TABLE OF OFFENCES AND PENALTIES

Abbreviations

[I]	On indictment
[S]	Summarily
Level 1 etc.	Fine at level indicated on standard scale
OAPA	Offences against the Person Act 1861
S.M.	Statutory maximum—currently £5,000 (Criminal Justice Act 1991, s.17)
*	Prosecution requires consent of Attorney-General
#	Prosecution requires consent of D.P.P.

Offences and source	Mode of trial	Maximum penalty
Chapter 2—Assault Offences		
Common assault	[S][1]	6 months and/or fine Level 5
Assault on a constable (Police Act 1964 s.51(1))	[S][2]	6 months and/or fine Level 5
ditto with a firearm (Firearms Act 1968 s.17(2))	[I]	Life
Obstructing a constable (Police Act 1964 s.51(3))	[S]	1 month and/or fine Level 3
Assaulting a Customs officer (Customs and Excise Management Act 1979, s.156(1))	[I] [S]	2 years 3 months and/or S.M.
Obstructing a Revenue officer (Inland Revenue Act 1890 s.11)	[S]	Fine Level 3
Assaulting a court officer (County Courts Act 1984 s.14(1))	[S]	3 months and/or fine Level 5
Assaulting a prisoner escort officer (s.90(1) Criminal Justice Act 1981)	[S]	Fine Level 5[1]
Assaulting a secure training centre officer (s.13(1) Criminal Justice and Public Order Act 1996)	[S]	Fine Level 3[1]

293

Offences and source	Mode of trial	Maximum penalty
Assault with intent to resist arrest (OAPA s.38)	[I]	2 years
	[S]	6 months and/or S.M.
ditto with a firearm (Firearms Act 1968 s.17(2))	[I]	Life
Threats to kill (OAPA s.16)	[I]	10 years
	[S]	6 months and/or S.M.

Chapter 3—Assaults Resulting in Injury

Offences and source	Mode of trial	Maximum penalty
Assault occasioning actual bodily harm (OAPA s.47)	[I]	5 years
	[S]	6 months and/or S.M.
ditto with a firearm (Firearms Act 1968 s.17(2))	[I]	Life
Making threat to internationally protected person (Internationally Protected Persons Act 1978 s.1(3))	[I]*	10 years[3]
Wounding or inflicting grievous bodily harm (OAPA s.20)	[I]	5 years
	[S]	6 months and/or S.M.
ditto with a firearm (Firearms Act 1968 s.17(2))	[I]	Life
Wounding etc. with intent to do grievous bodily harm (OAPA s.18)	[I]	Life
Attempting to choke etc. (OAPA s.21)	[I]	Life
Using chloroform etc. to commit an indictable offence (OAPA s.22)	[I]	Life
Maliciously administering poison etc. so as to endanger life (OAPA s.23)	[I]	10 years
Maliciously administering poison etc. so as to injure etc. (OAPA s.24)	[I]	5 years
	[S]	6 months and/or S.M.
Ill-treatment of mentally disordered (Mental Health Act 1983 s.127)	[I]#	2 years
	[S]#	6 months and/or S.M.
Causing bodily harm by gunpowder (OAPA s.28)	[I]	Life

Offences and source	Mode of trial	Maximum penalty
Causing explosion etc. (OAPA s.29)	Life	
Placing gunpowder near building with intent to injure (OAPA s.30)	[I]	14 years
ditto with a firearm (Firearms Act 1968 s.17(2))	[I]	Life
Causing explosion likely to endanger life or property (Explosive Substances Act 1883 s.2)	[I]*	Life
Attempt to cause an explosion (Explosive Substances Act 1883 s.3)	[I]*	Life. Obligatory forfeiture of explosives
Making or possessing explosives (Explosive Substances Act 1883 s.4(1))	[I]*	14 years. Obligatory forfeiture of explosives
Possession of articles for suspected terrorist purposes (Prevention of Terrorism (Temporary Provisions) Act 1989, s.16A)	[I]	10 years
	[S]	6 months and/or S.M.
Destroying etc. aircraft (Aviation Security Act 1982 s.2)	[I]*	Life
Destroying etc. air navigation facilities (Aviation Security Act s.3)	[I]	Life
Possessing dangerous articles in an aircraft	[I]	5 years
(Aviation Security Act 1982 s.4)	[S]	3 months and/or S.M.
Endangering safety at aerodromes (Aviation and Maritime Security Act 1990, s.1)	[I]*	Life
Endangering safety of ships etc. (Aviation and Maritime Security Act 1990, s.11)		
Developing etc. biological weapon etc. (Biological Weapons Act 1974 s.1(1))	[I]*	Life
Using etc. chemical weapons (Chemical Weapons Act 1996, s.2)	[I]*	Life
Offences involving nuclear material (Nuclear Material (Offences) Act 1983, s.2)	[I]*	14 years[3]
Setting spring gun to cause grievous bodily harm (OAPA s.31)	[I]	5 years

Offences and source	Mode of trial	Maximum penalty
Placing wood etc. on railway (OAPA s.32)	[I]	Life
Throwing stones etc. at railway carriages (OAPA s.33)	[I]	Life
Endangering safety of persons on a railway (OAPA s.34)	[I]	2 years
	[S]	6 months and/or S.M.
Endangering safety of Channel Tunnel (Channel Tunnel Act 1987, s.11)	[I]*	Life
Torture (Criminal Justice Act 1988, s.134)	[I]*	Life
Female circumcision (Prohibition of Female Circumcision Act 1985 s.1(1))	[I]	5 years

Chapter 4—Murder

Murder	[I]	Life (mandatory)
Solicitation to murder (OAPA s.4)	[I]	Life

Chapter 5—Manslaughter

Manslaughter	[I]	Life
Causing death by reckless driving (Road Traffic Act 1988 s.1)	[I]	5 years. Disqualification obligatory for 12 months

Chapter 6—Suicide

Aiding and abetting suicide (Suicide Act 1961 s.2(1))	[I]#	14 years
Genocide (Genocide Act 1969 s.1(1))	[I]*	(Life (if death results)) (14 years (otherwise))

Chapter 7—Abortion, Child Destruction and Infanticide

Attempting to procure a miscarriage (OAPA s.58)	[I]	Life
Acts preparatory to abortion (OAPA s.59)	[I]	5 years
Child destruction (Infant Life (Preservation) Act 1929 s.1(1))	[I]	Life
Infanticide (Infanticide Act 1938 s.1(1))	[I]	Life

Offences and source	Mode of trial	Maximum penalty
Chapter 8—Offences against the Young		
Wilful cruelty to person under 16 (Children and	[I]	10 years[4]
Young Persons Act 1933 s.1(1))	[S]	6 months and/or S.M.
Exposing a child (OAPA s.27)	[I]	5 years
Exposing child under 12 to risk of burning	[S]	6 months and/or S.M.
(Children and Young Persons Act 1933 s.11)	[S]	Fine Level 1
Tattooing of minors (Tattooing of Minors Act 1969 s.1)	[S]	Fine Level 3
Chapter 9—False Imprisonment and Kidnapping		
False imprisonment	[I]	Life
Kidnapping	[I][5]	Life
Child abduction by parent (Child Abduction Act 1984 s.1)	[I]#	7 years
	[S]#	6 months and/or S.M.
Child abduction by other persons (Child Abduction Act 1984 s.2)	[I]#	7 years
	[S]#	6 months and/or S.M.
Hijacking (Aviation Security Act 1982 s.1(1)) (and Aviation and Maritime Security Act 1990 s.9)	[I]	Life
Seizing control of fixed platforms (Aviation and Maritime Security Act 1990, s.10(1))	[I]	Life
Hijacking a Channel Tunnel train (Channel Tunnel (Security) Order 1994, Art. 4(1))	[I]*	Life
Seizing control of Channel Tunnel system (Channel Tunnel (Security) Order 1994, Art. 4(1))	[I]*	Life
Taking of hostages (Taking of Hostages Act 1982 s.1(1))	[I]*	Life
Piracy:	[I]	Death if committed in an aggravated form[6]; otherwise Life

[1] Also triable on indictment in certain circumstances—see text paras. 2–003–2–005
[2] Information must be laid within six months of offence.
[3] Unless substantive offence carries a lesser maximum term.
[4] Two or five years if committed before September 29, 1988 see text para. 8–014.
[5] Consent of D.P.P. required in certain circumstances—see text para. 9–015.
[6] See para. 9–067.

INDEX